D0648608

STEALTH AT SEA

STEALTH AT SEA

The History of the Submarine

Dan van der Vat

HOUGHTON MIFFLIN COMPANY

BOSTON · NEW YORK

1995

For information about permission to reproduce selections
from this book, write to Permissions,
Houghton Mifflin Company, 215 Park Avenue South,
New York, New York 10003.

Library of Congress Cataloging-in-Publication Data
Van der Vat, Dan.
Stealth at sea : the history of the submarine / Dan van der Vat.
p. cm.
Includes bibliographical references and index.
ISBN 0-395-65242-1
1. Submarine boats — History. 2. Submarine warfare —
History.   I. Title.
V857.V35 1994
359.9'3'09 — dc20   94-40105
CIP

Printed in the United States of America

MP 10 9 8 7 6 5 4 3 2 1

In memory of my mother

Contents

Illustrations

[1] General Dynamics
[2] Imperial War Museum
[3] Illustrated London News
[4] VSEL
[5] Salamander
[6] Conway Maritime Press
[7] US Navy

Maps in the text

Preface

THE END OF THE COLD WAR offers a natural break in the history of the submarine which made such an astounding technological advance and played so great a part in it. The world is left with more than 700 submarines. The 400 and more which run on conventional diesel-electric power carry on much as before, providing nearly fifty nations with the option of exploiting stealth at sea in a crisis. But nearly 300 submarines are powered by nuclear energy, including scores armed with the nuclear ballistic missiles which became the principal deterrent in the Cold War – the ultimate, first- or second-strike weapon which could be used even after a massive nuclear exchange of landbased or air-launched weapons. All other nuclear boats are "hunter-killers", built to attack ballistic and other submarines, surface ships and targets on land.

The technological gap between advanced conventional boats and nuclear submarines is slowly but surely closing, and the former, complete with the latest concealment aids, electronics and weapons, cost half as much as the latter. The reactor-powered underwater warship has begun to look like a white elephant, if not a strategic dinosaur, just when it had established itself as the "true" submarine, independent of the atmosphere as it took its oxygen from the sea, under which it could stay for months. Nuclear boats cost too much, are hardly indispensable and pose insoluble environmental problems when they have to be paid off. At this hiatus in their short but spectacular history, the five nations which own them seek to suppress decidedly mixed feelings about the huge investment they represent.

As the world awaits a reassessment of their role, the historian has a chance to review how the submarine progressed from a gleam in the eyes of Fenian Irishmen, intent on damaging the British Navy, to the most intricate technological system devised by man, capable of surviving in a supremely hostile environment, whether natural or man-made.

It is the only technology which makes a spaceship's look relatively straightforward.

This book is a history of the idea of the submersible man-of-war, from the earliest imaginings to the dangerous game of hide-and-seek which still continues among the leading navies, Cold War or no. It is written for the general reader and its emphasis is operational, on how submarines have been used in war and planning for war. But the book also explores the technological, political and diplomatic background to the development of the submarine, its weaponry and the strenuous efforts to contain and defeat it, to give as rounded a picture as possible in the space available of a fearsome yet fascinating weapons system.

That the theme is fascinating is shown by the widespread and growing interest in what we may call submarine archaeology. The discovery of a U-boat in a Turkish Black Sea coalmine, the raising of another in the entrance to the Baltic, the revelation that submariners from a third stole ashore in New Zealand to milk a herd of cows in the last months of the Second World War – all these discoveries command space in the media. So do worries about nuclear radiation from Soviet boats lost in thousands of feet of water, about nuclear-submarine graveyards and the disposal of the nuclear waste they have generated. More and more submarines are on show at museums, from the tiny HMS *Holland I*, Britain's first commissioned submarine at Gosport in England, via U-boats at Kiel and Chicago to USS *Nautilus*, the world's first nuclear boat, at Groton in New England. More and more people visit them.

Although this volume takes a broad view of a subject with many facets, it does not encompass miniature or midget submarines, underwater pleasure-boats, "human torpedoes", robots, bathyscaphs, deep-diving submersibles or other highly specialised underwater craft, although some are mentioned in passing when they touch on the main topic. Since most of the earliest experimental and even operational submarines were very small indeed, the distinction may appear a fine one at first; but there is a demonstrable and unbroken progression from the earliest, one-man attempt to attack from under the sea in the American War of Independence to the nuclear flotillas of today's principal naval powers. The Prologue covers the origin of the submarine and the book goes on to describe the leading part it played in two world wars. The Epilogue outlines its growing role in the nuclear age and the Cold War, until the USSR collapsed under the strain of the arms race, in which nuclear submarines also helped to make the USA the world's leading debtor.

In less than a century of serious deployment, the submarine as a weapons-system has matched or overtaken, outlasted or seen off, the battleship and battlecruiser, the aircraft-carrier and cruiser, the strategic bomber and even the landbased missile in its silo. From being the most vulnerable constituent of the fleet it has become the most dangerous. How it did so is a unique story, one of the most pervasive strands in the history of the century now drawing to an uncertain close.

This factual history of the submarine is drawn from primary research in the archives of America, Britain, Canada, Germany and Russia, and a mass of published material on general naval history as well as the specific works listed in the bibliography. The length of the latter shows how much I owe to so many earlier books on the subject.

I should like to express my gratitude for the invaluable help I received from the following individuals and institutions. Annette Boon, who went to Russia on my behalf; Stephen Cook; the late Captain John Coote, RN (retd); Graham H. Gavert of General Dynamics (Electric Boat Division); Stephen Hill; Stephen Howarth; Dr Roger Knight of the National Maritime Museum, Greenwich; Kathy Lloyd and colleagues at the US Naval Historical Center in Washington, DC; Helen Martin and staff of the *Guardian* library; William D. Moore, President of the South-East Connecticut Chamber of Commerce; Tom Pocock; Captain (2nd grade) Mikhail Shadrin of the Russian Navy; John E. Taylor and colleagues at the National Archive, Washington; G.R. Worledge, RAN (retd), of Turramurra, Australia; the staffs of the London Library, the Public Record Office, Kew, Surrey, and Twickenham (Middlesex) Public Library. Ion Trewin, my London publisher and co-originator of the idea, and my agents, Michael Shaw and Peter Ginsberg of Curtis Brown, as usual provided essential and unstinting support in fair and foul literary weather.

Any error is my responsibility alone.

Grateful acknowledgment is due to the following for quotations from copyright works: Bernard & Graefe Verlag, Koblenz, for *Memoirs*, by Karl Dönitz; Cassell & Co, London, for *History of the First World War*, by Sir Basil Liddell Hart; HarperCollins, London, for *One Hundred Days*, by Admiral Sandy Woodward; Little Brown of Boston, Mass, for *History of the US Naval Operations in World War II*, by Samuel Eliot Morrison; US Naval Historical Center, Washington, DC, for *History of US Naval Operations: Korea*, by James A. Field; Weidenfeld & Nicolson for *War Memoirs*, by David Lloyd George.

PROLOGUE: 1465–1900

Inventions and devices

THE UNDERWATER WARSHIP which relies on stealth and is today's ultimate weapon derives from a miscellany of experiments in which hope often, but usually not for long, triumphed over experience. Many false starts, whether comic, tragic or merely spectacular, were made by individual inventors working independently and prepared to defy the forces of nature in the most unlikely vessels. To find among them sailors, scientists, ships' carpenters and speculators is hardly surprising. But the presence of several clergymen, including a bishop, on the list of early submariners is surely at least as remarkable as the absence of Leonardo da Vinci, who envisaged so many other technological developments, both military and maritime.

A Nuremberg inventor named Keyser is said to have designed a diving boat in 1465, but the concept of a vessel which could submerge to evade an enemy was first formulated in 1578 by the English polymath William Bourne, mathematician, scientist, inventor, gunner and naval theorist. His specification, in a collection of articles entitled *Inventions or Devices*, had all the confidence of the theorist who never attempted to put his idea into practice: "It is possible to make a Ship or Boate that may goe under the water unto the bottome, and so to come up again at your pleasure." Bourne also went into considerable detail on how his submersible would descend and ascend by filling and emptying ballast tanks on either side, a key feature of submarines to this day. A German teacher called Pegelius, of Rostock, did duty for Leonardo by drawing an array of futuristic machines, including a submarine, in 1604, but no practical experiments ensued.

The first submersible boats were made to Bourne's design by a Dutchman who served for a time as tutor to the children of the King of England – Cornelis Drebbel from Alkmaar in Holland, another man of many talents. Physicist, alchemist, teacher and inventor, Drebbel was to become the Royal Navy's adviser on explosives before turning his versatile hand to running a public house near London Bridge. A personal friend of his wrote a brief account of experiments with his first three submersibles. These were closely studied later in the seventeenth century by two great scientists, the Dutch Christiaan Huygens and the Anglo-Irish Robert Boyle, both interested in the physics and chemistry of air.

Drebbel built all his craft on similar lines, if in different sizes, in 1620. Each vessel looked like two conventional boats, one inverted on top of the other, the whole covered in leather to make it as watertight as possible. Drebbel cut holes for oars in either side of the lower hull (twelve altogether in the largest craft) and fitted glass windows in the upper section for the oarsmen, who faced the stern, and the master, who stood with his back to them in the bow. Each oar-opening was fitted with a heavily greased, watertight leather sleeve. Although it is likely that Drebbel had read Bourne, he did not use ballast tanks. He preferred to rely on heavy weights to keep his boat, made of wood and braced with iron, awash in such a way that the efforts of the oarsmen drove her under. Even now submarines dive by reducing their buoyancy and propelling themselves below. To go up or down vertically is much harder and takes far longer.

Drebbel found the courage in 1620 to stage a public demonstration in the Thames before a large crowd by sailing underwater from Westminster to Greenwich. He reportedly persuaded his patron, King James I of England and VI of Scotland, to accompany him on one trip. Boyle accepted hearsay evidence that Drebbel had managed to stay underwater for several hours at a depth of twelve to fifteen feet. This is impossible to believe because of the inevitability of leaks and above all the constant need for breathable air.

Yet attached to the Dutch pioneer's work is a tantalising claim which is only sketchily recorded. He is said to have relied on a bellows arrangement of two pipes and two valves to expel foul air and suck in fresh, an idea which, no less than effective water-pumps, was certainly within reach of contemporary technology (it also foreshadowed a much more important Dutch submarine invention three centuries later – the schnorkel). But Boyle had learned from an unspecified source that Drebbel's principal secret was an air-freshening "liquor" carried in bottles. Drebbel would "for ought I could gather" (Boyle), open one whenever an injection of "quintessence of air" into the fetid atmosphere seemed necessary. Since Drebbel, a practising alchemist, claimed in 1608 to have discovered a process for regenerating air involving the heating of saltpetre (potassium nitrate), there may be something in Boyle's account – even if oxygen as such was identified only a century and a half later! Drebbel took his secret to the grave in 1633.

A year after his death two French priests called Mersenne and Fournier envisaged (but did not build) a spindle-shaped, metal submersible closely foreshadowing experimental craft built 200 years later.

Next on the uncrowded scene of submarine pioneers was Dr John Wilkins, churchman and scientist, Warden of Wadham College, Oxford (and later Master of Trinity, Cambridge). He was also Oliver Cromwell's brother-in-law, a founder-member of the Royal Society and Bishop of Chester – a kindred spirit to the Vicar of Bray. In his *Mathematical Magick* of 1648 he presented what amounts to a remarkably detailed, if entirely theoretical, vision of an "ark for submarine navigation". It would be invisible, safe from storms, icebergs, pirates and other enemies, able to attack conventional ships, relieve sieges and deliver surprise assaults on land, find wrecks and treasure and generally engage in scientific experiments. But Wilkins also left the hard work of putting his conception into practice to others.

One such was a Frenchman called de Son, who sold to the unexpectedly gullible (or perhaps merely desperate) Dutch the idea of a submersible warship during the first Anglo-Dutch War of 1652–4. Built at Rotterdam in 1653, the vessel is shown by contemporary engravings to have been a mighty construction of wooden beams and planking reinforced by iron girders. As a design it is chiefly remarkable for its close external resemblance to experimental types built of iron two centuries later. De Son's boat was designed to operate awash. It was shaped like an angular spindle, each pointed end iron-tipped for ramming, and was powered by a clockwork paddlewheel amidships. De Son made ludicrous claims for his invention as it took shape: it would sink 100 ships in a day, make a return run to London in a similar time and reach the Dutch East Indies in six weeks. Topped by a small deck complete with handrail, the de Son boat was seventy-two feet long and had cabins fore and aft. When launched it assumed its awash posture exactly as designed. Unfortunately the clockwork was far too weak to shift such a weight, the paddlewheel refused to budge and the de Son submersible became a motionless exhibit for a while, perhaps to recover some of the money wasted on it.

Not to be outdone by the Anglicans, the Italian Catholic priest and scientist Father Giovanni Alfonso Borelli bequeathed to the world a detailed design for what he described as a diving bell. His interest was aroused by the desire to view marine life. The design was included in his *De motu animalium* (on the motion of animals), published in Rome in 1680, one year after his death. He drew on the ideas of Bourne and Drebbel, including an assemblage of goatskin bottles as buoyancy tanks in what looked like a pair of conventional boats joined gunwale to gunwale and covered in leather. The vessel was to be powered by eight oars protruding from leather sleeves.

In 1691 a German princeling, the Landgrave of Hesse, commissioned a submersible from the French scientist Denis Papin. It had a ballast tank, a bilge pump, an airlock and an air pipe to the surface. It was successfully tested at least once.

It was not until 1747 that Nathaniel Symons, a joiner, built a "Borelli" in the River Dart in Devon. His design drawing is a mirror image of the Italian prelate's, obviously copied in every detail. According to a contemporary issue of the *Gentleman's Magazine*, Symons conducted successful trials in the Thames, staying under water for forty-five minutes. What became of his work is unknown, but it seems that when the ballast bottles were full there was not enough room for the oarsmen to move ... Yet Bourne's concept of the ballast tank had at least been put to the test and not found wanting.

In 1772 another German ruler, Wilhelm Count of Schaumburg-Lippe, commissioned a diving boat from his chief engineer, Johann Christian Pretorius. Armed with a single cannon, it was shaped like a fish and was supposed to propel itself by fishlike movements of its "tail". It was completed, and it did float, but no underwater trial is recorded.

Another craftsman in wood, a ship's carpenter named Day, built a submersible on the Norfolk Broads and took it to a depth of thirty feet near Great Yarmouth in 1773. On the strength of this success he persuaded investors to put up £340 for more experiments and the purchase of a sloop (which may count as the first submarine tender). His underwater vessel featured an air-chamber amidships and carried an external ballast of large stones, attached to the hull by ringbolts capable of release from the inside. He took his new craft to Plymouth Sound and made a successful descent in shallow water in summer 1774. Thus encouraged, he tried a third descent for a bet – but in twenty-two fathoms (132 feet) of water. Completely ignorant of the rapid increase of water pressure with depth, Day and his crew were killed, presumably in an implosion, in the first submarine disaster. A Dr Falcke of London who witnessed Day's last dive tried to raise the boat, believing it might be possible to revive the crew who would, he hoped, have been preserved by the cool temperature below and the air trapped in the hull. Bad weather put an end to the rescue effort.

The first attempt to sink a surface ship by a submersible craft was made by the American David Bushnell in 1776. It was also the first, but hardly the last, manifestation of anti-British sentiment as an important motive for developing means of attacking ships by stealth at sea. The Royal Navy was the world's strongest for 300 years, and the submarine, once it was taken seriously, came to be widely regarded as the weapon of the weak, a maritime "equaliser".

Bushnell, born in Westbrook, Connecticut, in 1742, spent some of his time at Yale University in the 1770s, when tension between the American colonists and Britain was rising, looking for ways of damaging the all-powerful British Navy which alone sustained the sovereignty of King George III across the Atlantic. When the American Revolution began in 1776 the Royal Navy duly blockaded the freshly promulgated United States. Bushnell's answer was the *Turtle*.

This first midget submarine was egg-shaped with the pointed end below. Above was a "crown" with four portholes, three sleeved armholes and the access-hatch on top. There were two hand-operated screws, one horizontal on top to propel the craft downwards or upwards and one vertical at the middle to move it forwards or backwards. A foot-operated valve in the bottom admitted water to help the descent and a foot pump expelled it for ascent. The *Turtle*, built of thick wood, was held upright by 700 pounds of lead ballast at the bottom. Among the other minimal fittings were a compass, an air-pressure gauge and a vent to freshen the air when at the surface (otherwise the air inside lasted barely half an hour). There was also a gauge to show the amount of water ballast in the tank.

The craft was to approach the target in an awash condition and submerge under its hull to attach the 150-pound explosive charge contained in the detachable magazine above the rudder. The operator sat on a saddle with his head in the crown. In front of his nose on the outside was an internally operated vertical drill, to be used for boring a hole in the bottom of the enemy ship for a hook to hold the charge. The magazine was buoyant and the operator used the sleeves in the crown to position it. Finally he would pull a string to trigger the clockwork time-delayed detonator, which released a sprung hammer on to a percussion cap after thirty minutes, during which the operator was to make good his escape.

Having proved at trials in Long Island Sound that the *Turtle* would indeed go up and down as planned, and also that it was possible to detonate a large gunpowder charge underwater, Bushnell's brother was to take it into action but fell ill. Thus it came to pass that the first man to attack a warship from underwater by attempting to blow it up was a soldier – Sergeant Ezra Lee of the Patriot Army. The *Turtle* was hauled overland from the Sound to the Hudson River in August 1776 for launching against HMS *Eagle*, the sixty-four gun flagship of Admiral

Earl Howe, then blockading New York. Two longboats towed Lee down-stream on the ebb – which swept him past his objective. When the tide turned he painstakingly wound himself back towards the frigate, moored off Governor's Island in Upper New York Bay. But Lee's hand-operated gimlet failed and the gallant sergeant was forced to withdraw. He was sighted as he did so. The British launched boats, but Lee primed and jettisoned his magazine, which blew up in their path. He got away on the tide as the pursuers abandoned the four-mile chase in confusion.

Two similar attempts were made later but failed. The British not only took New York in September 1776 but also captured and destroyed the *Turtle*. The French Navy, however, had so reduced Britain's command of the transatlantic route that the Americans won their independence anyway. Bushnell returned to the charge with an improved "Turtle" during the Anglo-American War of 1812. An attack was attempted on HMS *Ramillies*, a seventy-four gun ship of the line, off New London, Connecticut – future home from home of the United States submarine service – in July 1813. The approach was detected, an alarm gun was fired and *Ramillies* weighed anchor; the brave but unidentified sub-mariner still managed to attach himself to the keel for half an hour – only to have his drill break. Even so, he was able to get away, at three miles per hour.

Bushnell's underwater craft, the first submersibles to go into battle, stretch the already elastic definition of the word "submarine" beyond its limits, but they undoubtedly helped to raise awareness of the potential of stealth at sea and the surprise attack from beneath the waves.

The next inventor to try his hand at underwater navigation produced a craft several steps closer to what the modern world would recognise as a submarine. He was Robert Fulton, another American, born in the Pennsylvania town of Little Britain (now known as Fulton in his honour). Of Irish extraction, he had Fenian sympathies (for Irish inde-pendence from Britain). He arrived in England in 1794 to study engin-eering, supporting himself by helping to dig canals. A restless character with many skills, Fulton was persuaded by a compatriot to move to France in 1797 during an armistice in the Napoleonic Wars which, in naval terms at least, amounted to the first global war. He took a job as an engineer with the French government. Fulton spent his free time working on a submersible warship and an explosive "torpedo". Curi-ously, his motive was the opposite of what it seemed: he was totally opposed to war and wanted to find a way to neutralise the warship, the principal means of transmitting aggression round the world. The obvious target for an Irish nationalist was the British Navy, a motive he shared with Bushnell and the father of the modern submarine, John P. Holland.

Already in 1797 Fulton was conducting experimental underwater explosions in the Seine outside Paris. On 13 December he wrote to the Directory then ruling France. He proposed deploying a submarine against the blockading British fleet. The name he gave it remains the most famous in the factual as well as fictional history of submarine navigation: *Nautilus*. From ancient Greek via Latin, it is borrowed from an underwater mollusc mentioned by Aristotle. His suggestion was rejected (also by the Dutch); but after Napoleon became First Consul at the end of 1799, an almost empty French treasury found 10,000 francs for Fulton's experiment. Had he had his way the prototype would have been the first of a flotilla.

Nautilus, designed in 1798, was laid down at Rouen late in 1800 and completed in May 1801. The vessel had a copper skin reinforced with iron stays, was twenty-one feet long and seven in diameter at her widest, near the gently pointed nose. The overall shape was like a slug, round-bodied and tapering slightly towards the stern, where there was a hand-cranked propeller for underwater power. The first submersible to have separate methods of propulsion on and under the surface, *Nautilus* also carried a folding mast and collapsible sail. There was a rudimentary but recognisable conning tower, hemispherical and made of metal, as was the keel (detachable in emergency for rapid surfacing) and a curved bulkhead reinforcing the bow from within. On top of the "tower" there was a vertical spike to hold the vessel under the enemy's hull while an explosive charge was attached. The craft could accommodate three men, was equipped with horizontal and vertical rudders for controlling depth as well as course and was remarkably hydrodynamic in design. The horizontal rudder anticipated the diving plane of the modern submarine. *Nautilus* had ballast tanks and a glass scuttle in the hull for illumination, to obviate the need for air-exhausting candles. Her armament was a "torpedo" – a term which meant no more than an underwater bomb or mine until Robert Whitehead invented the self-propelled underwater missile we know today.

After one false start when the tide in the Seine estuary disrupted her maiden voyage, the *Nautilus* descended to her designated depth, about twenty-four feet, on 3 June 1801, staying under for an hour with three men aboard. Fulton's next refinement was to supply his craft with bottled, compressed air at a pressure of 200 pounds per square inch, enabling her to stay under for five hours. Thus encouraged, Fulton sent *Nautilus* under a schooner to attack her by detaching the "torpedo", a twenty-pound gunpowder charge with a delayed-action detonator stowed under the hull at the stern, and fastening it to the old ship's bottom in Brest harbour. The 500-yard approach was made at just over two knots and the craft sank her target and returned to her starting point submerged. However, despite the fact that Brest was feeling the pinch of the British continental blockade, the local prefect withheld permission to attack the Royal Navy. Even so, the inventor made several passes at a British frigate, but missed because she constantly changed position.

The French Ministry of Marine formally and finally dismissed Fulton, turning down his proposal for a bigger and faster *Nautilus* Mark II. He had also demanded an officer's commission and official recognition as a belligerent (a form of life-insurance in the event of capture). The ground for rejection of the *bateau-poisson* (fish-boat) was that underwater warfare was underhand, a weapon too terrible to use against an unsuspecting enemy, even one trying to starve the French into submission...

Meanwhile rumours swept England, not only of invasion by "Boney" and a secret French Channel tunnel, but also of a terrible machine capable of destroying entire fleets at a stroke. The Francophile Lord Stanhope, scientist brother-in-law of Prime Minister William Pitt (the Younger), warned of the threat in the House of Lords in 1801. This did not prevent Stanhope from becoming Fulton's patron when the disgusted inventor swallowed his anti-British principles and returned incognito to England as "Mr Francis" in May 1804.

Pitt appointed and even chaired a commission to examine his work. Fulton spectacularly sank the brig *Dorothy* off Walmer in Norfolk at a demonstration in 1805. But although the youthful premier was keen on the invention, the Royal Navy in general, and Admiral of the Fleet Earl St Vincent, First Lord of the Admiralty (navy minister), in particular, dismissed Fulton's idea as "a mode of warfare which those who commanded the seas did not want and which, if successful, would at once deprive them of it" (i.e. command of the sea). This was a rare occasion indeed historically: the two leading nations in the world, the superpowers of their day locked in worldwide conflict, in quick succession turning down a weapon because it was too lethal.

The British considered granting Fulton £50,000 to develop a boat driven by clockwork and his "sub-marine torpedoes". But when St Vincent's protégé, Nelson, broke the French fleet in his decisive victory at Trafalgar in October 1805, they all but lost interest in submarines (although they remained interested in the "torpedo"). Fulton demanded £100,000 to suppress his invention for fourteen years. He failed to secure this lavish gag, although the Navy did meet all his expenses, and returned in high dudgeon to his native United States in 1806.

In 1810 he persuaded Congress to put up $5,000 for a steam-powered submarine. The prototype very nearly brought off a staggering technological advance – an armoured vessel over eighty feet in length with a beam of twenty-one and a draught of fourteen, so quiet that it was named the *Mute*. But Fulton died before its teething troubles could be cured and it was left to sink at its moorings. Just before his death in 1815, Fulton completed the world's first steam-powered surface warship, all of thirty-eight tons and powered by a central paddlewheel – USS *Fulton*. Her inventor had come within a whisker of going down in history as the true progenitor of the submarine, having tackled and in some cases solved many of the principal technical problems associated with it.

In England Fulton's idea was taken up by a most colourful character, Captain Thomas Johnstone, sometime Channel pilot, privateer and spy against the French, part-time smuggler and habitué of debtors' prisons. Johnstone met and worked with Fulton after he brought the *Nautilus* to Dover. According to Tom Pocock who researched Johnstone's history, the adventurer was responsible for "the Chelsea submarine".

He may have taken part in a British submarine attack on the French at Brest in 1806, an abortive effort hinted at by St Vincent and others, which may also have involved Fulton himself. Johnstone persisted with the idea of a mechanically powered submersible and in or about 1812 appears to have completed a working model powered by clockwork. In 1813 a government figure – possibly Frederick Duke of York, Commander-in-Chief of the Army – offered (but did not pay) £100,000 for the real thing, capable of attaching a "torpedo" to a ship's bottom. The Admiralty may well have vetoed the project, given its hostility towards such ideas, but Johnstone commissioned an engineer to build a porpoise-shaped vessel with pointed ends out of sheet-iron, about twenty-seven feet long and lined with wood and cork. There was to be a central chamber large enough for a crew of two. There were also to be Fulton-style sails for surface work, but underwater Johnstone reverted to oars. Compressed air was to increase endurance to twelve hours submerged. Work started near Wallingford on the upper Thames in 1813. The "torpedo" at least gave every satisfaction in independent trials, but the government, having blown hot, once again blew cold in 1815 as the boat was close to completion. The Admiralty wrote to remind Johnstone that he had "no authority from their Lordships". So much for his hopes of securing for himself the £100,000 once reputedly promised to Fulton (or certainly demanded by him) for his silence.

Captain Johnstone was not sufficiently assiduous, apparently, in turning aside the blandishments of French and American agents who expressed interest in his work. He was arrested in London and questioned before being released for lack of evidence. He carried on with his boat or boats, at least one of which was successfully tried in the Thames near Woolwich in 1815.

The final victory over Napoleon at Waterloo in that year, and the long peace which followed, ended serious British interest in submarines for the rest of the century. Johnstone however carried on with his experiments, on his own account or quite possibly for unidentified clients interested in searching for sunken treasure.

One strong rumour had it that Bonapartists, interested in spiriting away their hero from his enforced exile on the island of St Helena in the South Atlantic, approached Johnstone with an offer of £40,000. When he was working on a biography of Walter Greaves, Tom Pocock found tantalising details among the papers of this Chelsea artist of "a mysterious boat built on the Chelsea Meadows that was intended to go under water, having air-pipes above". Greaves's father would have been a boy of nine at the time and might well have seen or at least heard of the launch one dark November night. It seems that government agents boarded the vessel below London Bridge and Johnstone threatened to shoot them. "But they payed [sic] no attention to his threats, seized her and, taking her to Blackwall, destroyed her." It is mildly surprising to record that Johnstone, builder of the mysterious "Chelsea submarine", managed to die peacefully in his bed in 1839, having extracted £4,735 11s 6d from an exceedingly reluctant Admiralty in April 1820 for his unsolicited efforts on its behalf! The St Helena expedition was aborted for ever by Napoleon's death in 1821. One cannot help regretting a sensation uncaused.

No less ready to offer his services to any interested party was the next notable submarine pioneer, the Bavarian Wilhelm Bauer. As a corporal in the Prussian artillery in 1849 he helped to keep blockading Danish naval vessels at a respectful distance during the long border dispute over Schleswig-Holstein. In tedious watches on the coast, Bauer conceived another method of discomfiting the blockaders – an attack from underwater. Although only a non-commissioned officer, Bauer acquired remarkable influence over those in authority in a very authoritarian state. At any rate he managed in 1850 to persuade the Howaldt-Werke at Kiel, one of the most important naval shipbuilders in Germany, to construct a boat twenty-seven feet long, eight feet at its broadest and about eight feet high, displacing thirty-nine tons and called *Brandtaucher* (incendiary diver) – the earliest *Unterseeboot* (undersea or submarine boat, *U-boot* for short) worthy of the name.

In profile Bauer's first U-boat looks like the oblong head of a sperm whale and is not so different in size or colour (matt black). The use of the present tense is justified as the craft is miraculously preserved at a German military museum. Her riveted, sheet-iron sides are flat, curving gently towards a vertical bow and stern. Right forward, like a wart on the whale's nose, is a tiny conning tower shaped like a horse's head. Top and bottom are flat with curved edges. There is a long vertical rudder at the stern under the propeller, which consists of three slightly overlapping metal arcs set at narrow angles to each other on the shaft. This was driven by a treadmill slightly forward of amidships inside the boat, powered by two of the crew of three. Access was gained by two hatches in the sides and there were ballast tanks inside the double bottom, their water content adjustable from within by valves and pumps. For trim Bauer's boat contained a new feature – a metal weight which slid along a horizontal rod aligned fore and aft inside the hull.

Completed in December 1850, the *Brandtaucher*, on trial in the Kiel Fjord, made a feint at the open sea which was enough to persuade the Danes to abandon their close blockade in favour of a more distant one. But on 1 February 1851 Bauer took his boat into deeper water; on descending, the weight slid forward and the craft hit the bottom at nearly sixty feet. Rivets started and several plates were stove in. Bauer proved to have iron nerves; overwhelming the natural panic of his two crewmen by sheer force of personality, Bauer made them wait six and a half hours as water slowly leaked in, until the air pressure inside the craft matched the external water pressure – whereupon the hatches could be opened. All three submariners shot up to the surface in their own air bubble. This discovery of how to escape from a sunken submarine could hardly have been made at a better moment. Fortunately the internal bulkheads did not collapse and would-be rescuers failed to smash the little portholes on top, which would have burst Bauer's bubble and killed the three men. A dredger rediscovered the wreck in 1887. She was salvaged, cleaned up and put on display in various museums until reaching her present home in Dresden in 1973.

Discredited in Germany but unabashed, the restless Bauer vainly tried his luck in Austria-Hungary before moving on to Britain, where he was awarded £7,000 to develop a new underwater craft, a large diving boat exploiting his unforgettable principle of the trapped bubble of air. The craft was to be propelled by the feet of its crew along the bottom for clandestine operations against the Russians in the Crimean War just begun. But several men died in the experiments and the idea was abandoned. The United States Navy proved even more sceptical than the British, so Bauer betook himself to Russia in 1855.

There he built a larger, cylindrical version of the *Brandtaucher* at St Petersburg. The *Diable Marin* (sea-devil), fifty-two feet long, twelve wide and eleven high, was launched late in 1855, starting sea-trials in spring 1856. The Russian Navy was looking for a means of countering the Anglo-French naval blockade of the Baltic in support of their Crimean campaign. The new boat had horizontal rudders as well as a sliding weight for trim and was powered by the same method, a treadmill turning the propeller shaft. Bauer truly made his name, on Tsar Alexander II's coronation day in September, by submerging in the principal Russian naval base at Kronstadt with a dozen crew and observers plus a four-piece brass band, which could be clearly heard playing the national anthem underwater. But he did not get on with the Russians, who disparaged him as "the little corporal" and disdained his blunt manner. In a later demonstration the *Diable Marin* ran aground while passing under a ship and the screw was fouled, forcing Bauer once again to resort to his tried and tested escape procedure. The curmudgeonly inventor moved on to France. The Emperor Napoleon III showed some interest in his ideas, but the Crimean War came to its untidy end in 1857, whereupon Bauer returned to his native Bavaria.

In the renewed war with Denmark in 1864 he designed the submersible *Küstenbrander* (coastal incendiary) for Prussia, complete with guns and powered by a sort of internal combustion engine designed to function underwater by generating its own oxygen, a technical goal which was also to elude his compatriots eighty years later. But he fell out with the Prussians too and it was never built. After working with some promise of success on an underwater paraffin engine he died poor, ill and unsung in 1875, although a monument to him was eventually put up in Munich, the Bavarian capital. A little less suspicion on the part of the inventor and his Prussian patrons alike might have enabled Bauer to surpass in advance the achievements of Nordenfelt and Holland.

It was in the adventurous and desperate hands of the shortlived Confederate States Navy that the submersible warship made the transition from theory to practice during the American Civil War (1861–5). Once again the "underdog" Southerners' motivation was to undermine a blockade: the siege of the key Confederate port of Charleston, South Carolina, by the United States Navy. The first large-scale maritime conflict in half a century brought several advances in naval technology, including steam power unaided by sail as well as the armour carried by the new "ironclads" of both sides. The Southern ironclad *Merrimac* sank two wooden ships off Norfolk, Virginia, in March 1862 before taking on the US ironclad *Monitor* in an inconclusive slogging match. The latter (which would lend her name to a shortlived type of small warship with a pair of outsize guns for coastal bombardment) was herself semi-submersible, reducing her profile with ballast tanks which rendered the main deck awash for duels with shore batteries.

In 1862 a new impetus to the development of a viable underwater warship was given by the wealthy engineer Horace L. Hunley of Mobile, Alabama. He studied earlier submarine experiments and put up the money to build one for the South. The *Pioneer* was thirty-four feet long, powered by three men cranking a propeller shaft by hand. She was lost in the Mississippi estuary, either when trying an attack during the North's occupation of New Orleans or else scuttled in 1865 to prevent capture (the few sources on these early underwater craft are often sketchy and sometimes contradictory). Her successor, also iron but only twenty-five feet long, was presciently designèd to be driven by a battery-powered electric motor, but no suitable power-unit could be found. Hand-cranked, she sank without loss off Mobile while trying an attack.

In parallel was developed the semi-submersible *David* (to take on the Goliath of the US Navy). This was a steam-powered vessel which had a cylindrical main hull ten feet long and about seven in diameter. Her two long, pointed, conical ends earned her the contemptuous nickname of "cigar-boat". To the nose was attached a spar with a 134-pound explosive charge and contact-detonator at its tip, a fitment which gave the craft her final length of some sixty feet from "torpedo" to propeller. She had a retractable funnel and ballast tanks which enabled her to reduce her outline to a shape only a few inches high and ten feet long when going in to the attack. There was a single, slightly raised hatch on the top, which prompted a Northerner to describe the craft when awash as "a plank with a cylinder on top". The prototype sank when a passing steamer swamped her in her awash condition as she crept out of Charleston for an attack. All three crewmen were lost although the captain, Lieutenant John Payne, survived.

But the *David* was recovered; Lieutenant W.T. Glassell, CSN, and three volunteers took her out on a second sally on the evening of 5 October 1863. They attacked the USS *New Ironsides*, 3,486 tons, flagship of Rear-Admiral John Dahlgren, USN, who had just taken over command of the Charleston blockade, by the simple if hair-raising expedient of ramming the armoured flank under her broadside of eight guns. As the *David* came in at her top speed of five knots for the attack, Acting Ensign C.W. Howard, USN, sighted and hailed her from the deck of the target. He was killed by a shotgun blast from the attacker's hatch and thus became the first fatality in the history of submarine warfare. The spar torpedo exploded spectacularly and rocked the ship, starting many leaks and flooding her engine-room. One man suffered a broken leg but the *New Ironsides*, dented at the waterline, survived. The *David* however, was all but swamped by the turbulence she had caused and two of her crew were captured. Glassell and the fourth man got away.

Two other steam-powered "Davids" each made an attack on a Union ship, causing superficial damage on both occasions. Their main and not inconsiderable strategic effect was to diminish the confidence and efficiency of the blockaders, who felt obliged to keep on the move and were prone to false alarms. Several incomplete "Davids" were found after the war and one, the famous *Pioneer*, can be viewed in New Orleans.

The most dramatic naval exploit of the American Civil War came on 17 February 1864, when a different and rather bigger type of submersible, fittingly named the *H.L. Hunley*, achieved the first sinking of a surface warship by an underwater one. For this larger craft the Confederates had chosen manual power.

The CSS *Hunley* carried a crew of nine, of whom no fewer than eight cranked the propeller shaft. Unlike the "Davids" the vessel was to attack submerged rather than awash, which explains why steam power was abandoned. She was meant to endure up to three hours underwater. The boat was equipped with ballast tanks and lateral rudders, rudimentary hydroplanes, to help with diving and surfacing. Instead of a "torpedo" on a spar at the bow, the *Hunley* towed what we would call a mine, now coming into its own as a significant underwater weapon, at the stern. Confusingly, the early mine was known as a "torpedo" (the name of an electric eel capable of administering a shock). It proved itself viable in the Civil War in its free-floating, captive and shipborne (or towed) forms. Beer barrels floating just below the surface, stuffed with gunpowder and equipped with contact fuses, accounted for many ships on both sides, especially towards the end of the war, when seven Union ships were lost in three weeks off Mobile. There were also wired mines set off from shore by an electric current when a ship passed over them.

The *Hunley* was to approach as near as possible on the surface and then pass under the target trailing the mine, which would detonate on contact with the enemy hull as the attacking craft drew clear on the other side. But the *Hunley*, which must have been extraordinarily robust, sank no fewer than five times in trials, with the loss of forty-one lives including Hunley's. Yet there was no shortage of fresh volunteers for the sixth foray under Lieutenant G.E. Dixon, CSN. He had decided to dispense with the treacherous and unruly towed mine in favour of a proven "David"-style spar torpedo at the bow. He would also approach awash rather than underwater. And so, on 17 February 1864, he did, choosing as his target the USS *Housatonic*, 1,400 tons, a new, wooden-hulled, copper-bottomed sloop powered by steam. The Yankee crew, fully aware of the threat from the "Davids", was on the alert and the attacker was sighted 100 yards off. The sloop had steam up, slipped her cable and began to back off, but it was too late. Her guns could not be depressed sufficiently to hit the craft, which kept on coming and finally struck amidships. The explosion of the "torpedo" set off a magazine, tearing a hole below the waterline and causing the sloop to settle upright in shallow water within five minutes. One officer and four men died aboard the first vessel to be sunk by underwater attack. Others scrambled up the rigging to wait for help.

The *Hunley*, having become the first submersible warship to sink an enemy vessel, promptly became the first such craft to be lost in action. Probably swamped in the turbulence caused by the unexpectedly violent explosion, the vessel sank with the loss of all nine aboard. The wreck was found about 100 feet from that of its victim during postwar clearance work at the mouth of the Charleston harbour.

Interest in submarine warfare undoubtedly grew after the Civil War, the first in which submerged attacks had been delivered successfully. The idea of stealth at sea had now progressed far enough for it to be clear that there were three fundamental problems to be overcome if the underwater assault craft was to progress from marginal special operations, conceived in despair and of interest only to underdogs, to a strategic role capable of changing the nature of naval warfare. The main deficiencies were: underwater endurance, reliable propulsion whether submerged or surfaced, and a serious weapon. They were made good in reverse order.

The shortlived enthusiasm for modernisation evinced by the Imperial Austrian Navy when it briefly entertained the difficult Wilhelm Bauer also brought forth Captain Giovanni Luppis in 1867. He constructed a miniature "boat", complete with ram at the bow (in keeping with contemporary warship design), keel, propeller and rudder. This unmanned device was to be powered either by steam or by clockwork and was guided by lines running from the rudder to the point of launch, which seriously limited its range and reliability. In its bow it carried an explosive charge, which was to be set off when a small, two-bladed screw at the nose, rotated by the device's motion through the water, hit the target. The screw was attached to the trigger of a pistol inside the body which was pointed at the explosive charge so as to set it off when fired. This method of torpedo detonation was to remain in use for the best part of a century, although the pistol was soon replaced by a more sophisticated, purpose-built detonator – a "cap" of fulminate of mercury struck by a firing-rod protruding from the nose. The "fan" or miniature propeller at the tip unscrewed itself along the rod until the latter was held back from the cap only by a shearing pin, which broke when the torpedo struck home. The "unscrewing" process was completed only after the first 100 yards of the torpedo's run, in order to protect the firer from accidental detonation on board or a premature blast on firing.

But Luppis's self-propelled sea-bomb was deemed unsatisfactory by his masters, who wanted it to be self-guided as well. So he turned for help to a Lancastrian engineer who was managing a marine engineering company at Fiume (now Rijeka in Slovenia, part of the Austrian Empire until 1918).

Robert Whitehead (1823–1905) made Luppis's excellent idea viable by turning the powered torpedo into a completely self-contained missile. Their joint experiments began in 1868 with a cylindrical, round-nosed model, the essential shape not only of all its successors but also, for half a century, of the submarines which carried them. The device was powered by compressed air at a pressure of 700 pounds per square inch, travelled 200 yards at six knots and weighed 300 pounds, including a charge of eighteen pounds of dynamite. A later prototype, powered by air compressed to 1,200 pounds per square inch, had a range of about 300 yards. Both travelled in a line more or less straight but were very erratic in depth-keeping. Whitehead took a great step forward by adding a "balance-chamber mechanism" to keep the torpedo at an even depth, at first little more than a weight on a vertical lever attached to a horizontal rudder. This was known simply as "the Secret" and was governed by a hydrostatic valve set to respond to a predetermined water pressure; it remained the secret of the torpedo's success until 1910. In 1868 White-head also made the first torpedo-launching tube, powered by compressed air, with a cap at the front and a door at the back. The first Luppis-Whitehead production model was ready by 1870: sixteen feet long, with a charge of seventy-six pounds of guncotton to be detonated by a Luppis pistol, a range of 400 yards and a speed of eight knots.

The Austrians did not wish to go to the expense of patents to protect the new weapon. Instead they invited representatives of foreign navies to Fiume. The Royal Navy took a close interest in 1869 when officers from the Mediterranean Fleet came to Whitehead's factory. Their favourable report led to an invitation to the inventor to return to Britain with two torpedoes and his launching tube in 1870. The tube was fitted to the deck of a warship at the bow and more than 100 test firings were made off Sheerness in Kent. "The government, acting with the most unusual promptitude, at once came to terms with Mr Whitehead, and bought the rights of manufacture for £15,000," future improvements included, as

Commander Sueter noted in an early history of the submarine.

As the inventor worked on constant refinements to his weapon, the Navy began experiments with defensive measures: weighted nets on booms, to be swung out from a ship's sides when in port or at anchor. The wooden corvette *Aigle* was fitted with them, though chains were prudently passed under her bottom in the River Medway in case she sank after all. The test torpedo, launched from 400 yards, brushed past the end of a net and blew a hole twenty feet by seven in her side, below the waterline, with its charge of sixty-seven pounds of guncotton. A second, smaller torpedo detonated on hitting a net, blasting it against the ship's side without inflicting serious damage. So the British adopted nets, regarding them as no more than a nuisance of little worth until it became clear that many Russian ships had been saved by them in 1904–5. Against this, the Imperial Japanese Navy, closely modelled on the British, crippled or sank five battleships and four heavy cruisers with torpedoes in the Russo-Japanese War. Nets attached to ships were abandoned during the First World War as too cumbersome, although they remained in use as fixtures in harbours.

Despite the short range of early torpedoes they proved extremely effective, albeit fired only from surface ships for some twenty years. These soon came to include the new torpedo-boat (1877), which promptly conjured the "torpedoboat-destroyer", also equipped with torpedoes, into existence against itself (1885). The two types soon merged; but the very small, fast motor torpedo-boat made its bow in the 1920s. Soon all sizes of warship, including even capital ships, were to be fitted with torpedo tubes. The first real torpedo attack was made in the Black Sea in 1878 by the Russians, who sank a Turkish revenue-cutter with one shot from each of two torpedo-boats. Chilean government gunboats torpedoed an ironclad battleship in the hands of rebels at Valparaiso in 1891: it sank in six and a half minutes. The Japanese were already making devastating use of fast torpedo-boats against major Chinese warships in 1895. The arrival of the torpedo put an end to gun actions at close quarters, encouraging the development of bigger and bigger guns, with ever-longer ranges, for capital ships. The torpedo transformed naval strategy and tactics well before the submarine caught up technologically with its natural weapon.

Whitehead torpedoes, which met little lasting competition, were adopted with remarkable speed by nearly all the leading navies. Most of them were initially made at Woolwich for the British and at Fiume for the rest, or else, as in the case of the US Navy (at Newport, Rhode Island), under licence from Whitehead. His Mark II torpedo was fourteen and a half feet long with a diameter of fourteen inches and a range of 1,000 yards at thirty knots, or 1,500 at twenty-four – a remarkable advance from his earliest experiments with Luppis. Development continued apace; by 1907 the air propellant was stored at a pressure of 2,250 pounds per square inch, which gave much greater range: 4,000 yards at thirty-six knots, for example, with a warhead of up to 300 pounds of guncotton.

A Mr L. Obry of Trieste, not far from Fiume, invented the gyroscope and sold the idea to Whitehead, who began to fit this device to his missiles from 1898 to govern their course and depth. This automatic steering system, soon adopted for other navigational purposes, proved indispensable to the reliability of the weapon. The relevant property of a spinning gyroscope (essentially an axis-rod with a flywheel at its waist) is that its axis seeks the perpendicular. The axis could thus be linked to the steering in such a way as to keep the torpedo on a straight course or, as the Royal Norwegian Navy discovered before the end of the nineteenth century, a curved one, enabling the missile to behave like a swung ball in cricket or baseball and making it harder to evade. A vessel firing several torpedoes at different angles from various tubes could have them adopt parallel courses shortly after launch by appropriate advance settings of their gyroscopes.

Range was first increased by heating the compressed air with a built-in burner. Then torpedoes got their own motors, initially tiny copies of a steamship's triple-expansion engine, later the much lighter turbine.

Among Whitehead's few rivals was the Schwarzkopf company of Berlin, whose comparable products were tested by the Americans and used by the Imperial German Navy. One initial advantage these early German torpedoes had over others was their salt-resistant, phosphor-bronze casing and internal parts, to counter corrosion.

We have seen how the idea of the submersible warship enthused an English bishop and French and Italian priests. The next man of the cloth to take an interest was an Anglican curate in south Lancashire, the Reverend George W. Garrett. Unlike his clerical antecedents who remained cloistered in the realm of theory, Garrett actually built a small submersible in 1878. In the following year he made a craft nicely named the *Resurgam* (I shall rise again), spindle-shaped in the manner of the Confederate "Davids". The central part of the hull was a cylinder fourteen feet long and less than half that in diameter, capped by a rudimentary conning tower with hatch. Each end came to a point, giving an overall length of some forty-five feet. The central section was made of wood covered by steel plate. The internal diameter of the hull was only five feet, little enough for a crew of three and the steam engine. She had ballast tanks and hydroplanes at the sides. Garrett's most interesting idea was to use stored energy for propulsion underwater. On the surface the craft would be propelled by steam. For submergence, full steam would be raised before the hydroplanes deflected the craft under the surface. Submerged, the boat could travel ten miles at up to three knots on the steam stored in pressure cylinders. Experiments in the Mersey off Birkenhead went very well; but *Resurgam* failed to live up to her name in rough water off the north Wales coats. *"Resurgam" non resurrexit,* as the disappointed Latinist might have said.

But Garrett took his idea to Thorsten Nordenfelt, a Swedish gunmaker and patron of inventors. He started work on the *Nordenfelt I* at Stockholm in 1882 – the first submarine to be fitted with a tube (on deck) for a single Whitehead (there was also a one-inch Nordenfelt gun). Garrett's angular spindle shape was smoothed into a cigar, but the rudimentary conning tower was retained, as was the idea of stored steam power. The two funnels were folded down for submerging. The craft, built of iron plate, was designed to withstand a depth of fifty feet. It measured sixty-four feet with a diameter of nine and a displacement of sixty tons. On each side amidships was a sponson (short fixed wing) about eighteen inches wide supporting a small horizontal propeller. These were to push the boat underwater; its natural buoyancy reserve of up to 800 pounds was to bring it back to the surface like a lift (descent and ascent were thus to take place without the advantage of forward motion). The *Nordenfelt* was designed to have a range of 150 miles surfaced and fifteen at four knots underwater. Steam power was also used to eject water from the ballast tanks and to expel smoke through underwater vents (for concealment) while running on the surface.

This first properly armed submarine was a remarkable advance, even though she suffered many teething troubles before and after her first public trials. These took place, in the presence of several of the crowned heads of Europe and observers from as far away as Japan and Brazil, at Karlskrona, Sweden, in 1885. Smoke, carbon monoxide and carbon dioxide (a curse of all pre-nuclear submarines) built up inside the hull. The boat was at best a semi-submersible, happiest when working awash. The Reverend Captain Garrett was overcome by fumes when demonstrating *Nordenfelt* in the Solent and needed three weeks to recover. Yet the vessel was sold to the Greek Navy in 1886 for £9,000 after an impressive demonstration in the Bay of Salamis.

This inaugurated the first submarine arms race: in 1887 Turkey, Greece's mortal enemy, ordered two "Nordenfelts" to be built at Chertsey on the Thames. These Mark IIs were 100 feet long, displaced 160 tons and had a range of 900 miles. They were capable of a remarkable eleven knots surfaced (five submerged) and carried two torpedoes, mounted externally, as well as two one-inch guns. The vertical screws were, however, aligned fore and aft instead of across the beam, which made a steady submergence almost impossible. The boats were built in sections and transported to Constantinople by ship. Captain Garrett, gazetted an honorary commander in the Imperial Ottoman Navy for the occasion, and his team from England had to conduct the trials in the Sea of Marmara; Turkish sailors were wisely reluctant to volunteer. Small wonder, as the boat proved very difficult to stabilise, or indeed keep submerged at all. The ballast tanks were too big and the lurching water inside them added to the instability; the bow jerked up to the surface when a torpedo was fired, whereupon the water in the tanks shifted sternwards and the boat went down stern first. The conning "tower" was so low in the water that almost anything passing and larger than a rowing boat tended to swamp the craft when she was surfaced. But the first of the pair was reluctantly accepted by Turkey. She was never used and rotted at her moorings in the Golden Horn; the second was never completed.

Undeterred, Nordenfelt, now linked with the Barrow Shipbuilding Company (at the yard where Britain's ballistic submarines are built today), went on to make a Mark III, 125 feet long, capable of diving to 100 feet and of making fourteen knots on the surface. She had two steam engines, a range of 1,000 miles and armour up to one inch thick, displacing 160 tons surfaced and 230 submerged. She was the first submarine to have internal torpedo tubes (two). This boat took part in the massive Spithead Naval Review of 1887 for Queen Victoria's golden jubilee. She was painted grey and when awash – her preferred operating depth – presented a target one-thirteenth of the size of a conventional torpedo-boat. The Russians were so impressed, despite her inherited, unstable depth-keeping, that they bought her on the spot. Unfortunately on the delivery run it was the turn of Providence to desert the Reverend Garrett: the "Russian Nordenfelt" ran aground off Jutland. Although nobody was hurt and the vessel was salvaged two weeks later, the Russians refused to accept her and she was scrapped. The British Navy did not take up Nordenfelt's design.

While he and Garrett were at work in England, a pair of British inventors called Ash and Campbell came up with the answer to the problem of underwater propulsion. In 1885 they started work on a spindle-shaped submersible with an electric motor, to be powered by 104 accumulators in two "batteries" of fifty-two each, capable of delivering eight knots over eighty miles. This boat, named *Nautilus* in honour of Fulton, was fundamentally unstable and stuck in the mud of Portsmouth harbour on submergence trials in 1888. The crew of six had to rush in a body from bow to stern and back again to rock the boat free, a technique which was to come in handy as late as the Second World War. Another British inventor called Waddington built an ellipsoid submersible in 1886 on Nordenfelt lines, but with an electric motor run on forty-five accumulators. It too was unstable; but the idea of using a battery-powered electric motor underwater was one of the great breakthroughs in submarine history: an electric motor needs no air.

In practical terms early submarine development was mainly Anglo-Saxon. But in the mid-nineteenth century the French led the world in shipbuilding, and from that time they began to make a major, and often the leading, contribution to the development of the submarine. They were doubtless urged on by Jules Verne's *Twenty Thousand Leagues under the Sea*, the adventures of Captain Nemo in the *Nautilus* (1870; another reason why it is the best-known submarine name). The French made the finest sailing ships and laid down the world's first ironclad powered jointly by steam and sail – *La Gloire* – in 1858. In the same year a Captain Bourgois produced a design for an air-powered submarine and the Ministry of Marine put it out to tender.

The competition was won by a certain M. Brun: his *Le Plongeur* (diver) was launched at Rochefort in April 1863. She was 140 feet long with a beam of twenty feet and a draught of ten. In profile she was not unlike a swordfish (the ten-foot "sword" being a spar torpedo). Without the spar, the design looks quite modern except for the small conning tower. The craft was made of iron plates with a heavy iron keel, contributing to an unprecedented displacement of 420 tons. There was a deck aft complete with railing; a lifeboat (with room for twelve and sealed buoyancy chambers) was housed in a recess on top amidships and held in place by bolts. *Le Plongeur* was powered by compressed air stored at 180 pounds per square inch in twenty-three tanks. There were water tanks and disposable cannon-balls for ballast. Despite her horizontal rudders and propeller the boat was impossible to control vertically and hopelessly underpowered for her bulk. But she made a graceful exhibit in model form at the Paris Exhibition of 1867.

The ingenuity of French shipbuilders and engineers was inexhaustible at this period. Having been first with breech-loading guns and steam boilers, they were also the first to launch an electrically powered submersible. Claude Goubet, a civil engineer, built the *Goubet I*, sixteen and a half feet long and five feet nine inches in diameter, shaped like an American football and made of bronze. The craft, eleven tons deadweight, was to be carried on a battleship and was meant to operate awash. There was a small periscope. Two charges were carried externally, to be attached to the target's hull. Inboard there was a tank of compressed air and bottles of oxygen to increase the endurance of the crew of two, who sat back to back. There was a retractable steel bar in the bow with cutters at the tip, to deal with enemy nets. Despite the fact that she too was almost impossible to control vertically, the Brazilian Navy bought her for £10,000.

The *Goubet II* was laid down in 1886 and launched three years later. She was twenty-six feet long and six in diameter with a heavy keel which could be detached in an emergency (when one arose, the bolts had rusted solid!). In an early trial the electric craft stayed under for a record eight hours; but she too lacked stability in the vertical plane. Even so the boat was still giving tourists rides in Lake Geneva as late as 1908. A British company bought the patents but won no orders and therefore built none.

Another Frenchman, Gustav Zédé, took up Goubet's ideas, backed by Admiral Aube, the submarine enthusiast who put and kept France in the lead despite powerful conservative opposition in the Navy. The *Gymnote* (electric eel), displacing thirty-one tons, was sixty feet long and six in diameter and has a strong historical claim to be the first "modern" submarine. Powered by a battery of 564 small accumulators with a total weight of one ton, she also had water tanks for ballast which were emptied by compressed air, soon to become a standard feature of all operational submarines. The boat made six and a half knots surfaced and six submerged. Trials at Toulon in 1888 were not a great success for the usual reasons of vertical control, but the *Gymnote* remained in use as a testbed for refinements into the new century.

The *Gustave Zédé* was launched at Toulon in 1893 by the recently deceased inventor's assistant, Romazzotti, who designed her in 1890. With her length of 148 feet, diameter of eleven and displacement of 266 tons, the boat was too large for contemporary technology. But she had a real conning tower five feet high and her surfaced profile resembled much more recent boats. She carried three torpedoes for her single tube in the bow, launched by compressed air. The original 720 bulky accumulators weighed no less than 130 tons but technical improvements soon made it possible to halve their number. Once again depth-holding proved difficult. On an early trial she hit the bottom at sixty feet with some force. Refinements such as extra horizontal rudders and buoyancy tanks were added and she eventually performed very well on attack trials. The bronze-hulled boat carried a crew of two officers and ten men and served for at least fifteen years.

The next submarine to join the French fleet was the *Morse* (walrus), which had a periscope nearly twenty feet high, a bronze hull and a range of 100 miles at seven knots, one below her top speed. This boat was 118 feet long and displaced 136 tons on the surface. Within months, in 1899, the *Narval* was launched. The designer, Laubeuf, won a competition run by the Ministry of Marine for a submersible capable of ten miles submerged at a speed of eight knots and a surface range of 100 miles at twelve. The displacement limit was 200 tons. Laid down at Cherbourg in 1897, the *Narval* was the first submersible to feature two viable propulsion systems for surface and underwater and comfortably surpassed all specifications. The boat proved to be capable underwater of twenty-five miles at eight knots and seventy-two at five knots, on her electric motor. On the surface the triple-expansion steam engine with its oil-fired boiler was capable of 250 miles at eleven knots or twice that at seven and a half. When the boat was running on the surface, the electric motor, powered by the main engine, acted as a dynamo for recharging the batteries, a most ingenious refinement which was universally imitated thereafter.

The remarkably advanced *Narval* had a double hull, the inner circular for strength and the outer flattened on top with a recognisable conning tower. The ballast, water and fuel tanks, all small to eliminate "slurping", were between the two hulls; there were even compensation tanks to fill with water as the oil tanks emptied, for the sake of trim. The ballast tanks were once again emptied by compressed air. The four torpedoes were fired from external frames, two on each side. The one great drawback was the near-vertical diving procedure, which took a minimum of fifteen minutes and normally twenty, even after improvements: the funnel had to be folded, the boiler shut down, the steam cooled and a great deal of water taken slowly into the ballast tanks. There were also problems with the oil-fired boiler, but the installation of an internal combustion engine brought great improvements in both reliability and range for the world's first "ocean-going" submarine. The hull, fitted with a ram like almost every other warship of the day, was of unprecedented strength.

The French instituted far-reaching naval reforms in 1899, after years of neglect of the fleet in favour of the Army, which had lost its pre-eminence in Europe to the Germans in 1870. Identifying the Germans and the British as their strongest potential enemies at sea, they were confident of matching the former on the open sea in *guerre d'escadre* (squadron actions). Unable to challenge the Royal Navy's supremacy, they adopted the *guerre de course* (cruiser warfare on commerce) against the British. For the first time submarines now formed an integral part of a major power's strategic planning: they were to defend France's coasts and harbours. Also of interest was the idea of the submarine as an "equaliser" for the weaker naval power, especially for France, which also had to make contingency plans against Italy and Austria in the Mediterranean. Submarines were "in": the newspaper *Le Matin* raised 300,000 francs from its readers for two identical boats, the *Français* and the *Algérien*, thus forming the first "class" of submarine. Next came the "Farfadet" class of four, reputedly capable of diving in ninety seconds. The 1901 budget provided for twenty boats of Romazzotti's "Naiade" class, which had two petrol engines and an electric motor. The heterogeneous French submarine force now began to profit from the advantages of standardisation; but new experimental types were still coming off the stocks in quick succession. In 1904–5 three, known only as *X, Y* and *Z*, were launched within twelve months and four more prototypes were building. By 1906, 800-ton boats were being designed with a range of 2,500 miles and an underwater speed of ten knots as France, the world's leading submarine power by a large margin, deployed its new weapon in flotillas in the Channel, the Mediterranean and even Indo-China. The first flotilla had been formed before the nineteenth century ended.

Russia, as we saw, flirted briefly and inconclusively with Bauer and his design. It was not until 1876 that the Russo-Polish engineer Drzewiecki began to earn his place in the history of submarine development. He built a turtle-shaped submersible in that year but in 1879 adopted the increasingly popular cigar shape for his second attempt, a pedal-powered boat armed with two external fifty-kilogram (110-pound) mines, to be deposited under the target and detonated by a suitably lengthy electric wire. The Russian government fell over itself to order fifty of these in the same year, after successful trials in which the Drzewiecki craft managed up to four knots at a depth of fifteen feet. Later he added an electric motor and batteries, reduced the crew from four to two and raised underwater speed to five knots. Then the Navy abandoned its policy of coastal defence by submarines; they were reduced to serving as pontoons and the like. Unfazed, Drzewiecki carried on at the drawing board and in 1896 invented his "drop collar" method of launching torpedoes carried on a submarine's deck. The French promptly bought the right to use his idea.

In 1903 the Russian petrol-driven submarine *Delfin*, a 200-ton boat 175 feet long, sank on trials at Kronstadt with the loss of twenty-four men, including many young trainees, the worst submarine disaster yet. A faulty valve which should have been capable of simple repair caused panic and in the rush to escape one man managed to jam the hatch open, swamping the boat.

A flotilla of "Lake" submarines bought from the United States was in place at Vladivostok, the main port on Russia's Pacific coast, in time for the war with Japan in 1904–5. Although teething troubles, inexperience and indiscipline rendered the craft ineffectual, the Japanese kept well clear of the port for fear of them. The Japanese had also secretly taken delivery of their first five "Holland" submarines from America by the end of 1904 but did not deploy them.

The last decade of the nineteenth century in the United States, where underwater warfare began, gave the final impetus to the development of a viable submersible torpedo-boat. The US naval budget for the year 1893–4 included a sum of $200,000 for the construction and testing of an experimental submarine. Tenders were invited and there were just three entrants: Mr Baker, Mr Lake and Mr Holland.

Baker's boat was a forty-foot egg, made of oak covered in waterproof cloth. It displaced seventy-five tons and had dual steam and electric power. The "conning tower" was a hemispherical blister on the hull and the chief novelty was the pair of screws, one on each side, which could be swung through 180 degrees to propel the craft forward and/or downward or upward. The craft was unable to maintain a steady depth.

Simon Lake built *Argonaut*, a craft chiefly notable for her two large wheels in line, enabling her to run along the bottom at depths down to 150 feet. She was made of steel plate and had a powerful searchlight and a flexible air pipe with a float to hold its end above water. When the boat was submerged, her petrol engine would suck in air for the crew of five by means of this ancestor of the schnorkel. She could operate comfortably fifteen to seventy-five miles off American shores on the continental shelf.

Lake's *Protector* was rather larger, with three torpedo tubes (one in the stern) and a relatively spacious conning tower containing the novelty of an airlock. This enabled a diver to get in or out to cut cables, destroy mines and even communicate with the shore via the telephone in his helmet and an underwater cable. The airlock was also envisaged as an escape hatch and for salvage purposes. The petrol and electric engines were capable, working simultaneously, of ten knots submerged. The electric motor offered slow but silent running when needed and the four hydroplanes conferred exceptional stability underwater. The wheels had a partly pneumatic, partly hydraulic suspension system for smooth running. The boat was notable for her ability to submerge in stately fashion on an even keel using her ballast tanks.

The "Lake" boats were envisaged for coastal defence; Russia bought the *Protector* in 1904, with an order for four more, from the Newport

News Shipbuilding Company in Virginia. The chief weakness of the
remarkable design was the craft's dependence on her breathing tube –
and a sea bottom on which to rest her wheels!

But Lake could not withstand the competition from John Philip
Holland, an Irish schoolmaster born in County Clare in 1840 who
emigrated to New Jersey in 1873. Holland, another Fenian sympathiser
originally inspired, like Bushnell and Fulton, by the desire to do down
the almighty Royal Navy, started work on his first underwater craft in
1875. He later set out his objective:

The submarine boat is a small ship on the model of the Whitehead torpedo,
subject to none of its limitations, improving on all of its special qualities
excepting speed, for which it substitutes incomparably greater endurance. It is
not like other small vessels, compelled to select for its antagonist a vessel of
about its own or inferior power; the larger and more powerful its mark, the
better its opportunity.

What he had in mind was a juicy British battleship. His first craft was
puny, only sixteen feet long and slightly ovoid in section, with a beam
of twenty inches and a depth of two feet, shaped like a cigar with a point
at each end. Her rudder was slung under the exposed propeller at the
stern. She was pedal-powered by her one-man "crew" and anticipated
the "human torpedoes" of the Second World War. The "driver" sat in a
kayak-like cockpit wearing a diver's helmet and breathing the compressed air stored in the hull, which also contained ballast tanks. Though
hardly classifiable as a submarine and soon scrapped as impracticable,
she had the efficient hydroplanes, water ballast and compressed air which
were key features of all the "Holland" boats that followed, each bigger
and better than the last.

Holland's second effort, launched in 1882, was financed by the Fenians
and known as the *Fenian Ram*. She boasted a petrol engine and a
pneumatic gun which fired a nine-inch-diameter torpedo six feet long,
also the work of the inventor. She was still only thirty-one feet long
with a displacement of nineteen tons and her torpedo was a complete
failure. The Fenian Society gave up its grand plan for smuggling a
flotilla of "Rams" in the holds of merchant ships to British waters
and unleashing them against Her Majesty's ships, took possession of
Holland's creation and ran her aground at New Haven, Connecticut.

But the inventor had already discovered the secret which enabled his
later submarines to overcome the competition and drive almost all others
from the seas. His boats did not descend or ascend by their own weight,
finely adjusted by complicated and time-consuming fiddling with valves

and ballast tanks. They *dived*, by tilting their large hydroplanes, mounted, near the stern, and propelling themselves under by their own engine-power, against a small reserve of buoyancy. Once at the desired depth they remained there with hydroplanes level, surfacing by driving forward with the hydroplanes tilted in the opposite direction.

Holland's next client was the United States Navy, which, despite competition from Nordenfelt, placed an order for his seventh model in 1895, when the Holland Boat Company was founded. This vessel was launched in 1897 as the USS *Plunger*, displacing 140 tons on the surface and 165 when submerged. Her two triple-expansion engines were powered by petrol-fired boilers, delivering a remarkable fourteen knots on the surface while the electric motor provided eight knots submerged. This matched the performance of a typical First World War submarine; those in the Second were not much faster. But the boilers raised the temperature inside the hull to all but unbearable levels in the eighty-five foot boat. Work was suspended and in the end Holland gave the US government its money back.

His next model was built speculatively, with financial backing (in exchange for rights to his patents) from the Electric Storage Battery Company, which now became the Electric Boat Company, henceforward principal supplier of submarines to the US Navy. Known simply as the *Holland*, the new boat was rather shorter than *Plunger* at fifty-four feet with a surface displacement of seventy-five tons. It was powered by a single Otto petrol engine capable of seven knots and an electric motor delivering five and a half submerged. Launched in 1897, two years before the French *Narval*, she was the first submarine capable of recharging her own batteries at sea. Trials were completed in 1899 and the US Navy finally bought her in 1900 for £150,000, making the United States the second power after France to commission a submarine into its fleet. *Holland*'s armament was a bow tube with three torpedoes, plus a pneumatic gun firing fused dynamite charges for use on the surface.

The first "Holland" production-model, the inventor's ninth, was based on this and ordered by many navies. The original length was sixty-three feet four inches with a maximum diameter of eleven feet ten inches. The 160-horsepower, four-stroke Otto engine not only powered the dynamo which charged the batteries but also operated an air-pump to refill the compressed-air tanks. The boat carried air flasks with a total capacity of forty-two cubic feet, equivalent to a cubic mile of air at normal pressure, enough to enable nine men to breathe for nine weeks. This air was used to blow the ballast tanks for rapid surfacing, to charge the torpedoes with compressed air and also to fire them. Even the inevitable leaks from the flasks were turned to advantage: they improved the quality of the atmosphere underwater and raised the internal pressure to help keep water-leaks under control.

Each boat had a main ballast tank and an auxiliary one, with two more tanks for trim, fore and aft. The level of water in the auxiliary tank depended on the number of men aboard (seven to nine), and the weight of stores and fuel. Air was used to move water between the fore and aft trim tanks according to need, as indicated by the spirit-level amidships. When awash, the small conning tower provided 300 pounds of positive buoyancy. This was enough to bring the boat to the surface as soon as her forward motion stopped. Turning the hydroplanes upward with the motor still running made for a quicker ascent; blowing the tanks as well was even faster.

The US Navy ordered four "Hollands" in 1900, two to be built at Elizabeth, New Jersey – Adder and Moccasin – and two at San Francisco, Grampus and Pike (almost all subsequent US boats until the nuclear age were named after fish). The pair named after snakes were unlucky: on their joint sea-trials their towline broke as they were being taken out to sea in rough weather and the two boats collided, damaging each other seriously. Earlier, when the Adder struck the bottom hard at twenty feet, the crew had crowded into the stern and Captain F.T. Cable blew the tanks to surface again; undeterred, they refilled the tanks and the air flasks and sailed another fifteen miles underwater. The West Coast pair did well from the start, needing only four minutes to dive out of sight. Designed to withstand depths of 100 feet, the Porpoise, one of three "Hollands" ordered in 1901, went down to 127 feet on her trials in 1903, whereupon some valves failed. The ballast tanks had to be pumped out by hand and twenty minutes were needed to regain buoyancy, but the boat finally shot to the surface undamaged.

By this time Holland was working on a Mark II, exploiting the lessons learned from the first commissioned boats. The prototype, Fulton, was sold to Russia in 1904 and the US Navy ordered four in 1905–6.

Thanks above all to John Philip Holland, the theory of the submersible torpedo-boat had been turned into a practicable, if fragile, weapons system at the turn of the century, as shown by the fact that several important navies were taking the submarine seriously.

ACT I: 1900–1918

Scene i: The race to arm

THE POWERS WHICH WERE to be the chief antagonists at sea in the coming war, the United Kingdom and the German Reich, although they owned respectively the greatest and the most advanced navies in the world, disdained the submarine even as their naval arms race accelerated.

Mr Hugh Oakeley Arnold-Forster, Parliamentary Secretary (junior minister) at the Admiralty told the House of Commons at the end of 1900:

The Admiralty are not prepared to take any steps in regard to submarines because this vessel [sic] is only the weapon of the weaker nation. If, however, this vessel can be rendered practical, the nation which possesses it will cease to be weak, and will become really powerful. More than any other nation, we should have to fear the attacks of submarines.

The orthodox naval view was expressed in 1901 by Admiral Sir Arthur Wilson, VC, a future First Sea Lord. The submarine, he declared, was "underhand, unfair and damned un-English". He was soon to recommend that submarine crews captured in wartime should be hanged without trial as pirates. But attempts at the first of two disarmament conferences at The Hague, in 1899, to persuade twenty-six governments to outlaw both the submarine and the torpedo had failed as completely as all other serious arms-limitation proposals. And the British noted the enthusiasm with which the French and American navies had adopted the submarine. So by spring 1901, in the naval estimates for 1901–2, there was provision for five "Holland" boats, at £35,000 each. Arnold-Forster said at the time: "One thing stands between the submarine boat and efficiency, and that is the motor by which it is propelled; but there is no disguising the fact that if you can add speed to the qualities of the submarine boat, it might in certain circumstances become a very formidable vessel." His nephew, Lieutenant F.D. Arnold-Forster, RN, would soon take up his post as the first captain of the first submarine in British service, *Holland I*.

The British came late to the submarine but, despite the distaste of the traditionalists, adopted it with the same kind of enthusiastic pragmatism as they had shown rather more promptly for the torpedo. The greatest admiral of the day, Sir John Fisher, First Sea Lord from 1904 to 1910 and 1914 to 1915 as well as progenitor of the fleet which was to decide the outcome of the First World War, had no doubts as he took supreme command: "I don't think it is even *faintly* realised – *the immense impending revolution which the submarines will effect as offensive weapons of war*" (this exceptionally prescient, self-made man was notorious for over-emphasis). Fisher also foresaw the decisive importance of airpower.

The Royal Navy's first submarines were virtually identical to the American "Hollands". Their construction under licence at the Barrow-in-Furness yard of Vickers Sons and Maxim (now Vickers Shipbuilding and Engineering Ltd) was supervised by the American Captain Cable, who ran the pre-acceptance trials. His Majesty's Submarine Torpedo-Boat *Holland I* was commissioned early in 1902 under the aegis of Commander (later Admiral Sir) Reginald Bacon, RN, the first Inspecting Captain of submarines, who also made the periscope standard equipment. By then the Admiralty had already placed an order for the first four larger boats of the "A" class, largely designed by Bacon: 100 feet long, displacing 180 tons submerged, with speeds of eleven knots surfaced and seven and a half submerged.

There were to be thirteen "A" boats. The first, *A1* (Lieutenant Loftus Mansergh, RN), was terminally unlucky on 18 March 1904. Fresh from the previous day's triumphs on manoeuvres in the Solent, where submarines had scored four "hits" on battleships, the *A1* submerged to "attack" the cruiser *Juno*. She never returned. Shortly afterwards the SS *Berwick Castle* reported a hit from an unarmed torpedo and then two or three bumps under her hull. The liner had apparently run over the *A1*. The Navy concluded that the boat had been in a collision and sprung a leak. A gunboat saw large bubbles of air at the spot but stood by helpless as no means of assistance could be found. The hatch at the top of the conning tower of all other "A" boats and later British submarines was supplemented by another at the bottom.

The Navy none the less began to work its way through the alphabet, each letter signifying a new class of submarine larger and usually better than the last. They took delivery of the first "B" in 1905, the first "C" in 1906, "D" in 1910 and "E" in 1913. All these, eventually totalling some 130 boats, were directly descended from the "Holland" design.

From *B1* onwards all British submarines had the type of conning tower standard around the world until beyond the end of the Second World War. From *D1* (1914) they had much more efficient (and less detectable) diesel engines for surface propulsion. Alphabetical order was thrown overboard for a while from 1913 when the British decided to try other types of boat, notably the "S" class of three, the first double-hulled boats in the Royal Navy, a British variation on an Italian design (the Scott-Laurenti type). Future British boats were to enjoy the immense gains in strength and "survivability" to be had from the double hull, which dominated submarine design until 1945.

The British "Hollands" gave sturdy and reliable service for a decade and more, a remarkable tribute to the quality of a pioneering design. Indeed the first is still in harness. *Holland I* foundered without loss of life on the way to the breaker's yard in 1913. The boat was located off Plymouth by a minesweeper only in 1981. After sixty-eight years submerged the Royal Navy's first submarine was still sound enough to salvage. She was restored as a unique exhibit at the Submarine Museum at Gosport near Portsmouth, where she can be inspected from within. The visitor will be surprised by the modernity of the spartan interior – and probably amazed by the thought that nine men at a time went to sea in her without harm.

During a debate on the Imperial Navy in 1901, Admiral Alfred von Tirpitz, State Secretary at the Navy Office since 1897, when he initiated the forced expansion of the fleet, declared: "Germany has no need of submarines." The Navy itself thought otherwise and was ready when he changed his mind.

Wilhelm Bauer had been the first real German submariner. The next, Friedrich Otto Vogel, built a small, steam submersible at Dresden in 1867–70, but it sank on trials. The Germans bought a licence from Nordenfelt for the construction, in Kiel and Danzig, of two boats of his design, completed in 1890. They were not impressed, any more than by an experimental craft built by Howaldt at Kiel in about 1891.

The same yard constructed a boat designed by the torpedo expert Karl Leps in 1897. Its hull was a cylinder with a round nose and a pointed stern and its main dimensions were forty-two feet by eight. This overgrown torpedo was strengthened by watertight bulkheads. Observation was effected through a diver's helmet attached to the hull, which had a horizontal stabilising rim sixteen inches wide round it and horizontal and vertical rudders. Tests were disappointing and the craft was scrapped in 1902.

In the same year the Spanish engineer R.L. d'Equevilley, who had worked with Laubeuf on the *Narval*, came to Germany when the French government showed no interest in his designs for new submarines. It will have become clear that, in the small circle of obsessive, early submarine inventors, loyalty attached less to a flag or cause than to whomsoever could be persuaded to show interest (and money). It is inconceivable, regardless of subsequent denials, that d'Equevilley avoided applying what he had learned (and contributed) in France, while at work in Germany. When he left France, his mentor Laubeuf was working on the *Aigrette* (egret), which had diesel and electric propulsion (the first application of the combination used in all non-nuclear submarines from 1913).

Krupp of Essen, the leading German steel and munitions conglomerate to whom d'Equevilley offered his services, had just acquired the Germaniawerft yard in Kiel on the Baltic. The *Forelle* (trout) was laid down in February 1903 and completed in four months. She was a cigar-shaped craft some forty feet long, displacing fifteen and a half tons and powered by batteries. The tests went so well that Kaiser Wilhelm II came to inspect her; his brother, Prince Heinrich, a serving admiral, took the helm in an underwater trial. Germaniawerft was already at work on the design of a 200-ton boat for the Royal Netherlands Navy, but the Dutch withdrew and built their own "Holland" variant (*Luctor et Emergo* – I struggle and emerge – later restyled *O1* (for *Onderzeeboot*, underseaboat, number one)).

The Russians, however, were as interested in German designs as in French and American, and placed an order in Kiel for three 205-ton boats which eventually formed their "Karp" class – on condition that they could take the *Forelle* with them in the meantime. Thus the first operational boats built in Germany were not for the House of Orange, still less the Hohenzollerns, but for the tottering Romanovs. Despite the interest of the Kaiser himself, and of his Navy's own Torpedo Inspectorate, Tirpitz and the staff were dismissive, absorbed in the spectacular expansion of their battlefleet as it rapidly developed, technologically and ship for ship, into the finest fleet in the world.

Germany, which already fielded the world's most formidable Army, was now locked in a naval arms race with Britain, which it was trying, successfully at first until the British awoke to their danger, to overhaul. For a century Britain had no naval strategy except the "two-power standard": to maintain its fleet at a strength equal to the second and third strongest naval powers combined, plus ten per cent for the Empire. There was no active maritime policy but only a reactive one, to maintain naval supremacy in support of worldwide imperial trade. When the French launched the world's first ironclad in 1859, the British laid down their first, HMS *Warrior*, in 1860. When the French, and then the

Americans, went in for submarines by the turn of the century, the British copied. Only when Fisher's reign at the Admiralty began did they develop a coherent strategy backed by planned construction. The world's first "all big-gun" battleship, HMS *Dreadnought*, built in a year and a day and launched in 1907, made all other capital ships in the world obsolete overnight.

Now it was the Germans' turn to adopt a reactive policy with their own "Dreadnought" programme. Their individual ships were better, but the British, once they remembered that sea supremacy was a matter of life and death for them when faced with a restlessly ambitious Germany, simply used their much greater shipbuilding capacity to outstrip the Germans. They abandoned the two-power standard in favour of staying sixty per cent ahead of Germany overall (fifty per cent in the North Sea zone). When the Germans started building dreadnoughts, Britain laid down super-dreadnoughts with bigger guns.

Tirpitz was still telling the Reichstag in spring 1904, despite a growing U-boat lobby, that submarines were of little foreseeable use to the High Seas Fleet. But in July he changed his tune and minuted: "I intend to have a submarine built by the Navy Ministry and authorise [the Technical Department] to execute the construction." If Britain was building them, Germany had to follow.

In autumn 1904, therefore, the naval engineer Gustav Berling was employed by the Torpedo Inspectorate to lay down the *U1*, completed in September 1906. Benefiting from lessons learned in meeting the order from the Russians, the first operational German submarine was double-hulled, like all her successors for forty years. Kritzler, Germaniawerft's chief engineer, supervised the construction and abandoned petrol propulsion for paraffin. The *U1* had two screws and was 139 feet long with a beam of twelve feet, displacing 238 tons (283 submerged). She was capable of about eleven and seven knots, had one torpedo tube and a crew of nineteen. *U2*, completed at Danzig in 1908, was similar but somewhat larger and quicker, with four tubes, two each at bow and stern.

The next two boats, *U3* and *U4*, from Danzig, formed a class and featured a two-inch gun on deck, as did their successors. *U5* to *U8*, built at Germaniawerft, and *U9* to *U12*, from Danzig, formed the next class. Successive boats generally incorporated improvements in size, performance and refinement. Starting with the *U19* class of four, completed at Danzig from 1913, all German submarines were diesel-powered. The "U19s" measured 210 feet and displaced 650 tons surfaced or 837 submerged; their engines came from Maschinenfabrik Augsburg-Nürnberg (MAN). The reliability and endurance of diesel power turned the submarine from an essentially defensive, tactical weapon to a potentially strategic one – potential only, because hardly any admiral except Fisher (in restive retirement between 1910 and 1914) fully understood the possibilities.

The great navies were dazzled by the technological achievement embodied in the "Dreadnought" line-of-battle ship and her lighter but faster cousin, the battlecruiser. Their main armament, the giant gun in its massively armoured turret, was soon to be capable of hurling a broadside of shells, each as heavy as one of the new horseless carriages, from one side of the Channel to the other. These were the strategic armaments and ultimate deterrents of the day. They were given flotillas of destroyers to protect them and to engage in high-speed, close-range torpedo attacks during "fleet actions"; light cruisers to reconnoitre for them and lead and protect the destroyers; recoverable seaplanes to catapult from their decks for long-range reconnaissance and spotting the fall of their massive shot; mountains of coal and later lakes of oil in huge reserves to fuel them; great shipyards to maintain, repair and replace them; and radio stations to control their movements. It cost as much to build one dreadnought as to raise an Army corps of two divisions or 25,000 troops.

By the time war broke out in August 1914, the main powers' strengths in dreadnoughts alone were as follows. Britain had twenty-three battleships in commission and thirteen more building (plus eight battlecruisers in service and one building); Germany had thirteen battleships, five more under construction (and five battlecruisers with two more building). France had four battleships at sea and three on the stocks; Italy had three built and three building; Austria had two in service; Russia had completed one battleship and laid down another, with two battlecruisers at sea and six more on order. Turkey had none: the two battleships it had ordered from Britain were brusquely commandeered by the Royal Navy in 1914.

Of the leading non-European navies, which were to play minor roles in the coming war, Japan had one battleship plus two building and two battlecruisers with two more building. The United States, neutral until April 1917, commissioned no battlecruisers but had ten battleships in service with seven more in hand when war broke out in Europe.

All these fleets had heterogeneous auxiliary forces, including heavy or armoured cruisers for showing the flag in distant parts; gunboats for similar purposes where cruisers could not go; coastal defence vessels, torpedo-boats and patrol boats; minelayers and minesweepers; depot and repair ships; and submarines.

Before the war submarines were seen strictly as auxiliaries. The Russians and the French in particular had acquired them for the defence of coasts and harbours. The British and the Germans saw them as stealthy adjuncts of the battlefleet: to spy on enemy ships and harbours, to reconnoitre secretly, to locate the enemy or else to act as a defensive screen to give early warning of enemy movements. Sometimes they accompanied surface formations but their low speed made this the exception rather than the rule. The rival navies on the North Sea also planned to use their submarines as minelayers.

But their main effect, reinforced by that of the mine, on prewar strategic planning was a momentous one indeed, far greater than the role envisaged for them: they had done well enough on manoevres to instil fear into every admiral, a nightmare no less real for being initially unacknowledged most of the time, and often glossed over by commanders and umpires on exercises. Because of the new threat the British abandoned their original strategy against Germany of close naval blockade, traditional in wars with continental powers. At the eleventh hour, in July 1914, they prudently opted for a distant blockade, enabling them to keep their squadrons together for the anticipated "Trafalgar" while using cruisers and submarines as forward sentinels.

The tactical consequences of the submarine threat were no less farreaching. The commander of the Grand Fleet, Admiral Jellicoe, realising in the last days of peace that his main base in Scapa Flow, north-east of Scotland, was completely defenceless against U-boats, resolved to keep the big ships on the move to prevent them becoming sitting targets. "Dreadnought" was already a serious misnomer in the new age of the mine and the submarine – well before the true nemesis of the battleship, the aircraft, had become a factor at sea.

The Germans did not fancy their chances of winning a Trafalgar and began the war with a strategy of attrition. Anticipating a blockade, they resolved to concentrate locally superior force against individual ships or small formations involved in enforcing it. Their idea was to erode British numerical superiority until they could take on the enemy's residual main strength on roughly equal terms for the decisive fleet action. Until then there was to be no pitched battle. For the Germans the Navy's role was secondary to the Army's, which was confidently expected to decide the issue by a swift defeat of France in a repeat of 1870, before dealing with Russia, the main enemy. For Britain, with its small professional Army, the Navy retained strategic primacy. While the much bigger French Army, reinforced by British divisions, held the Germans on land, the Royal Navy would confront them at sea and help the French Navy to deal with the Austrians and the Germans in the Mediterranean. All this was arranged in prewar staff talks.

The causes of the war were numerous and complex. The Germans wanted supremacy in Europe and more colonies. The French, aggrieved by their relegation to second place on the Continent in 1870, wanted revenge and the return of Alsace-Lorraine. The British, as ever, opposed domination of Europe by any power, and feared German ambitions there, at sea, in colonial territories round the world and economically. German ambition, French revanchism and British anxiety were brought to a head, as Bismarck had predicted, by "some damned foolish thing in the Balkans", where the crumbling Austrian and Russian Empires clashed over local nationalisms. The Austrians were in the Triple Alliance with Germany and Italy (which dropped out), the Russians in the Triple Entente with France and Britain. Then a Serbian nationalist's pistol at hapless Sarajevo detonated the power-keg.

The Balkan rivalry of Russia and Austria was exacerbated by the accelerating dissolution of the Ottoman Turkish Empire, which in its heyday had dominated the region as well as the Near and Middle East and North Africa. In October 1912, Serbia, Montenegro, Bulgaria and Greece attacked the "sick man of Europe" in pursuit of various territorial and/or political goals. After two months the major powers helped bring about an armistice, but in January 1913 the Bulgarians attacked again. To their mutual astonishment and even pleasure, Britain, France and Germany, working smoothly together through their diplomats in London, brokered a settlement in the Balkans and doused this spark. When Bulgaria rounded on its erstwhile anti-Turkish allies in June it was brought to order in a matter of weeks.

These Balkan wars were otherwise notable for an event of special interest here. On 9 December 1912 Lieutenant-Commander Paparrigopoulos of the Royal Hellenic Navy took his submarine to within 550 yards of the Turkish light cruiser *Medjidieh* and fired one of his four eighteen-inch torpedoes at her as she emerged with five destroyers from the Dardanelles into the Mediterranean. The Greeks had just two submarines, *Delphin* and *Xiphias*, each of the Laubeuf-Schneider, diesel-electric type with a displacement of 460 tons, delivered by France in 1911 and 1912 respectively. On this first wartime operational patrol they executed the first underwater attack on a warship on the high seas. But the torpedo veered off course and did not explode.

In the 100 years between the decisive naval battles of Trafalgar, when the British smashed the French fleet in 1805, and Tsushima, when the Japanese destroyed the Russians' in 1905, there had been very few noteworthy actions for the leading navies to learn from. During that century, however, the advances in naval technology had been stupendous. First iron, then steel, then armour-plate, instead of wood; steam instead of sail; oil-fired turbines; breech-loading guns whose power grew almost exponentially; high explosives; precision range-finders; wireless; mines; torpedoes; aviation; and of course submarines. On land, developments in war technology had been less visibly spectacular, but the effect of the magazine-rifle and (especially) the machine-gun, smokeless powder, accurate and mobile long-range artillery on the ability of armies to kill and maim much greater numbers of the enemy simultaneously was no less fundamental. As humanity marched with increasing speed towards the global conflict which shaped the twentieth century, it also tried, though with markedly less energy and enthusiasm, to alleviate the consequences of its own malign ingenuity. Serious attempts were made to extend a version of the Queensberry Rules, applied to boxing in 1867, to the battlefield – an attempt to reconcile homicidal aggression with gentlemanly conduct.

Moved by the suffering of the wounded after the French defeat of the Austrians at Solferino in 1859, the Swiss philanthropist Henri Dunant instigated the conference which engendered both the Red Cross and the Geneva Convention in 1864. The latter, ratified as part of international law only in 1906, when the requisite number of states had endorsed it, set standards for the treatment of enemy wounded and prisoners, and outlawed methods of warfare that caused "unnecessary suffering", such as expanding bullets. The first Hague Peace Conference of twenty-six nations in 1899 is directly relevant to our story because one of the three conventions it produced extended the Geneva Convention to war at sea. It also considered, but rejected, outlawing submarine warfare.

The second Hague Conference of forty-four nations took place in 1907 and lasted twice as long (four months). It also spent more time on naval warfare, in an atmosphere of general expectation that such conventions as it might manage to formulate could be needed at any moment. The rules of war at sea provoked more controversy than any other topic. The British pressed for unrestricted right of capture in support of their customary strategy of blockade; the Germans pressed for the recognition of mines and submarines as legitimate weapons against blockade. The conference produced no fewer than eight naval warfare conventions on such issues as the declaration of minefields, giving warning of shore bombardment, international prize courts, detention of shipping caught by war in enemy ports, contraband in wartime and the rights and duties of neutrals at sea. This work was clarified by the London Declaration of 1908, the result of a follow-up conference on the naval aspects of The Hague.

Most important from our present viewpoint was the imposition on submarines of the same Prize Regulations as applied to cruisers and other surface ships engaged in war on commerce – the principal target, alongside the enemy fleet (usually found in the same place), of navies since time immemorial. Under "prize rules" submarines, the frailest and slowest of warships, were obliged to sacrifice their one advantage, tactical invisibility, just when it was most valuable: at the moment of attacking enemy shipping (unless the merchantman was armed); and this in the new era of marine wireless.

A submarine could stop and search an enemy or neutral merchant vessel on the high seas for contraband (strategic material bound for or owned by the enemy), a process which could be carried out only on the surface. If such was found the submarine was entitled to sink the offending ship, provided passengers and crew were allowed off first, with the means (lifeboats, food and water, charts and navigation instruments or else a passing neutral ship) to reach a safe haven. Neutral ships with contraband could only be escorted into internment. Armed enemy ships, whether naval or mercantile, were held to be fair game for surprise attack once war had been declared (merchantmen were not supposed to be armed unless officially converted into auxiliary cruisers; Germans and British alike fitted large merchantmen with gun-mountings before the war).

The fleet exercises of March 1904, in which HM Submarine *A1* was lost, were also the Royal Navy's first crude attempt at anti-submarine warfare. The tragic accident, first of eight before 1914 in the British service in which a total of seventy-nine submariners were killed, may have distracted admirals from the unpleasant truth: half a dozen submersible torpedo-boats, despite their lack of speed, had scored far too many "hits" on major warships with impunity and had hamstrung the fleet on manoeuvres. Until 1910, therefore, British submarines on exercise had to be escorted by a surface vessel flying a red flag, the naval equivalent of the similarly equipped pedestrian required to precede the earliest cars.

Nothing could have expressed more vividly the reputation among "real" sailors of submariners in the navies which employed them. Even in an age when personal hygiene had not been elevated to a fetish by the advertising industry, submariners were noted for the personal atmosphere they created, which they all too often carried around with them unawares on working days. Like that other new breed of military eccentric, the aviator, they tended to wear unorthodox clothing, usually for much too long. A few hours underwater was enough to fill a boat with a stench made up of damp from condensation, treacherously unreliable

toilets, sweat, unwashed feet and clothing, battery acid and the ubiqui-
tous fumes of oil. A wash at sea was a rarity, certainly much rarer than
the doubtless extremely welcome free tot of rum which remained the
daily consolation of the entire British Navy until the latter part of the
twentieth century.

While the Germans were sensible enough to issue their submariners
with leather clothing and warm underwear from the outset, the British
had to make do with calf boots, ordinary dungarees and the famous
"frock", the white (!) rollneck sweater made of heavy, oiled wool. The
few waterproofs aboard were, perforce, for communal use. Sleeping
facilities were primitive to non-existent. Despite the higher pay (a large
percentage of a small principal) soon awarded to them as in most navies,
early British submariners were collectively known to the rest of the fleet
as "the Trade" and their officers as "unwashed chauffeurs". Thus did the
snobbish Navy of a nation unique for the subtlety of its class distinctions
choose to categorise a service which was a world apart in every Navy: a
strange new coterie run by obsessive and smelly enthusiasts supported
by maritime troglodytes marinated in oil. Opportunities for mutual
non-communication and incomprehension abounded.

What ideas did the belligerents of 1914–18 develop for countering the
new threat? Briefly, none. Almost all concerned had seriously underestimated its potential, so there was little spur to invention before 1914.
Desultory experiments in underwater detection had been going on at
HMS *Vernon*, the Navy's (shorebound) torpedo school, since 1882.
Some work was done on the electrical detection of submerged metal
objects. In 1894 Captain C.A. McEvoy of *Vernon* produced a "hydrophone", a device to pick up underwater sound such as the noise from a
propeller. The first version was an adaptation of telephone technology, a
platinum strip inside a heavy bell placed on the seabed with air trapped
inside. The underwater sound moved the air and vibrated the strip,
which sent a signal shown on a galvanometer and heard through an
earpiece. A strong signal would alert the watch by closing an extra
electric circuit, which lit a lamp, rang a bell and fired a gun!

Nearer the mark by far was the work of two Americans, Elisha Grey
and A.J. Mundy, in the 1890s. Their hydrophone was developed from a
telephone earpiece, a "bell" with a diaphragm and a carbon microphone
attached. This was first fitted in a wooden pod, towed well astern of a
ship to minimise the sound of her own propellers. Later two such devices
were fitted internally forward, on either side of a ship's hull in small,
sealed water tanks which served to cut out most of the ship's own noise.
This system was used as an aid to navigation, picking up signals from

bells attached underwater to lighthouses, sandbanks, wrecks, buoys and lightships. When the intensity of the signal in each receiver was the same, you knew the bow was pointed at the source. By 1913 a transducer for transmitting and receiving underwater Morse-code signals had been developed. Its inventor, Professor R.A. Fessenden, also produced an electro-magnetic coil detector in April 1914, to locate a submerged metal object up to two miles away. These ideas held promise, but contemporary ignorance of underwater acoustics in general and how to determine the direction of an underwater sound-source in particular were the major obstacles to real progress. Hydrophones of three experimental types had been fitted to forty-five British warships and one submarine in 1911, but were intended as navigational aids and for short-range, ship-to-ship telegraphy (not so readily overheard as wireless). No Navy could detect a submerged submarine in August 1914.

But what if one revealed its presence by surfacing at the wrong moment, firing a torpedo or showing its periscope? No Navy was capable of destroying a submerged submarine either, unless it was near enough to the surface to ram or hit by gunfire (no easy matter when the target was so small). The Admiralty set up a Submarine Committee in 1910 to look at anti-submarine measures as well as improvements to the boats themselves. Some wondrous ideas were put forward among the 14,000 suggestions from the public. Serving sailors were offered £5 to £15 for ideas. A ship could discharge glutinous fluid designed to gum up a periscope. Or it could use a very long boathook to loop an explosive necklace round the periscope. A destroyer could trail a grapnel with an explosive charge and try to snag a periscope. Or it could throw a net across the path of a suspected submarine which, when snared, would cause a red flag (again!) to pop up on the buoy attached to the net. Thereupon the warship would dash up and drop another net festooned with explosives. Elaborate attempts were made to use sea lions as submarine detectors and seagulls as periscope spotters. More promising than these was a series of experiments in 1911 with *Holland II*, testing the effect of hand-grenades as miniature depth-charges on submarines. More interesting still, in 1912 a seaplane of the kind now being routinely supplied to major warships for reconnaissance was used to search for periscopes and submarines on or near the surface.

But on the eve of war the Royal Navy, which had the most to fear and the most to lose from submarine warfare, had no anti-submarine strategy, detector or weapon. The Grand Fleet, which as a unit sustained no loss to U-boats, and military transports (very seldom attacked) adopted the tactic of sailing in synchronised zigzags inside a destroyer screen. For the rest, the best the Admiralty could do was deploy "anti-submarine picket-boats" in Scapa Flow, imaginatively equipped with strong paper bags and hammers. The idea was to pop the bag over the enemy's periscope and belabour it with the hammer until the lens shattered. No instruction was given on how to persuade the attached submarine to keep still during this indignity. Other navies, including the German and French, had nothing to offer against the submarine.

The British, having spent five per cent of their shipbuilding budgets on submarines since 1906, had the world's largest underwater fleet when war broke out: seventy-five boats in commission and twenty-eight on the stocks. Of the former only twenty (the eight "D" class and the first twelve "E") were diesel-powered, boasted a gun, displaced more than 550 tons and could therefore be regarded as ocean-going. The thirty-seven "Cs" and ten "Bs" were around the 300-ton mark and petrol-driven, the latter of little use except for training, the former certainly capable of coastal work. No British boat was yet equipped for minelaying.

France had sixty-two in service and nine building, of several types. Some half-dozen were clearly ocean-going and fourteen were powered by steam on the surface; thirty-three belonged to the loosely defined "Laubeuf" class.

Russia had an even more varied collection of thirty-six boats, having bought from America, Britain, France and Germany. Nineteen more were in construction. Eight were of the American "Lake" type and five were Mark II "Hollands". The Russian Navy functioned as an adjunct of the Army and its submarines were therefore destined to be among the most notable under-achievers deployed by the major belligerents.

Germany had the fourth-largest, and the newest, submarine fleet, with twenty-eight in service and seventeen on the stocks. Of the former, some twenty were operational and eight in training; ten were ocean-going diesels with the world's best range and depth performances and a surface displacement of 650 tons. German mines were also rather better than British, though no U-boat could lay them until 1915. The Germans planned to wage war on enemy commerce from the first day of war – but with naval and auxiliary cruisers.

Austria had just six boats operational and two building, a small but effective service based on German technology and the best efforts of the still busy Whitehead factory at Fiume. The other Adriatic Navy, Italy's, had twenty-one boats with seven more under construction in 1914. Many of these were classified by the contemporary *Jane's Fighting Ships* as "non-effective". The United States had thirty boats in service and ten on the way while Japan had thirteen and three; but these rising navies remained on the sidelines, gaining hardly any experience of submarine warfare in this conflict.

In January 1914, Lord Fisher, still chafing in retirement as the war-clouds gathered, wrote: "There is nothing else the submarine can do except sink her capture ... this submarine menace is a terrible one for British commerce and Great Britain alike, for no means can be suggested at present of meeting it except by reprisals." Nobody heeded the apoplectic Cassandra. Shortly before the outbreak of hostilities, Winston Churchill, First Lord of the Admiralty since 1911, complacently said of unrestricted submarine warfare on merchant shipping: "I do not believe this would ever be done by a civilised power."

Scene ii: the north

THE LATE SIR BASIL LIDDELL HART, strategist and historian, identified the decisive naval moment of the First World War as 29 July 1914 – nearly a week before the United Kingdom took up arms against Germany. The well-named Grand Fleet with its new C-in-C, Admiral Sir John Jellicoe, had gathered with its reserves in the Solent on England's south coast for a test mobilisation on 10 July. This complex and unprecedented exercise, necessitating the call-up of 20,000 reservists, displaced the customary summer manoeuvres because war seemed imminent. The thus reinforced battlefleet formed the greatest display of naval firepower yet seen when King George V came to review it at Spithead a week later. The ships of the Reserve Fleet then dispersed to their home ports but were still fully manned when Prince Louis Battenberg, the First Sea Lord, decided on the evening of Sunday 26 July to keep them so, in view of the crisis over the Balkans. His political chief, Winston Churchill, First Lord of the Admiralty, was away for the weekend, leaving the decision to Battenberg. The Grand Fleet itself was ordered to stay together, and on the 29th it was dispatched in a body to Scapa Flow, the main fleet anchorage in the Orkney Islands, north-east of the Scottish mainland.

The grey line of armoured steel eighteen miles long, the bulk of the Navy which was as ever Britain's shield in time of war, sailed up the Channel and the North Sea to its war station. "From that moment Germany's arteries were subjected to an invisible pressure which never relaxed," wrote Liddell Hart in his *History of the First World War*. He is not alone in regarding this blockade as the most important contribution to the ultimate defeat of Germany. The Royal Navy's immaculate mobilisation on the eve of war could not, however, frustrate the Schlieffen Plan, whereby the Germans, in a vast outflanking manoeuvre through Belgium, set out to seize Paris and force a quick end to the war in the west before the showdown with Russia. The southern North Sea

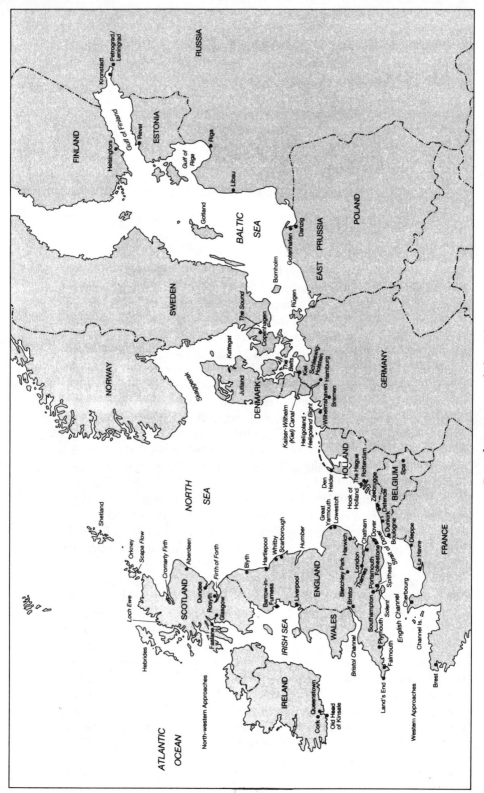

British Waters and the Baltic

was covered by the Harwich Force of destroyers, light cruisers and submarines; and the Straits of Dover by the Dover Patrol of destroyers and light craft, backed by Admiral Sir Cecil Burney's Channel Fleet. This pre-dreadnought force was to cover the transport to northern France of the British Expeditionary Force, initially six divisions. The "contemptible little army", as the Kaiser famously called it, a fraction of French strength, was discounted by his General Staff (which had operational control of the Navy), so that no plan existed for impeding its delivery.

The opening naval move by Britain bottled up the High Seas Fleet, which could now hope to influence events only by attacking the numerically superior British fleet with its long and illustrious record. Unfortunately that was precisely why it had been built. The Germans planned to use locally superior force against elements of the Grand Fleet, until it was so reduced that the High Seas Fleet could take it on with a fair chance of winning a decisive, set-piece battle. The Royal Navy, whose shore facilities had hitherto been concentrated on the south coast against France, had only recently acquired bases on the long east coast facing Germany. Even Scapa Flow was virtually undefended, without gun emplacements or nets; subsidiary bases in the firths of Cromarty and Forth were incomplete and inadequate after a decade of obsession with expensive, "all-big-gun" dreadnoughts. Shamefully, and for the familiar British reason of false economy, the big gun had no holster. The Grand Fleet lacked a safe haven for a war against Germany, and mustered only forty destroyers against the High Seas Fleet's eighty.

The day after the Grand Fleet sailed for Scapa, the High Seas Fleet took an entire day to pass the newly widened Kaiser Wilhelm (Kiel) Canal from the Baltic to the North Sea across Schleswig-Holstein. Consigned to the rear were most of Germany's twenty operational U-boats, attached to the fleet commanded by Admiral Friedrich von Ingenohl. Another clue to their status in the Imperial navy was the rank of the fleet's Führer der Unterseeboote, Hermann Bauer, a mere commander, albeit an extremely able one (Roger Keyes, Britain's Inspecting Captain of Submarines since 1910, bore the courtesy title of Commodore).

The High Seas Fleet submarines, whose forward base was the fortified isle of Heligoland, were on war-alert from 31 July and deployed on the surface in a defensive screen in the Heligoland Bight on 1 August 1914. On that day Germany, having failed to force the Tsar by ultimatum to stop mobilising against Austria-Hungary in support of Serbia, declared war on Russia. Three days later the latter's partners in the Triple Entente,

France and Britain, declared war on Germany when it failed to guarantee the Belgian neutrality its massed armies were about to breach.

In the northern waters which this chapter covers – the North Sea, the north-eastern Atlantic and the Baltic – caution prevailed on both sides, suppressing any serious thought of an instantaneous Trafalgar. The Germans were aware of being outnumbered by five to three in big ships; the British were not going to risk this margin by gratuitously running on to mines and torpedoes. The Grand Fleet found nothing in the waters between Scotland and Norway when it responded to a false rumour of a German raid on the Shetland Islands. Meanwhile its reconnaissance forces were on patrol in the North Sea in distant support of the Channel Fleet's unchallenged escort of the first British divisions to northern France, begun on 6 August.

On the same day, chafing over the maritime inactivity at the outset of what was meant to be a short sharp war, Commander Bauer won permission to take ten submarines of the First U-boat Flotilla to sea on an aggressive sweep. If the British Navy was not after all to carry out the anticipated pre-emptive assault on the narrow German North Sea coast, then the U-boats might as well try to beard the enemy in his lair. He took personal command of the ten boats, *U5*, *U7–9* and *U13–18*, and chose the ultimate challenge for the untried arm: the main units of the British fleet in and around Scapa Flow. Only capital ships would do; lesser vessels were to be ignored if possible.

The chosen boats all ran on paraffin and emitted sparks and flames, clouds of smoke and steam. They were escorted eighty miles out to sea by two light cruisers, two destroyers and a torpedo-boat. As in the British service, they were almost invariably skippered by a lieutenant-commander – Kapitänleutnant (all submarine captains named in this book held such rank unless otherwise stated). *U5* (Lemmers) and *U9* (Otto Weddigen, of whom much more later) were forced to turn back after two days at sea with serious mechanical breakdowns. *U13* (Arthur Graf von Schweinitz) was lost without trace to an internal explosion or other catastrophe. She failed to reappear as ordered at Heligoland on 11 August.

The shooting star of Bauer's less than dazzling debut was Pohle in *U15*. He wandered hopelessly wide of the front of advance, in line abreast seven miles apart towards Scapa. As a result, on the morning of 10 August he sighted a squadron of three dreadnought battleships on gunnery practice near Fair Isle, halfway between Orkney and Shetland – *Ajax*, *Monarch* and *Orion*. Pohle submerged and fired a single torpedo at HMS *Monarch*, which missed but caused consternation in the squadron, and shortly afterwards throughout the Royal Navy. The British had not expected to meet a U-boat so far from her base and so near to theirs. Pohle escaped eastward on the surface.

But not for long. His treacherous Körting engines broke down and he was forced to heave to for repairs. At 3.40 a.m. on the 11th, the new 5,440-ton light cruiser *Birmingham* (Captain Arthur Duff, RN), reconnoitring for the Grand Fleet, spotted the boat, opened fire and came on to ram. *U15* was cut in half and sank with all hands, the first submarine to be lost to enemy attack. The underwater torpedo-boat as realised by John P. Holland had yet to claim a victim, but had been blooded – in its own blood. Bauer's bold but abortive raid had lost two boats out of ten; two more had broken down.

Four diesels from the Second U-boat Flotilla (*U19*, *U21*, *U22* and *U24*) left Heligoland on 8 August to look for heavy ships covering a rumoured British landing on the coast of northern Flanders. In fact the Channel Fleet was further south, and the U-boats caught only glimpses of the enemy destroyer screen before returning home, unscathed but still unscoring, on the 11th. Fortunately for the British Army, the Germans soon gave up the idea of such attacks but began to ponder different possibilities. Pairs of U-boats ventured across the North Sea during the rest of August but sighted only the occasional British patrol and attacked nothing.

Justly pleased though Duff and his crew were with the first sinking of a U-boat, the Navy as a whole succumbed to the new disease of "periscopitis". As the bulk of the Grand Fleet lay majestically at anchor in the Flow at dusk on 1 September, a light cruiser suddenly opened fire, her guns at their lowest angle. Jellicoe ordered steam up as several more ships expended a hail of shot at other "targets" in what wags later styled "the first battle of Scapa". The rulers of the waves dispersed into the gloaming in an undignified scramble and slunk back to their berths only after daybreak.

On the afternoon of 5 September another small cruiser, the ten-year-old HMS *Pathfinder*, 2,940 tons (Captain Martin Leake, RN), was on patrol with destroyers of the Eighth Flotilla at the mouth of the Firth of Forth in calm, sunlit waters when the ship suddenly shuddered to a colossal detonation. The obsolete warship was torn apart by an explosion in her forward magazine, despite a lookout's warning of a periscope and a torpedo track and an order for an engine-assisted emergency turn. The ship was crawling along at the "economical cruising speed" of six knots and would thus not have been able to avert her fate, even if her engineers had not dismissed the telegraphed order for full astern on one engine and full ahead on the other as an error and ignored it ... The false economy was remedied by a standing order imposing a minimum patrol speed of fifteen knots. Meanwhile *Pathfinder*'s bow and forward deck were already under water, most lifeboats were smashed or unusable, bulkheads were going down like dominoes; 259 of the crew were doomed as the cruiser's ram touched bottom and her stern rose into the air. Captain Leake emerged dazed from an upper-deck meat store, into which he had been hurled by the blast, and was the last of the nine survivors to leave the ship, which took four minutes to sink. HMS *Pathfinder*, the first vessel ever sunk at sea by a submarine, blazed a very long and unhappy trail.

An unnoticed periscope rose and fell with the swell, trained on the chaos from less than a mile off as two destroyers raced to the aid of their leader. Lieutenant Otto Hersing, aged twenty-eight with barely a year's submarine experience, was the first captain of the new, diesel-powered *U21*. He was "looking over his shoulder" as his boat made off. He had fired one torpedo from 1,200 metres (3,800 feet), four times the maximum range then recommended for an attack. But it had been aimed at an easy target, which it hit amidships, its effect compounded by the "sympathetic explosion" in the magazine, which tore the heart out of the ship. *U21* fought on throughout the war, foundering in 1919 on the way to surrender. Her first captain soon became an "ace", commanding the boat for a three-year marathon of twenty-one war patrols. They sank thirty-six ships, including two battleships and two cruisers.

Commodore Roger Keyes boarded HMS *Maidstone* in the Humber on 30 July 1914 and led his other depot ship and the Eighth "Overseas" Flotilla of HM submarines to their war station at Harwich, down the English east coast, by the 31st. The combative "Commodore (S)" had cancelled all leave on his own initiative on the 26th and won consent to taking direct operational command of the one British ocean-going flotilla of diesel "D" and "E" class boats. Only ten of the seventeen boats were on station and ready for sea. No desk pilot, Keyes felt that the best place for a submariner was within striking distance of the Heligoland Bight. Elsewhere the British had three smaller and older boats in the Far East, six in the Mediterranean and forty-two on coastal defence round Britain, particularly in the Dover Strait.

The Royal Navy's first submarine war patrol left Harwich in the early hours of 5 August. *E6* (Lieutenant Cecil Talbot) and *E8* (Francis Goodhart) were towed out to sea by destroyers from Commodore Reginald Tyrwhitt's forty-strong Harwich Force of two flotillas. The pair spent two days in the Bight observing shipping movements and returned on the 11th. Four more boats repeated the exercise a week later, and another three returned with more information on the 23rd. On the latter sortie *D5* (Lieutenant Godfrey Herbert) had gone so far as to fire two torpedoes at a light cruiser. But, set for dummy peacetime warheads, they ran deep.

Now very well informed on dispositions at the enemy's forward base in the Bight, Keyes pressed for a hit-and-run raid. The Admiralty approved an attack by light surface forces and submarines led by the two Harwich commodores. Heavier units from the Grand Fleet, they were told, would *not* take part. Tyrwhitt was to take thirty destroyers, led by two light cruisers, to Heligoland to engage their opposite numbers. This should lure German cruisers out to sea, where Keyes's boats would wait submerged to attack them coming out and going back. The plan was slap-dash; its executants were thrown into confusion when Vice-Admiral Sir David Beatty's Battlecruiser Squadron, the Navy's biggest and fastest capital ships, burst upon the scene, escorted by Rear-Admiral W.E. Good-enough's Light Cruiser Squadron, on 28 August, despite the Admiralty's assurance. As on so many later occasions, often disastrous, the Admir-alty's wireless signal of the change of plan never reached the addressees. Nobody thought of asking or waiting for an acknowledgment. As a result, British submarines caused their own battlecruisers to scatter and open wildly inaccurate fire on them, while British destroyers twice identified their own light cruisers as enemies. German light cruisers and destroyers profited from this by coming out and beating up the light cruiser HMS *Arethusa* and British destroyers, without sinking any.

The eight submarines had been ordered to surround Heligoland and lure the Germans out. In this they had been only too successful. The battlecruisers had steamed over the horizon when the British light forces sank a destroyer. Then the impetuous, overbearing Beatty, whose dash to join in was approved only retrospectively in London, led two battle-cruisers into the mêlée to sink three German light cruisers in short order. The submarines fired a few torpedoes but achieved little and hit nothing. Essentially they got in the way; they were as much of a danger to their own side as to the enemy. Keyes, who could not influence the battle from his post on a destroyer, was forbidden to lead his boats into battle again. Nevertheless the almost disastrous skirmish was transmogrified into the Battle of the Heligoland Bight and presented to the British public as a dashing naval tweak of the Kaiser's nose.

The U-boat arm saw the *Pathfinder* as handsome revenge for the *U15*. The Germans, urged on like the British by a chauvinistic press, were just as keen to get their own back for the three cruisers sunk by the British in the Heligoland raid. The U-boat men were even keener to strike a new blow after the British trumpeted the exploit of HMS *E9* in sinking the old light cruiser *Hela* and the destroyer *S116* during mid-September patrols in German waters. The skipper, Max Horton, RN, celebrated these deeds by hoisting a skull and crossbones on his return to Harwich, inventing a tradition. Unbeknown to the new hero of the British submarine service and his superiors, his work had caused the Germans to cease using the German Ocean, as they called the North Sea, for fleet exercises, now transferred to the Baltic. They too were forced to mollycoddle their capital ships for fear of submarines.

The instrument of German vengeance turned out to be a frail one indeed: Weddigen's paraffin-powered *U9*, completed in 1910, displacing 493 tons surfaced and 611 submerged, armed with four forty-five-centimetre torpedo tubes and a single five-centimetre gun, capable of just thirteen and a half knots surfaced and ten submerged.

Otto Eduard Weddigen was born in Westphalia in 1880 and joined the Navy as an officer-cadet in 1901, transferring to the infant U-boat service in 1908. *U4* was his first command, as a lieutenant, in 1910; on 1 October 1911 he took over *U9*, and in April 1912 he was promoted to Kapitänleutnant. Despite the mechanical failure which aborted his participation in Bauer's drive on Scapa, his boat was regarded as one of the best run in the service. The engines of *U9* behaved themselves as Weddigen set off from Heligoland before dawn on 20 September for a lone patrol down the Dutch and Belgian coasts as far as Ostend. He was looking for supply-ships rather than big men-of-war or troopships, which were always escorted and thus seldom came to harm throughout the war, a fact which escaped the notice of most British admirals until 1917. Around dawn on Tuesday the 22nd, the *U9* was hove to on the surface some twenty miles west-north-west of the Hook of Holland, merrily exuding dense white smoke from the exhaust funnel in a strong equinoctial wind. Lieutenant Johannes Spiess, the First Officer (and future skilled commander of *U9*), scanned the sea with binoculars as Weddigen slept in his tiny "cabin".

Peering through his own boat's fumes Spiess thought he discerned black smoke on the horizon. Then he sighted a mast. Called to the tiny bridge on the conning tower, Weddigen ordered a dive and the periscope up. To his own incredulity, he soon identified not one, nor yet two, but three old British cruisers steaming in line abreast at a mere ten knots without even bothering to zigzag. So much for the order to patrol at fifteen knots, one and a half more than *U9* could manage flat out on the surface.

In fact Weddigen's targets would have had a difficult time sustaining such a speed. They were over fourteen years old, ancient by the standards of the time. "Used to be very good steamers but now getting worn out and only good for short spurts," *Jane's Fighting Ships* noted in 1914. They were the 12,000-ton armoured cruisers *Aboukir*, *Hogue* and *Cressy* of the reserve, manned mostly by part-timers. They were little more than lumbering mobile lookout posts, nicknamed the "live-bait squadron" by staff officers. Keyes at Harwich had written to the Admiralty urging their withdrawal. Battenberg, the First Sea Lord, regarded them as a liability. Only on 17 September Churchill had recommended that they should be retired. This just concern was not based on fear of submarines but of any sizeable modern German *surface* force. The fate of the *Pathfinder* was still held to be an unlucky fluke.

It took Weddigen thirty-five minutes to get within torpedo range. At 6.20 a.m. and 500 metres (1,640 feet) he fired a single missile. Crew members scrambled bruisingly to and fro through the cramped hull to prevent the boat bobbing to the surface after the sudden loss of weight. But they heard the dull clang when the torpedo struck home, followed by a huge explosion. The *Aboukir* listed, turned turtle and sank in twenty minutes. Captain Drummond thought he had struck a mine and, as senior officer, innocently ordered the two cruisers in company to close up and lower boats for survivors.

The *Hogue* therefore stopped to aid her stricken sister, despite suspecting the presence of a submarine and firing in all possible directions at a ghost army of periscopes. Weddigen kept his eye glued to the only real one present, now focused firmly on a grey steel wall, and fired two more torpedoes from 300 metres. He had to order an emergency turn to avoid a collision with the stricken *Hogue* as *U9* shuddered to the shock waves from her own shots. Forty-five minutes after the first, only one British cruiser remained amid the spreading debris, coal dust and oil of the heaving swell.

Twelve minutes later HMS *Cressy* loomed in the periscope's view-finder, blindly intent on picking up survivors from her two vanished sisters. Weddigen, his bow tubes empty, had put about. At 7.17 a.m. he fired both stern tubes from 1,000 metres. Captain Robert Johnson, RN, was alerted by lookouts to the twin tracks and ordered full speed ahead. Only one torpedo struck. But by 7.35 a.m. Weddigen was able to administer a probably superfluous *coup de grâce* with one more torpedo from the bow. The third cruiser was gone in twenty minutes, one and quarter hours after the first.

The neutral Dutch steamer *Titan*, which saved 114 British sailors, was in the offing throughout. Captain Berkout reported:

I saw the three cruisers at a great distance on the horizon. After a little while one of them had disappeared; at first I thought she had steamed off, but when I looked carefully I discovered that a second had also disappeared. Smoke hung over the sea and I heard a muffled explosion. I immediately set course in the direction in which I had seen the ships. Then I lowered two boats ...

No such scene had ever been witnessed before in all the millennia since men put to sea: three ships blown away in swift succession by an invisible force. Fatal casualties totalled 1, 459 or sixty-six per cent, more British sailors than had died in the nation's greatest naval victory, at Trafalgar in 1805. Weddigen managed to hit each victim below her 2,100-ton girdle of armour.

U9 returned in triumph to her home port of Wilhelmshaven to be greeted personally on the quayside by Admiral von Ingenohl, commander of the High Seas Fleet. Every man aboard was awarded the Iron Cross, second class (before this decoration became so common that, as a cynical Austrian officer put it, one had to commit suicide to avoid it). Weddigen was awarded the first class as well and the Iron Cross motif was painted on the conning tower on the admiral's instructions. When Weddigen set off on his next mission after leave and a brief refit, Ingenohl could not resist signalling: "After E9 comes U9."

Just a week after celebrating Horton's deeds, the British public was plunged into gloom by the loss of a whole squadron of cruisers and so many sailors – the greatest British naval humiliation for a century. And it had been imposed by one paraffin-guzzling, flame-belching, smoke-wreathed boat with a crew of twenty-six.

The ever-cautious Jellicoe was particularly horrified by the implications. Unbeknown to the Germans, the U9 and the fear of mines had driven the Grand Fleet out of the North Sea. As makeshift defences were hurriedly being installed at Scapa Flow, the battlefleet took temporary refuge in Lough Swilly on the northern Irish coast. Its battlecruiser squadron lurked at the Isle of Mull off the north-west of Scotland. The light cruiser Amphion had been lost to a mine in the first week of the war off the Thames estuary. On 17 October in the Irish Seas, the battleship HMS Audacious, 23,000 tons, was also lost to a mine. Only a few men were killed from a crew of about 850, but British morale was severely damaged. The world's greatest fleet, Britain's ace of trumps, was skulking about, unable to take the initiative, vulnerable to cheap little mines and a handful of invisible U-boats. All it had managed was a muddled skirmish off Heligoland.

Amidst all the gloom in high naval places little attention was paid to the fate of the SS Glitra. This British tramp-steamer of 866 tons hove to when a shot crossed her bow off southern Norway on 20 October. U17 (Feldkirchner) then sent a boarding party to check the ship. The Germans politely ordered the crew to take to their boats, made sure they had retired to a safe distance, and saved ammunition by opening the seacocks in her bottom. This impeccable application of prize rules was the first time a submarine had ever sunk a merchantman. Schneider of U24, in the Dover Strait – the maritime lion's mouth – felt unable to afford this kind of chivalry six days later, when he torpedoed the unarmed *Admiral Ganteaume*, 4,590 tons, a cross-Channel steamer carrying 2,500 Belgian refugees. Miraculously only forty died; the ferry managed to make port. Schneider had given no warning, another unhappy precedent.

Feldkirchner won retrospective approval of his attack on the *Glitra* as his superiors began to ponder its implications. Thus encouraged, he went on to torpedo the battleship HMS *Formidable* on New Year's Day, 1915. The awful lesson of the three "Cressys" ensured that, in line with Admiralty orders, the *Formidable*, an 1898 relic of 15,000 tons, was left to die alone; 550 of her crew of 800 were lost in the wintry waters of the western Channel as other vessels kept well clear. War at sea with the new stealth weapons was proving nastier week by week. The fashionable word for the garishly reported horrors perpetrated by U-boats and mines at sea (and the German Army's atrocities in Belgium) was "frightfulness".

Fright without suffixes meanwhile was still the thinly disguised, prevailing mood in the homeless Grand Fleet and its Battlecruiser Squadron in Scottish waters in gloomy October, the third month of a war which was originally expected to end "before the leaves fall" or at latest by Christmas 1914. A U-boat's intrusion into Loch Ewe on the 7th robbed that alternative anchorage of its attraction. Briefly back at Scapa to replenish in September, the Grand Fleet manoeuvred violently and opened fire with much secondary armament on a "submarine" which turned out to be a seal. The fate of the unfortunate mammal is not recorded. In the Cromarty Firth Beatty's battlecruisers mistook a destroyer's bow-wave as evidence of a submarine and demolished some houses in the village of Jemimaville with wildly misdirected shells, fortunately missing the destroyer. It all added to the general atmosphere of helplessness and pessimism as autumn closed in.

So did Weddigen's deadly postscript to his destruction of the three "Cressys" – the sinking of the 1891 cruiser *Hawke* (7,350 tons) in the North Sea east of Aberdeen at noon on 15 October, in the presence of British destroyers and other vessels. To elude them he fled southward, circumnavigating the British Isles to get to Germany where the Fleet Command had given him up for lost. Nine days later the Kaiser gave him the order Pour le mérite, the highest gallantry award of the day, confirming his status as a national hero.

Admiral of the Fleet John Arbuthnot, first Baron Fisher of Kilverstone, for ever known to the lower deck as "Jacky", irrupted into the Admiralty for a second term as First Sea Lord at the end of October 1914. Prince Louis Battenberg, an excellent peacetime naval administrator, had succumbed to the triple burden of general criticism of the Navy's inglorious start to the war, specific blame for the loss of the *Audacious* and a whispering campaign about his German origin, from which deadly combination the malicious groundlessly and shamefully deduced divided loyalties.

Despite his chestful of decorations and titles, Fisher was a self-made man who started life at the opposite end of the social spectrum from his broken-hearted predecessor. The once and present First Sea Lord, with a volatile countenance like Charles Laughton's, stood out all the more in a service whose officer class was even more aristocratic than the peacetime British Army's. And while the British ruling class, including the Hanoverian-derived monarchy, Churchill and Battenberg, could not believe that the Germans would be so "uncivilised" as to launch a submarine war against commerce, Fisher's legendary foresight told him otherwise. Unfortunately he was seventy-three when he returned to office and his mercurial temper was well nigh uncontrollable. He shared too many characteristics with his political chief, whereas Battenberg had sometimes been able to restrain Churchill from yielding to his rasher impulses. But the thinly spread, dashing element among the admirals, including Beatty and Keyes, looked forward to more dynamic leadership.

Fisher had been back for only two days when, on 1 November, Graf Spee's Pacific Squadron of two heavy and three light cruisers destroyed Rear-Admiral Sir Christopher Cradock's elderly cruisers at the Battle of Coronel, off Chile. This first defeat in a century in a major gunnery action surpassed even the disaster of the three "Cressys" in its effect on public opinion. Fisher made retribution swift. Vice-Admiral Sir Doveton Sturdee was sent after Spee with two battlecruisers and four cruisers. Spee's squadron was destroyed in its turn at the Battle of the Falkland Islands on 8 December. Here at last was news of the kind the public had so long awaited from the Royal Navy. This, not the silent and inglorious blockade of Germany, was what the King's fleet was for.

But the blockade was biting, as Germany's bitter propaganda campaign of November 1914 confirmed. The British had ruthlessly extended the scope of their boarding of neutrals in search of "absolute" contraband – war matériel bound for an enemy port – to "conditional" contraband such as food, fodder, fuel, gold and coin in August and then strategic raw materials such as iron, copper and rubber in September, whether bound directly for Germany or via a neutral (Scandinavian or Dutch) port. The Germans, with some justification, took this as a breach of international law (the neutral Americans were none too pleased either). The British had not ratified the 1908 London Declaration (naval follow-up to the second Hague Conference) because its definition of contraband was too narrow for effective blockade.

To tighten their hold even further, the British "closed" the northern entrance of the North Sea – the main route to Germany from west and north – to neutrals bound for Holland, Denmark and the Baltic, forcing them to follow a designated route through the Dover Strait and up the English east coast. In the same first week of November Admiral Hugo von Pohl, High Seas Fleet chief of staff, submitted a memorandum to the German Chancellor, Theobald von Bethmann-Hollweg, advocating a counter-blockade of Britain by U-boat. Pohl himself had been urged on by Bauer, the increasingly influential U-boat chief, whose skippers had reported on the wealth of traffic in British waters. The Chancellor, the only true statesman on the German side, clearly foreseeing the adverse effect on neutral, especially American, opinion of a submarine war on commerce, held out against naval pressure as long as he could. But it mounted as German cruisers were swept from the seas by December. Tirpitz, the naval minister, who had never been a submarine enthusiast, was still in two minds about the potential of the U-boat, but also just as frustrated as his British counterparts by the inability of the capital ships to change the course of the war, thanks to the threat from enemy submarines and mines. Had he known that the British fleet was even more hamstrung than his own he might have taken a different view.

Considerable effort has been devoted to "proving" that the Germans intended unrestricted submarine warfare against merchant shipping all along, as part of their strategic planning for the 1914 war. *Kapitänleutnant* Ulrich-Eberhard Blum, of the U-boat Inspectorate created in March 1914, wrote a staff study in May 1914, concluding that 222 U-boats would be needed to strangle British seaborne trade. He was doing his job, in the same way as prewar staff officers of all nations had been set to explore the implications of war with any conceivable enemy.

Writing his memoirs in 1940, Hermann Bauer said that before the 1914 war "cutting England off from its sea supply by U-boats had in no way been considered, since such a submarine war against English sea trade would not have conformed with the London Declaration." In fact it had been considered – by a lieutenant-commander on the orders of a captain. The resulting paper had landed, with many another, on the desk of Tirpitz as political chief of the Navy he had built. There is no evidence that he was impressed. On the contrary, like all the other original belligerents, Germany expected a brief war, which it entered with one-tenth of the number of operational U-boats Blum postulated as necessary for an effective underwater "cruiser warfare" campaign against British commerce. It was only when these boats went to war that their commanders saw for themselves just how vulnerable Britain was, knowing how Britain's blockade was affecting almost landlocked Germany. Pressure grew in the Imperial navy to make maximum use of the new arm, whose strength was slowly being augmented by better boats (*U38* being the last to be completed in 1914).

By the end of that year stalemate had already been achieved on the Western Front. In the east the Germans had inflicted terrible losses on Russia; but the failure of the Schlieffen Plan to knock France out of the war also denied them the concentration of force needed for total victory in the east. The two great dreadnought fleets had all but vacated the North Sea without fighting the battle for which they had been built. The main reason for this was the unexpected deterrent effect of the submarine. In these waters in 1914 U-boats sank seven secondary warships (including five old cruisers) and ten merchantmen totalling about 20,000 tons. They had lost five boats: two to Channel mines, two to ramming off Scapa Flow, one to unknown cause. The British had lost four (two for reasons unknown, one mined off the east coast, one torpedoed by a U-boat in the Bight) for Horton's two small warships.

Britain's allies, France and Russia, also started the war with considerable submarine fleets. One or two French boats joined their British counterparts but contributed little or nothing: the main preoccupation of the French fleet, by prewar agreement, was the Mediterranean. French concentration there enabled the British to reinforce the Grand Fleet from the Mediterranean Fleet, whose residual strength was to be subordinated to the French C-in-C.

The Russian Navy took the keenest interest in submarines after Tsushima. In the prewar decade it kept up with the explosion in submarine construction, having acquired forty-eight by 1913 (third in numbers after France and Britain). After Tsushima a rift opened in the Naval Staff between the "Old School", which favoured a strong battlefleet, and the "Young School" which wanted *guerre de course* against enemy trade and a defensive "mosquito fleet" of small vessels with torpedoes, including submarines, to harass invaders. The compromise between the two and shortage of funds left Russia with an inadequate battlefleet and inadequate light forces by 1914, rather weaker than the Germans in the Baltic. But the Navy had opened a submarine training school in 1906 at Libau (now Liepaja in Latvia), where officers learned the uniquely Russian "hands-on" approach to command, still prevalent today and made necessary by the poor education of their sailors. The Baltic Fleet got the first "brigade" (note the Army term) of submarines to join the colours, in 1907. M.P. Nalyetov developed a minelaying submarine in 1908, although the first joined the Black Sea Fleet only in 1915.

The 1912 naval construction programme produced the "Leopard" class, designed by Bubnov, the most effective Russian boats of the war and as good as any French, American or Italian class. Two dozen were ordered, eighteen to be built in Baltic yards. They were ocean-going boats of 650/784 tons, with speeds of eighteen and 9.5 knots. The first twelve had German paraffin engines but the war saw to it that the second batch had inferior local ones. They had four torpedo tubes and eight drop-collars. The Russians started the war with a miscellany of nine classes, including several "one-off" experimental boats, compared with the Germans' three.

While the Pacific Fleet based at Vladivostok took no part in the war as a formation (its submarines and ships were used to reinforce elsewhere), the Baltic Fleet was mobilised in a defensive posture behind minefields, with coastal artillery at its back. Only a few submarines operated outside the mine barrier, lying in wait. The one offensive task envisaged was to lay mines in German waters and if possible to blockade the Baltic end of the Kiel Canal. The Gulf of Finland leading to Kronstadt and Petrograd was closed by mines. When it was clear that the German battlefleet was not coming, mines were laid offensively off East Prussia with submarines protecting the minelayers, and the entrance to the Gulf of Riga was also closed. Although the Baltic Fleet boasted three "Leopards" and nine other submarines at the beginning of the war, the first British boats to get through at that stage far outdid them in aggressiveness and initiative. The German Baltic C-in-C, Prince Heinrich, remarked that a British submarine was worth a Russian heavy cruiser.

One of the Germans' most significant naval setbacks of the entire war occurred, unknown to them, in the Baltic on 26 August 1914, when the elegant, four-stack light cruiser SMS *Magdeburg* ran aground in a fog in the Gulf of Finland. By the time Russian men-of-war and troops arrived to demolish the ship, her secret equipment had been destroyed. But among the dead in the water was found a warrant officer with a heavily bound volume in his death-grip, marked "top secret". It was handed to the British two months later in a priceless act of solidarity: the signal book of the Imperial Navy.

At about the same time a British armed trawler recovered the Germans' equally secret numbered-grid charts of the North Sea from the wreckage of a destroyer. On these fortunate foundations was built the decryption section of Naval Intelligence at room forty in the Old Building ("Room 40 OB") of the Admiralty. It was staffed by a small group of gifted eccentrics under the new Director of Naval Intelligence, Captain (later Admiral Sir) Reginald Hall. The British were now able to eavesdrop on the High Seas Fleet, and also to glean information about U-boat movements, for the rest of the war, an intelligence coup surpassed only by the frontal assault on Axis ciphers in the Second World War. The finds also led to the development of systematic wireless interception as well as location of ships by cross-bearings on their transmissions (direction-finding or DF), the foundations of modern signals intelligence ("sigint"). Before the war was three weeks old Churchill wrote to the Russian C-in-C, Grand Duke Nicholas, with a proposal to send capital ships into the shallow Baltic – without consulting the Cabinet. He was to try to revive the idea in 1939–40, and on both occasions was restrained by his admirals, who rightly regarded the intricate shallows of the Baltic and its sole doorway to the open sea, the Kattegat, as lethally dangerous for warships.

At a review of the war at sea aboard Jellicoe's flagship *Iron Duke* in Loch Ewe in mid-September, British naval leaders politely but firmly stifled Churchill's plan, approving a suggestion from Commodore Keyes to send submarines instead. It was a typical Keyes wheeze, all gung-ho and no staff work, and it naturally appealed to Churchill. Two Eight Flotilla boats, *E1* and *E5*, rather gave the game away by a botched reconnaissance of the Kattegat at the end of September. *E1* broke down for a while; the weather was hostile; German merchant skippers reported their presence. They turned back before exploring the Sound, the waterway (less than ten miles wide at its narrowest) between Denmark and Sweden, through which boats must pass to penetrate the Baltic proper. The other route, the Belts east-north-east of Kiel, had been heavily mined by the Germans. Once in, the boats would have to stay in because it was so easy to close their exit. They therefore needed a Russian base. This consideration failed to prompt Keyes, not famed for his intelligence, to tell Admiral N.O. von Essen, the Russian Baltic C-in-C, that his boats would be coming.

Such were the inauspicious beginnings of one of those improvised "private wars" by small forces behind enemy lines which became a British twentieth-century speciality. It was to achieve results out of all proportion to the modest initial investment: *E1* (Noel Laurence, senior officer), *E9* (Horton) and *E11* (Martin Nasmith). They left Harwich on 15 October 1914, plagued as usual by mechanical troubles, showing that British engineering was inferior to the Germans' who had fewer problems with their U-boats on much longer patrols.

The Germans raised the alarm on the 18th, when *E1* fired one torpedo at the 1897 German armoured cruiser *Viktoria Luise* (5,800 tons) but her torpedoes too were still set for dummy warheads and ran deep.

The German Baltic command reacted by ordering destroyer patrols in the Kattegat and the Sound to be doubled. Heavy merchant traffic forced Horton in *E9* to submerge so often, and finally to lie on the bottom for hours, that he was much behind schedule. He resumed his crawl along the Sound after dark on the surface, the lesser of two evils, because his batteries needed recharging. Towards midnight he was south of Copenhagen, about to emerge into broader waters, when he sighted a destroyer 150 yards away. An emergency dive took the boat down fifteen feet, when she hit bottom and then crept ahead until she found a depression fifty feet deep to hide in. Horton, hampered by the breakdown of one diesel, needed two more days to join Laurence in Libau on 21 October.

The bemused Russians did not know whether to be pleased or alarmed by these unexpected allies, whose arrival had been proclaimed only by a few signal flares and an outsize British naval ensign hoisted as each entered harbour. The German Army was closing in on the port, which had already been mined by the Germans on the seaward side. Meanwhile Nasmith's *E11* gave up and went home on the 22nd, after engine failures and evading merchantmen, destroyers, a seaplane and a submarine, which Nasmith tried to torpedo. He missed, which was fortunate as the boat was Danish. At least one of the destroyers was German because it tried to ram him. He did not manage to enter the Sound. Churchill and Fisher were infuriated by Keyes's carelessness with his most efficient submarines.

The German U-boat arm had not been idle in the Baltic, sending *U23*, *U25* and *U26* to the western end of the Gulf of Finland to look for Russian warships. *U26*, having narrowly missed one armoured cruiser, sank another, the *Pallada* (7,900 tons), on 11 October with a single torpedo which set off a magazine. The Russian Navy now withdrew eastward, abandoning Libau. German cruisers none the less arrived to bombard it in mid-November, losing their flagship, SMS *Friedrich Karl*, to a mine on the way. They could have saved themselves the trouble as the Russians had already destroyed the docks. The two British submarines were berthed at Revel (now Tallinn) in Estonia (then Russian) some 300 miles to the north-east.

In the ensuing winter Laurence and Horton patrolled little, saw almost nothing of the enemy and sank nothing at all beyond generous helpings of Russian vodka. But their mere presence amid the constricting ice-floes obstructed the Germans' planned advance on Petrograd (St Petersburg) by sea and disrupted their shipping in the north-eastern Baltic. They therefore felt obliged to take the sensible step of routinely sailing all ships in convoy, which showed their admirals to be more intelligent than the British. Despite the cold, constant mechanical problems, shortages of spare parts, a drought of the rum which fuelled the Royal Navy and a dearth of sinkings, the two British boats had already made a strategic contribution out of all proportion to their strength.

The Germans lost a light cruiser and several light craft to mines but tended to blame all such losses on the British boats, the hated and much publicised Horton in particular. The disputed waters became known as "Horton's sea" and German intelligence went to the lengths of sending a beautiful spy to Tallinn to poison him. The siren reputedly fell for Horton's charms and allowed herself to be "turned", eventually fleeing to England. Horton and Laurence were promoted full commanders at the turn of the year, although their first Baltic sinkings did not come until June 1915, when Horton caught a merchantman and soon afterwards wrote off a destroyer and a collier with "borrowed" Russian torpedoes. On 2 July Russian and German cruisers clashed in fog off the Swedish island of Gotland. The Russians got the upper hand, damaging three German men-of-war. The two British boats were in attendance, and Horton seriously damaged *Prinz Adalbert*, one of two armoured cruisers sent as reinforcements. She was repaired, only to be sunk by HMS *E8* in October 1915.

At the end of July *E1* was at last blooded when Laurence sank a German merchantman converted for minesweeping. His persistence was further rewarded on 19 August, near the Gulf of Riga, when he was astounded to get a periscope view of the greater part of the High Seas Fleet. Grand-Admiral Prince Heinrich had ten battleships, three battle-cruisers, nine light cruisers and two dozen destroyers under command to help the German Army take Latvian Riga, then under Russian rule.

Vice-Admiral Ehrhard Schmidt took two battleships, four cruisers and twelve destroyers into the Gulf of Riga while the rest stayed outside. He drove off the only substantial Russian unit present, the old battleship *Slava*, which managed to limp away after disrupting German minesweeping. As the rest of the outgunned Russian fleet was in Kronstadt and other distant bases, Schmidt withdrew after shooting up the shore. The westbound Germans then sailed past Laurence's end of a waiting patrol line of four submarines, two Russian and two British. Laurence fired at Vice-Admiral Franz Ritter von Hipper's three German battle-cruisers, conveniently sailing in line abreast. Missing the nearest, SMS *Seydlitz*, which sounded the alarm, he hit the second, *Moltke*, forward, causing her to ship 450 tons of water and slowing her, and the squadron in sympathy, to fifteen knots. Under orders from his brother not to risk his ships unnecessarily, Prince Heinrich withdrew them all the way to Kiel, for fear of further submarine attack. The Germans abandoned the operation against Riga, which was never captured in the war. Strategists and historians on both sides concluded that this saved Petrograd and even Russia itself (until 1917) – all for one torpedo.

Meanwhile Keyes had sent two more boats: *E8* (Goodhart) and *E13* (Geoffrey Layton) left Harwich on the 14th. Goodhart got through the Sound in an ordeal similar to Horton's. Layton took a run at the treacherously shallow strait and ran aground on a sandbank in neutral Danish waters. Given twenty-four hours to save herself unaided, as international law required, and having spent the night in vain efforts to get off, the boat illegally came under fire from German destroyers. They ceased only when Danish torpedo-boats intervened, by which time fifteen British sailors had been killed while abandoning the battered hulk. The other half of the crew, including five wounded men, went into Danish internment, from which Layton eventually escaped to England. The boat was sold for scrap to the Danes after the war.

In September two more boats arrived, bringing the total in the Baltic to five. Robert Halahan arrived in *E18* and F.N.A. Cromie in *E19*. The latter was caught by nets in her first patrol off the German island of Rügen on 2 October, coming under fire from a patrol vessel, but Cromie got away unscathed. He became expert in economising on torpedoes by boarding and scuttling his victims or else bombarding them with gunfire, disposing of eight freighters in October. Despite German diplomatic protests they included iron-ore carriers bound for Germany from Sweden, obliging the Germans to reinforce their patrols with vessels from the High Seas Fleet.

Horton sank four merchantmen in mid-Baltic in late summer and early autumn. The cruiser *Prinz Adalbert*, damaged earlier by Horton, was dispatched by Goodhart with a single torpedo on 23 October. A magazine exploded and pieces of armour rained down on *E8* as she dived for cover. Fifteen days later the light cruiser SMS *Undine* fell victim to two of the torpedoes Cromie had been saving up, sinking off Sweden's Bornholm Island. Cromie torpedoed a destroyer and sank two more merchantmen for a final tally of ten. He also destroyed two U-boats, one in November and one in December, achieving by far the best score in the Baltic. Russian submariners were impressed by the example set by Horton and the no less flamboyant Cromie, but made little or no destructive contribution to the harassment of the Germans in the enclosed sea.

In the following month Horton went home to take command of the new *J6*. Laurence left Tallinn a few days later but was given command of the first boat in this new, large and fast class, HMS *J1* (1,210 tons surfaced, 1,820 submerged). Hubert Vaughan-Jones relieved Horton;

Laurence was replaced by Athelstan Fenner in command of *E1*, while
Cromie took over as Senior British Naval Officer. Noel Laurence went
on to distinguish himself in his new boat by seriously damaging two of
the latest German battleships – *Grosser Kurfürst* and *Kronprinz* – with
a single salvo of torpedoes in the North Sea a few weeks after the Battle
of Jutland.

For Britain the peak of achievement in the Baltic was now past. The
Germans had hermetically sealed the entrance, forcing the British to
send smaller submarines to northern Russia and transport them overland and by canal to the Baltic. But, since the generals ultimately controlled the Russian Navy and wanted it to guard their flanks on land,
the fleet mostly stayed in port for fear of German submarines. Such
offensive action as there was came mostly from a handful of mechanically unreliable British submarines. These nevertheless proved quite
enough, with the dense Russian minefields, to deter the German Navy,
hugely superior in the Baltic whenever it wished to be, from major
undertakings eastward of its own heavily patrolled patch in the western
Baltic. And all this in waters often barely deep enough to allow the
passage of anything larger than a coastal steamer, or else widely frozen
for months on end.

Here as much as anywhere the startling deterrent effect of the submarine, all but universally discounted before the war, was unmistakably
demonstrated, even before it could submerge for more than a few hours
or had reliable torpedoes, propulsion or location equipment. These early
boats, frail, shortsighted and almost deaf, had already added an entire
new dimension at sea to the ancient military stratagem of surprise.

As the British submariners bumped and ground their way into the Baltic,
the German U-boat men were let off the leash in the north-eastern
Atlantic before the first winter of the war was over.

On 3 November 1914 the High Seas Fleet had embarked on pro-
vocative, coat-trailing raids across the North Sea. Vice-Admiral Hipper's
five battlecruisers, a category in which the Germans had a qualitative
superiority as pronounced as in submarines, were assigned this task with
a suitable escort of light cruisers and destroyers. Their mission was to
provoke the British by minelaying and hit-and-run attacks on the
English east coast. Hipper had the edge in speed to avoid a clash with
larger British forces, while picking off smaller ones if the chance arose.
But Room 40 discovered in advance that he would be out on 15 December,
and eight submarines helped to set a trap.

Yet the British, content to send Beatty's battlecruisers and a squadron
of battleships against Hipper, did not discover that the main body of

Ingenohl's High Seas Fleet was out as well. When the destroyers clashed on the 16th, Ingenohl put about and left Hipper to it, missing the best opportunity of the war of destroying a British heavy force and swinging the balance of power at sea in Germany's favour, as Tirpitz had envisaged.

Ignorant of this distant clash or even of his chief's presence, let alone his decision to convert it into an absence, Hipper, also unaware that the two British squadrons were out , confidently divided his force in two and shelled Hartlepool, Whitby and Scarborough, inflicting hundreds of civilian casualties, before turning for home at about 9.30 a.m. Jellicoe belatedly dispatched two more squadrons of battleships from Rosyth and Scapa. Hipper was sailing, did he but know it, between two British forces, each with much more firepower than his own. He never found out because the perennially overrated Beatty now perpetrated one of his mighty errors. By sending an opaque and misleading signal to the British light cruisers, he broke off the incipient clash instead of following it up.

Had it not been for the news of the Royal Navy's clear victory against Graf Spee a week earlier, heads would surely have rolled in the wave of public anger over the bombardment of defenceless civilians and the Navy's failure to grasp the opportunity of punishing the perpetrators. In Scarborough, the coroner at the inquest on the eighty-six dead asked, in an outburst without precedent: "Where was the Navy?"

The German war leadership was no less angry about Ingenohl's own missed opportunity to smash a large but inferior enemy force, which he might well have done in the hours before Grand Fleet reinforcements arrived. Tirpitz, still navy minister, blamed Ingenohl for failing to win the war in its fifth month. Neither the U-boats nor Keyes's submarines took part in the narrowly missed fleet action, which offered each side in turn the chance of an early strategic victory at sea. Here was more evidence that tactical collaboration between submarines and battlefleets capable of much higher speeds was impracticable.

Hipper came out again on 23 January 1915 with four of his battlecruisers, hours after Room 40 had divined his intention. The presence of the hybrid *Blücher*, whose guns were only of 8.2-inch calibre, and the absence of one of his true battlecruisers made Hipper's force inferior to Beatty's, now increased to five, of which three carried the latest 13.5-inch guns. Beatty raced down from the Firth of Forth to link up with Goodenough's Grand Fleet light cruisers (and Tyrwhitt's destroyers from Harwich) near the Dogger Bank in the southern North Sea at daybreak on the 24th. The opposed light cruisers sighted each other and began firing. By the time the British capital ships arrived Hipper was already bound for home, having abandoned his apparent intention of bombarding the English coast again.

Once more a confusing signal from Beatty's flagship, HMS *Lion*, led the British into serious tactical error, leaving one German ship unengaged and thus free to shoot without distraction. The *Lion* was therefore seriously damaged by fifteen hits and fell out of the line. So did Hipper's flagship, the *Seydlitz*, which narrowly escaped destruction by her own magazines. The *Blücher* was less fortunate and eventually sank under a hail of British shot, the only fatal casualty of the action.

Beatty was reasonably convinced that he could catch and destroy the rest of Hipper's squadron in the 200 miles between it and safety. But at this favourable moment in the Battle of the Dogger Bank the submarine, or more precisely the fear of it, "periscopitis", took a hand and reduced a major action to an indecisive skirmish. On a reported sighting of a periscope the British admiral ordered a ninety-degree evasive turn, fearing he was being led into an underwater trap. Hipper was therefore able to escape, helped on his way by yet another signalling mix-up which led the British to focus their fire on the clearly doomed *Blücher*, instead of on the retreating German survivors before they got out of range. But it was Beatty's second-in-command, Rear-Admiral Archibald Moore, who was dismissed – for obeying the bad signal. Jellicoe, who might have been able to seal Hipper's fate had he not lost three hours in coming up in support, did however draw attention to Beatty's past neglect of gunnery practice.

On the defeated German side, Hipper actually gained in stature for escaping a superior force and bringing home the shattered *Seydlitz*. His chief, Ingenohl, was condemned for lack of initiative in not supporting his battlecruiser commander with the battleships. Early in February, therefore, he was relieved by his chief of staff, Admiral Hugo von Pohl.

This taciturn, physically frail but decisive and aggressive officer was by now utterly convinced that an underwater version of all-out cruiser warfare against British seaborne trade, nothing less than unrestricted submarine attack, was the key to victory. When the Kaiser came to Wilhelmshaven on 4 February 1915 to review his battlefleet, which he was intent on preserving at almost any cost as a bargaining counter, the new C-in-C won the "All-Highest Warlord's" approval for the only means of taking the war to the enemy now open to the Imperial Navy. The leash was taken off the U-boats in Pohl's order declaring the seas round the British Isles, as far north as Shetland and west of Dutch coastal waters, a war zone. Any ship found there on or after 18 February faced sinking without warning. A neutral flag was no guarantee of safety. The threat to neutrally flagged ships, which angered United States opinion, was prompted by the ruse of Captain William Turner of the Cunard liner *Lusitania*, in flying the Stars and Stripes in the Irish Sea on 31

January. His explanation was that he had many American passengers, and a U-boat (Hersing's *U21*) was in the area. U-boat skippers were now under orders to be absolutely sure a ship was neutral before sparing it; they were not ordered to sink neutrals regardless but rather not to accept a mere flag as proof of neutrality.

Hersing, nemesis of HMS *Pathfinder*, had destroyed three freighters with explosives under prize rules on the previous day and had cheekily shelled Barrow-in-Furness, headquarters of British submarine construction, on the 29th. Between the outbreak of war and the day British waters became a German free-fire zone on 18 February, U-boats had sunk one Allied and eleven British merchant vessels, one old battleship, four old cruisers, one light cruiser, a seaplane-carrier, a gunboat and the submarine *E3*. They had lost seven U-boats but commissioned fifteen new ones and ordered forty-three more.

This respectable score had been achieved with an average operational strength of fewer than thirty submarines, of which the majority were still small, non-ocean-going boats and only one third were actually on patrol at any one time (the rest being either outward- or homeward-bound). The conduct of German submariners in British waters henceforward was indistinguishable from that of British submariners in the Baltic and the Dardanelles, the specific threat to neutrals, prompted by Captain Turner's deception, always excepted. The only substantive differences lay in the quality of the submarines engaged and the quantity of targets the Germans found in the world's busiest waters. This accounted for the sheer scale and unique strategic significance of their campaign, especially when it reached its peak in 1916–17. By then Britain's very fate depended on the outcome.

By the end of April 1915 the U-boats, at a cost of three more of their number, destroyed another thirty-nine merchant ships, together with the lives of hundreds of seamen and passengers. This destruction was a mere foretaste of the "frightfulness" to come. In January they had sunk 47,900 tons (including six ships in a single week) and in February 65,000; in only two weeks of May they were to send 120,000 tons to the bottom. Among the most notable early incidents was the death of an American among the fifty-seven passengers and forty-seven seamen killed when *U28* (Freiherr von Forstner) sank the British liner *Falaba* on 28 March. Forstner, whose two sons were to captain U-boats in the Second World War, had already killed sailors and passengers abandoning a ship he was trying to sink by gunfire a few days earlier. An American tanker captain died in an April attack which failed to sink his ship; US opinion was inflamed further on the destruction by torpedo of the British steamer *Harpalyce*, 5,940 tons, flying a white flag and banners proclaiming her intent of fetching American food for the starving in Belgium. The small coastal boat *UB4* (Lieutenant Gross) sent her to the bottom without warning a few miles off the Belgian coast.

One of the few British anti-submarine successes in these early days was a most spectacular one and particularly satisfying for the Royal Navy. It came on 18 March, when Vice-Admiral Sir Doveton Sturdee, the Falklands victor, was leading his Fourth Battle Squadron on exercise off north-east Scotland. Sighting a U-boat on the surface, his flagship, HMS *Dreadnought*, prototype of all modern battleships, "turned on a sixpence" and managed to ram a vessel with just one-thirtieth of her displacement. As the boat rose in the water for a few seconds before disappearing for ever, the number *U29* was clearly visible on the conning tower. It was the newly promoted Commander Otto Weddigen, erstwhile captain of the immortal *U9* which had sunk four British cruisers. British coyness about how they had destroyed his new boat led to rumours in Germany that he had fallen victim to an unworthy trick. But it was the old-fashioned ram, still the only successful British anti-submarine weapon of the time, which had done for him; not one U-boat had been sunk by gunfire.

The incident which stands out, not only in this first period of unre-stricted U-boat warfare or even in the First World War as a whole but also in the entire history of submarine operations, took place on 7 May 1915. Walter Schweiger was on patrol in *U20* in the Western Approaches, the busy waters south of Ireland and west of England. He had sunk three ships on the 5th and 6th and, left with only three torpedoes for his four tubes, was bound for home by the 7th. Thoroughly pleased with himself, his crew of thirty-eight, his boat and the world in general, Schweiger was catching the lunchtime sun on the conning tower and routinely scanning the horizon when he sighted the huge smoke cloud of a very large, black-hulled ship with white trim and four tall red funnels striped and tipped in black; obviously a Cunard transatlantic liner, eastward bound off the coast of south-west Ireland.

Six days earlier in neutral New York, a sensation had been caused by the publication of advertisements signed by the German Embassy. They carried the blunt reminder that any ship was liable to destruction in British waters: "Travellers sailing in the war zone ... do so at their own risk." The stark warning appeared just under the customary Cunard Line notice of that day's sailing to Liverpool by the RMS *Lusitania*. The 30,396-ton liner had been built in 1906 and won the "Blue Riband" for fastest transatlantic voyage in 1907.

Captain Turner, nicknamed "Bowler Bill", dismissed the German threat. A vastly experienced seaman of fifty-eight with a curt manner and a hearty dislike for the fare-paying passengers, whom he was wont to describe as monkeys, Turner proffered the protection of the Royal Navy and the "unsinkable" qualities of his ship with her honeycomb of watertight compartments, double bottom and four screws delivering a top speed of twenty-six knots. His confidence helped to offset the ghoulishness of reporters who swarmed aboard just before sailing to record the start of what they proclaimed her "last voyage".

It began at noon on May Day, two hours late by the time the last reporters and wellwishers had gone down the gangways. There were 1,257 passengers aboard, of whom 197 were US citizens, including Alfred G. Vanderbilt of the railroad and shipping family, a multi-millionaire amateur horseman aged thirty-seven. Three German stowaways – one may deduce that either they were spies or they did not read newspapers – were found in a steward's pantry shortly after departure and detained for questioning in Liverpool. Like so many others they did not arrive there, leaving just one of many mysteries associated with the loss of the liner.

The greatest controversy surrounded her status under international law. As contemporary editions of Brassey's *Naval Annual* unequivocally confirm, the sister-ships *Lusitania* and *Mauretania* belonged, like several other fast liners, to the Royal Naval Reserve. Cunard received government aid for their construction and an annual subsidy in return for allowing their conversion to auxiliary cruisers in wartime. Each therefore had reinforced decks for eight six-inch guns. The manifest listed among her cargo a total of 173 tons of rifle ammunition and shrapnel shells, as well as fulminate-of-mercury detonators as used in mines and torpedoes. The *Lusitania* was not armed; but the dangerous mixture of passengers and munitions she carried seems in retrospect cavalier.

So does Captain Turner's disregard of naval advice to zigzag, to maintain high speed and to stay clear of coastal waters whenever possible, especially after he received two warnings of submarine activity off south-west Ireland from the Royal Navy at Queenstown (now Cobh) within an hour on the evening of the 6th. The alert was tardy, given that Room 40 had located at least one U-boat in the area early on the 5th. As we have seen, Schweiger had sunk three ships in short order well before sighting the *Lusitania*. Turner had the opportunity to take extra precautions but preferred to reduce speed from twenty-one to eighteen knots to be sure of being able to take his deep hull over the Mersey Bar next morning without having to wait for the tide. But he did double the lookouts, darken ship, close as many watertight doors as possible and have the lifeboats swung out of their davits for swift launching. The night passed without incident.

Schweiger threw the rest of his lunch overboard when he got his sighting, some fifteen miles off the Irish coast due south of Cork. Turner was heading due north for the Old Head of Kinsale to take a navigational fix. By the time the liner turned east again, Schweiger had managed, by going flat out on the surface on a parallel course, to reach the ideal position for a shot at the ship's starboard side from the near-perfect range of 700 metres when *Lusitania* turned across his bow, as he knew she must. The torpedo, fired at 21.15 p.m., struck amidships ten feet below the waterline. *Lusitania* had eighteen minutes to live.

Among the many controversies which arose from her destruction was whether Schweiger fired a second time, or whether the huge second explosion noted by many witnesses was the munitions going up "in sympathy". In fact coal-dust in her bunkers was almost certainly the reason. Schweiger died in command of *U88*, lost to a mine in September 1917, but veterans of *U20* insisted that only one torpedo was fired.

Two lookouts saw it coming but there was nothing Turner could do in the minute it took to strike home, tearing the guts out of his ship. Although the torpedo hit aft of the bridge, dives on the wreck revealed that the main damage was a great hole in the hull well forward of it. The *Lusitania* listed to starboard as her wireless operator tapped out his forlorn message: "SOS. Come at once. Big list. Ten Miles south Old Head Kinsale. SOS . . . " Also going down rapidly by the bow, the ship was driven under by the death-throes of her own great engines.

To starboard the lifeboats were swinging too far out from the side for unathletic passengers to board. To port they swung inboard and could not be lowered into the water. Horrific scenes ensued as port-side life-boats full of screaming passengers slithered over other people who had lost their footing on the tilting deck, only to smash against more solid obstacles. The explosions had sent a column of debris 150 feet into the air to rain down on the hulk. One American forced a seaman to cut a boat loose at pistol point, while Mr Vanderbilt, who could not swim, gave the last minutes of his life to helping children. Finally the bow hit bottom and the stern rose steeply before falling back in an appalling cacophony of disintegration, as plates parted, bulkheads collapsed, heavy machinery broke loose and great gouts of air forced their way to a surface covered in debris, coal dust and bodies. Among the 1,198 fatal casualties were 413 crew and 785 passengers, including ninety-four children and 128 Americans. It was all terribly reminiscent of the even more catastrophic loss of the *Titanic* only three years earlier, but that was merely a disaster. The sinking of the *Lusitania* was a deliberate act of war against unarmed civilians.

It was followed by a ferocious propaganda battle. On hearing the news of this unprecedented "frightfulness" at sea, President Wilson burst into tears and sent a telegram of protest to the Kaiser. Americans were booed and hissed as "cowards" in London streets, theatres and restaurants as their country stayed out of the war. Some Germans claimed that Churchill had abandoned the *Lusitania* to her fate so as to draw the United States into the war. The German authorities pointed out that they had issued the clearest possible warning, that the *Lusitania* was carrying war matériel, that she was in a declared war zone and that Schweiger had actually forborne from firing again when he saw so many people in the water. The U-boat skipper reportedly denied that he had recognised his target before firing (which seems either specious or irrelevant: her size and her Cunard livery made it clear he had a liner in his sights, whatever her name. The denial may have been his government's rather than Schweiger's own).

The overall tonnage lost to submarines in May 1915 was a record 120,000, as noted above. But after the *Lusitania* horror, the U-boat campaign eased off. Churchill was unwise enough to boast that it had failed. He was soon proved wrong.

Both sides in their different ways experienced the crisis of this first unrestricted submarine campaign on the anniversary of the war, in August 1915. After May, U-boat activity picked up again month by month, until in August 185,800 tons of shipping were destroyed, 165,000 by submarines. This was not only a new record but also an ominous turning point for the British. For the first time tonnage sunk exceeded Britain's monthly shipbuilding capacity. Clearly this was no freak result but an established trend; as the U-boat fleet expanded, sinkings would increase, and as losses grew, Britain's ability to supply herself and her armies would decline, reducing her ability to wage war or even feed her people.

But on 19 August the "*Lusitania* factor" came to Britain's aid. Rudolf Schneider's *U24*, one of three boats operating south of Ireland, was on the surface shelling a freighter fifty miles south of Kinsale when a much bigger ship loomed up from the east, zigzagging at speed but heading towards him. Schneider, perhaps thinking he was about to be rammed, dived and fired a single torpedo. The White Star liner *Arabic*, 15,800 tons, sank in ten minutes with the loss of forty-four passengers and crew – a remarkably light toll in the conditions. Only three of the dead were Americans, but they were enough to arouse new indignation. President Wilson duly protested again, more sharply.

British leaders were now seriously worried by the U-boat threat, to which they had no answer. Nor did they have the remotest inkling that their German opposite numbers were just as anxious, and deeply divided on what to do next. The politicians and the diplomats, Chancellor Bethmann-Hollweg to the fore, were convinced that it was only a matter of time before the United States, with all its manpower, natural resources and industrial capacity, came into the war on the Entente side if the unrestricted submarine campaign continued. The Kaiser and his staff wanted to press on with the counter-blockade, especially Admiral Henning von Holtzendorff, Chief of Naval Staff, who promised that the British would collapse in six months, if he had a free hand at sea, before any US intervention could take effect. This was no idle boast but a cool assessment of Britain's dependence on its transatlantic lifeline and inability to staunch the haemorrhage of its shipping; his calculation was accurate and was vitiated only by changes in the circumstances on which it was based. But the Chancellor prevailed; the Kaiser told his Navy not to attack passenger ships after the end of August except under prize rules. This was now far too risky in British waters, and the ever-present possibility of confusing liners with other ships led the U-boat captains to refrain rather than attack when in doubt. But it needed only one blunder by a single U-boat captain to revive the issue.

Sinkings round Britain meanwhile diminished sharply in September, and on the 20th of the month, seven months and two days after the opening of the unrestricted campaign, U-boats withdrew from British waters, except for the southern North Sea where reconnaissance and minelaying continued. The focus of the U-boat onslaught on Allied shipping now shifted to the Mediterranean, where there were plenty of targets and virtually no Americans. The haemorrhage ceased but the British Merchant Navy bled on, the effect of every lost ton of capacity and cargo being exactly the same for Britain wherever it occurred. By the end of the year 855,000 tons of shipping, 748,000 of it British, had been lost in the war thus far, for a mere twenty U-boats sunk.

A grim harvest of ninety-four ships was also reaped by German mines in 1915, the bulk of them sown by specially built, small "UC" submarines (originally 168/183 tons; higher numbers were larger) operating under the independent command of the Flanders Flotillas from the occupied Belgian ports. Also stationed there from 1915 were even smaller "UB" types (originally 127/142 tons; later boats were larger), specially designed for coastal work and often sent in sections overland to their bases.

One of these, UB29 (Lieutenant Pustkuchen), resurrected the Lus-itania factor on 24 March 1916, when he fired a torpedo at the small

French cross-Channel ferry *Sussex*, 1,350 tons, carrying 380 passengers from Dieppe to Folkestone in calm, clear weather. The oddly named Pustkuchen (puff pastry) later claimed he had seen uniformed men on deck and deduced it was a troopship. Holed in the bow, the ferry was taken in tow and beached at Boulogne (where torpedo fragments were found in her hull) as a British destroyer and a French trawler picked up some 300 survivors. Among the eighty or so killed were twenty-five Americans. In Washington the German ambassador, Johann Heinrich Count von Bernstorff, was summoned to the State Department for a dressing-down. He suggested that the *Sussex* had hit a mine; unfortunately for him the *Salybia*, a British freighter heading for the Thames from the West Indies, had unquestionably been torpedoed in the same area two hours after the ferry was hit, so the Count was not believed.

Washington protested by a Note on 20 April, unprecedented because it contained a threat: "Unless the Imperial Government should now immediately declare and effect an abandonment of its present methods of submarine warfare against passenger and freight-carrying vessels, the Government of the United States can have no choice but to sever diplomatic relations." In its bitter and unrepentant reply Berlin wrote:

The German Government cannot but reiterate its regret that sentiments of humanity, which the Government of the United States extends with such fervour to the unhappy victims of submarine warfare, have not been extended with the same feeling to the many millions of women and children who, according to the avowed intention of the British Government, are to be starved, and who by suffering are to force the victorious armies of the Central Powers into an ignominious capitulation.

But on 24 April Bethmann-Hollweg once again overcame Admiral Holtzendorff and the U-boats were ordered to observe prize rules, effectively withdrawing from British waters altogether. On 4 May the Germans sent a Note to Washington bowing to its demand, thus averting American intervention for another year. In the preceding twenty-one months 131 ships totalling 442,000 tons had been lost to U-boats' attacks; Britain alone had lost more than a million tons of shipping to all causes in the war so far, with untold quantities of goods, munitions and food, at a total cost to Germany of just thirty-two U-boats and fewer than 1,000 submariners. The counter-blockade was proving more effective than the surface blockade which inspired it. Unfortunately for the Germans, the effect of the British blockade was invisible (though no less real) and long term, death by a thousand cuts in rations for an incalculable number of people. The effect of torpedoes and mines was all too spectacular and instantaneous, involving the simultaneous deaths of hundreds and the destruction of ships and cargoes.

The intermission in unrestricted submarine warfare was an enormous relief for the British. There was to be no remission in their blockade of Germany, or in their increasingly desperate efforts to find an answer to the U-boat threat.

Since the Royal Navy had gone to war without a submarine strategy, it comes as no surprise to learn that it had no anti-submarine strategy either. The first weapon deployed against the U-boat in 1914 was money. Weddigen's *U9* had been sighted by an English fishing-boat on 21 September, the day before the massacre of the three "Cressys", but the skipper did not make his sighting report until the 25th. To encourage a proper sense of urgency the Admiralty, on posters in every port, offered £80 for a firm sighting of the tiny *U1* or *U2* and £160 for *U21* and upwards. A sighting leading to a "kill" would fetch £1,000; one leading to a chase was worth £200. Fishing vessels were offered £1 per diverted mile to deliver urgent sighting reports. Rewards of up to £10 were paid for the destruction of enemy mines. But there was only a thin harvest of reports; fishermen put their own safety and their catch above acting as impromptu picket-boats. There were also very few boats to be reported; the rest was periscopitis. The only sightings of real value were those reported at once by wireless, which was not carried by contemporary small vessels.

For reasons of ignorance and snobbery, Britain was already seriously short of young scientists and technicians before the war. The self-made entrepreneurs who prompted the Industrial Revolution bought country estates and sent their sons to exclusive schools, where they learned to disdain the hard work which brought world economic domination between Britain's defeat of Napoleon I and German unification after the defeat of Napoleon III. The shortage was compounded by the British Army's indiscriminate wartime use of highly qualified young men, whether graduates or skilled tradesmen, as cannon fodder. The twice-beaten French did not make this mistake.

In Paris a Bureau of Inventions for National Defence was set up in 1914 under Paul Painlevé (soon known as "Minister of Inventions") to coordinate military and naval research. At Toulon the engineer Paul Langevin tested his pioneering ultrasonic underwater echo-ranging devices, an early stab at sonar. Other anti-submarine and naval research was carried out at Cherbourg and Brest.

The impasse on the Western Front, the growing submarine threat – and Sir Maurice Hankey, the former Royal Marine officer and secretary of the Committee of Imperial Defence (later of the "War Council" or inner Cabinet) – drove the British to follow suit in 1915. One result was the Advisory Council on Scientific and Industrial Research run by the War Office and the Ministry of Munitions; another was the Admiralty's shortlived Board of Invention and Research (BIR), chaired by Fisher after he resigned as First Sea Lord in May 1915.

The BIR seemed set fair to make progress when it started. Its chief was as forceful as ever, and was supported by such powerful figures as Sir Charles Parsons, the great Tyneside engineer, Sir Ernest Rutherford, one of the world's leading scientists, and many other experts. Each of six sub-committees had a naval officer as secretary and boasted half a dozen top scientists; the submarines and wireless sub-committee concerns us most. Public interest in the war and how to win it is shown by the fact that the BIR received 38,000 suggestions from individuals (hardly any were of value).

"Submarines and wireless" was mainly concerned with anti-submarine warfare (ASW). It took another look at the unlikely possibilities of harnessing birds, sea lions and dowsers to find submarines but also initiated serious research into underwater acoustics, the key to detection. The most promising researcher was Commander C.P. Ryan, a torpedo and wireless expert who had left the Navy in 1911 for the Marconi wireless company after indifferently commanding a destroyer flotilla. Recalled on the outbreak of war, Ryan, then forty, started developing hydrophones to detect U-boats at the Admiralty's experimental station at Hawkcraig in Fife, Scotland, before the end of 1914. Rutherford sent two scientists from Manchester University to join him. It was an unhappy partnership because the abrasive Ryan typified the bluff, no-nonsense approach to technology of the Royal Navy (or those corners of its that took any interest at all). He concentrated on practical devices rather than the theoretical research which might improve on them. Nor did the "Silent Service" like sharing its secrets with outsiders, a category which seemed to embrace not merely the rest of the world but also any other branch of the Navy. It was this unbridgeable rift between academics and technical officers which brought down the BIR before the war ended.

"Peace talks" were held at the Admiralty in March 1916, leading to the appointment of Professor W.H. Bragg, a Nobel prizewinner in physics, as resident director of the civilian scientists at Hawkcraig. He was soon complaining of the "Gilbert and Sullivan opera" run by the Navy. At the end of the year the civilians left the field to acting-Captain Ryan, whose establishment was subordinated to the Admiralty's new Anti-Submarine Division (ASD). The scientists set up a theoretical research station at Tyrwhitt's base in Harwich. All these organisations worked on underwater detection by sound.

It was Ryan who set up the shore-based system of listening for submarines underwater. He also developed wired mines with microphones, for detonation by an electric current from shore when a U-boat was heard. These inventions were hampered by sensitivity to extraneous noise, short range and inability to determine the direction of the sound-source. They worked best in dead calm conditions and were adopted for the lack of anything better.

In 1915 ASW picket boats began to be fitted with the "Portable General Service hydrophone" or "drifter set" which could detect the presence of a submarine but not its bearing, still less its position. From 1916 submarines in their turn began to listen for ships, with directional hydrophones fitted in pairs at the bow. One was sensitive to high pitch, the other to low, and the instruments, tested and "tuned" by musicians, detected direction by measuring variations in the strengths of vibrations picked up by the two microphones.

The main difficulty with the first directional hydrophones was their inability to tell whether sounds were coming from ahead or astern. The source might be on a given bearing or its reciprocal, opening the possibility of a 180-degree error. Almost nothing was known about the properties of sound in water, where it travels at about four times its speed in air and is highly susceptible to changes in motion, pressure, temperature, density and depth.

While A.F. Sykes did important theoretical work on directional hydrophones at East London College, the French naval Lieutenant G. Walser developed his "sound lenses", a pair of blisters near a ship's bow, each incorporating a fly's-eye pattern of diaphragms monitored by ear-trumpets. The diaphragms giving off the strongest vibrations would be at right angles to the source. It was tried but eventually rejected as too fragile. The Americans were also working on hydrophones before they came into the war in April 1917; their main early contribution was the double multiple hydrophone array, a non-electrical "stereophonic" system which was an aural equivalent of the optical rangefinder. The British and Americans worked independently, and later cooperated, on arrays of hydrophones towed in special containers well astern of the ship's own sound.

The Germans, not surprisingly, were much more interested in listening devices for, rather than against, submarines. Early U-boats had hydrophones similar to British ones, based on those developed for navigational purposes by the American Submarine Signalling Company. Initially microphones were installed on either side of the boat, with the whole hull acting as the sound-sensitive diaphragm. Later German hydrophones were much more sophisticated, capable of "hearing" at up to twenty-five miles, directional and able to distinguish between types of sound. German equipment needed silence on board, a commodity more readily available on a lurking submarine than on any surface ship, even when motionless. The Germans focused their work on "passive" sound detection during and after the war and in the Second World War, while the Anglo-Americans, driven by their ASW needs, moved on to "active" detection by sound impulses.

The depth-charge, or "water-bomb" as the Germans called it, was developed in Britain in 1915 but was not widely deployed until spring 1916 and claimed no victim until July that year. The ram and the gun could be used if the U-boat stayed on the surface for long enough, or else sweeps with explosives attached might be towed at high speed (and high risk) by several small vessels and released over a U-boat's suspected position in the hope of blowing a hole in it. Otherwise the British were reduced to laying their nets and low-quality mines or stepping up patrols (3,000 small ASW vessels were already in use by the end of 1916). More and more merchant ships were armed with naval guns, an expedient which only encouraged the U-boats to attack without warning.

So did the "Q-ship", the most famous ASW weapon of the First World War. The "Q" may derive from Queenstown, the naval base in the south-west of Ireland, but so much secrecy surrounded them that one cannot be sure. Not even the precise number deployed is known, though it was over 200. The Q-ship was a small mercantile vessel, trawler or similar with relatively heavy armament concealed behind false or removable upperworks. The idea was to lure the U-boat to surface and use its gun on an apparently helpless target. Then the Q-ship would hoist the naval White Ensign, drop its screens and blast the U-boat out of the water. This ruse worked at first, but within weeks the overall effect was to make U-boat captains more ruthless. The first victim was *U36*, sunk by Lieutenant W.P. Mark-Wardlaw's coaster *Prince Charles* on 24 July.

The most notorious incident was the sinking of Wegener's *U27* by Lieutenant Godfrey Herbert's *Baralong*, a 4,200-ton tramp-steamer with a trio of concealed twelve-pounders. Herbert was hoping above all to exact revenge for the loss of the *Arabic* to *U24*. On 19 August 1915 he was sporting the Stars and Stripes south of Ireland when he saw *U27* in the act of attacking the merchantman *Nicosian*. Witnesses said later that Herbert attacked the U-boat, which sank inside a minute, without bothering to exchange the American flag for a British one; yet he had hoisted a signal declaring his intention to rescue survivors from the

Nicosian. Six unarmed German survivors scrambled aboard the abandoned freighter, where they were massacred by a boarding party from the *Baralong.* Wegener himself was also shot dead in this nasty incident.

The most famous Q-ship commander was Captain Gordon Campbell, decorated for his exploits with the two highest British gallantry awards, the Victoria Cross and the Distinguished Service Order. His first success was to sink the *U68* in the Western Approaches in 1916.

A uniquely unlucky victim of the German anger which such "dirty tricks" aroused was Captain Charles Fryatt of the British Merchant Navy. Sighting a U-boat off the Belgian coast, he tried to ram it but failed. He was captured by a German boarding party, court-martialled and shot at Bruges as a *franc-tireur* on 27 July 1916.

In February 1916 the ailing Admiral Pohl was replaced as High Seas Fleet C-in-C by Admiral Reinhard Scheer. He soon reverted to the original German strategy of making forays into the North Sea to seek and destroy inferior British formations so as to erode the superiority of the Grand Fleet. He came out in strength on 24 April 1916 in (very) distant support of the Easter Rising in Ireland. We may note in passing an early, perhaps the earliest, example of the use of a submarine for a clandestine mission. A U-boat landed Sir Roger Casement, formerly of the British Consular Service, in Ireland that month with a consignment of arms to lead the rebellion (he had gone to Germany to seek help for the Fenian cause on the outbreak of war). He was caught, tried and hanged for treason. Vice-Admiral Hipper's deputy, Rear-Admiral Friedrich Bödicker, led the battlecruisers for a hit-and-run bombardment of Lowestoft and Yarmouth on the 25th, while Scheer and his battleships lurked north of the Dutch islands, hoping to trap Beatty's battlecruisers or some other substantial British unit.

Room 40 once again primed Harwich Force and the Grand Fleet. The British destroyers rushed northward, to find and engage the German Second Reconnaissance Group of four light cruisers escorting Bödicker. The destroyers were driven off, but Bödicker withdrew instead of taking the chance to cut down Tyrwhitt's light forces. Scheer in his turn headed for home; the Grand Fleet did not come within 300 miles of the Germans.

Scheer next planned a raid on Sunderland in mid-May, sending submarines to lie in wait for the big ships off Scapa Flow and the Firth of Forth when the Grand Fleet came out to face him. Zeppelins were sent up to help Scheer locate and destroy Beatty before the British battleships could join him. As one German battlecruiser was not ready for sea before the U-boats ran out of endurance, they were recalled and the Sunderland raid was abandoned in favour of a sweep up the west coast of Jutland by the battlecruisers, followed at a discreet distance by the battleships. The objective once again was Beatty's force, which was to be crushed between the two German groups before Jellicoe could arrive to turn the tables. The result was the vast, maddeningly inconclusive, eternally controversial Battle of Jutland on 31 May and 1 June.

As no submarines were involved on either side, the details of the gigantic mêlée in the North Sea, a huge missed opportunity for each side, need not detain us. The result must. Tactically the Germans had the best of it. They lost one battlecruiser, one pre-dreadnought, four light cruisers and four destroyers (6.79 per cent of their strength); the numerically superior British forfeited three battlecruisers, three cruisers, one light cruiser and seven destroyers (8.84 per cent). Hipper was the best admiral present; Beatty blundered badly. Strategically it was rather different. The Germans had taken much more damage, rendering the High Seas Fleet unable to put to sea as an integrated body for three months. Jellicoe however reported the Grand Fleet ready for sea at four hours' notice on 2 June. He had two dozen undamaged dreadnoughts to the Germans' ten; the man who, in Churchill's memorable phrase, "could lose the war in an afternoon" had carefully refrained from doing so. Jellicoe thus set the seal on British surface mastery of the North Sea and the entire Atlantic. The blockade tightened its invisible grip on Germany; the High Seas Fleet never came out again to challenge the Royal Navy until the twelfth hour was at hand and it was too late.

In a remarkable reversal of roles, the most startling attestation of the "arrival" of the submarine as a strategic maritime weapon, the High Seas Fleet was soon effectively reduced to supporting and escorting the U-boats in home waters. They were now Germany's last card at sea. Yet it was a wild card, which came hair-raisingly close to trumping the British ace of blockade.

The Mediterranean

Scene iii: the south

THE FIRST WORLD WAR embroiled the Canadian Army and the Royal
New Zealand Navy and needed the weight of the United States to force
a conclusion, but was essentially a European conflict. It is customary to
describe the war from the geographical viewpoint of the Central Powers:
the decisive Western Front was western only for Germany. For France
it was northern; for Britain it was to the east. Germany's Eastern Front
was western for Russia, whose southern front faced Germany's ally
Turkey. The Ottoman Empire in its turn fought on its western, northern
and eastern fronts. Italy, though a member of the prewar Triple Alliance
with them, was not obliged to support Germany and Austria unless they
were attacked. Since they did the attacking, Italy initially remained
neutral, joining the Triple Entente in May 1915 and opening a new front
against Austria.

All this made the Mediterranean the undoubted southern front of the
war at sea, just as the north-eastern Atlantic was the northern front.
Subsidiary fronts were opened in the Baltic and in the Black Sea. For the
Russians these two enclosed seas, where their principal foe was Germany,
represented the maritime extremities of their transcontinental front,
which straggled from the far north to the far south of Europe. The
Russians were not involved in the Mediterranean.

That enclosed body of water, 2,200 miles long from Gibraltar to the
Dardanelles, was bounded to the south and east by the French, Turkish
and British empires. Britain controlled Gibraltar and the Suez Canal,
the western and eastern gateways to the open sea, and Malta in the
middle. By prewar agreement with Britain, the French fleet was almost
entirely concentrated in the Mediterranean, leaving the British free
to focus on the main naval struggle in the north. But their residual
Mediterranean Fleet of three battlecruisers, four heavy cruisers and
supporting ships guarded their imperial interests, including the short
route to India via Suez. Italy and Austria maintained considerable navies;

Turkey's was moribund; Germany deployed Rear-Admiral Wilhelm Souchon's Mediterranean Division of one battlecruiser and one light cruiser to show the flag.

On the outbreak of war the British Mediterranean Fleet was to come under French supreme command. But the French Navy would initially concentrate in the western basin (west of Italy) for its first task, covering the passage of the French XIX Corps from North Africa to the south of France, en route to its place in the line against Germany. During this phase the British would watch for any move by Austria down the Adriatic into the eastern basin. The Entente expected Italy would stay neutral and believed the hopelessly outnumbered Germans would run westward for home and be annihilated in the process. The French and British Mediterranean fleets together comfortably outgunned the combined naval strengths of Italy, Austria and Germany were they to effect a conjunction. The safest stratagem was to ensure they did not. Nobody in the French or British fleets or in their governments had given a thought to ramshackle Turkey, except to discount it as a likely neutral.

Germany had other plans, as did a revolutionary group of Turkish Army officers led by Enver Pasha, who wanted to revive the Ottoman Empire. While the British and French enjoyed their extra-territorial privileges in Constantinople and looked down on the Turks, the Germans wooed them, completing a railway link between Berlin and Baghdad (the Middle East being then under Turkish rule).

In the opening days of the war Admiral Souchon boldly shelled the French North African coast, disrupting troop movements. He eluded the French and British fleets before taking refuge at Messina in Sicily for coaling. The Allies assumed he would try to break back to the west, which meant sailing north-about from Messina. This made it all the easier for him to elude a singularly lacklustre British pursuit when he ran south, rounding the heel of Italy and making as if to join the Austrians in the Adriatic. During the night of 6–7 August Souchon turned south-east. Leaving behind his solitary British shadow, the brilliantly handled light cruiser *Gloucester*, he was lying off the entrance to the Dardanelles by the late afternoon of the 10th, demanding a pilot.

The reason for his run east was that the Germans had secretly concluded an alliance with the Enver faction on 2 August. Although German officers under General Otto Liman von Sanders were effectively running the Turkish Army (including the Dardanelles garrisons), it was far from ready for war. To activate the new alliance, the sole strategic coup by the Kaiser's diplomats, the Germans needed to deliver a visible sign of their commitment and a genuine reinforcement for their precarious command of the Narrows between the Mediterranean and Black seas. So on 3 August Tirpitz ordered Souchon to make for Constantinople.

The result was a catastrophe for the Triple Entente. Souchon exchanged his cap for a fez, to become C-in-C of the Turkish Navy (displacing the British Rear-Admiral Arthur Limpus) and the Germans "sold" his two ships, the battlecruiser *Goeben* and the light cruiser *Breslau*, to the Turks. Impatient with their reluctance to take an active part in Germany's war with Russia, Souchon hoisted the Turkish ensign on the *Goeben* with the connivance of Enver and led the entire serviceable strength of the Turkish Navy into the Black Sea on 29 October 1914, to shell the four principal Russian ports there. Russia declared war on Turkey on 2 November; Britain and France followed suit three days later.

The Dardanelles, route for over ninety-five per cent of Russia's inward and outward trade, were closed. Her allies could now deliver muchneeded munitions only via the far north-west or the Pacific coast of Russia, 8,000 miles from the front. The British would get no Russian grain deliveries via the Mediterranean and France. This left them even more reliant on North America and therefore the transatlantic route, under attack by U-boats. The war spread over the Middle East and ultimately drew in Bulgaria, Romania and Greece. Most immediately and horrifically, Souchon's stroke led to the Dardanelles campaign, in which the submarines of both sides played dramatic roles, and the tragedy of Gallipoli, special not least because it was completely unnecessary.

The British Navy, having underestimated Souchon, court-martialled (but acquitted) Rear-Admiral Thomas Troubridge, who had decided not to attack the *Goeben* with his four old cruisers amid a welter of confusing orders from the Admiralty. The French echoed the plaint of the Scarborough coroner: *Que fait donc l'armée navale?* The Navy had done nothing, but joined the British in an attempt to force the Dardanelles. This failed for lack of resolve; the admirals could not bring themselves to risk their ships for strategic ends, even when specifically ordered by Churchill to do so, and even after Commodore Keyes took personal charge of the very necessary minesweepers. It was later discovered that the Turco-German defenders had been reduced to their last eight armourpiercing shells. But it was their mines that frightened off the attackers, with heavy losses in old yet expendable ships.

Having seen the Army of Africa safely across to France, the French fleet, whose C-in-C was Vice-Admiral Augustin Boué de Lapeyrère, assembled at Malta on 12 August 1914. On that day, at midnight, Britain and France went to war against Austria. Three days later Lapeyrère took a force of battleships and cruisers to join Troubridge's heavy cruisers for a sweep up the Adriatic. They drove the Austro-Hungarian fleet, commanded by Admiral Anton Baron von Haus, back into port at the northern end of the Adriatic, sinking a light cruiser. The French took over the watch on the mouth of the Adriatic while the British stood guard off the Dardanelles. The navel sieges of these two Mediterranean offshoots, which were to last as long as the war, were thus in place at the end of the first fortnight of hostilities. Both blockading forces were supported by submarines, British and French. Vice-Admiral S.H. Carden became Senior British Naval Officer, Mediterranean, relieving Troubridge in command of the Dardanelles force on 20 September. Keyes was officially transferred from the Harwich submarine command as his chief of staff in February 1915. Carden was to sink any warship, German or Turkish, coming out of the Strait.

The British, left to deal with the Turkish problem, adopted Churchill's idea of a purely naval attempt to force the Narrows in January 1915. Fourteen British and four French pre-dreadnoughts, a British seaplane-carrier and two British dreadnoughts, including the brand-new super-battleship *Queen Elizabeth* with her fifteen-inch guns, plus supporting cruisers, destroyers and submarines, were to reduce the Dardanelles forts to rubble. It was to be done in three stages, at long, medium and short range, starting on 19 February. There was soon rubble a-plenty, but the Turks and Germans kept on firing. Admiral Guido von Usedom had come from Germany with naval specialists to strengthen the defences. Naval guns were unshipped and used as reinforcements while German artillerymen supported their Turkish counterparts with mobile howitzers firing plunging shot.

Stage one went well enough, but stage two, the medium-range bombardment, entailed entering the Narrows, where dense minefields had been laid. Carden was elderly, sick and tired and lacked resolve; Anglo-French shooting was poor, the naval reservists manning the minesweepers lost their nerve under fire. The deafening bark of bombardment proved much worse than its bite against the resolutely manned defences; even the biggest shells needed direct hits to score. Carden resigned on 16 March, to be replaced by Vice-Admiral John de Robeck. He instituted an unprecedented cannonade two days later, led by twelve battleships. A French battleship and then a British battlecruiser were lost to mines and an old British battleship knocked out for six weeks; a similar veteran was lost altogether trying to help her. This new havoc was caused by just twenty mines, laid at night on 8 March by a Turkish colonel from a small steamer, in an area used by the Anglo-French fleet for manoeuvring. De Robeck retreated and called off the naval assault altogether, ignoring Churchill's plea to finish the job.

The Allies next decided to invade the Gallipoli peninsula, on the European side of the Narrows leading into the Sea of Marmara. They were however in no hurry to arrange it, leaving the Germans and Turks more than five weeks massively to reinforce the single, thin Turkish infantry division which had been there in mid-March. British, Australian, New Zealand and French troops landed on 25 April and were locked into a compressed version of the Western Front impasse by 9 May, complete with inert generals. Two nights after that a small Turkish destroyer, manned largely by German sailors, torpedoed the British pre-dreadnought *Goliath*, which blew up with the loss of 570 lives and provoked a crisis in London. Fisher resigned over Churchill's plan to send massive naval reinforcements, which the old admiral regarded as throwing good money after bad. The press demanded that heads roll for the "incompetence in high places" exposed by the Dardanelles fiasco, defending Fisher and attacking Churchill. After a very long week in British politics, the Navy's political and operational chiefs had gone. The admirals were sentimental about the ignominious downfall of Fisher but openly delighted to be rid of Churchill, who was unable to identify good advice, or to delegate.

Meanwhile, three tiny British submarines, based at Mudros on the island of Lemnos from December 1914, had begun to probe the Narrows, determined to make their mark ahead of their three French counterparts based at Tenedos. From its entrance to the Sea of Marmara the Strait is thirty-five miles long and only one and a half wide at its narrowest. The initial British commitment was small indeed: *B9, B10* and *B11*, all dating back to 1906 (aeons in contemporary submarine terms). They were small, slow coastal boats with two tubes, four torpedoes and a crew of two officers and fourteen men apiece.

Lieutenant Norman Holbrook braved the perpetual outflowing current and the mines in *B11* on 13 December. Near the northern end, off Chanak, he sighted the old Turkish battleship *Messoudieh* (10,000 tons) at anchor: he submerged, approached to within 1,000 yards and sank her with a single torpedo, which set off a magazine. Holbrook failed to force the Dardanelles completely but was readily excused after such an exploit. *B11* survived a hair-raising return journey with periscope, compass and engine playing up. Holbrook was awarded the first Victoria Cross in the history of the submarine service. Officers and crew shared (according to rank) a bounty of £3,500.

Three more British boats were transferred to Mudros from Gibraltar in the new year, followed by three larger E-types: *E11* (Nasmith, from the Baltic), *E14* and *E15*. The latter, under T.S. Brodie, was ordered to complete the forcing of the Strait in mid-April 1915. The boat ran aground and was captured; Brodie and six others were killed in an enemy bombardment. *B6*, British seaplanes and destroyers all tried to demolish the captive submarine. Finally the old battleships *Triumph* and *Majestic* were sent in to shell the wreck from six miles away. They failed too, but sent two motor-boats armed with torpedoes to finish the task on 19 April.

Henry Stoker, RN, was the next to try, in the Australian submarine *AE2*. On 25 April, as ANZAC troops were landing on Gallipoli, he sank a Turkish gunboat, spent a night submerged and broke into the Sea of Marmara at last on the 27th. Mishandled under fire in the Strait on the way back, the *AE2* foundered, just as *AE1* had done in the Pacific in the preceding December: Australia was left without a submarine for the duration. But seven British boats and one French were to follow the trail blazed by Stoker and his Australian crew in due course. E.C. Boyle won a VC in May for a spectacularly disruptive, three-week Marmara patrol, during which his sinkings included a transport with 6,000 Turkish troops aboard.

British and Allied submarines were not allowed to have it all their own way, however. Otto Hersing, the man who had sunk *Pathfinder* and shelled Barrow, had stolen into the Mediterranean in *U21* as the advance guard of the U-boat arm. Its arrival was another portentous result of the Dardanelles imbroglio initiated by Souchon. The German High Command had become impatient with Austrian tardiness in prosecuting the war at sea. Haus, who had refused to come out to help Souchon, decided to keep his severely outnumbered capital ships in port as a "fleet in being", to offset which the enemy would always have to keep on hand superior forces that would therefore be unable to operate elsewhere. After visiting the Austrians in the Adriatic, Hersing was sent to the entrance of the Dardanelles while his compatriots wrestled with the logistics of delivering prefabricated coastal "UB" and minelaying "UC" types overland in sections to Pola, the main Austrian naval base. On 25 May he torpedoed the old battleship HMS *Triumph*; two days later, despite the increased alert caused by his dramatic arrival, he coolly dealt a similar blow to another old ironclad, the *Majestic*. Both sank off the mouth of the Dardanelles.

So did Allied morale. The entrenched troops felt that their navies, which had begun to pull back for fear of U-boats even before Hersing arrived and all but vanished from sight thereafter, had deserted them. Hersing entered the Strait on 1 June and reached Constantinople on the 5th, showing the false number *U51* to confuse the many spies ashore.

U-boat strength at Constantinople was soon to reach a half-flotilla, variably consisting of four to six boats. Their efforts from the Dardanelles for the rest of the war never matched the promise of Hersing's spectacular stroke, thanks to Russian mines in the Black Sea and huge British counter-measures at the Mediterranean end, including nets, mines and patrols by swarms of small craft. The heavy British and French ships on guard against a foray by the *Goeben*, now styled *Yavuz*, kept well clear.

The Germans also built up their submarine strength in the Austrian Adriatic bases of Pola (now Slovenian Pula) and Cattaro (now Kotor) to a flotilla apiece, with devastating results for Allied, especially British, shipping. The Austrian fleet never strayed far from base but its submarine service made its own distinctive mark in the Adriatic and beyond.

Nasmith's *E11* came to dominate the Sea of Marmara for much of the rest of 1915 in a one-boat campaign of unique ingenuity and improvisation. Nasmith twice recovered torpedoes for re-use by sealing them so that they surfaced rather than sank after missing their targets, enabling him to collect them once the pursuit had gone home. He once charged his batteries in broad daylight by lashing a captured sailing boat to his conning tower as camouflage. Eventually Nasmith passed the Golden Horn off Constantinople and reached the entrance to the Bosporus, leading into the Black Sea. In June he was awarded the VC, the third to be earned in Turkish waters; in August Lieutenant Guy D'Oyly Hughes, his "number one", earned the DSO for landing with a party of ratings from a small boat to blow up a railway line. Nasmith became the "Scourge of the Marmara" and the leading British submarine ace of the war, with 122 vessels , mostly small, sunk by torpedo, gun or boarding in 1915. His colleague, K.M. Bruce, sank a total of thirty-seven vessels, mostly small, with *E12*.

In September Lieutenant A.B. Cochrane, RN, lost his boat, *E7*, in a remarkable duel with Heino von Heimburg. The skipper of *UB14* had already made his name in the Adriatic in command of *UB15*, destroying an Italian submarine. He sank a large British troopship in the Aegean with his second boat on the way to Constantinople. Heimburg sailed to the northern end of the Dardanelles on learning that the Turkish nets had ensnared a British submarine. He rowed to the spot in a dinghy and waited while a rating dipped a plumbline to locate the trapped boat. Heimburg then had a mine with a delayed-action fuse lowered against the hull and retired to await the explosion. The badly damaged *E7* surfaced long enough to hoist the white flag; the crew went over the side after setting scuttling charges. Cochrane was last out as the conning tower sank out of sight under his feet.

The cunning Heimburg struck again in November. Lieutenant Ravenel's French submarine *Turquoise* had run aground in the Marmara on 30 October and was captured in good enough condition to be taken over by the Turkish Navy; which also found papers about a rendezvous with the British *E20* (C.H. Warren) planned for 5 November. *UB14* was under repair but was hurriedly patched up and sent to keep the tryst in the Sea of Marmara. One torpedo was enough; of a British crew of thirty only nine survived, including the captain, who was on deck having a wash at the time. In all, three French and four British boats were lost during the Dardanelles campaign, which ended on 8 January 1916 in the withdrawal, without a single extra casualty, of the Allied troops from Gallipoli. Allied submarines had almost starved out the Turks and Germans in the ultimately victorious defence, destroying seven Turkish warships, nine troop-transports, seven supply-ships, thirty steamers and 200 sailing vessels.

The French had generally failed to distinguish themselves off the Dardanelles but initially tried harder in the Adriatic. Their fleet flagship, the super-dreadnought *Jean Bart*, was damaged by an Austrian submarine torpedo during a sweep into the Adriatic in December 1914. This prompted their submarine arm to retaliate. The Franco-Irish Lieutenant Gabriel O'Byrne took the new diesel submarine *Curie* up the Adriatic to probe the reinforced defences of Pola in mid-December 1914. He was caught in the anti-submarine nets; forced to scuttle, O'Byrne and his crew of thirty surrendered. The Austrians salvaged, thoroughly overhauled and modernised the boat, renamed it *U-XIV* (the Roman numerals were used to distinguish Austrian from German U-boats) and relaunched it under their most famous ace, Lieutenant Georg von Trapp. Five more French boats were lost in the opening months of the fighting in the Adriatic, whose clear waters aided efficient and assiduous Austrian airborne ASW patrols, the first systematic use of aviation against submarines.

When Italy came into the war on the Anglo-French side in May 1915, the French sent a mixed flotilla of steam and diesel submarines plus destroyers under Captain Henri de Cacqueray to base itself at the southern Italian port of Brindisi. It was a most uneasy three-cornered *ad hoc* alliance which took up station at the entrance to the Adriatic, a coalition rich in possibilities for mistrust and misunderstanding. Four French boats gallantly penetrated the defences of Cattaro in August 1915, only to be let down by unreliable torpedoes; they escaped unscathed. But Lieutenant Deville brought the steam-powered *Arch-*

imède from Harwich and proved himself by sinking four Austrian troop-transports in autumn 1915.

In September of that year the Allies set up the Otranto Barrage across the narrow part of the southern Adriatic, forty-four miles wide from Italian Otranto south-east to the Greek Ionian island of Fano (now Othonoi). It originally constituted a series of nets slung along a chain of sixty British drifters. Despite the arrival of 100 more in 1916 and other reinforcements, the "barrage" consisted largely of gaps and was intermittently maintained and guarded by British motor launches, with Italian and French submarines lurking to north and south respectively and surface ships in distant support. It seldom proved much more than an inconvenience for German or Austrian U-boats. More and stronger nets, bigger boats and keener patrols by destroyers and aircraft might have driven home this spatchcocked maritime siege. The U-boats were able to pass over, under or through it almost at will throughout the war as the flimsy barrier itself became a focus of irregular skirmishes involving the light forces and submarines of both sides. Even the arrival in June 1918 of thirty-six American submarine-chasers equipped with hydrophones – the last plaster on an open wound – made no real difference to the effectiveness of the Otranto Barrage. American claims of success there in the last months of the war were subsequently disproved.

The British-run barrage, like the Adriatic campaign as a whole, was ineffectual because of Allied lack of will. Italian destroyers, which should have supported the British light craft on the barrage, tended to stay in port. The French and the Italians would not agree to put their ships under one command. Either fleet, especially with the British ships on hand, would have been enough to deal with any breakout by the bulk of the Austrian fleet.

But without precise agreement on who was to do what, Allied forces much larger than necessary were kept idle while submarines and smaller warships did all the work in an inconclusive and strategically marginal "private war". Admiral Haus was free to choose between staying in port with his "fleet in being", risking his heavy ships in a pointless dash for the Dardanelles or to attack the Greek coast round Salonika. He let the submarines have their head and ordered the occasional raid by light surface ships. Given that there was no German surface presence in the Mediterranean and that Italy, Austria's only other erstwhile ally at sea, elected to join the Entente in May 1915, this was his best option. At the same time, fear of mines and U-boats clearly deterred the not very united Allies from attempts to bombard the Austrian fleet in its bases.

An early Austrian success was scored at the mouth of the Adriatic by

Lieutenant von Trapp in his first command, the tiny "Holland" type *U-V*, at the end of April 1915, when he sank the French armoured cruiser *Léon Gambetta* (12,500 tons). Only one in six of her crew of more than 800 survived the devastating attack with two torpedoes; the main units of the French fleet immediately withdrew to the Ionian islands, while the four British pre-dreadnoughts on hand based themselves at Taranto inside the Italian "heel". Trapp's missiles had been made by the factory and submarine plant at Fiume, until recently run by Robert Whitehead, inventor of the torpedo, to whom Trapp was related by marriage. The barrage made no difference to his career after he took over *U-XIV* in October: all his victims were sunk outside the barrier built to confine him and his colleagues to the Adriatic. The small Austrian submarine force, Trapp to the fore, achieved a proud record. They mounted seventy-nine torpedo attacks during the war; on every occasion at least one torpedo hit and only about one torpedo in every ten fired was wasted. The Austrians also did much effective minelaying off the Italian coast; all in all a remarkable achievement by the small navy of an essentially landlocked power.

The Italians, with their limited force of small and technically backward submarines, sank one Austrian boat but lost six of their own in the Adriatic. One German and one Austrian boat were destroyed in the barrage; a second Austrian boat may have met the same fate. The Austrians lost the hospital ship *Elektra* (Captain Quarantotto) to the French submarine *Ampère* (Lieutenant Devin) on 18 March 1916. Fortunately this blunder led to only two fatalities on the converted steamship, which was beached. One Italian and two French destroyers were sunk by U-boats in the area; so was an Italian heavy cruiser, the *Amalfi* (10,600 tons), dispatched by Heimburg's *UB15* in July 1915, and an auxiliary cruiser. Three British light cruisers were badly damaged by U-boat attacks but did not sink. Sixteen British drifters were destroyed in Austrian hit-and-run raids led by light cruisers, notably *Helgoland* (Captain Hermann Seitz), which also sank two French submarines, and *Novarra* (Captain Nikolaus Horthy de Nagybánya), which specialised in destroying drifters, particularly in the great raid of May 1917. They were able to evade much larger Allied forces, which had managed to place themselves between the Austrians and their bases at the time of the raid but failed to catch the cruisers on their way home.

The British could only spare half a dozen small, old "B" submarines for the Adriatic from October 1915, based at Venice under Commander Wilfrid Tomkinson, a non-submariner on the staff of Rear-Admiral Cecil Thursby, commanding the British Adriatic Force (replaced by Rear-Admiral Mark Kerr in June 1916). The little boats made eighty-one patrols but achieved nothing measurable. *B10* had the unhappy distinction of becoming the first submarine to be sunk by aircraft on 9 August 1916, when a dashing Austrian air-raid on Venice caught her in harbour. The crew escaped. Three modern "H" boats came out as replacements for all the "Bs" but did no better, even when moved south to Brindisi to reinforce the barrage. The one positive contribution by the H-boats – and indeed the entire British submarine presence in the Adriatic – was the destruction of the German *UB52*, on 23 May 1918 near the barrage, by Oliver North in *H4*, which scored hits with two torpedoes. This helped to compensate for the sinking in error in April 1918 of the Italian *H5*, just acquired from Britain, by Heaton's HMS *H1*. Even the half-dozen members of the trusty "E" class, which carried out "guest" patrols in the Adriatic from time to time on their way to or from the Dardanelles, failed to add to this lowest score in any theatre by British submarines.

Bulgaria came into the war in September 1915, helping the Germans and Austrians to overrun Serbia. When an Anglo-French force failed to stop this, Rear-Admiral Troubridge, now head of the British Military Mission to Serbia, redeemed his failure to tackle Admiral Souchon by leading a difficult evacuation of the Serbian Army to Salonika, in the month of the withdrawal from the Dardanelles (January 1916). A substantial Allied force was to sit out the war in Salonika, ensuring that the British naval covering force in the eastern Mediterranean could not be much reduced after the retreat from Gallipoli. Greece entered the war on the Entente side under Prime Minister Venizelos in June 1917, once the Allies had deposed King Constantine, of German origin.

The third and most secluded of the "private wars" on the disjointed southern maritime front of the First World War was between the Turco-German fleet and the Russians in the Black Sea. The campaign here, as with those in the Adriatic and at the eastern end of the Mediterranean, was essentially military. Warships, submarines and naval auxiliaries were the protagonists as participants and victims alike, even though there were inevitably some mercantile casualties (troop-, supply- and even hospital ships, for example). These subsidiary conflicts were much less significant strategically than the onslaught on merchant shipping in the Mediterranean proper and on the northern naval front. The latter were geographically separate but strategically one and the same. They constituted a single "tonnage war", as the Germans came to call it: we noted above how the loss of every ton of shipping and cargo was of precisely the same importance to Britain and its allies no matter where or how it occurred. We shall return to the general Mediterranean U-boat campaign.

The Black Sea is effectively a lake, fed by great rivers whose waters pass into the Mediterranean via the Sea of Marmara and the Dardanelles, through a single narrow exit, the Bosporus. The question at the end of 1914 was whose ships would dominate an area of water of obvious importance as a means of supporting the armies of both sides fighting around its shores.

Admiral Souchon's ruthless exploitation of his escape into the Straits and its appalling consequences have already been noted. The defence of the Dardanelles remained chiefly in the increasingly capable and confident hands of the Turkish Army and its German mentors while Turco-German naval forces played only secondary roles. But Souchon had no intention of sitting out the rest of the war: there was an enemy fleet at each end of the Straits. He would have no sea-room if he attempted a foray against the Anglo-French forces to the south-west. But to the north-east the Russian Navy, recently trounced by the Japanese, had Vice-Admiral A.E. Eberhard's squadron of five ancient pre-dreadnoughts. Even collectively these were hardly a match for the formidable *Goeben/Yavuz*. Eberhard also had two crumbling ironsides in reserve, as well as two cruisers, twenty-six destroyers (nine capable of thirty-three knots), two gunboats, four small torpedo-boats and eleven submarines. For all her superior speed, armour and firepower the *Goeben* could not be everywhere at once (and was plagued by boiler trouble); leaving her aside, the Russians outgunned, sometimes heavily, the Turco-Germans in every type of warship. And at the Nikolayev yard on the Black Sea they were slowly completing three second-generation dreadnoughts, any of which, at least in firepower, would have the edge on *Goeben*.

Russian naval incompetence in the war with Japan had misled the other leading navies into investing in the "big guns" which won at Tsushima and thus overlooking the success of mines and torpedoes in the same war – and the possibilities they raised for submarines. What happened after Tsushima was a classic case of military leaders preparing for the next war by planning to re-fight the last. HMS *Dreadnought* may have made all her predecessors obsolete at a stroke; but within a decade the submarine had already checkmated her and all her successors, until naval aviation developed enough striking power to drive the "big-gun" capital ship from the seas.

In the Black Sea the Russian strategy was sound enough: to close the Bosporus by mines laid at close range, backed by submarines and finally surface ships. The Russians' last naval redoubt was to be the north-east of the Black Sea and the Sea of Azov, behind the Crimea. The execution of the Bosporus plan however left much to be desired. The Russians placed too much faith in too few mines and underestimated their enemies. The arrival of the Germans in Turkish waters led Eberhard to decide that his surface ships would be too far from their home bases on the Crimean coast if they operated off the Bosporus. Only submarines were therefore to reinforce the thin minefield in the first instance. But on 4 November 1914 the Russians laid mines off their own northern Black Sea ports and sent their battleships and cruisers to sow more fields off the Bosporus. They also shelled the Turkish harbour of Zonguldak in the south-west of the Black Sea and sank three transports on the way home. Two weeks later they bombarded Turkish Trabzon (Trebizond) to the south-east, fending off the *Goeben* and her supporting ships, which tried to cut them off from their bases.

The Russians may not have been able to lay many mines; but they still surprised the Germans on the first Christmas Day of the war, when the *Goeben* shuddered to the blast of two large explosions, first on the starboard side, then on port (correcting the list caused by the first mine). The Germans had thought they were safe from moored mines (invisible from the surface) in 600 feet of water, but the Russians had managed to anchor some in this unprecedented depth. Only the German battlecruiser's double bottom and strong construction enabled her to limp back to port, where it took nearly three months to make her seaworthy. She thus missed the naval struggle for the Dardanelles, although from time to time Souchon had her moved by tugs as she emitted huge clouds of black smoke, to persuade Constantinople spies that she was about to intervene. The Allies were completely unaware of her parlous condition; otherwise the intrepid British submariners would surely have tried to finish her off.

Russian Black Sea submarines acted in a purely defensive manner, not seeking the enemy but waiting for him to come to them, which he mostly failed to do. The fact that only two boats at a time, out of a notional eleven in 1914, were usually available for the most important submarine task in the area strongly suggests that Eberhard's flotilla was in poor condition. Many of them had been built elsewhere and delivered in sections overland for assembly on the Black Sea. They therefore had rust built in when they were assembled and could not descend to their design depths. Only when the Nikolayev yard near Odessa started to launch warships in 1912 did the Black Sea Fleet acquire its own submarine-construction facility. Six very small boats were built there in 1912 and six larger "Leopard" types were ordered from the yard in the same year.

It was only in March 1915 that regular Russian submarine patrols began off the northern entrance of the Bosporus, usually by a pair of small boats. By the end of June they had managed to sink two small Turkish craft. The submarines were confined to small, predetermined patrol areas which they covered with all the imagination of sentries guarding the barrack gates at night. Only when the first Russian dreadnought, *Imperatritsa Maria*, made her maiden voyage from Nikolayev to the main fleet base at Sevastopol in summer could Eberhard scrape together four submarines to guard the Bosporus. But they laid new mines, and in July 1915 the *Goeben*'s faithful escort, the light cruiser *Breslau*, hit one and was dragged into a floating dock just before she sank.

Inconclusive surface clashes continued, the *Imperatritsa Maria* giving the *Goeben* a nasty fright with her ten twelve-inch guns in January 1916 on her first war outing. Unaccountably the Russians failed to press home their advantage, not even when their second dreadnought, the *Yekaterina II*, joined the fleet in April. In October 1916, as they continued to lie idle in Sevastopol, the *Imperatritsa Maria* succumbed to a mighty explosion, apparently spontaneous. It was as if aggressive warfare, or merely taking the war to the enemy, had been expressly forbidden by the General Staff – as in effect it had. The Russian Black Sea Fleet was used as an adjunct to the Russian Army on land, guarding its southern flank just as the Baltic Fleet motionlessly guarded the northern.

Echoing the reversal of roles in the German High Seas Fleet after Jutland, the Russian Black Sea submarines were supported by the *Imperatritsa Maria* in July and August 1916 in a renewed attempt to block the Bosporus by mines. By this time an average of seven submarines at a time were seaworthy, capable of cruising for between five and twelve days. Small groups reaped a meagre harvest of lesser enemy vessels (there being no large merchantmen to sink). The minelaying effort was desultory enough for the scratch Turco-German minesweeping force to counter with ease. Mines were the Russians' principal weapon in the Black Sea; they even floated some down the Bosporus on the perpetual current, hoping to hit something in Turkish waters; in vain.

Indeed the mines briefly became a bigger threat to the Russians than to their enemies in September 1916, when a huge storm tore many of them free of their anchors. By the Revolution late in 1917 the operational strength of the Russian submarine flotilla in the Black Sea had reached sixteen; in the preceding year they made about thirty patrols in all – not quite two each – and sank over ninety small vessels. As in the Baltic, the submarine force fell hopelessly short of its potential; but not as short as the surface fleets in both seas, which achieved very nearly nothing. The death of the Imperial Navy and the birth of the Red Fleet in 1917 were accompanied by the almost complete disappearance of the Russian flotillas, scuttled, seized by the Germans or left to rot.

The metaphor of the Russian submarine as inflexible sentry is made especially apposite by the fact that Army minds lay behind the deployment of the Black Sea Fleet. The General Staff saw it as a static, coastal-defence and reconnaissance force; the admirals compounded the weakness of the Russian Navy before the war, and its remarkable under-performance during it, by splitting into two factions. The pre-revolutionary uprising, notably in the Black Sea Fleet, after the Japanese victory in 1905 forced Tsar Nicholas II to concede a parliament, the Duma, where fierce public debates took place on the Navy's role, how and at what cost it should be reconstructed. With the "Old" and "Young" schools wrangling themselves to a standstill before the war and running out of funds, it is hardly surprising that non-Russian commentators dismiss the role of the Russian Navy in the First World War in a few lines. The disproportionate effects of the haphazard deployment of a handful of mechanically treacherous British submarines in the Baltic and the Dardanelles show up Russian naval missed opportunity and under-achievement as nothing else. The uncomprehending rigidity of the General Staff and the paralysing split in the Naval Staff responsible for this failure were one more symptom of the moribund condition of the Tsarist regime, which lost the war with Germany and fell to the Revolution when it finally came in 1917.

In the Mediterranean, the German U-boats first arrived by land when four small coastal "UB" and then three not much larger minelaying "UC" types were brought in sections by rail to Austrian Pola, where they were assembled for onward passage to the Black Sea from late in 1914. Others followed to fight alongside the Austrians in the Adriatic itself, based mainly at Cattaro, well down the coast from Pola.

But the front door to the Mediterranean is the Strait of Gibraltar, just fifteen miles wide: nevertheless the British, with their base at Gibraltar, were never able to make the Strait submarine-proof, even in the Second World War. The first ocean-going U-boat to pass through was Hersing's *U21*, on her way to wreak havoc at the Dardanelles and beyond. In U-boat terms he had the eastern Mediterranean to himself until the war was more than a year old. But in August 1915, as the dispute raged about unrestricted warfare around Britain, the German Naval Staff took an increasing interest in the "American-free" Mediterranean. On the 23rd, Waldemar Kophamel arrived at Cattaro from Germany in *U35*, accompanied by *U34* (Rücker). Gansser's *U33* and *U39* (Walther Forstmann) soon followed; in November *U38* (Max Valentiner) joined the German Cattero flotilla. This formidable force of (initially) five boats from the same new class included two of the three skippers who would become the leading German "aces" of the First World War.

Originally under the command of Hans Adam, a mere *Kapitänleutnant* and German liaison officer at Pola, the Cattero boats became a separate command at the end of 1915, when Kophamel was given the three full stripes of *Korvettenkapitän* (commander) and put in charge of the new Mediterranean flotilla. He handed over *U35* to the aristocratic Lothar von Arnauld de la Perière, who ended the war as the most successful submarine captain of all time, a record which still stands. The cunning Forstmann was to become the U-boat arm's second-highest scorer; the bloodthirsty Valentiner, one of nature's Waffen-SS men ahead of his time, was to win third place in tonnage sunk but soon took an unbeatable lead as grimmest reaper of lives at sea. In August he had sunk a record thirty vessels in five days in the rich waters south of Ireland. But by the end of 1915 the centre of gravity of the German submarine campaign had shifted with a vengeance from the Atlantic to the broad Mediterranean. In the last quarter the Allies forfeited eighty ships totalling 293,000 tons to Mediterranean U-boats – more than four-fifths of their global loss in that period.

Valentiner left his bloodstained calling card outside the gates before entering the Mediterranean. He sank the British *Woodfield* off Morocco by torpedo after a one-sided exchange of fire with the freighter's pop-gun on 3 November. Later the same day, still off Morocco, he took on the rather larger and better-armed British troopship *Mercian* (6,300 tons) but was driven off by her guns. Reverting to the tactic of attack without warning which had served him so well in Atlantic waters, Valentiner passed the Strait and torpedoed a French troop-transport off Marseilles on 4 November, killing more than 700 colonial soldiers. The shocked French confined all Mediterranean shipping to port for the time being.

Slowly proceeding towards Cattaro, Valentiner first sank another French troop-transport (fortunately unladen) and then, on 7 November, sighted the Italian liner *Ancona*. To get round the fact that Italy had been at war with Austria-Hungary since May 1915 but was not engaged in hostilities with Germany, Valentiner surfaced and ran up the Austrian ensign before his attack, initially under prize rules. Ordering the captain and the ill-disciplined crew to clear the ship, he opened fire amid scenes of chaos and was accused of shooting at the passengers in the water. Eventually he submerged, having purportedly seen another ship approaching, and torpedoed the liner, with the loss of hundreds of lives. The Mediterranean may have been "American-free" when it came to ships, but it was not devoid of American passengers, of whom twenty went down with the *Ancona*. On the 9th, Valentiner compounded his offence by pursuing the small Italian steamer *Firenze* under his Austrian flag and finally torpedoing her, killing a similar number of Americans and many more Italians.

The *Lusitania* factor returned in strength. A four-cornered international wrangle ensued, involving Italy, Austria, Germany and the United States. Admiral Haus, the Austrian C-in-C, was quite happy to carry the German can, to the acute embarrassment of the Vienna foreign ministry. The Italians accused the Germans of flying false colours (common practice on both sides). The Americans wanted a straight answer to a straight question: was the U-boat which sank the two Italian ships German or Austrian? By the time it was put, *U38* had joined the Austrian naval order of battle with the connivance of Haus, conveniently backdated to 21 October. The Germans let their Austrian allies take the blame; Vienna, being completely dependent on Berlin for its survival in a war much too big for the creaking Habsburg Empire, acquiesced, blamed the Italians for panicking on the *Ancona*, pretended to punish the unnamed U-boat commander and paid compensation to the Americans at the end of December. The British, when they learned who was responsible, put Valentiner on their wanted list of war criminals, to be prosecuted after the war for, *inter alia*, sinking their liner *Persia* between Crete and Libya, killing 334 more civilians without warning, on 30 December 1915. At the time Germany, Austria and Turkey all denied responsibility. The issue might have been clearer had the *Persia* not carried a gun rather bigger than *U35*'s.

The German High Command chopped and changed the rules of engagement for submariners, first permitting attacks without warning on all kinds of merchantmen if armed, then bowing to diplomatic pressure by moderating the rule and excluding liners whether armed or not. Once again, as in the North Sea, this led most skippers to adopt a "when in doubt, don't" policy, especially when the Admiralty ordered merchant ships to hide their guns. This sharply reduced the numbers sunk from the early months of 1916 because there was no infallible way of telling which liners were carrying non-combatants and which troops. The German self-denying ordinance did not apply in areas where no liner would be found unless carrying troops (such as the Aegean). Otherwise only hospital ships were instantly identifiable everywhere by their big red crosses.

January 1916 brought the Allied retreat from the Gallipoli Peninsula and the evacuation of the beaten Serbian Army to Salonika, where they were joined in spring 1916 by hundreds of thousands of British and French troops. An Allied conference in Paris in December 1915 had divided the Mediterranean into eighteen patrol zones. These were distributed among the various Allied navies in an attempt to prevent the U-boats from reaching "secret shore-bases", which they neither needed nor even possessed. The Allies with their less efficient submarines had no idea that the U-boats now routinely stayed at sea for weeks. Much time and effort was wasted by countless patrol craft seeking these mythical havens.

The British, for example, were allocated the Aegean zones, with the duty of sealing the Dardanelles and covering Salonika. Even when the number of zones was reduced to eleven at another naval conference on Malta in March 1916, there was no discernible improvement, because the whole anti-submarine strategy was wrong. Allied admirals, already hamstrung by the absence of a truly unified command, persisted in guarding shipping lanes by patrols rather than protecting the ships themselves. In other words the movement of naval traffic was operationally entirely discrete from that of merchant shipping. All the U-boats had to do was hide from the former, whose patrols conveniently revealed the whereabouts of the latest "protected" route, until the coast was clear to attack the latter. Even 3,000 patrol vessels could not begin to provide adequate protection in two million square miles of ocean on this basis. As a result very few ships were accompanied by men-of-war (although those that were proved strangely immune from attack); even troopships were often left to fend for themselves. Only capital warships were routinely accompanied by escorts; not one was sunk in such conditions. British and French troops travelled as far as possible by rail to the Near and Middle East, a precaution which threatened to overburden the already strained French, Italian and Greek railways.

Just what could be done by a submarine commander despite all the vacillations of the Kaiser and his High Command was shown by Lothar von Arnauld, who not only followed prize rules punctiliously but also imposed a self-denying ordinance on his main ordnance. Under his command *U35* fired just four torpedoes, one of which missed. He preferred the boat's 105-millimetre gun, which in his hands became a precision instrument. When possible he would send a boarding party to place charges in the hulls of his victims. Otherwise he would surface and fire a few shells from a safe distance, wait for the crew and passengers to abandon and then close in to dispatch the victim with point-blank shots. Arnauld, a would-be naval airman diverted to submarines, had just turned thirty and served as adjutant to the C-in-C of the High Seas

Fleet before inheriting a first-class boat and crew from Kophamel when the latter became flotilla commander. In five weeks in April and May 1916 he sank twenty-three ships totalling 68,000 tons. This astonishing haul was promptly surpassed by his four-week patrol in July and August, when he sank fifty-four vessels – two a day – with a total tonnage of 91,150. In the end, under three captains, *U35* accounted for 224 ships of 536,000 tons, including three warships and five troopships. Arnauld meanwhile took command of *U139*, a "U-cruiser" with three times the displacement and two mighty 150-millimetre guns, in March 1918. In her he raised his personal score to 454,000 tons, including two warships, five troopships and 187 merchantmen (one-third of them sailing vessels).

This astounding record, never equalled, shows as nothing else can the importance of the character of the commander to the success of his boat. In the First World War, as in the Second, fewer than five per cent of skippers accounted for the majority of total sinkings. Arnauld, an aloof autocrat in the Prussian manner but totally trusted by his crew, was also a complete professional. There was no room in his world for the casual, upper-class ignoramus or "gifted-amateur" approach of one common variety of British officer (many of whom had no real light to hide under this kind of bushel). Arnauld had prepared for war by going to England to learn the language of the chief potential enemy. At sea he developed a knack for finding victims based less on instinct than on thorough reading, observation, intelligence by wireless (much of it intercepted aboard), on for ever keeping all sections of the crew up to the mark and on mastering every technical aspect of submarine operation. Not one individual was harmed on any unarmed vessel he caught. Chivalry was not entirely extinguished, even in this cruel new form of warfare, and Arnauld's Pour le mérite or "Blue Max", the highest decoration at the Kaiser's disposal, was as well earned as any he placed round an officer's neck.

The U-boats' Mediterranean depredations caused the Admiralty to start diverting shipping round the Cape of Good Hope rather than risking the short route to and from the Far East and Australasia via Suez. Traffic with India continued to use the Canal, which had been built for that very purpose. Serious thought was given to asking Japan, Britain's ally since 1902, to send destroyers to the Mediterranean to help in the hunt for U-boats (it sent two excellent flotillas in April 1917). Meanwhile diversion via the Cape meant that much more tonnage was needed to maintain the same rate of delivery of troops, supplies and goods by the long route.

Allied losses in the Mediterranean passed a million tons before 1916 was eight months old. Yet only from August was it possible for the

Germans, thanks to the arrival of three more ocean-going boats, to keep more than one long-range U-boat on patrol at a time. By autumn the Germans had ten ocean-going, three coastal and nine minelaying submarines operating in the Mediterranean. The tenth in the latter category, which bore the tasteless generic nickname of "children of sorrow", was *UC12* (Lieutenant Fröhner). This ill-starred little boat scored an own goal with serious diplomatic consequences when she ran on to one of her own mines just off the southern Italian port of Taranto in March 1916 and sank with the loss of all fifteen hands. The Italians eventually raised, repaired and recommissioned her as *X1*. In the process they found German uniforms and much other incontrovertible evidence that the 168-ton boat was of German construction and under German command; but there were as many Austrian flags as German aboard. Here at last was proof that the Germans had been using false colours to attack Italian targets. Italy finally declared war on Germany over this issue on 27 August 1916.

Rear-Admiral George Ballard, who had just succeeded Arthur Limpus in command at Malta, was almost certainly not the first to think of an idea, which went back to Roman times if not beyond, but he seems to have been the first flag officer to suggest it during this war. On 14 October 1916 he urged the Admiralty to suggest a convoy system to the French C-in-C, still in nominal supreme command in the Mediterranean. Vice-Admiral Rosslyn Wemyss, then C-in-C, East Indies and Egypt, did likewise in December. Neither the Admiralty nor the French was interested. As a result the haemorrhage of shipping continued in the Mediterranean well into 1917, the year in which the U-boats, so recently derided as the weapon of the weaker power, came within weeks of defeating the stronger side.

Scene iv: the crisis of 1917

ADMIRAL REINHARD SCHEER, C-in-C of the High Seas Fleet which had knocked itself out in winning its purely tactical victory at Jutland in mid-year, bluntly declared in his report to the Kaiser soon after the battle that the U-boat would now have to play the decisive role in naval strategy. His partial success in giving the Royal Navy a bloody nose gained Scheer the mantle of authority which had belonged to Tirpitz until he resigned from the naval department in March 1916. The old admiral had been discredited by his opportunistic "conversion" to the U-boat in 1915 after so many years of ignoring it and promoting a huge surface fleet which had notably failed to undermine British seapower. Already in 1915 at Wilhelmshaven, chief port of the High Seas Fleet, this street-cry could be heard:

> Our country needs to care for naught:
> The Fleet is fast asleep in port!

The next of many leaders on both sides to lose office over the military impasse of 1916 was General Erich von Falkenhayn, the competent but colourless Chief of General Staff. Transferred to the Balkans in August, he briskly conquered Romania, the new belligerent, thus securing much-needed corn and oil for Germany and temporarily easing the blockade, to the consternation of the Allies. He was replaced at the Kaiser's Grand Headquarters in Spa, Belgium, by the team which had trounced the Russians in East Prussia in 1914: Field Marshal Paul von Hindenburg, living symbol of the Prussian officer corps, as Chief of the General Staff, and General Erich Ludendorff as Quartermaster-General, the brains and real leader of the partnership. The "Hindenburg Programme" of total mobilisation, launched at the end of August, made it difficult for the Navy to step up submarine construction because of the Army's prior claim to limited resources. Scheer wanted at least 350 U-boats, to force

The Atlantic, also showing the "airgap" of the Second World War

Britain to sue for peace before any American intervention caused by their deployment could take effect. But the best the Navy Office could do in 1916–17 was to scrape together 172 million marks for forty-six U-boats over and above the dozen or so then being built per month. The same old argument over unrestricted submarine warfare broke out again in summer 1916. It gained added weight from the latest types of long-range U-boats. Members of the "U51", "U57" and "U63" classes were able to make lengthy patrols into the broad Atlantic, well away from British home waters. In an unsubtly intimidatory display *U53* coolly sank five Allied merchant ships in a few days just outside American territorial waters; within sight of the Nantucket lighthouse, as David Lloyd George noted in his *War Memoirs*.

At about the same time the U-boats scored a propaganda triumph of a different order altogether which impressed many Americans. The unarmed submarine freighter *Deutschland* (Captain Paul König of the Merchant Navy) surfaced in Chesapeake Bay and sailed past Washington to anchor off Baltimore, Maryland, on 9 July. The boat, displacing an unprecedented 1,512 tons surfaced and 1,875 submerged, had sailed from Kiel with 700 tons of cargo, including chemicals, precious stones and mail, on 23 June. The Admiralty's Room 40 knew within twenty-four hours and alerted Vice-Admiral Sir George Patey's North American and West Indies Squadron. But the lumbering *Deutschland*, barely capable of twelve knots on the surface, where she passed almost the whole of her crossing, was not intercepted. The British fared no better between 2 and 24 August, when the *Deutschland*, fêted throughout her stay by German-Americans, completed the return passage with a cargo of rubber, nickel and tin worth ten times her building cost. For this her crew were regaled a second time in Bremen. An identical submarine named after that port was damaged – either by a mine or in an accidental collision while submerged with a passing British ship – north of Scotland on her maiden voyage to Norfolk, Virginia, in late summer. *Deutschland*, however, repeated her exploit in autumn with a successful return voyage to New London, Connecticut.

Had the British sighted one of these boats, flying the German mercantile tricolour rather than the Kaiser's ensign, and sunk her as Patey intended, they would have been guilty of the same crime they were constantly laying at the Germans' door: sinking an unarmed merchantman without warning. König's boat eventually "joined the Navy" in February 1917 with six other members of what became the "U151" (Oldenburg) class of "U-cruisers", equipped with a pair of heavy 150-millimetre guns as well as torpedoes. They were thus able to contribute to the next round of unrestricted U-boat warfare from the beginning.

The idea of merchant submarines did not surface again seriously until after the Cold War came to an end in 1989.

In Britain disenchantment with the war leadership went all the way to the top. Herbert Asquith, Prime Minister and leader of the Liberal Party since 1908, was tired as well as habitually indecisive, and in September his son was killed in France. David Lloyd George, a temperamental but brilliant Welsh Liberal with boundless energy and ideas, now launched a bid for power. His aim was not to be premier but merely to run the war, as leader of a revitalised War Committee or "War Council". Asquith had founded this a year or so earlier as an inner Cabinet of three – himself, Lloyd George as Secretary for War and Arthur Balfour as First Lord – but it had succumbed to Whitehall disease and grown in numbers as it shrank in effectiveness, with Asquith ever keener to defer difficult decisions by adjourning. Lloyd George had been President of the Board of Trade (commerce minister) and then Chancellor of the Exchequer (finance minister) before the war, but confirmed his outstanding ability by founding and making an administrative triumph of the Ministry of Munitions before moving to the War Office. There he tried in vain to overcome the stubborn inflexibility of the generals led by Sir William Robertson, Chief of the Imperial General Staff, and Sir Douglas Haig, C-in-C of the British armies in France.

Events came to a head in London over conscription of labour for the war economy, over the German victory in Romania and above all the huge losses of ships and cargoes to the U-boats. Allied war losses exceeded 500 ships or one million tons by the end of 1915 and more than 1,000, or two and a third million, in 1916. Germany had begun 1916 with fifty-eight boats operational and ended it with 140, after two dozen losses to all causes (only seven to enemy action). From October the U-boats were back in strength in British waters, albeit under prize rules, with a ban on passenger ships and free fire allowed only against obviously armed merchantmen. Virtually unrestricted warfare continued in the Mediterranean and losses were mounting in mid-Atlantic. The bulk of the lost Allied tonnage was British. Neutral ships accounted for a quarter of the overall loss worldwide; their owners understandably became reluctant to carry British cargoes – despite the government's generous war-risk insurance scheme, introduced by Chancellor Lloyd George in 1914 – just as British shipping dwindled four times faster than it could be replaced. The life-expectancy of a merchant ship at the end of 1916 was less than ten ocean voyages.

Fisher, sidelined at the Bureau of Inventions and Research, wondered aloud, "Can the Army win the war before the Navy loses it?" Walter

Runciman, President of the Board of Trade, told the War Council on 10 November 1916 that, if sinkings continued at the current rate, there would be a complete breakdown in shipping by the middle of 1917. A few days later he revised his estimate – downward. In the following month Holtzendorff, German naval chief of staff, forecast during the revived debate on unrestricted use of the U-boats that a sinking rate of 600,000 Allied tons per month would scare off 1.2 million tons of neutral shipping and force Britain, its imports slashed by forty per cent, to sue for peace in five months. Here at least was one point on which the two principal belligerents agreed completely

To grasp Britain's desperation at the turn of the year it is only necessary to review the stark facts and figures. In 1913 the country imported fifty-five million tons, roughly half food and half raw materials, and exported 100 million tons in coal and manufactures. The British ocean-going merchant fleet (ships of 1,600 tons or more), which carried the bulk of this huge trade, consisted of 8,600 steam-powered vessels totalling more than fourteen million tons, forty-three per cent of the world's shipping stock. In the war Britain's allies – France and then Italy in the Mediterranean, and to some extent Russia – relied on the British merchant fleet for deliveries of cargoes largely imported from North America. Before the war the Admiralty overestimated the threat from German cruisers and armed merchantmen and prepared protective measures which had the desired effect after just eight months of war. But this was far more than merely offset by almost universal underestimation of submarines.

Convoy, which had been compulsory in the Napoleonic Wars, was now anathema for several reasons. Shipowners and masters saw it as a waste of time, fuel and money. Naval officers thought wireless and the steamer, with its giveaway column of smoke, had made it impossible to conceal shipping. Merchantmen would also be unable to keep station, the convoy would be forced to sail at the speed of its slowest constituent and there were not enough cruisers to counter enemy cruiser warfare. Besides, and this was the key issue for many officers, convoy was an unmanly, defensive tactic.

The Admiralty resolved to minimise the one threat it identified – enemy cruisers – by dispersing the merchant fleet and concentrating its own cruisers for the protection of the main sea-lanes round Britain. The only idea it had when the U-boats entered the fray was more of the same, plus (ineffectually) mining enemy ports, installing nets in the Dover Strait, using Q-ships, arming merchantmen and, from summer 1916, deploying hydrophones and depth-charges, both new but few.

The Admiralty even had a statistical case against convoys: relying on figures from Customs, it pointed to 5,000 shipping movements in and out of British ports *per week*. Not only did this make the very thought of marshalling all that traffic seem impossible; it also made losses to U-boats look trifling to all but the most enquiring of naval minds. Lloyd George pleaded in vain at the War Committee meeting of 2 November 1916 for convoy, the first time the idea had risen so high. Jellicoe, about to take over as first Sea Lord, and Rear-Admiral Alexander Duff, director of the new Anti-Submarine Division, attended another War Council on the 22nd, but remained unmoved, trotting out all the usual arguments.

One of the many curiosities in this stubborn attitude was the fact that in the Napoleonic Wars convoys of hundreds of cumbersome sailing ships had managed to keep station with only the unpredictable wind for power and only visual signalling for guidance. Another was that the Royal Navy's supreme hero, Admiral Lord Nelson, and his colleagues won many a glorious engagement arising out of escorting those very convoys. "The Admiralty stubbornly refused to consider adopting the convoy system and thus extending to the merchant marine the same guardianship as that upon which they relied for their own safety in the Grand Fleet," Lloyd George wrote. To say nothing of innumerable troopships escorted all the way by the Navy. Not even Commodore Andreas Michelsen's flotillas of coastal U-boats, based in the Flanders ports, could make the slightest impression on this traffic, which did not lose a single soldier to enemy naval action.

In the first eight months of 1916 Britain lost about 600,000 tons of shipping; in the last four she lost 632,000 tons. The monthly building rate stood at 52,000 tons, hardly a third of the peacetime figure. At the end of the year, with 738 ocean-going ships totalling over 2.3 million tons lost to the country, the Merchant Navy was said by Runciman to have less than fifty per cent of the tonnage required for imports of "irreducible needs". The neutrals barely covered half this gap. There were not enough ships to collect the crops from India and Australia: of the 100 ships per month required, fewer than thirty were available in Britain. There was barely one week's sugar. Of the more than ten million tons of merchant shipping needed for non-military purposes, just over seven million were available early in 1916. Of the total stock at Britain's disposal (British, Dominion and neutral) at the end of 1916 – 3,731 ships totalling 16,600,000 tons – 2,231 were on war work, leaving 1,500 of 7,082,000 tons for all other purposes. Small wonder that freight rates had risen by up to twelve times. In January 1917 Britain lost another 154,000 tons, keeping up the average of the last four months of 1916.

On 17 January Room 40 intercepted a top-secret telegram from Arthur Zimmermann, State Secretary at the German Foreign Office, to the head of mission at the German Legation in Mexico City, copied to Count Bernstorff, the German Ambassador in Washington. Naval Intelligence could do this because the Navy had systematically cut all marine cables to Germany at the beginning of the war, so that all overseas telegraphic traffic had to be sent via the powerful wireless transmitter at Nauen, west of Berlin. The references to U-boats in the "Zimmermann telegram" make it a seminal text in submarine as well as diplomatic history.

We intend to begin unrestricted U-boat warfare on February 1. The attempt will however be made to keep the US neutral. In the event that this should not succeed, we offer Mexico alliance [to reconquer Texas, New Mexico and Arizona] ... and add suggestion [to the President of Mexico] to invite Japan to join on its own account and simultaneously to mediate between us and Japan. Please inform the President that ruthless deployment of our U-boats now offers the prospect of forcing England to [make] peace.

Grasping at straws and fearful of American intervention in the war, the German government was now weaving a fantasy of drawing Mexico into an alliance against the United States for the recovery of territory acquired by the Americans only a few decades earlier. Hindsight makes the hopeful reference to a Japanese change of sides for the sake of gaining US territory in the Pacific look rather less unrealistic, not to say prophetic. But Japan remained true for the time being to its alliance with Britain; and the post-revolutionary Mexican government was sensible enough not to provoke its great northerly neighbour. Instead the notorious telegram merely fanned American irritation over the constant provocations of the U-boat campaign into anger. The effect was compounded when Washington was officially notified of German plans for all-out submarine warfare in a bitter note from Berlin two weeks later, on 31 January. The reason was predictably given as the British blockade. British intelligence had first heard of the resurgence of the "hawks" in Berlin before the end of 1916, when Bethmann-Hollweg was still fighting his rearguard action against the inevitable resumption of unrestricted warfare. The hardliners were gaining because the unspoken belief was spreading that blockaded Germany could not win a war of attrition by any other means; and to be effective, the counter-blockade had to be pressed home before the increasingly likely American declaration of war could influence events at the front. A hungry Britain would sue for peace and Germany would at last get the upper hand in Europe.

In October 1916 the U-boats sank 337,000 tons of shipping (British and foreign). From November to January 1917 inclusive they sank 961,000 tons. On the reintroduction of unrestricted U-boat warfare on 1 February, the Germans sank thirty-five ships or an average of five per day in the first week, towards a global total for the month of 520,000 tons (sixty per cent more than in January). Britain's shipping losses were 311,000 tons in February – twice as much as in January – and 352,000 tons in March, another record. More than a million tons had gone in under nine weeks of unrestricted warfare.

The Germans began 1917 with just 105 operational boats. By April the full horror of what they were poised to achieve was there for all who knew to see (those in the know did not include the public): Britain lost 564,000 tons (over 300 ships or ten per cent *in a single month*) out of a worldwide total to all causes of 881,000. The British, masters of propaganda, concealed the true extent of the losses by exaggerating them. They released the names of all British ships over 1,600 tons lost at sea but ignored all other losses (including damage, which affected as many ships again). To this limited information was added, without comment, the total of sinkings claimed by the Germans. This was invariably inflated by optimistic U-boat commanders in the heat of battle, if not more so by German propaganda. The public was left with the impression that all enemy claims were absurdly exaggerated, instead of only marginally worse than the horrific truth. This ploy was a classic example of Whitehall economy with the truth.

Holtzendorff's forecast of a British collapse by June looks positively pessimistic in German terms given the real figures. The life-expectancy of an ocean-going ship was now down to four return voyages. But in this worst month for shipping in the entire history of warfare (not even the Second World War produced a month quite so destructive at sea), the factor which tipped the balance in the Allies' favour had also been thrown on the scale. The United States Congress, enraged by the Zimmermann telegram and mounting "frightfulness" at sea, finally declared war on Germany on 6 April.

But, unless something drastic was done, the Germans still stood to win their gamble. The U-boats could yet starve Britain out before the US mobilised. They could also make it well nigh impossible for the US Navy to find the ships to deliver the American Expeditionary Force to the front. On 25 April 1917 something drastic was done.

Two days earlier David Lloyd George, Prime Minister since 7 December 1916, lost patience with the admirals after they had once again rejected convoy. They had agreed in February to abide by the results of experiments on the routes to France and Norway after reading a Cabinet

Office memorandum urging the case for convoy. Lloyd George and Hankey, the Cabinet Secretary, had a working breakfast on 13 February with Jellicoe, the First Sea Lord, and his equally stubborn ASW chief, Duff. Also present was Sir Edward Carson, hopelessly ineffectual as First Lord of the Admiralty but politically dangerous as the leading opponent of Irish Home Rule – an issue shelved, with disastrous results, for the duration of the war. Between that barren breakfast and the Cabinet crisis meetings on the shipping disaster in April, however, the premier quietly consulted relatively junior officers, notably Commander R.G.H. Henderson, RN.

Lloyd George was reminded that the French relied on Britain for half their coal, having lost Alsace-Lorraine with its coalfields to the Germans in 1870. They expressed concern at collier losses caused by Michelsen's Flanders flotillas; Henderson was ordered to help. On 7 February he instituted "controlled sailings" to Brest, Le Havre and Cherbourg, covered by humble armed trawlers. He knew better than to call them convoys, but that is what they were. Over the ensuing quarter just one collier was sunk for every 450 sailings. This problem solved, Henderson betook himself to the new Ministry of Shipping, set up by Lloyd George as part of his anti-submarine programme, and investigated the shipping movement statistics. It will be recalled that at the beginning of the war the Admiralty had accepted the Customs figure of 5,000 movements per week. Henderson found to his amazement that this included any movement by any vessel, whether ocean liner or dredger, oil tanker or fishing smack. If a coaster called at ten ports in a week, twenty movements (ten in, ten out) were logged. Stripping the records of everything but arrivals and departures of ocean-going ships upwards of 1,600 tons, Henderson came up with an average of about twenty inward and twenty outward movements per day – fewer than 300 per week. In his *War Memoirs*, Lloyd George wrote of the admirals: "The blunder on which their policy was based was an arithmetical mix-up which would not have been perpetrated by an ordinary clerk in a shipping office."

Early in April 1917 Admiral Beatty, now C-in-C of the Grand Fleet, took a hand. He initiated convoys, diplomatically styled "protected sailings", on the Norwegian route, which passed dangerously close to Germany's front doorstep. Losses were running at an appalling twenty-five per cent of sailings, a life-expectancy of just two round trips per ship. But from 21 April, sinkings sank dramatically to one for every 400 sailings, or one per cent of the former rate.

Jellicoe may have avoided "losing the war in an afternoon" at Jutland, but he very nearly became the man who lost the war altogether in the first four months of 1917. It was Lloyd George who provided short-term salvation while waiting for the Americans to supply the long-term assurance of victory.

At another crisis meeting of the War Cabinet (now an officially constituted, five-man inner council chaired by himself) on 25 April, Lloyd George won approval for a memorandum to Carson at the Admiralty. It gave notice of his intent to call on the 30th, to enquire about anti-submarine measures. The threat was unmistakable.

Carson was a lawyer, perhaps the most skilled advocate of his time. He was also a bigoted Ulster Protestant and derived his political influence from the support of Conservatives opposed to Irish Home Rule – nearly half the party in the House of Commons. His gifts did not include the administrative ability to run the only government department that was also an operational headquarters. Lloyd George, head of a coalition, had to give Carson a real job, despite his lack of ministerial experience, and made him First Lord of the Admiralty. The hidebound admirals, knowing Lloyd George's impatience with the entire military leadership and his "fixation" on convoys, could scarcely believe their luck when Carson said he was "very much at sea" in naval affairs and would leave all technical matters to them. Lloyd George, who wanted a new, "hands-on" political style to overcome military inertia and intellectual bankruptcy, had appointed the ultimate "hands-off" amateur to run the Admiralty, for party-political reasons. For this only Lloyd George can be blamed. It was doubly unfortunate that Jellicoe replaced Sir Henry Jackson as First Sea Lord two days before Lloyd George formed his government. Jellicoe was anxious and tired, lacking the vision to rethink an obviously inadequate ASW strategy.

The news that the Prime Minister was coming in five days, with the express intention of summoning any official with ideas on beating the U-boats, electrified the Admiralty. Reports from British submariners complaining about enemy convoys were dusted off. The day after Lloyd George's self-invitation, Admiral Duff, Director of the Anti-Submarine Division, conceded to Jellicoe that the time had arrived "when we must be ready to introduce a comprehensive scheme of convoy at any moment." It might be against their better judgment, but the admirals knew they had to bow to the politicians answerable to the electorate. Duff's memorandum was endorsed, without enthusiasm, by Jellicoe on the 27th. So when Lloyd George swept into the building three days later he found no battle left to fight.

He unveiled a six-point programme for reversing the trend at sea: convoys; arming all merchantmen; priority for new methods of locating and destroying submarines; more shipbuilding in Britain and much more in the United States; more efficient use of existing shipping; and import substitution, especially in food by means of radical farming reform.

Among his earliest moves as premier Lloyd George had appointed two "dictators": Sir Joseph Maclay, as Shipping Controller at the head of a new shipping ministry; and Lord Devonport, as Food Controller with a new food department. Maclay's responsibilities included standardisation of merchant shipbuilding, economising on the use of cargo space, arming merchantmen and decongesting the ports. Other non-politicians were appointed to take charge of construction and the deployment of industrial manpower in a drive for efficiency inspired above all by the U-boat threat to the British war economy.

It was only on 2 May 1917 that the Prime Minister took a grip on the Admiralty by making Sir Eric Geddes Controller of the Navy (theoretically in charge of warship construction but appointed as a catalyst for reform). Geddes had superbly reorganised Army transport on the Western Front, even winning the admiration of General Haig. But Lloyd George did not feel free to oust Carson until July, when the crisis at sea was on the wane. Geddes lived up to his reputation by galvanising the department, a process ultimately enhanced by his abrupt dismissal of Jellicoe at the end of the year in favour of Admiral Wemyss. Carson joined the War Cabinet without portfolio, a post more appropriate for a man of his forensic abilities and lack of administrative talent.

That the loss of 600,000 tons of shipping worldwide (345,000 tons of it British) in the single month of May should have occasioned relief at the Admiralty shows how desperate the position at sea had become. The Admiralty's approval of Beatty's Scandinavian experiment on 11 April and Commander Henderson's safe deliveries of coal to France helped to account for the fall of not quite one-third in shipping losses; the fact that Lothar von Arnauld and his colleagues were recuperating after their supreme effort in April was just as significant. Global sinkings rose again to 685,000 tons (399,000 British) in June, the second-worst month of the war, and eased to 550,000 (360,000) in July. The monthly total exceeded the half-million mark for the last time in August, when Britain alone lost a third of a million tons.

Lloyd George's victory on convoy might appear on the basis of these figures to have been pyrrhic: no miracle cure here. But convoys were introduced only piecemeal by a still sceptical Admiralty. The first, seventeen vessels escorted by two Q-ships – hardly the best choice – left Gibraltar on 10 May, arriving unscathed. The first transatlantic convoy, twelve ships, set sail from Hampton Roads (off Long Island) on 24 May 1917. Two could not keep up and were sent back to Halifax unescorted;

one was torpedoed. The other ten and their escort, the cruiser HMS *Roxburgh*, were met by destroyers from Devonport for a safe passage through the dangerous Western Approaches. Station-keeping, even when zigzagging in formation, had been "excellent", the *Roxburgh's* Captain F.A. Whitehead reported. The first twelve convoys to reach Britain collectively lost just one ship sunk, plus one damaged but towed to port.

The laggard admirals were reluctant to release destroyers, the ideal escorts, for convoy duty: only thirty out of 279 in home waters had been made available by June, necessitating another explosion by Lloyd George. On the 6th of that month, Fleet Paymaster (later Rear-Admiral Sir) Eldon Manisty, RN, was appointed "Organising Manager, Convoys", reporting to the Director of the Trade Division at the Admiralty. But he had to scour the building himself for an empty office and a handful of staff. In September Captain Whitehead became Director of Mercantile Movements, an office last filled in the Napoleonic Wars, taking over the supervision of Manisty's Convoy Section. A similarly named department at the Ministry of Shipping, headed by Mr Norman Leslie, worked hand in glove with Manisty, the latter organising the escorts and the former the merchantmen.

Their seaborne "empire" was still slow to expand. Only on 2 July were convoys set up for homeward-bound transatlantic traffic and on the 26th for shipping from Gibraltar. In August convoys started sailing to and from Dakar in West Africa. The US Navy initially proved as reluctant as the Admiralty to run convoys, despite strong advocacy from Rear-Admiral William Sims, commanding US naval forces in Europe since America's declaration of war, who had been stunned by his old friend Jellicoe's revelations of the true losses. Sims was largely responsible for the detachment of nearly eighty US destroyers for convoy duty by the end of the war.

The South Atlantic had to wait until September; the Mediterranean, with its divided Allied naval command, until November, despite its special notoriety as a drain on shipping. There was little point in running a convoy from Britain to Gibraltar when the ships had to cross the Mediterranean unescorted. The same lack of logic prevailed in coastal waters until the new Admiralty statistical department, set up by Geddes, noticed that ten per cent of sinkings in British waters towards the end of 1917 were within ten miles of shore, whereupon coastal convoying was introduced, in December.

Like most people U-boat captains preferred the softest option. When convoys were introduced in one part of the oceans, they moved to fresh pastures. When outward-bound convoys were instituted they switched to inward-bound, where sinking were four times higher until a two-way system was in place. When convoys began to spread across the globe they looked for the gaps in the system: when ships were sailing to join up or, better, when they dispersed to their destinations after a safe crossing. And when all else failed, there were still indefensibly large numbers of ships sailing independently. Convoy never did become compulsory in either world war. In the last eighteen months of the First, 16,657 sailings were made in ocean convoys to and from Britain, of which 154 were lost, or less than one per cent. They included thirty-six which had lost touch and were really sailing alone, and sixteen sunk in storms and accidents. Combined they represented a much smaller loss than in the blackest month, April 1917. From then until the end of the war there were about 88,000 sailings in convoy worldwide; just 436 (257 British) ships were lost, a rate of 0.5 per cent. But nearly six per cent of independent sailings were sunk in the same period, accounting for the overwhelming majority of British losses (eighty-five per cent, or 1,500 ships) in the last year and a half of the war.

The desperate search for new ASW methods finally led the British to follow the Austrian example in the Adriatic and deploy aircraft in all their new-fangled forms against the U-boats. They had already been used against surface ships, notably at the Dardanelles, though with little effect. But their most successful contribution at sea was in scouting from capital ships. By April 1917 scores of airships and seaplanes were already on ASW and anti-ship patrol round Britain. From that time, landbased aircraft began to join in. Early aircraft had no ASW weapon (the airborne depth-charge had yet to be invented; the torpedo was only of use against surface ships; contemporary bombs were useless at sea) and they could communicate only by the pilot's free arm, by Morse lamp, circling or waggling their wings. But their mere presence over shipping forced a submarine to dive or risk attack from warships. Convoys covered by plane suffered virtually no losses at all, notably on the Anglo-Dutch route which lay between the German and Belgian U-boat bases.

At the end of 1917 nearly 100 airships, 291 seaplanes and twenty-three aeroplanes, over 400 aircraft, were on ASW duty. At the end of the war there were still 100 airships and 285 seaplanes but also 272 aeroplanes, a total of 657. The Germans were forced to abandon surface attacks by day, to introduce upward-looking periscopes (altiscopes) and to move further into the Atlantic to get out of range of aircraft.

But the formation, in April 1918 from Army and Navy squadrons, of the Royal Air Force with a virtual monopoly of military flying has been described as the Royal Navy's greatest defeat. An early example of the

ensuing disadvantages was the refusal of the fledgling RAF to release
any of the new long-range bombers for ASW. They were kept for other
tasks, such as bombing the Flanders submarine pens, where not a single
boat was sunk in ever-increasing raids in the last months of the war (a
mistake to be forgotten and therefore repeated in the Second World
War).

Not only was convoy introduced with agonising slowness as the
admirals were dragged into the twentieth century via the end of the
eighteenth; it was also subjected to double standards by its opponents.
Men who had shrugged off dozens of sinkings per week made a fuss
about one loss under escort. In October 1917 disaster struck a convoy
whose leading escort was HMS *Mary Rose*. A dozen ships on their way
from Bergen, Norway, to the Shetland Isles were attacked by two light
cruisers, which first sank the two destroyer escorts and then nine merchantmen inside an hour. Some conservative admirals could not resist
saying, "I told you so" over the loss of 10,248 tons of convoyed shipping –
just over one-third of the average *daily* loss in April. The disaster showed
that convoys were no panacea; fortunately it prompted reflection on
tactics against superior surface forces. Against submarines, convoys had
to stay together and rely on their escort; against strong surface attack
the best defence was to scatter. No remedy was found for simultaneous
submarine and surface attacks, something which never arose in this war.
Even the most fervent advocates of convoy never said it was infallible.

The most noticeable decline in Allied shipping losses was between
August and September 1917: some fifty per cent. Sinkings then rose and
fell rhythmically in alternate months to the end of the war, on an overall
downward trend. But it was only from August 1918 that monthly
shipping losses undercut the average for 1916. Even so the British alone
lost 144,000 tons that month. New building in British yards doubled in
1917 to 1,229,000 tons for the year – a mere third of British losses in
the period – and rose again to 1,579,000 tons in 1918, still 52,000 tons
below British losses in the last year of war. In these figures lies the best
justification for the claim by a few bombastic Americans to have "won
the war" for the Allies. But for the output by United States yards of so
many ships, including hundreds of the standardised "Hog Islander" type,
based on a British design, the U-boats would clearly have forced Britain
to end the war on German terms. The ships mattered at least as much
as the two million men of General Pershing's American Expeditionary
Force. They arrived in heavily escorted transports: only one such ship
was lost.

*

The Germans commissioned 344 submarines to add to the twenty-eight with which they began the war. At the Armistice on 11 November 1918, 226 were under construction; 212 more had been ordered under Admiral Scheer's accelerated building programme. Only during the last six months of war did U-boat losses exceed new construction, roughly coinciding with the period when the Allies at last outbuilt shipping losses. About 178 U-boats were lost to all causes, with 4,716 submariners killed (1,400 were captured), an overall casualty rate of about a third of those who served in what the Germans came to call the "iron coffins". A similar number of boats were surrendered; a handful were scuttled or "sank" on their way to surrender.

They destroyed worldwide during the war, by gun, scuttling charge or torpedo, 11,135,000 tons of shipping, 4,837 merchantmen, of which 7,662,000 tons were from Britain – fifty-five per cent of the prewar strength of its merchant fleet and sixty-nine per cent of the total lost. The overall loss of shipping to all causes exceeded thirteen million tons; of the other two million, a high proportion was lost to mines laid by U-boats.

The British Merchant Navy lost 15,313 men in this struggle, or about five and a half per cent of its total wartime manpower; the Royal Navy lost four per cent or 22,811 men killed at sea, including several thousand merchant seamen seconded to it on requisitioned vessels such as trawlers and drifters, equivalent to another two per cent of the merchant service. One third of Royal Navy fatalities was ascribed to the defence of trade.

It remains to review briefly events on the various submarine fronts in the last phases of the First World War. In the Baltic, Laurence's successor as Senior British Officer, Commander Cromie, cut a dash as a dandy and got on very well with the Russians but sank no ships after his 1915 exploits. The front door to the Baltic having been slammed shut by the Germans, four small "C" class coastal submarines were towed out of Chatham in south-east England on 3 August 1916 to Archangel on the White Sea in the Russian north. There they were loaded on to barges for transfer to Petrograd by canal overland, arriving on 9 September. While on leave there in March 1917 Cromie got caught up in the first Russian Revolution but got back to the Russian depot ship servicing his small flotilla – to find her flying the Red Flag. Since the revolutionary sailors, a key element in the March and October Revolutions, were prone to kill their hated officers, Cromie, promoted acting captain, had to intercede to save lives.

A foray by a German light cruiser and eleven destroyers into the Gulf of Finland in November 1916 led to the loss of seven of the latter to

Russian mines. This was a spectacular return on the sowing since 1914 of 25,000 mines in the eastern Baltic. Six American-built "Hollands" delivered to Vladivostok and five more built under licence eventually joined the Baltic divisions; but during 1916 only five boats hunted enemy merchantmen, and three of those were British. A harsh winter terminated naval activity until May 1917, by which time Russia was in turmoil.

There was a burst of minelaying in June and a Russian boat sank a German coaster in August 1917; then naval activity dwindled, ending altogether after the Bolshevik Revolution in November.

The Germans closed in on the Gulf of Riga in September; three British "C" boats failed to reduce a strong German surface force. One ran aground and was blown up by her crew while the other two were damaged and only just reached the new British base of Helsingfors (Helsinki) in still-Russian Finland. The four "E" and three "C" boats left in the British flotilla were scuttled there in April 1918 as the Germans extended their grip to the Gulf of Finland.

In the Mediterranean, life was suddenly transformed at the end of 1917 for a young submariner called Karl Dönitz, as he recalled much later in his memoirs:

The oceans at once became bare and empty; for long periods at a time the U-boats, operating individually, would see nothing at all; and then suddenly up would loom a huge concourse of ships, thirty or fifty or more of them, surrounded by an escort of warships of all types ... The lone U-boat might well sink one or two of the ships, or even several, yet that was but a poor percentage of the whole ...

The Mediterranean did not always offer enough searoom for convoys. This and the divided Allied command helped to account for the fact that the U-boats fought on, undeterred and most effectively, to the end in the landlocked sea. It was here too, in answer to the frustrating convoy tactic, that the Germans began in the final months to experiment with a stratagem of attack by U-boats operating in small groups. The escorts could be distracted sufficiently by one or more members to give others a clear shot at the convoy. This was not Dönitz's idea; but he saw its worth and filed it away in his mind.

The title Dönitz would hold soon after the outbreak of the Second World War – *Befehlshaber* (commandant) der U-boote – was created in June

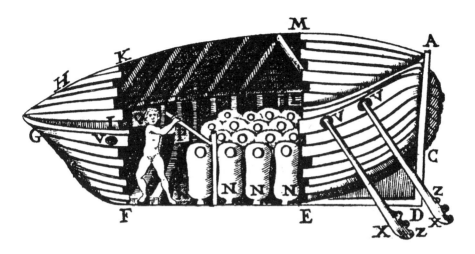

Father Giovanni Borelli's theoretical "diving bell", published in 1680 (above), obviously inspired the craft built in 1747 by Nathaniel Symons (below), which submerged in the River Thames for forty-five minutes.

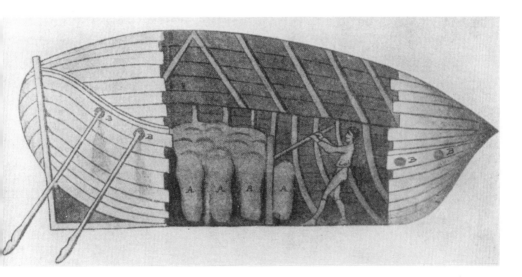

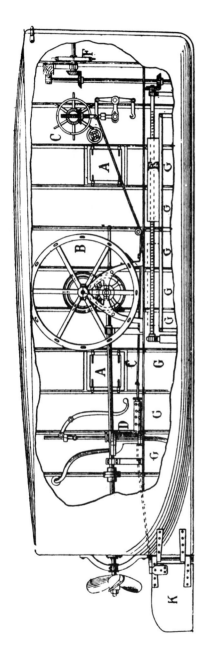

Brandtaucher, designed by the Bavarian Wilhelm Bauer in 1850 (above), was the first "U-boat" and can be seen today in Dresden. The second of many boats called *Nautilus*, built by the Britons Ash and Campbell in 1888 (below), was the first to run on batteries underwater.

END VIEW.

HMS *Holland I*, the Royal Navy's first submarine, at her launch; she is still in harness as a museum exhibit. Her inventor and father of the modern submarine, John Philip Holland, is shown with one of his early experiments.

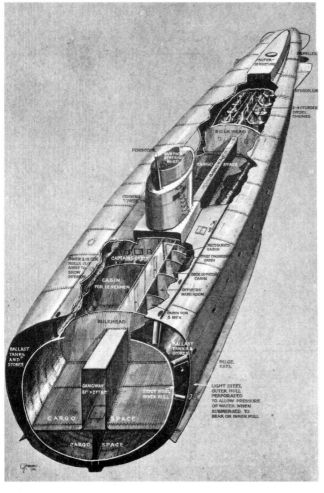

The first minelaying U-boats belonged to the "UC1" class (above). Another German innovation, a short-lived sensation, was the mercantile U-boat *Deutschland* of 1916, armed and converted to *U155* in 1917.

An artist's impression of the loss of the *Lusitania*.

The British *E11*, in which Martin Nasmith dominated the Dardanelles and won the VC in 1915, shows her bows on launching (above). So does Britain's *K4* in less happy circumstances – an unlucky member of a disastrous class.

The experimental British *M2*, with a sawn-off battleship's gun (above in 1918), and some ten years later, with the gun replaced by a crane to hoist a seaplane aboard.

A typical convoy scene, photographed from a British battleship early in the Second World War.

Part of the second U-boat fleet proudly on display with a depot-ship at Kiel in 1939.

1917 for Commodore Andreas Michelsen of the Flanders flotillas, to whose pennant were now added the German-based boats previously led by Hermann Bauer (promoted admiral of a squadron) as *Führer der U-boote* in the High Seas Fleet. The new chief was not prepared to preside over a withdrawal; on the contrary, he planned to take the campaign to the new enemy, across the Atlantic.

The weapon was soon to hand: the big new submarine cruiser or *U-kreuzer*, conceived in 1916. As we saw, the Germans converted seven merchant submarines, *U151–U157*, arming them with heavy guns and torpedoes. The *Deutschland* (1916) became *U155*; five were commissioned in 1917 and *U157* in 1918. Even larger and also faster were the three purpose-built cruisers of the "U139" class, which displaced 1,930 tons surfaced and 2,483 submerged, all completed in 1918 (though *U141* never saw action). Arnauld was given *U139*; Kophamel took on *U140*. The nine U-cruisers that went into service carried one large gun forward and one aft of the conning tower, giving them a unique profile. At economical surface speed these boats could sail round the world without refuelling. One member of an even bigger class of nine, *U142*, 2,158/2,785 tons, was not commissioned; the rest were scrapped. The big boats were very comfortable for their time, with extra space and safety features such as thicker hull plates, watertight bulkheads and armour in the conning tower.

In the last nine months of the war the cruisers roamed the entire Atlantic, laying mines off the American east coast and lying in wait for ships sailing alone. After the flurry on the US east coast over *U53* in summer 1916, almost two years went by in which Americans were lulled into a false sense of security. The arrival of the cruisers caused consternation. *U151*, under a Prussian aristocrat with an even longer name than Arnauld's, Commander Heinrich von Nostitz und Jänckendorff, opened the attack in May by laying mines off the coast of New England. Later that month he boldly retraced the underwater route of the *Deutschland* into Chesapeake Bay to lay more, between Washington and Baltimore: there had not been a intrusion like it since the British came in the war of 1812. His mines sank four ships, causing widespread panic. In his thirteen-week patrol Nostitz also sank twenty-three ships, totalling 61,000 tons, by gunfire and cut telegraphic cables, escaping unscathed from a depth-charging by an American warship. On the way home he boarded a neutral Norwegian ship and seized as contraband the invaluable copper in her cargo, using it as ballast. Like Arnauld he observed prize rules.

The six boats which carried out one patrol each off the coasts of Canada and the United States accounted for forty-five American and fourteen Canadian ships totalling 167,000 tons. The 1904 heavy cruiser USS *San Diego* (15,000 tons) was lost to a mine sown by *U156* off New England. The U-cruisers sank 174 ships of some 361,000 tons, over three per cent of the total sunk by U-boats in the war, a not inconsiderable haul given the lateness of their arrival, the strain on a crew of up to eighty men set by a marathon patrol and the prevalence of convoy in 1918. One, *U154*, was sunk by HMS *E35* off Morocco in May 1918 and four months later *U156* became one of the tiny handful of victims of the colossal northern mine barrage between Shetland and Norway.

The barrage was one of several American initiatives in the war at sea which promised much but achieved little, such as the ineffectual sub-chasers sent to the Otranto Barrage – much less useful than the two dozen destroyers sent by Japan in 1917 to escort Mediterranean convoys.

As the U-cruisers took the war westward to American waters, the United States Navy advanced eastward, lending a battle squadron to the Grand Fleet and starting to send destroyers for convoys in May. Without them the system, slow to grow as it was, might not have stopped the rot in time for American intervention to tip the scales in favour of the Allies. That invaluable Anglophile, Admiral Sims, saw more clearly than most that in this context the best form of attack is defence: if the enemy targets your commerce, give your warships their best chance of attacking him by placing them alongside his objective, forcing him to take them on or withdraw. A Navy's dual role was and is to protect the nation and its interests and to attack the enemy. Convoys enable it to do both at once. To appease the slighted "offensive spirit" of the anti-convoy school it has been argued that convoy protection is intrinsically offensive. This is an offence only against semantics. Convoy gives sailors the chance to counter-attack the enemy, thus satisfying their aggressive urge; but there can be no denying that convoy is a defensive stratagem. The real point is that this is one of the quintessential duties of navies and therefore never was anything to be ashamed of in the first place.

The American escorts knocked out their first U-boat on 17 November 1917, when the destroyers *Fanning* and *Nicholson*, covering eight freighters, depth-charged *U58* west of Lundy Island in the Bristol Channel. The American submarine service was no less anxious to join the fray, even though it lacked the experience which more than three years of war had conferred on its main ally and main enemy alike. Its boats were backward as a result. Submarine Division Four of small coastal boats advanced to the Portuguese Azores in mid-Atlantic in October 1917 to hunt U-boats. The four boats were too small for ocean work and achieved nothing. Submarine Division Five, of seven boats, arrived in Bantry Bay, Ireland, in December. The Submarine Force, Atlantic Fleet (engineering staff officer: Commander Chester W. Nimitz, USN) patrolled in the Atlantic, British waters and even the Mediterranean. These larger boats also proved not to be up to the job; they had come too late to the front.

The British also built outsize boats but for a different role, which their classification as "fleet submarines" made clear. In seeking a surface speed of twenty-four knots at the design stage in 1915, the Admiralty and the builders, Vickers, made the mistake of going back to steam propulsion for this "K" class of 1,883/2,565 tons, mostly completed in 1917. Of the seventeen commissioned during the war, no fewer than eight were to be involved in accidents. Three sank with much loss of life after collisions, in some cases on exercise with other "K" boats in the North Sea; two more foundered. One of the latter was K13, which was lost with twenty-five sailors near Faslane, the submarine base in south-west Scotland, and was raised and renumbered K22. The many flaws in these unfortunate boats, 338 feet long but with a beam of only twenty-seven feet, included low underwater endurance, poor manoeuvrability, a dangerously complex and slow diving procedure (they had to shut down steam engines and retract funnels before submerging) and instability underwater not experienced since the days of Nordenfelt. No real thought had been given to their role, vaguely conceived as with the fleet, but in the event reduced to almost pointless and unsuccessful anti-U-boat patrolling. A "much improved" K26 was completed in 1923 but all the survivors of the class were sold off in the 1920s. The real freak of the British submarine service was the "M" class, of which two out of a total of three were commissioned in 1918. These 1,600/1,950-ton monsters were submersible monitors, equipped with a single twelve-inch gun worthy of a dreadnought. The first, M1, was entrusted to Horton in August 1918 but saw no action. Both were lost in tragic accidents between the wars. They were intended for shore bombardment which, however, the Royal Navy eschewed in case the Germans did the same!

This weasel argument was the real reason why the Navy did not bombard the Flanders U-boat nests, something Lloyd George never understood. The German fleet and its submarine arm had after all already tried coastal bombardment at the beginning of the war. The U-boats obviously had better things to do thereafter than gratuitously revealing their presence by shelling the shore of Britain.

But Roger Keyes, in command at Dover since New Year's Day 1918, decided something had to be done about the fifty or so Flanders U-boats which proved such a persistent nuisance in the southern North Sea and the not altogether "English" Channel. The Germans used Ostend as a forward base and Bruges, linked to the sea by the canal to nearby Zeebrugge, as their main lair. Keyes drew up a plan which was simplicity itself: to shut down both ports by sinking blockships across their mouths. Two attempts on Ostend failed.

Zeebrugge was to be raided to cut the railway viaduct between the coast and the Zeebrugge mole, a curved stone breakwater outside the port, and to block the entrance to the canal at the same time with the hulks of three old cruisers on St George's Day, 23 April. Another elderly cruiser, HMS *Vindictive*, and a pair of old cross-Channel ferries of shallow draught were to land marines to storm the battery covering the mole. The tiny eleven-year-old submarine *C3* (Lieutenant R.D. Sandford, RN) was loaded with five tons of dynamite to be blown up against the viaduct. A second boat with a similar assignment did not arrive in time. *C3*'s crew of six had two small motor-boats for their escape. In fact they waited until their boat struck home, and had to row for it in the riddled remains of one launch under heavy fire from German troops. The viaduct was demolished in a huge explosion and the six submariners, three wounded including Sandford, were rescued by his elder brother Francis, a lieutenant-commander on Keyes's staff who had planned the raid and requisitioned a launch on his own initiative for that very purpose. The younger Sandford was awarded the Victoria Cross and all five of his crew received high decorations. Keyes was awarded a barony.

But: the blockships could not be sunk in the right place; the canal and its lock were not blocked; there were more than 500 British casualties in a fierce and confusing action at the mole, comfortably won by the defenders. Nor did it take the Germans long to repair the viaduct and resume U-boat activity. But the dashing "Zeebrugge raid", a rare display of old-fashioned buccaneering after three and a half years of war, did wonders for British morale. The Admiralty wildly exaggerated the results of an episode which provided as much cheer as any exploit by the Royal Navy in the war. The U-boats sank 214,400 tons of British shipping that month, their highest score for four months, and 179,400 tons in May.

The British surface blockade continued relentlessly as the convoy system narrowly held the U-boats in check. The naval strangulation of Germany was reflected in a collapse of morale among the men of the High Seas Fleet, whose mutiny in October 1918 signalled the end of the war. Unlike their British counterparts, these sailors lived ashore in barracks unless actually going to sea. The German dreadnoughts were significantly stronger for not having to sacrifice bulkheads to create large compartments suitable for messing, but this meant life aboard became intolerable after a few days. Living ashore, however, brought contact with the hungry civil population and with revolutionaries inspired by events in Russia.

The last case of U-boat "frightfulness" was the sinking of the ferry *Leinster* in the Irish Sea with the loss of 450 lives, including many Americans. President Wilson promptly stepped up his pressure on the Germans to sue for peace, demanding an immediate end to unrestricted submarine warfare.

The German boats abandoned the Belgian coast at the beginning and the Adriatic at the end of October. All U-boats at sea were ordered home by Scheer on 21 October, the day after Germany accepted Wilson's "Fourteen Points" and called off the unrestricted campaign. Scheer planned to use some of them in support of a last throw against the Royal Navy, planned for the 29th. But when the time came the neglected High Seas Fleet rebelled and would not set sail. Only crews which had been constantly at sea – the U-boat and destroyer crews – remained loyal. It therefore fell to Commodore Michelsen, commandant of U-boats, to quell a mutiny on two battleships in the Jade estuary. He boarded *U135* (Johannes Spiess, Weddigen's erstwhile lieutenant) and, backed by a handful of other boats and destroyers, faced down the mutineers by placing *U135* at right angles between the two looming dreadnoughts on 6 November, with a view to torpedoing them at point-blank range if necessary. The mutineers backed down and the ringleaders were arrested; but the battleships were sent through the canal to Kiel, where rebellious sailors "infected" other ships.

Lothar von Arnauld had almost been undone by his last victim, an ancient Portuguese gunboat, when it sank over his head just before Scheer's recall signal. When he brought *U139* into Kiel on 14 November he found the Baltic port in turmoil with Red Flags flying everywhere and drunken sailors threatening officers. So the ace of aces put on a civilian suit and went home.

The last throw of the U-boat arm was similar to its first: an attempt on the Grand Fleet's base. *UB16* (Kurt Emsmann) entered the now heavily defended Scapa Flow from the south and got as far as Hoxa Sound. Shorebased operators listening in to hydrophones on the seabed detected the boat. They waited until the invisible intruder was passing over a field of submerged, captive mines and flicked a switch, which destroyed the boat and its crew of thirty-four. The only other German boat – Heinrich von Hennig's *U18* – ever to penetrate the Flow had been sighted at almost the same spot on 23 November 1914 by a trawler and a destroyer, which opened fire and came on to ram. The damaged submarine ran on to rocks in the Pentland Firth and was abandoned in a sinking condition. These two gallant efforts were not forgotten in Germany.

Of the vast total of sinkings achieved by 372 operational German submarines, thirty per cent were done by four per cent of the U-boats, and sixty per cent by just twenty-two of the 400 or so who captained them. The British deployed 150 boats under about 300 captains during the war. Of the latter, forty-six seized, sank or damaged 346 enemy merchant vessels (two-thirds of them too small to be described as ships) as well as fourteen surface warships and seventeen U-boats; eight captains got 281. Martin Nasmith, VC, was the leading British ace. In general the British were left behind by the Germans in every department of the first submarine campaign except one: anti-submarine warfare. The last submarines completed by Britain during the war included the ten members of the "R" class, the world's first purpose-built ASW submarines, or hunter-killers as they are known today. These little boats (420 tons surfaced, 500 submerged) had six bow tubes, a four-inch gun and a single crew. Their most remarkable feature was their unheard-of underwater speed of fifteen knots, compared with just 9.5 on the surface. But these boats, in many respects the most advanced in the world, came too late. With their streamlined hulls and rounded angles they were the ancestors of all modern fast submarines and were technically surpassed only twenty-five years later – by the Germans. But the ASW-submarine concept did not come into its own until well after the Second World War.

Hydrophones, depth-charges and aircraft were in widespread if not always effectual use against submarines by the time of the Armistice. In June 1917 an Allied Submarine Detection Conference took place in Washington. There the British and Americans decided to cooperate with the French (thanks to Paul Langevin, leaders in the field) in developing an active underwater detection system. It was based on the newly invented quartz transducer, capable with an amplifier of picking up echoes from ultrasonic underwater radio signals. His Majesty's Trawler *Ebro II* was chosen as the first ASW vessel to be fitted with "ASDIC" (reputedly an acronym derived from Allied Submarine Detection Investigation Committee). As ASW officers went into Asdic training from summer 1918, work on the trawler was completed, five days after the Armistice. At that point the British took the lead in this new technology, brought to fruition just too late to be tested in combat. Allied cooperation in this area faded after the war. The British jubilantly locked their secret away; the Americans started work on their own "SONAR" (*so*und *na*vigation *a*nd *r*anging), now the generic term for the technology.

*

The U-boats were not defeated but only frustrated. The threat they represented to a power heavily dependent on seaborne trade had only been staved off by the time the British blockade and the failure of the German Army's formidable last offensive in 1918 forced Germany to sue for peace. It was not the fault of his U-boats that the Kaiser's Reich fell; they very nearly brought him victory in a war in which Germany was grossly outgunned even before the Americans joined in. But for the U-boats this intervention, after which the Americans supplanted Britain as leading world power, would not have been necessary. But for the U-boats, the war might have ended before it brought on revolution in Russia. It was the British blockade by surface seapower which won the war; and it was the counter-blockade of Britain by U-boat, reducing it to just ten days' supply of staple foods, which came closest to turning the tables, emptying the British treasury in the process.

The unparalleled losses inflicted by an untried and grossly under-estimated weapon offered, at the end of the largest war so far known, a clear and most painfully acquired historic lesson: never again to under-estimate the submarine. The Allies forbade Germany to own or build submarines in the Treaty of Versailles. Only the loser, Germany, by far the most proficient exponent of submarine warfare, absorbed the lesson fully, even as it ignored others. The failure of the other powers to remember it meant that in the Second World War, which began only twenty-one years after the end of the First, the vastly expensive learning process had to be undergone all over again. In this case, the classic military error of preparing for the next war by planning for the last would have been much less damaging than repeating the greatest naval blunder of 1914 – underestimating the submarine.

INTERMISSION: 1919–1938

Breaching the peace

IF THE GERMANS thought the Armistice was tough, the Treaty of Versailles which formally ended the war in June 1919 was harder still. The Germans were effectively told in that month, as they jibbed at signing after seven months of negotiation, to take it – or leave it and face a renewal of hostilities. The treaty was no harsher on the Germans than they had been on the Russians in the Treaty of Brest-Litovsk in March 1918. The Allies forbade the Germans from manufacturing or acquiring military aircraft and submarines. Their Army was limited to 100,000 and the Navy to 15,000 men including 1,500 officers. They were to have no more than six armoured ships displacing up to 10,000 tons each; they could have six cruisers up to 6,000 tons, twelve destroyers of up to 800 tons and twelve torpedo-boats up to 200 tons. Anglo-American proposals to outlaw the submarine altogether were scuppered by the French, who insisted that this weapon of weaker powers should remain available to them, provided it was used in accordance with prewar conventions.

Britain put seven submariners, including Max Valentiner, on its list of eighteen Germans wanted for war crimes. The German authorities added two junior U-boat officers involved in the sinking by *U86* (Helmut Patzig, listed by the British) of the hospital ship *Llandovery Castle* west of Ireland in June 1918, whose survivors were fired upon. The Reich Supreme Court at Leipzig tried the five officers traced out of the total of nine, gave the *U86* officers four years each and the others up to ten months each, in June 1921.

The Allies sent a Control Commission to Germany to administer the application of the treaty; in September 1924 the Naval Section, satisfied that its work was done, was dissolved. Most submarines found in German yards had been shared among the victors, while the rest and all partly built boats were broken up.

It is necessary to bear in mind when considering the inter-war years that, while postwar German politics quickly subsided into uproar and then violence between converging right-wing forces and a fatally divided left, virtually all Germans regarded Versailles as iniquitous, worthy only of subversion by any means. Reparations, heaped high by the vengeful French, were justified by a clause laying the blame for the war at Germany's door. The payment burden was eased by printing money, which led to the runaway inflation of 1923. But currency reform, American-led easing of reparations and a revival of industry brought a brief flowering of hope to the Weimar Republic, the fascinating but fragile first German democracy, until the Wall Street crash of October 1929 and the great economic depression which followed. A weakened Germany was affected more than any other industrial economy by the consequent social problems, which gave Hitler and the Nazis their opportunity.

Abroad, Germany was the first country to grant diplomatic recognition to the Soviet Union, by the Treaty of Rapallo in 1922. In the same year the French, alarmed by this rapport between pariahs, used Germany's tardiness with reparations and its appeal for a moratorium as excuses to occupy the Ruhr (the rest of the Rhineland was already occupied by them and the British). German nationalism and hatred of Versailles were only encouraged by this move. But the campaign of passive resistance – an unlimited general strike in the Rhineland during which the German government paid the workers by printing money, the immediate cause of the "Great Inflation" – had to be abandoned by the Stresemann government in September 1923. Yet the currency reform successfully ensued, as did the softening of reparations under the Dawes Plan, backed by American credits. Five years after the war the Versailles Treaty had finally been made workable. The French withdrew from the Ruhr in August 1925; the Rhineland remained demilitarised.

President Wilson had proposed the League of Nations to run the postwar world order. But the US Congress lapsed into isolationism and did not join, while Germany and Russia were at first excluded. The organisation fell apart in the late 1930s when it failed to make any impression on a series of international crises. These included Japanese aggression in Manchuria; the Italian conquest of Abyssinia; and the Army revolt against the republican government of Spain. The latter led to a dreadful civil war: the Soviet Union inadequately aided the government, the Fascist powers successfully supported General Franco and the democracies pursued a feeble policy of "non-intervention".

Germany and Russia were excluded from the naval conferences called by the Anglo-Saxon powers between the wars in an attempt to limit the strategic armaments of the time. Big-gun ships retained this status despite the far greater depredations caused by submarines during the war, and rapid developments in aircraft (and carriers) after it. Negotiations led to fixed tonnage-ratios among the principal naval powers: America, Britain, France, Italy and Japan. The key ratio was the Anglo-American-Japanese one, as Japan fell out with its wartime allies in its relentless pursuit of national ambitions. So did Italy. Meanwhile Russia quietly decided to acquire the largest national force of submarines in the world; and Germany resolved, long before Hitler, to remain the builder of the world's best submarines, Versailles or no.

To summarise the postwar positions of the once and future enemies on submarines: the Anglo-Americans tried to outlaw or at least to restrict them, confident that Asdic or sonar offered a complete defence should they ever be deployed in strength again; meanwhile the principal wartime losers, Germany and Russia, respectively put their faith in quality and quantity of new submarines. While the west held to its belief that it had overcome the submarine threat, the Germans secretly preserved their technological lead, loyally aided, as in so many other breaches of the military provisions of Versailles, by Stalin's Soviet Union.

In many respects the greatest beneficiary of the First World War was Japan. It had been awarded the "certificate of respectability" of an alliance with the British in 1902 – the end of the Empire's "splendid isolation" – because Germany's growing power and ambition forced an already comparatively declining Britain to concentrate its naval strength in European waters. The Japanese suffered negligible casualties in delivering the promised assistance, taking over German colonies in China and the Pacific, escorting Australian and New Zealand trooping convoys and finally sending destroyers to the Mediterranean. Their reward was not only permanent occupation, under League of Nations mandate, of several of the ex-German island territories in the Pacific, some of which were of great strategic value, but also a seat at the top table at Versailles.

Any feeling in Japan that the 1868 revolution, which committed it to taking on the West at its own game (whether in industrialisation or imperialism), had thus been vindicated soon went sour. The first "non-white" world power was treated as second class by the West, both at Versailles and Geneva, seat of the League. Insofar as the leading powers, America, Britain and France, had a war aim other than putting an overweening Germany in its place, it had been self-determination for small nations. This turned out to mean small *European* nations: Belgium,

Finland and the new states which emerged in eastern Europe and the Balkans in 1919. But the "big three" unanimously viewed those with yellow or darker skins as naturally subject peoples. The British went so far after the war as to liberate part of the United Kingdom itself – the future Irish Republic – but gave no thought to freeing India, which had sent an Army to the Western Front, or "their" third of Africa. The French held on to Indochina and their own third of Africa. The Americans found this kind of colonialism, which they had thrown off in 1776, repugnant, but kept the Philippines and other territories seized from Spain in 1898. They also viewed China as a natural target for economic imperialism, thus clashing head-on with Japanese ambition.

Japan's burning desire to copy the West had already made it a major naval power; but it also wanted a large colonial empire, the one talisman of world-power status even more important than a powerful fleet. Victories over China in Korea in 1895, and then Russia in 1905, followed by the cheap winnings of 1914–18, hugely enhanced the status of Army and Navy. In a country where further constitutional reform (in 1889) had given the General and Naval Staffs a status parallel rather than subordinate to that of the Cabinet, takeover of the government itself by the generals, abetted by the admirals of the junior service, gradually followed. These leaders may have copied western military institutions and methods, but they also harked back to the bushido code of the samurai warrior, or those parts of it which suited their growing lust for power. This code decreed all to be fair in war, including surprise attack without declaration of war, and viewed surrender, retreat and even being captured as, quite literally, capital crimes. If an enemy committed them he could expect to be summarily executed; if a Japanese did so, he was required to commit suicide. Poetry and calligraphy were encouraged, absolute obedience demanded and independent thought outlawed. This ultra-machismo among the real rulers of Japan (the worshipped Emperor was a figurehead and the civilian government was hamstrung) made it very dangerous to thwart them. Merely to disagree with Japan's stated position on an issue was taken as an insult and a national humiliation. Compromise was anathema because it amounted to surrender. Not to prevail in "negotiation" meant loss of face.

This terrifying intransigence, first met at Versailles where the Japanese rightly saw themselves as victims of racialist discrimination, soon became all too familiar on the world stage. It was on view again when Charles Evans Hughes, the US Secretary of State, invited nine nations, including the five leading maritime powers, to Washington in November 1921. This conference was the first attempt to meet the Versailles call for general disarmament, in addition to what had been imposed on Germany. Germany and Russia being uninvited, the conference soon became an attempt to contain Japan.

Budgetary constraints on the Americans and (especially) the British led them to propose limits on numbers and tonnages of capital ships and naval construction, so as broadly to retain existing strengths. The two leading navies wanted new dreadnoughts but political objections in both countries prevailed. Britain, which had once maintained first a "two-power standard" for the Royal Navy (as strong as the next two navies combined) and then Germany plus sixty per cent, now accepted a "one-power standard"; equality with the strongest foreign fleet. That meant the United States, which already had a distinct edge in modernity and whose catchword became "a navy second to none". As his predecessor, Lord Wemyss, had done at Versailles, Admiral Beatty, now First Sea Lord, proposed a ban on submarines, only to be frustrated by another French veto.

The Washington Conference did quite well as a first postwar attempt to regulate and defuse international rivalries by negotiation. It produced nine treaties and a dozen resolutions. The nine powers, including China, agreed to respect each other's interests in that country, which had the effect of limiting Japan's while encouraging America's. This was to become a principal cause of the war between them.

The five main naval powers signed a treaty fixing the ratio of capital-ship tonnage at 5:5:3 for America, Britain and Japan, and 1.65 each for France and Italy. No ship was to displace more than 35,000 tons, and there was to be a ten-year "naval holiday" during which no new ones were laid down. For the three leading navies this entailed cancelling orders, dismantling partly built, and scrapping commissioned ships. The ratio for aircraft carriers was to be $10:10:6:4\frac{1}{2}:4\frac{1}{2}$. Cruisers were not limited in numbers of total tonnage but only in individual size, up to 10,000 tons, and in armament (eight-inch guns); but "experimental" guns of greater calibre were permitted. This "limitation" merely led to a race to build as many as possible. Merchant ships could be designated auxiliary cruisers and readied in peacetime for fitting guns of up to six-inch calibre in wartime. No limits were placed on smaller warships, including submarines; but the latter were once more subjected to the prewar code of prize rules by another treaty.

The Japanese Navy promptly split into "treaty" and "fleet" factions, the former for and the latter against "Washington". The fleet faction all but went to the barricades for 10:10:7 rather than 5:5:3, but its underlying view was that any limit on the right of the Emperor (i.e. his admirals) to build any ships he liked was, tediously, an insult and a national humiliation. Japan had until 17 February 1925 to scrap ten ships and stop work on six more, to come down to a capital strength of 300,000 tons. The Americans scrapped fifteen and stopped eleven while the British scrapped twenty-four and stopped four, to get down to 500,000 tons apiece. France and Italy did not need to scrap any ships to achieve their targets. The naval treaty was to remain in force until the end of 1936. Its ratification at Westminster formally ended the world supremacy of the Royal Navy which, because of the greater average age of its battlefleet, was effectively overtaken by the US Navy in 1925. But the fiction of "equality" was maintained with increasing desperation by the British service.

The gap widened further as the Americans pulled ahead in naval aviation (a field in which Japan, however, far outstripped the US by 1930). This British failure was to prove extremely damaging in the Second World War, not least in the second struggle with the U-boats: hence the claim that the foundation of the RAF was the Royal Navy's worst defeat. On the formation of the world's first autonomous Air Force on All Fools' Day 1918, the Navy lost about 2,500 aircraft and 55,000 personnel of the Royal Naval Air Service. The RAF did form Coastal Command for landbased work with the Navy, but this opened two decades of inter-service wrangling about priorities, roles, manning, tactics, equipment, aircraft types, training, supply and maintenance. Another struggle broke out over the Fleet Air Arm, which flew and maintained Britain's modest and backward collection of carrier aircraft. The Air Ministry naturally gave precedence to RAF Bomber and Fighter Commands whenever it could. The first chief of Coastal Command, Air Vice-Marshal A.V. Vyvyan, in a memorandum to the Admiralty on the first anniversary of the Armistice, saw anti-submarine patrols and aerial convoy escort as undesirable because "purely defensive". Already the incalculably costly lesson of the importance of convoy in both checking and attacking the enemy at sea was being seriously eroded from a new direction.

The United States did not acquire an autonomous air force until after the Second World War, which did not prevent it from deploying the most effective strategic-bombing and naval air forces in that conflict. As the air-marshals and admirals argued about aviation in London, US Navy captains in their forties and fifties, such as Ernest J. King and William F. Halsey, queued to earn their "wings" in order to qualify for command of the new aircraft-carriers, the contemporary "smart career-move" in their more go-ahead service.

It was not only the fledgling RAF in Britain which seemed to want to draw a veil over the effects and lessons of the almost victorious U-boat onslaught. The Admiralty did not even bother to commission a history of the disastrous campaign. The shipping and cargoes lost to the U-boat drained Britain's wealth and helped to ensure the transfer of naval (and world) primacy across the Atlantic. A civil engineer temporarily attached to the Admiralty, Commander Rollo Appleyard, RNVR, had the wit to analyse convoy effectiveness and tactics from when the system started in 1917. One of his most important findings was that bigger convoys were safer than small ones. Largely unread (because largely unreadable), *The Elements of Convoy Defence in Submarine Warfare*, instead of being classed as essential reading for all sea-going officers, gathered dust as an Admiralty "confidential book" and was scrapped altogether in 1939, just when most needed.

But serious sea-trials of Asdic began in great secrecy in July 1920. A year later the main teething troubles seemed to have been resolved and euphoria swept the Admiralty. Despite the fact that not one exercise in protecting a mercantile convoy against submarine or aircraft attack took place in the Royal Navy between 1918 and 1939, and that Asdic could not detect a submarine on the surface (or even submerged if in the immediate vicinity of the searching warship), the submarine problem was regarded as solved. Large numbers of admirals reverted to their disastrous antipathy to convoy itself as "infra dig" because purely defensive. ASW remained a poor relation in Admiralty terms; fortunately a cadre of officers expert in Asdic was available by 1928. The Americans did practise convoy protection; they also tried their sonar on exercise, and did not rate it as highly as the British their Asdic. The air threat, especially from torpedo-bombers, was also underrated and/or regarded as checkmated by the new naval anti-aircraft guns, of which the Admiralty bought far too few. As before the war, the underfunded and underappreciated British submarine service reverted to being a world apart from the rest of the Navy, which showed little interest in its potential and hardly ever manoeuvred with the boats. Once again the Admiralty took the view, when the German Navy began its revival, that the main threat to British commerce was the surface raider.

The next attempt at arms limitation, the 1927 Geneva Disarmament Conference, began in June at the League of Nations. Its authority had just been enhanced by the accession of Germany, relieved of the Allied Control Commission in January 1927. The central naval issue was cruisers. Britain wanted recognition of its special needs in policing a worldwide Empire and protecting the world's largest merchant fleet as justification for exceeding the cruiser ceiling of 300,000 tons proposed by the Americans. Cruisers were the principal area of Anglo-American rivalry since the Washington Conference had not restricted their total tonnages or numbers but only their size. On this occasion the Japanese were conciliatory and radical at the same time. They disingenuously proposed an indefinite moratorium on all naval construction, in the secret knowledge that from 1924 they had been building mighty cruisers which exceeded the 10,000-ton Washington limit by a third.

Their delegation nevertheless stood on the sidelines as Britain and America fought to a standstill on cruisers. The former wanted a limit of 7,500 tons per ship, proposing seventy for the Royal Navy, forty-seven for the US and twenty-one for Japan. The Americans, with Japan and vast Pacific distances in mind, wanted to keep the 10,000-ton limit and the 300,000 tonnage ceiling, which would have left the British with under forty cruisers, half the minimum they felt they needed. The conference ended in August without agreement.

But the atmosphere improved a year later on the signature in Paris of the Kellogg-Briand Pact – the International Treaty for the Renunciation of War – by fifteen nations (including Japan, Germany and Italy), later accepted by forty-seven others. The idea was to outlaw aggressive war as an instrument of policy: the economic repercussions of the Wall Street crash in October 1929 also encouraged disarmament, if only to save money.

The accession of a Quaker President in the shape of Herbert Hoover and a pacifist Labour Prime Minister, Ramsay MacDonald, at this uncertain period led to another attempt at arms limitation: the London Naval Conference in January 1930. Present were the five leading maritime powers; but this time the British and Americans were almost hand in glove while the Japanese were hell-bent on moving up from 5:5:3 to 10:10:7. Rivalry between France and Mussolini's Fascist Italy in the Mediterranean made the likelihood of agreement between them remote.

But the cruiser problem was solved by a triangular compromise. Britain abandoned its demand for seventy and accepted fifty. The Americans accepted for themselves an overall tonnage limit of 323,500 (339,000 for the British), a new category of 7,500-ton, six-inch cruiser, as well as the Washington 10,000-tonner with eight-inch guns, of which they were to have eighteen. Japan accepted a 5:3 ratio in the latter and extracted 10:7 in the lighter cruisers. Destroyers were limited to five-inch guns and 1,500 tons (except for flotilla leaders, 3,850 tons) and an overall tonnage of 150,000 for each of the two leading navies. The naval holiday was extended for six years (except for replacement and modernisation). Britain and America limited themselves to fifteen dreadnoughts each, and Japan to ten.

The three leading powers accepted parity in submarine tonnage (not numbers) at 52,700 tons each, with a generous upper "limit" of 2,000 tons per boat and a maximum gun-calibre of 5.1 inches or 130 millimetres. Parity in submarines was another boost for Japan. France as usual refused to countenance abolition as once again proposed by the Anglo-Americans. Submarines were yet again unrealistically subjected to the same prize rules as surface ships. The five-power Naval Treaty was signed on 22 April; like the Washington Pact it would expire at the end of 1936. Its most important consequences were political; a positive sea-change in Anglo-American relations and a regrettably shortlived victory for moderation in Japan. It was also the last successful exercise in naval arms limitation between the wars.

The General Disarmament Conference foreshadowed by Versailles finally opened in Geneva in February 1932. The auguries were poor. The British proposed reducing the future sizes of all classes of ship and abolishing naval and military aircraft; the Americans suggested a thirty per cent overall cut in armaments worldwide. The Germans demanded equal rights with the other major powers, which meant abandoning the already overstretched special limitations imposed by Versailles; when thwarted they walked out in September. Japan finally left the League in February 1933 after being condemned as the aggressor in Manchuria. Hitler came to power in January 1933, and in March Franklin D. Roosevelt entered the White House. Hitler tore up Versailles in May by giving two years' notice of renunciation, formally withdrew from the Geneva Conference in October and from the League itself shortly thereafter. The conference dragged on until June 1934, when it was adjourned indefinitely, without agreement.

Alarmed by German, Japanese and Italian naval construction, the British had by the end of 1933 abandoned their own "ten-year rule" (not to be confused with the ten-year naval holiday agreed at Washington). It required every defence budget to proceed from the assumption that there would be no war for ten years – an idea of Churchill's when Chancellor of the Exchequer. For the sake of greater numbers Britain concentrated on building light (5,000-ton) cruisers with six-inch guns within the overall tonnage limit. In the United States Roosevelt signed the National Industrial Recovery Act, which included large-scale naval construction and modernisation among economic measures (the New Deal) to counter the Depression. Two carriers, four cruisers, nineteen destroyers and four submarines were ordered by Washington in 1933 while the British kept to their pattern of the past few years with three cruisers, nine destroyers, five sloops (light escorts) and three submarines.

In 1934 both countries launched naval programmes unprecedented since the war, in all categories from battleships to submarines: the

American programme was inevitably much larger. The British opted for one carrier, four cruisers, nine destroyers, six sloops and three submarines; the Americans ordered seven battleships, one carrier, seven cruisers, eighty-nine destroyers and thirty-seven submarines. Japan, which had outbuilt both powers almost every year since 1918, contented itself with a carrier conversion, a seaplane carrier, two destroyers and one submarine while Germany laid down two battlecruisers, one cruiser, nine destroyers and twelve submarines. France ordered a battlecruiser and eleven destroyers while Italy ordered two battleships, two cruisers and four destroyers. Whereas the Americans ordered nothing more until their next great naval programme of 1938, the British outbuilt any other nation over the last five years of peace. Yet Britain came nowhere near achieving the strength needed to cope with the nightmare which prompted this acceleration: a possible combination of Germany and Italy and Japan against it, a much greater threat than had faced its larger Navy of 1914. From 1932 every destroyer got Asdic (as did various other categories of ship), but very little attention was paid to training. Most destroyers were assigned to fleet work; the sloops alone were specifically intended for convoy escort. Only in 1939 did the Admiralty wake up to the escort shortage and order twenty light destroyers and fifty-six corvettes (adapted from an old whaling-ship design) for the purpose. When war broke out the Royal Navy had 220 ships with Asdic: 165 destroyers, twenty trawlers and thirty-five escorts.

Hitler's notice to cancel Versailles took effect in May 1935. In June Britain broke ranks with the 1918 victors to connive at this annulment, with results which will be examined below. Meanwhile London, concerned by the fact that naval building had accelerated and that the Washington and London treaties were due to expire at the end of 1936, invited eleven nations to another naval conference: the five leading naval powers plus six British Commonwealth countries. They convened in London in November 1935 and were deadlocked within days. Japan withdrew in January 1936, rejecting all limitations on its naval construction and confirming its two years' notice of intent, given in 1934, to renounce the Washington and London limitations when they expired. The Germans were not invited (but were sent a copy of the draft treaty) because the French were angry about the annulment of Versailles and would not share a room with them; France also once again vetoed a British proposal to outlaw submarines. With one exception the results were meagre: some more tinkering with cruiser and carrier tonnage limits, sanction of the sixteen-inch gun for battleships (an American idea), the retention of the 2,000-ton limit on submarines, a ban on new construction between 8,000 and 17,000 tons. The treaty was signed in March 1936.

But there was a special protocol open to universal subscription: a complete ban on unrestricted submarine warfare against merchant shipping, to which Russia, Germany and Japan acceded, together with all other significant naval powers among a total of forty nations, in the course of 1936. Like the treaty, it was to come into effect in July 1937.

In the same year the Admiralty won a battle of crucial importance: it regained control of the Fleet Air Arm, with effect from May 1939, after twenty years of RAF neglect. By that time the Air Arm mustered barely 400 aircraft, mostly obsolete, whereas the US Navy had 2,000. British carriers were well behind Japanese and American in quality and effectiveness. Fortunately for Britain, Germany and Italy never commissioned any. Coastal Command remained under RAF control.

Apart from desultory arguments for and against abolition, submarines were a secondary issue at the conferences. A ceiling was eventually put on them, but only after and because all other main categories of warship had been limited. As memories of the stupendous losses to U-boats faded and confidence in anti-submarine technology grew, and as the leading naval powers became embroiled in arcane arguments about experimental guns and cruiser tonnages, the submarine was once again underestimated more and more. The world's admirals reverted to their fixation on big guns and dreadnoughts, endangered now not only by underwater warfare but also by aircraft. As early as July 1921 the American Brigadier-General "Billy" Mitchell sank a confiscated German dreadnought by aerial bombardment in twenty-five minutes. Aircraft had shown by 1918, to those who wished to see, how much they could inhibit submarines by their mere presence. That too was largely forgotten by the gunnery enthusiasts who ran all the major navies. In Japan, which had originally modelled its Navy on the British, the submarine was regarded as unmanly. So, of course, was convoy. In Germany, however, submarine technology was secretly forging ahead.

The story of the U-boat between the wars is little known but full of official skulduggery and deceit. The universal German contempt for Versailles gave comfort to those who set out to undermine it before the ink was dry on the treaty and encouraged the growth of amorality in political life. There is no more spectacular example of this trend than the secret development of the next generation of U-boats.

The records show that Germany surrendered eight U-cruisers, sixty-two U-boats, sixty-four "UBs" (coastal) and forty-two "UCs" (minelayers) to Britain for sharing among the five principal Allies. All of them adopted features from these boats in their later submarines. The treaty made no mention of blueprints and construction drawings, which the German yards retained, together with access to engineers and skilled workers.

The first customer was Japan, which acquired the blueprints for a U-cruiser and an ocean-going minelayer by 1920. The Japanese boats *I1–I13* and *I21–I24* were built in a Japanese yard under the personal supervision of Dr Hans Techel, doyen of German submarine designers and a few of his Krupp colleagues. A former U-boat skipper supervised the sea-trials.

Argentina invited Michelsen's successor as U-boat chief in Flanders, ex-Commander Karl Bartenbach, and two German designers to supervise the construction of a ten-strong submarine service in an Argentinian yard by a Kruppled consortium from 1921. In 1922 Italy and Sweden availed themselves of the expertise of German submarine designers. Spain was interested. Business appeared to be on the verge of booming. But Article 191 of Versailles said: "The construction and acquisition of any kind of submarine, even for trade purposes, is forbidden to Germany." How could Germany coordinate the exploitation of its technical supremacy when it was illegal to restart submarine construction inside the country?

The answer was to move to the neighbouring Netherlands. In July 1922 the innocuously named Ingenieurskantoor voor Scheepsbouw (IvS – engineer-office for shipbuilding) was formed with a nominal capital of 12,000 guilders, put up in equal parts by the AG Vulkan yard in Hamburg and the two Krupp-owned yards, Germaniawerft, Kiel, and AG Weser, Bremen. The technical director was Dr Techel and the commercial director was ex-Commander Ulrich Blum, late of the U-boat service. As they waited for the Dutch company registration to pass the bureaucratic and political obstacles, they worked quietly in a temporary office at the Germaniawerft, building up a technical team.

But Argentina changed its mind, Italy lost interest and fierce competition was developing in Spain over the country's grand plan to acquire forty submarines. *Kapitänleutnant* Wilhelm Canaris of the new Reichsmarine (Navy), who spoke Spanish, tried to win a share of this bonanza for IvS against America, British, French and Italian bids. The intimate relationship between the rump German Navy and IvS is demonstrated by the fact that the Navy itself persuaded Blohm und Voss, the Hamburg shipbuilders also dabbling in the submarine market, to assign their licence to install MAN diesels, which the Spaniards favoured, to IvS. But Spain too changed its mind in 1925 as IvS finally set up shop in The Hague, after failing to win a single firm order from fifty-three tenders.

The best hope now was for two small boats for Turkey, to be built at the Fijenoord yard in Rotterdam.

The three German yards behind IvS were in no position to boost the company's chances by providing the large subsidies it clearly needed for a breakthrough. The only other likely source was the German Navy, which was very keen to keep German construction skills alive. Since it could not for political reasons afford to be seen backing IvS, some of the secret funds available to the "Sea Transport Section" of the Navy, led by Captain Walter Lohmann, were channelled into IvS through a German dummy company set up by the Navy Office: Mentor Bilanz, purporting to be an accounting consultancy. It now became the fourth shareholder in IvS. Its director, it need hardly be said, was another former U-boat captain, but the real mentor was newly retired Lieutenant Hans Schottky, who was to liaise between Mentor, IvS and the Navy. At the same time Lohmann set up a front company called TebeG-mbH, German acronym for "technical advice and supply company limited", whose real purpose was to enable Germany to build submarines in the event of war. It was headed by a retired junior captain. Both front companies brazenly kept their registered offices in the same Navy building in Berlin. At the same time Captain Arno Spindler, a former U-boat flotilla commander still in the service, was given charge of a new "anti-submarine defence" section in the Navy Office, to lay the foundations of a new U-boat arm. Independently of IvS, Mentor Bilanz in 1927 set up a "technical department" – really the Navy's U-boat construction office-in-waiting.

Thus encouraged by the Navy and its secret submarine network, IvS got a firm order from Turkey for two medium submarines, derived from the "UBIII" type of larger coastal boat, displacing 505/620 tons. Both were completed at the Fijenoord yard by March 1927 and exhaustively tested at sea by "retired" German submariners before making their way independently to Turkey a year later. The German ex-officers who delivered them stayed on to found a submarine school.

In 1926 Finland ordered three boats, advanced versions of the "UCIII" design (a 493/715-ton minelayer), for construction in a Finnish yard under German supervisors, including Schottky. The contract took more than three years to complete because of the harsh winters and local inexperience. The Finns placed another order with IvS for a ninety-nine-ton minelayer in 1929, completed in the following year under Schottky's supervision.

Protracted negotiations with Spain from 1926 to 1929 led to the construction, under IvS auspices in Rotterdam (with engines and parts direct from Germany) for final assembly in Cadiz, of E1, a boat based on the experimental "UG" design of 1918. The establishment of the

Spanish Republic in 1932 meant that Madrid never bought the boat, financed by the German Navy from secret rearmament funds. But the experience was held to be worth the five million marks spent.

In the meantime, however, attempts to boost secret military funds by speculation led to press exposés, questions in the Reichstag and the resignation of the defence minister, Otto Gessler, early in 1928. The focus of the scandal was Captain Lohmann of Sea Transport, but the furore was about misuse of public funds, not secret submarine programmes. TebeG and Mentor Bilanz were wound up, Lohmann resigned and his department was abolished. When the dust settled, a new dummy company, Igewit GmbH (acronym for "engineer-office for economics and technology company limited") was quietly formed by the Naval Staff later in the year, directed by ex-Lieutenant Schottky, who also tidily succeeded the promoted Spindler as head of the "anti"-submarine section in 1929.

The Finns, satisfied with their first four German-built boats, in 1930 ordered a 250-ton, single-hulled coastal submarine from IvS (in business as before, ceasing to trade only on the liberation of the Netherlands in May 1945). It took three years to build and was Igewit's first design, loosely based on the "UF" experimental type of 1917 and codenamed "Lilliput". Once again German officers and ratings received clandestine training for submarine operation in the new "torpedo and signals school" at Flensburg, north Germany, before the boat's sea-trials, which they conducted.

This type, the larger one built for the Finns, and the Spanish E1 were regarded until 1932 as prototypes of the three classes the German Navy would order in the event of war; thirty-six each of the first two types and twelve of the third. But in autumn 1932, just before the Nazis came to power, the Navy and the defence ministry secretly decided on a six-year naval reconstruction plan, to include up to sixteen U-boats. For this a submarine development department, disguised as the "experimental motorboat section" (MVB), was set up. Plans were laid for building three types: MVBI (the Spanish E1), MVBII (the Finnish coastal model) and a third midway in size between the two, of about 500 tons. Throughout this period the German Navy's Torpedo Inspectorate had been working on new torpedo types, ostensibly for surface ships. The 53.3-centimetre (twenty-one-inch) "G7a" and "G7e" types were developed, the former powered by internal combustion and the latter by electricity. Unlike the submarines that would carry them, these missiles were by no means the best of their kind, as will be seen.

It is surely clear by now that Hitler's naval rearmament plans were not plucked out of thin air and did not represent a new departure or a decline in German standards of obedience to the Treaty of Versailles. The new element was the stridency with which the plans were proclaimed. Germany no longer concealed its rearmament.

The clandestine activities of German submarine builders and their alliance with "former" and serving naval officers could hardly be concealed altogether from the erstwhile allies of Versailles, who preferred in the main to turn a blind eye. But the submarine activity was only part of a much broader German interest in all areas of armament, whether naval, military or aeronautic. Before considering developments following the arrival of Hitler, we shall survey the context within which the foundation of a second U-boat fleet was laid, not least because it affected the plans of the Royal Navy and other foreign forces.

After Versailles the Reichsmarine had just 15,000 men but hardly any serviceable ships. But within a year the Navy gradually returned to running warships. Some older vessels within the Versailles limits were recommissioned and in 1921 the first order was placed for a 6,000-ton cruiser – the *Emden*. One 200-ton torpedo-boat was ordered in 1924, five more and another 6,000-ton cruiser in 1925 and six of the former and two of the latter in 1926, but nothing at all in 1927. The 1928 estimates, however, presented late in 1927, included provision for a "Panzerschiff (armoured ship) A". This purported to conform with the Versailles limit of 10,000 tons, and voluntarily (Germany not being a party to the 1922 pact) with the Washington ceiling. The eleven-inch, rather than eight-inch, guns of the future *Deutschland* were permissible as "experimental". They were in fact no more than updated versions of the trusty twenty-eight-centimetre gun of the High Seas Fleet, fitted in two triple turrets fore and aft. The ship had high speed and medium armour and was a triumph of German shipbuilding: only three ships in the British Navy could both outrun and outgun this first of three German "pocket battleships". They were not as miraculous as they seemed since their displacement was knowingly understated by a cool 3,000 tons.

There was uproar at home and dismay abroad. The British took the view that this super-cruiser could only have one role: as a commerce raider, one so powerful that every convoy would need a capital ship to protect it. The world at large saw the trio as symbols of Germany's will to rearm. In Germany "armoured ship A" became a bone of contention between the right, which wanted rearmament and an end to the country's diplomatic impotence, and the left, ever leery of the military and of defence spending. But the keel was laid in 1928, along with that of a light cruiser. In the same year Vice-Admiral Erich Raeder, commander in the Baltic, was made full admiral and Chief of the Naval Command (there being no "Naval Staff" after Versailles). Although never a sub-mariner, he believed that unrestricted U-boat warfare would be essential in another war with Britain.

Under his autocratic command the German Navy settled down after the postwar upheavals, avoiding rows with the government without surrendering its expansionist ambitions. Armoured ships B and C – the future *Admiral Scheer* and *Admiral Graf Spee* – were laid down in 1931 and 1932. But budgetary constraints saw to it that no further large ship was ordered until the Nazis took over in 1933.

In November 1932 General Kurt von Schleicher, the defence minister, sanctioned a secret naval reconstruction programme, referred to above; there was to be a small but ultra-modern battlefleet as well as sixteen U-boats and other light craft by 1938. A submarine depot was to be set up at Kiel and 100 officers and men were earmarked to start up the resurrected U-boat arm. Unlike almost every other state institution in Germany under the Nazis, the Navy had no need of *Gleichschaltung* (forcing into line): in marked contrast with the Army, the Navy of the Weimar Republic seamlessly became the Navy of the Third Reich, under the same unpurged commanders: only the name was changed, from Reichsmarine to Kriegsmarine (war navy).

Adolf Hitler, as leader of the largest party in the Reichstag, was demo-cratically invited on 30 January 1933 by the senile President Paul von Hindenburg to be Chancellor of Germany. He appointed General Werner von Blomberg as defence minister; and three days later addressed the most senior generals and admirals for two hours at the home of General Kurt von Hammerstein, chief of the Army Command since 1930. He declared that there would be no challenge to the military from the huge SA (Sturmabteilung), the Nazi Party's uniformed militia; but there would be massive rearmament at maximum speed. On the same day Blomberg sanctioned the inauguration, under the nominal auspices of the Torpedo Inspectorate, of a secret submarine training centre – dis-informatively styled the "anti-submarine defence school" – at Kiel, for the crews of the first two U-boats of the second generation, whose construction was scheduled to start on 1 October.

But Hitler himself halted the laying of the first two keels. It was not a cancellation: he had every intention of rearming regardless of Versailles, but the secret deferment of the no less secret new U-boat programme was the first of many moves to avoid alarming Britain. His plan to acquire *Lebensraum* (living space) in eastern Europe was enough by itself to alarm the British as a threat to the peace they were determined to maintain in Europe after the horror of 1914–18. The only German naval order in 1933 was for another light cruiser.

Hitler met Raeder in June 1934 to inflate the five-year naval building programme described above. Two more pocket battleships – "armoured ships D and E" – were uprated to full-size battleships with three times the original tonnage (the British classified the future *Scharnhorst* and *Gneisenau* as battlecruisers because of their speed); two super-battleships, armoured ships F and G (*Bismarck* and *Tirpitz*), were added, each of more than 45,000 tons unladen. A sixth light cruiser and nine destroyers helped to make 1934 the most important year in German naval shipbuilding for more than two decades. There were also to be two aircraft-carriers, four heavy cruisers, more light cruisers and destroyers, plus forty-six submarines. Nor was this the end of Hitler's naval notions.

The ever-changing submarine programme was top secret, but this very fact meant that any leak could have become a diplomatic disaster in the first months of the new regime. Nothing, for example, could be allowed to pose even the remotest threat to the intended effect of Hitler's speech of 21 May 1935, in which he planned to make Britain an offer it could not refuse.

Hitler had put the German Army on notice to treble itself to 300,000 by October 1934. His Minister of Aviation, Hermann Göring, set up the innocent-sounding "League for Air Sport" in which military pilots, trained in Russia courtesy of Stalin (see below), passed on their knowledge to volunteers as excellent aircraft were built in secret for a new Luftwaffe. Krupp increased production of armour and big guns; IG Farben, the chemical cartel, pressed ahead with plants for synthetic petroleum and rubber products. The Americans (but not their President) were in isolationist mood and took little official notice. The Anglo-French response was appeasement, a policy whose popularity in countries which had lost a generation of young men in the trenches should not be underestimated (nor was it ignoble to want to avoid a repetition, a fact on which Hitler played with consummate skill until he overreached himself).

Columns of tanks were being driven through the crumbling edifice of Versailles, but London and Paris in February 1935 offered Germany equality in armament and a general European settlement. This would have included an "eastern Locarno", extending to eastern Europe the agreement on Germany's western borders and on settling disputes enshrined in the Locarno Treaty of 1925, Hitler, with *Lebensraum* in mind, was evasive but not negative. Anglo-French anxieties were revealed only one month later by Britain's plan for judicious naval rearmament in response to world trends and a French decision to lengthen conscription from one and a half to two years to cover the wartime decline in the birthrate. Hitler's carefully calculated response was to snub the British Foreign Secretary, Sir John Simon, who wanted to see him; to let Göring announce to the London *Daily Mail* the birth of the new Luftwaffe; and to proclaim his plan for a standing Army of half a million.

Britain and France met Mussolini's representatives at Stresa in Italy in April to protest against this slighting of Versailles. On 21 May Hitler went to the Reichstag and bawled Germany's peaceful intentions at an all too credulous world. He specifically renounced any intention of repeating the Kaiser's blunder in taking on Britain, with its special imperial needs, in naval building. He offered to "limit" the new German Navy to thirty-five per cent of the British. Nobody was churlish (or alert) enough at the time to point out that, so far from making cuts, Germany would have to spend hundreds of millions of marks over ten years to reach this level. But when the offer was formally put in June the British fell over themselves to accept. The result was the Anglo-German Naval Agreement of 1935. The British did not inform their Stresa interlocutors in advance of their intentions to sign a pact which, as the first armament pact between one of the 1918 victors and Hitler, administered the *coup de grâce* to Versailles.

Germany was allowed five battleships, twenty-one cruisers and sixty-four destroyers (strengths it never attained, even in wartime). U-boat strength was not to exceed forty-five per cent of Britain's; but in circumstances of special threat the Germans could go to 100 per cent!

Meanwhile, far from the conference table and the political rally, U-boat plans were modified again: two small, 250-ton U-boats (now restyled type IIA) were to be completed in 1934, four in 1935, six more and two large 800-tonners (type IA) in 1936, to be repeated in 1937. In 1934 plans were revised yet again: there were to be ten IAs and eighteen IIAs in commission by 1938. But from the end of 1933 submarine components were being sent from the Ruhr via IvS in Holland to Kiel, a subterfuge which eliminated the risk of discovery through transport overland within Germany. The (unexpectedly lengthy) training of the first class of submariners went ahead as preparations were made for assembling the new U-boats in a secluded, covered shed at Kiel where work started on 1 February 1935. The world was stunned when the First Flotilla was paraded at the end of September, complete with three spanking new coastal boats and freshly appointed commandant, Captain Karl Dönitz, aged forty-four. Barely three months had passed since the Anglo-German pact.

*

The curious, double-edged relationship between Germany and Russia remained very much alive after Hitler's arrival. When the KPD, the German Communist Party, was formed in the early 1920s, the Russians saw it as their natural fifth column for the internal subversion of Germany, the only country with the potential to challenge the desired Soviet domination of Europe. Stalin and the Comintern (the Communist International through which the Soviet Union controlled foreign Communist parties) used the KPD so ineptly that the German left, the only force apart from the Army capable of stopping Nazism, was kept permanently divided, essentially the same mistake as the Russians made in Spain. German Communists, inspired at dictation speed, declared the "bourgeois" Social Democrats (SPD) to be "the real enemy", significantly helping Hitler to power.

At the same time the 1922 Rapallo Pact between the two countries concluded in Lenin's time led to a massive breach of Versailles (by the Germans; Russia was not a party to the treaty). This occurred only a few short years after the Germans had imposed the harsh Treaty of Brest-Litovsk on the desperate Bolsheviks in 1918 and then gone on to intervene in the Russian Civil War. The Germans were permitted to train with forbidden aircraft and tanks on a large scale in the great empty spaces of the Soviet Union, a fact exposed by the *Manchester Guardian* in 1926 after many months of rumour. The 1918 victors apparently preferred to turn a blind eye to this flagrant breach. By way of reciprocity, at least three classes of Soviet submarines were supplied by the Germans with MAN diesel engines, the best in the world. Soviet engineers copied and adapted them for at least one later class. The Nazi-Soviet Pact of August 1939 saw to it that Soviet naval cooperation remained closer with Germany (until Hitler invaded Russia in June 1941) than it ever became with the western Allies.

The Russian Navy, having contributed little to its country's war effort, withdrew from the seas after the October Revolution even more completely than the German Navy after the Armistice. The new Soviet Union in effect had no Navy. In the Black Sea Turkey had also been defeated so that there was hardly any naval presence. In the Baltic, newly independent Poland was hostile and Finland, also freed from Russian rule, was embroiled in its own civil war. Estonia, Latvia and Lithuania had also become independent and their ports were not available any more. The residual German fleet, though a shadow of its former self, was the strongest in the northern sea.

It was only at the tenth Communist Party congress of 1921 that the decision was taken to create a Red Navy, in the first instance for the Baltic.

There were twenty submarines in various conditions from scuttled but salvageable to almost seaworthy. Of these, ten members of the Tsarist "Leopard" class (650/784 tons) were found to be usable and redesignated $B1$ to $B9$ and $B25$. In the Black Sea one boat was seaworthy and another was raised and restored; four wartime "Hollands" delivered from America but unassembled were added by 1923.

Cutting their coat according to their cloth, the Communists took the view that these and a handful of refitted Tsarist surface ships were capable of fighting holding actions at best; and this duly became the little Soviet Navy's strategy. The main potential enemy was seen as Britain, which had intervened against the Bolsheviks and had much the biggest Navy in Europe. The Red Fleet, if such it could be called, would resist invasion with submarines, destroyers and smaller vessels, backed by coastal forts, artillery and old battleships deployed as floating batteries: a "fortress fleet" policy. The split between "old" (big ship) and "new" (small ship) schools within the naval officer corps survived the Revolution; the latter faction was winning by default and remained dominant until the late 1930s. But Professor Gervais of the Frunze Naval Academy in Leningrad was influential as the main proponent of a strong surface fleet, pointing out that submarines might be able to cut the other side's sea communications but could not protect one's own.

It was 1926 before the Soviet Union could afford even a handful of new submarines, the first six of Series I of the first Soviet class, "Dekabrist", numbered $D1–6$. They were about ten years behind western boats technologically. The six, displacing 920/1,318 tons, were commissioned between 1927 and 1931, whereupon work began on another six, Series II, numbered $L1–6$ and mainly minelayers with German engines. As before, yards at Leningrad and Nikolayev on the Black Sea built three each. The British $L55$, sunk off Kronstadt during the intervention in 1919, was raised in 1928 and joined the Baltic Fleet in 1931. For the Pacific, six boats styled Series XI and seven of Series XIII, slightly larger than their predecessors, were built in sections at Leningrad and shipped to Vladivostok for assembly.

The Pacific Fleet was re-established in 1932 with an aggressive and hostile Japan in mind. Alarmist rumours of a rapidly expanding Soviet submarine force began to appear in the Japanese and German press in the early 1930s and were echoed on both sides of the Atlantic. Soviet sources boasted of huge increases, but only in the meaningless percentages also cited for industrial production in general. Without the base figure, the claim of Admiral Nikolai Orlov, the C-in-C of the Soviet fleet, in 1936 that submarine tonnage had risen by 735 per cent since 1933 was at once startling and uninformative. Only now, as Soviet records become available, is it possible to calculate that the Soviet Navy had some twenty operational submarines in 1932 (with none in the Pacific), thirty-eight in 1933 (eight in the Far East), eighty-two (thirty-nine) in 1934, 106 (forty-five) in 1935, and 181 (seventy-four) boats in 1939, rising even further to 205 (eighty-seven) in 1940. By then it was by far the largest submarine fleet in the world, albeit distributed across four seas. German war construction apart, this quantitative lead was held for some six decades by the Soviet Navy and its new Russian heir.

The principal types which accounted for these great numerical leaps were the "M" (for *malodki* or small) coastal class (160/200 tons), known by its Cyrillic initial, for which we must use four Roman letters, "Shch". Six yards built nearly 100 between 1930 and 1948; the first four, styled Series III, displaced 577/704 tons but later boats were larger. The "Shch" and "M" classes were to bear the brunt, such as it was for Soviet submarines, of the Second World War.

The first attempt to construct large submarines, the three "Pravda" class boats displacing 955/1,671 tons and built between 1931 and 1936, was a technical failure, even though they were fitted with MAN diesels. The next long-range patrol submarines were the Series IX "Stalinetz" boats, very much more reliable. About fifty were built – to an IvS design of which the Russians bought the blueprints – between 1934 and 1948, displacing 840/1,070 tons and equipped with German engines or copies. The "Stalinetz" boats were somewhat enlarged first cousins of the type VII submarines which were to be the mainstay of Germany's second U-boat campaign in 1939–45. German engines were also fitted in the big Soviet Series XIV "K" class cruiser submarines, displacing 1,498/2,095 tons, Russia's last prewar submarine design. More than a dozen of these heavily armed boats were built in Leningrad; early experiments with small aircraft housed aboard were not successful. The "Ks" carried ten tubes and twenty-four torpedoes, twenty mines, two four-inch and two anti-aircraft guns.

More by accident than design, the Red Fleet had in ten years acquired a "two-power-plus" superiority in submarines, outnumbering the two next-largest underwater fleets of America and Italy combined – eloquent testimony to the influence of the "young school" before it fell victim to Stalin's terrible purges. But the fleet was very short of submarine support-ships, destroyers, minelayers, minesweepers (and mines). A strategically unsound, political compromise between old and new schools engendered a "Soviet school" in a fleet seriously inadequate in both large and small ships and for both defensive and offensive operations when war came.

*

On the other side of the Sea of Japan the Imperial Navy, which had broken the Tsar's fleet, expanded at a phenomenal rate from 1918. The Naval Staff, mostly in the hawkish fleet faction, and the navy ministry, mainly in the moderate treaty faction, were completely united behind Japanese plans to dominate Asia and the Pacific.

The Navy as a whole favoured a "southern strategy": expansion towards American, British and Dutch possessions in the western Pacific and south-east Asia. The reason for this preference was that such a strategy required a strong Navy. The Army, which by the early 1930s was the dominant force in the Empire, favoured a northern strategy, building on recent conquests in Korea and Manchuria to dominate China and humble the Soviet Union, seen by many generals as the main long-term enemy. The reason for this option was that it required a very large Army. The Army started its war in Manchuria in 1931, and went to war against China itself in 1937, without consulting the Emperor, the Cabinet or the Navy. The General Staff then agreed to a southern strategy for the 1940s, even though the Army was hopelessly bogged down in China and had been given a bloody nose in "border incidents" (including major clashes) with the Russians in Mongolia. The Japanese thus elected to make the same monumental error as the Kaiser in the First World War and Hitler in the Second – starting a war on two fronts.

The other main foibles shared by the future Axis partners included a belief that autarky or economic self-sufficiency was the way to escape a repetition of Germany's fate in 1918; underestimation of the enemy; and a belief in the inherent superiority of the race, which was intimately connected with the foregoing. The lesson selected for learning from the First World War by the Japanese military junta – autarky as insurance against blockade – was reflected in the widespread and rigid belief in the siege-minded Navy that an attacker could not overcome the Japanese fleet unless he had a naval superiority of at least fifty per cent. The 5:3 ratio gave the perceived main maritime enemy, the United States, an edge of sixty-seven per cent over Japan, whereas 10:7 reduced it to forty-three.

This curious obsession conveniently overlooked the fact that the United States had a two-ocean Navy with duties in the Atlantic as well as the Pacific, whereas the Japanese fleet needed only to concentrate in a relatively small and contiguous area of the western Pacific, on interior lines. To achieve autarky for a country with hardly any natural resources a land empire in south-east Asia was deemed necessary; but to fight the requisite wars of conquest in China and the Indies, Japan ever-increasingly relied on western, especially American, supplies of strategic raw materials, especially oil and steel. When these were cut off by embargoes, Japan went to war against the West.

By the time it did so, its fleet was the most formidable in the world, regardless of tonnage. It boasted not only by far the biggest battleships – two leviathans of 70,000 tons all up, with eighteen-inch guns – but also six of the world's best fleet aircraft-carriers plus light carriers and a large, landbased naval air service; the finest light cruisers; well over 100 destroyers and ancillary craft to match. The Zero fighter, with its enormous endurance, used by both Army and Navy, was the most deadly in the world at least until 1942, and the type 93, twenty-four-inch "Long Lance" far outclassed any other Navy's torpedoes in range and effectiveness. The submarine variant, the type 95, twenty-one-inch missile, had the amazing range of 37,000 metres at thirty-six knots, or 20,000 at fifty. Propelled by oxygen, it left no bubbles in its wake.

The Japanese began their postwar submarine programme by building ten large coastal boats between 1919 and 1922, displacing more than 1,000 tons surfaced but with short range. Balked of a big battlefleet at Washington, the Japanese took a greater interest in longer-range cruiser submarines. Like the French and prewar naval strategists, they saw submarines as adjuncts to the battlefleet, as underwater equalisers to reduce an enemy fleet by attrition so that what was left of it could be roundly defeated by the imperial line of battle. War against trade was dismissed by Japanese admirals as beneath them. The Japanese conference delegations were second only to the French in their opposition to outlawing submarines. Japan, having asked for 78,000 tons, adhered to the 52,700-ton overall submarine limit, equal to British and American quotas, but on opting out of treaty limitations in 1934–6, built well beyond it.

From 1924 to 1940 construction focused on three main types: a cruiser (with five-inch or even heavier guns and sometimes with aircraft) for reconnaissance and long-range independent operations; a fleet type for use with surface formations and against enemy warships; and a medium-sized boat for home waters. Because the Japanese wanted the maximum from their investment – heavy armament, long range, high speed – Japanese boats were unusually large, cumbersome and slow to dive, as well as few in number for the total tonnage built.

Some Japanese submarine commanders, discounted even more than in other navies, favoured distant deployment against enemy supply-lines (uniquely lengthy in the Pacific), against merchantmen and such strategic targets as the Panama Canal, the American link between the east and west coasts and their Atlantic and Pacific fleets. They were ignored.

By the time Japan went to war its Navy had sixty-four boats, of which twenty-one were obsolete; forty-one were of the heavy-cruiser and fleet types and only two of the latest medium coastal class. Twenty more submarines were under construction. The cruisers displaced 2,200 tons surfaced and 3,000 submerged (later boats were even bigger) while the less heavily armed fleet boats started at 1,800/2,300 tons. Both categories could manage twenty knots on the surface, a high speed for the time. Once the basic designs, derived from German, British and French models, were in use, they were not seriously modified. Minor improvements were introduced in each category, and the cruiser and fleet types became indistinguishable except in choice of armament. Their numbers were preceded by the letter "I". The prefix "RO" indicated the medium, home-waters type, displacing 940/1,200 tons and more. The first two modern members of the class – RO33 and RO34 – were built by 1937 and about forty more were added by 1945 out of a total wartime construction of 126 (of these, twenty-six were transport submarines). Japan went to war with only four minelaying submarines, broadly based on the German U122 design (1917) and built in the twenties, but unstable under water.

As in other things, the Japanese went to extremes in submarine construction. They built more than sixty midget boats before the war (and hundreds during it) and also by far the world's largest boats of their day: the "I400" class of submarine aircraft-carrier, displacing 5,223 tons surfaced and 6,560 submerged (bigger even than the first nuclear boats) but carrying only three bombers equipped with floats. These wartime boats were not deployed; they were developed from the four "Type A" boats built from 1938, which carried just one plane and were about half the size. In 1940 the Japanese abandoned work, begun in 1937, on a high-speed (twenty-five knots underwater) electric submarine, N71, remarkably similar to the fast U-boats developed by the Germans, too late to affect the outcome of the war. Fortunately for the Americans they did not return to the design, which was all their own work, until just before the end of the war, probably inspired by the German effort in this field, of which they were kept informed (like eavesdropping Allied cryptanalysts) by their ambassador in Berlin, Baron Oshima.

In general, Japanese submarines were too big, too vulnerable to blast from depth-charge, bomb or shell, too slow to dive and too easily detectable, whether by hydrophone, sonar or other Second World War detection methods. The Japanese were also well behind in such technologies, going to war without radar, radar-detectors or sonar (though with the finest night binoculars). With their customary disregard for comfort the Japanese failed to exploit the size of their boats to maximise living space, seriously reducing the endurance of submarine crews.

The Army, reflecting the inter-service hatred which distorted Japanese politics, diplomacy and the country's war effort, became the only one in the world to build its own submarines – twenty forty-ton clandestine cargo-carriers for beleaguered garrisons. The Navy was not consulted.

On the far side of the Pacific lay the power identified by Japan as the main enemy at sea, the only one in the world capable of frustrating its desire to dominate China and the Indies. Like the Japanese, the Americans were selective in the lessons they decided to learn from the First World War. For the Americans too, the submarine remained an adjunct to the battlefleet, not a commerce-raider or weapon against enemy communications. Its only other recognised roles were distant reconnaissance and defensive patrol against enemy warships. The huge distances in the Pacific and Atlantic led the United States Navy, with its small scattering of bases, to concentrate on endurance for lengthy patrols, which meant comfort for the crews, ample storage space for arms and food and relatively high speed. All this meant that American boats were distinctly larger, with unduly prominent conning towers, than European, displacing some 1,300 to 1,500 tons (so not as large as Japanese). They were faster on the surface at up to twenty knots but slower to dive, which would have made them very vulnerable to the kind of opposition faced by the Germans in the Atlantic and Mediterranean. But the Japanese paid no attention to anti-submarine warfare until it was far too late, which enabled the Americans to exploit their submarines' excellent torpedo-boat characteristics throughout the war. Had they been forced to duck and dive, twist and turn like German and British submarines it might have been a different story. American radar was also very good.

When the United States became a belligerent at the end of 1941 it possessed 112 operational submarines, a fleet second only to the Soviet Union's in numbers. There were eight of the "O" and nineteen of the "R" classes, direct descendants in the main of the "Holland" boats and designed and built at the end of the First World War. These were mostly used for training. The twenty-six boats of the "S" class still in service in 1941 had been built in four groups between 1918 and 1924, displacing up to 903 tons surfaced and 1,230 submerged. Capable of a modest fifteen knots on the surface and a useful eleven underwater, these boats lacked range and air-conditioning, features of later boats important in Pacific operations. Henceforward the US Navy named its submarines; the successor to the "S" boats was the "Barracuda" class of three, the first "fleet" submarines in American service, displacing 2,000/2,600 tons with a range of 12,000 miles at eleven knots. USS *Argonaut* was the only purpose-built minelayer ever produced by the Americans, derived from the "Barracudas" but displacing 2,710/4,164 tons. Of similar dimensions was the two-member "Narwhal" class (the other bore the recurrent name of *Nautilus*) built in the 1920s with German diesels, replaced just before the war. These largest boats in American service were too cumbersome for patrol work and were adapted for special tasks.

Six small classes of medium or fleet boats followed them, including the two of the "Cachalot" class built in 1931–3, interesting for being the first anywhere to have welded hulls. The Americans led the world in this field and all subsequent US submarines used a construction method which greatly strengthened hulls.

The last class built before the Americans went to war was also the most numerous and important: the double-hulled "Gato" class, of which seventy-three were ordered before the war (and 122 of the related "Balao" class during it). These submarines displaced 1,825 tons surfaced (2,410 submerged), were 312 feet long and twenty-seven across the beam, with four diesel and four electric motors delivering over twenty knots on the surface and up to nine submerged. They had a range of 11,400 miles and carried twenty-four torpedoes for six forward and four aft tubes, one or two deck-guns and two heavy machine-guns. They could also carry forty mines in place of spare torpedoes. This highly successful class was notable for its good seakeeping qualities, its comparative comfort (including air-conditioning) and the best array of surface weaponry of any boats in the world – which went some way to make up for the fact that they started the war with by far the worst torpedoes of any major belligerent.

The submarine arm of the Royal Navy had a lean time between the wars, when the constant need for budgetary economies and eventually reinforcements for the surface fleet made it an obvious target for skimping. Such tendencies were only encouraged by general loathing of the weapon inside and outside the Admiralty, based on traditional notions of fairness and recollections of the "frightfulness" with which the U-boat had almost won in 1917. The British still had the most to lose to submarines, which explains why they were keenest at the peace conference between the wars to abolish them, or at least shackle them with as many restraints as possible, blind faith in Asdic notwithstanding.

Britain, as an insular nation with worldwide colonial and shipping interests, presented the fattest target to an enemy's submarines. The British submarine service had no obvious reciprocal strategic role. The Mediterranean was still the most likely area to offer British submarines the opportunity to wage a generalised campaign against naval and mercantile shipping, as in the First World War.

When that ended, the British rapidly reduced their submarine fleet to some sixty boats in the early 1920s. These were a balanced mix of coastal and ocean-going boats plus the disastrous, steam-powered "K" class of fleet boats. They and the highly promising "R" class of small anti-submarine boats were soon scrapped; the latter decision seems with hindsight to be one of the more important errors of the period, a classic case of false economy, and was also influenced by overconfidence in Asdic. The first new postwar design owed a lot to the German cruisers: HMS X1 displayed 3,600 tons and proved surprisingly good at diving and manoeuvring. But her diesels were never satisfactory and nobody could think of an appropriate operational role for such a huge boat in British service, so she was scrapped uncopied in 1936.

For the rest the Royal Navy maintained three principal categories of boat: coastal, fleet and ocean-going and/or minelaying. The first new design was in the last category, the "O" class: HMS Oberon was commissioned in 1930. Nine of these 1,490/1,892-ton submarines were built. Three larger and exceptionally fast "River" class boats (2,165/2,680 tons; up to twenty-two knots) were designed for the fleet role in the 1930s, despite the fact that most naval opinion had nothing good to say of a function which had never worked well in any Navy. The chief problem was to build boats fast enough to keep up with the increasing speeds of surface vessels, even the lumbering battleships.

The British now dropped the fleet-submarine concept and concentrated on medium boats for the North Sea and larger ones for ocean-going and minelaying. In the medium category the "S" or "Swordfish" class of thirteen, built between 1931 and 1938, proved very reliable at about 900 tons and up to fifteen knots on the surface. The "Porpoise" class, 1,810/2,157-ton minelayers built around the same time, were technically even better. Both types were of relatively simply construction, making maintenance and wartime expansion easier; a case of economy leading to the right result. The same applied to the "T" or "Triton" class, upwards of 1,320/1,523 tons, whose twenty-two members were to be the ocean-going mainstay of the Royal Navy in the Second World War. The principal new coastal type was the "U" class, of which three were commissioned by 1938 and a dozen more ordered in 1939. This was another cheap, straightforward and robust design which was to perform particularly well in the confined waters of the Mediterranean, despite being technologically behind its equivalents in their leading navies. It lacked the double hull of other British classes, and was slow at 11.5 knots surfaced (nine submerged), but had excellent diving ability and manoeuvred very well.

When Britain went to war the Royal Navy had fifty-eight operational submarines, one more than Germany, of which eleven were of First World War vintage. By choosing unsophisticated but sturdy designs for three main categories of boat in the last years of peace the British Navy was well placed to expand its flotillas quickly for war tasks. These did not include as much *guerre de course* against enemy commerce as was available to their German and American contemporaries, but did include reconnaissance, attacking enemy warships, transports and communications, as well as special missions.

The French Navy, which had been the first to adopt the submarine into its strategy, was determined to hold on to this weapon, having understood its power as exercised by the Germans in the Great War. All the French theories about *guerre de course*, originally conceived for surface cruisers but now shown to be even deadlier when waged by submarines, had been vindicated. France made it clear at all conferences that it would not be denied, even though postwar economic restraints prevented it from rebuilding its flotillas on the scale its admirals would have liked. France received forty-four U-boats as part of its share of naval reparations and studied them closely, recommissioning ten.

After Washington in 1922 the French launched a new building programme of ocean-going boats (for reconnaissance and colonial patrol and against commerce) and coastal submarines for home waters; a third category, of ocean-going minelayers, was added in 1925. The first long-range boats, nine members of the 1,150/1,441-ton "Requin" class, did not compare in quality with their successors of the "1,500-ton" class, of which thirty-one were built by 1939: at twenty knots, the later members of this class were five knots faster. Thirty-four coastal boats in three classes, each better than its predecessor but all with a surface speed of about fourteen knots, were built between 1927 and 1939: the "600-ton", the "630-ton" and the "Minerve" types. The first minelayer, *Saphir*, was laid down in 1925 and commissioned five years later. Five more were added to this very sound and reliable class by 1937. By the time war broke out, France had seventy-seven submarines in commission with another thirty-six on the stocks or ordered (which would have brought parity with Italy, seen as France's main potential enemy at sea).

The most remarkable French development in the underwater-warfare field, the country's only venture into cruiser submarines, was the *Surcouf*, laid down at Cherbourg in July 1927 as by far the largest submarine ever conceived at that time (and for many years thereafter).

When submarine construction began again in 1922, Admiral Pierre Drujon, true to the post-Napoleonic development of the *guerre de course*, had proposed seven giant submersible raiders. Robert Surcouf, a privateer in the Napoleonic Wars, gave his name to the first, which the French could afford to start only five years later. The resulting monster was launched in November 1929, measuring 361 feet and displacing 3,304 tons (4,318 submerged). Despite her unprecedented size she was capable of only one hour submerged at just over eight knots (seventy miles or only fifteen hours at four and a half). She carried a pair of mighty eight-inch guns in an armoured turret forward of the "kiosk" (conning tower), two thirty-seven-millimetre cannon aft of it, a pair of machine-guns and ten torpedo tubes. Of these, four were internal for submerged use and six were mounted externally on a platform at the stern. Aft of the conning tower was a hangar for a single float-plane. The resulting long superstructure made her look like a completely sur-faced small submarine when she was in fact awash, and like a very large submarine with a conventionally sized one on her back when she was fully surfaced or in dock. She was the most heavily armed submarine so far commissioned and remained the world's largest until the Japanese produced their vast boats in 1944–5. She had a special compartment for up to forty captured enemy seamen and carried a crew of 130 men.

Commissioned only in July 1931, *Surcouf* never overcame her teeth-ing troubles and was never used for her intended purpose. The Sulzer diesel engines gave constant trouble, she was unstable and took two and a half agonising minutes to submerge; the aircraft and the big guns persistently failed. As she was such an extraordinary boat we may complete her sad story here.

Stationed in the French West Indies on the outbreak of the Second World War, *Surcouf* was recalled to Brest for overhaul and escorted a British convoy from Jamaica in September 1939 under Captain Pierre Martin. The overhaul was still not complete when France was overrun and Martin slowly sailed his giant boat to the British base at Plymouth in June 1940. The repairs were completed with enormous difficulty as there were naturally no suitable parts in Britain. Her executive officer, Pierre Ortoli, relieved Martin when he refused to serve under British command. The boat finally sailed to Canada in February 1941 with a demoralised Free French crew and a three-man British liaison team. From Halifax she helped to escort two convoys to Britain. An unfounded rumour spread among British seamen that she had sunk some of the merchantmen on the eastbound crossing (in fact none was lost). Since nobody except the escort commander on the British battleship *Ramillies* had been told the French boat was joining the convoys, such a *canard* was hardly surprising.

He detached *Surcouf*, ordering her to go ahead to Devonport (near

Plymouth), which only strengthened the rumours. She arrived on 17 April. Following yet more repairs she sailed for Bermuda and the Royal Navy's Americas and West Indies station, arriving in mid-June 1941. After an ineffectual patrol the boat was sent for another overhaul at Portsmouth, New Hampshire. In November she collided with an American boat at Groton, Connecticut, the US Navy's main submarine base. By December she was in Halifax. The British had always found her an embarrassment and kept her on only to appease General Charles de Gaulle, the Free French leader based in London. Previous embarrassment was as nothing, however, when *Surcouf* joined three Free French corvettes in bloodlessly liberating St Pierre and Miquelon, the tiny islands at the mouth of the Canadian St Lawrence River which are all that remain of the French Empire in North America, from their Vichy French administration on Christmas Eve, 1941. The Americans were furious.

The Admiralty exercised operational control of Free French naval forces and the Flag Officer, Submarines, Vice-Admiral Sir Max Horton, sent *Surcouf* as far away as possible – to the French colony of Tahiti in the south Pacific. She set off on 12 February 1942, after yet more repairs at Bermuda and was never positively sighted again. She was almost certainly hit by the American SS *Thompson Lykes* (Captain Henry Johnson) on the late evening of the 18th, some seventy-five miles northeast of the eastern entrance to the Panama Canal. The 6,763-ton freighter was moderately damaged as the unidentified object scraped along her port side. Muffled explosions were heard and patches of oil were seen in the ship's searchlight, but a thorough check of the area yielded nothing else. The only warnings of the unavoidable collision had been a white light which suddenly appeared dead ahead and a single cry of "help!" in English. On the morning of the 19th three US Army Air Force planes from Panama claimed to have sunk an unidentified "enemy" submarine near the canal entrance by bombing. *Surcouf* had never fired a shot in anger.

France's rival in the Mediterranean was Italy, which had assembled a considerable fleet under Mussolini's Fascist government, in power from 1922. At the end of the First World War Italy had fifty-six coastal submarines in service, few of which had gained much experience beyond coastal patrols in the Adriatic campaign, on which Italy concentrated as an ally of Britain and France. Some forty boats survived into the 1920s, to be replaced from 1925. The first new type was the successful medium "Mameli" class of four, closely followed by the similar but unstable "Pisani" class, also of four. A similar number of ocean-going "Balilla" class boats were built simultaneously. Two medium minelayers of poor design entered service in 1931 among a succession of prototypes and short series. But over the next ten years, fifty-nine boats of a new "600-ton" (surface displacement) class, specially designed by the experienced engineer Bernardis as short-range Mediterranean boats, were supplied to the Italian Navy (and a few more for export to South America). This successful class was by far the most numerous built by the Italians and bore the brunt of Italian submarine operations during the Second World War.

Among a bewildering array of other types tried by the Italians, few achieved anything noteworthy, whether in the occupation of Abyssinia or the Spanish Civil War. Their ocean-going types were poor, especially when compared with their German contemporaries: German naval men were amazed when they first saw these boats with their very prominent conning towers, complete with enclosed bridge and generous observation windows. Even so, they were impressed in May 1938 when, in honour of Hitler's visit to Italy, eighty submarines surfaced at the same time in the breathtaking Bay of Naples to fire a salute in a unique display.

Their torpedoes were reliable; the Italians profited from inheriting the Whitehead factory upon their annexation of Fiume from the Austrians in 1919. Italian mines were unreliable and little used. Their submarines had no radar or active sonar; although they were to acquire the latter during the war, only a German radar-detector of limited effectiveness was fitted. The most original Italian contribution to underwater warfare was the brilliant attacks by pairs of frogmen on torpedo-like assault craft against enemy harbours; seven submarines were equipped to carry the craft, known as "pigs".

When Italy declared war on 10 June 1940, it had eighty-four boats operational, two on trials and twenty-nine in dock. Seven of the 115 were entirely obsolete, thirty-nine ocean-going with a surface tonnage of 1,570 to 950 tons and sixty-nine "Mediterranean", displacing 600 to 950 tons on the surface.

The foregoing account of the development between the wars of the submarine flotillas of all the main naval powers would not be complete without a review of some of the tragic setbacks which accompanied the rapid progress in this most dangerous branch of naval technology.

The British naval historian Edwyn Gray, in his exhaustive work, lists forty-three submarines as having sunk between November 1918 and September 1939. The two largest navies of the period, the British and American, accounted for thirteen each. Five more (almost certainly an understatement due to lack of information) are known to have been lost by the Soviet Union, four by Japan, three by France and two by Italy.

Germany lost one. Human error overwhelmingly but not surprisingly dominates the list of causes; within that, collision equally naturally takes first place. Perhaps the most remarkable fact about Gray's list is that only four are known to have sunk as a result of mechanical failure.

The two disasters that stand out during this period occurred within days of each other on opposite sides of the North Atlantic, three months before Hitler began the Second World War in Europe. One had a comparatively happy ending; the other did not.

On 23 May 1939 USS *Squalus*, the 192nd submarine commissioned by the American Navy, began her eleventh day of sea-trials off Portsmouth, New Hampshire, where she had been built. Lieutenant Oliver Naquin was in command of four officers and fifty-one sailors; three civilian technicians were also aboard. She was a 1,450/2,350-ton ocean-going boat in the second group of the "Salmon" class of eight submarines, a direct ancestor of the great "Gato" class. She was 310 feet long and had a beam of twenty-seven feet; her maximum operational depth was 256 feet.

It was fortunate therefore that the water off the Isle of Shoals in which Naquin chose to try an emergency dive was sixteen feet shallower. Having signalled her precise pre-diving position to Portsmouth Navy Yard, the *Squalus* took sixty-two seconds to reach fifty feet. At that point sea water was reported to be flooding into the engine-room. Naquin ordered all watertight doors closed and blew his ballast and forward buoyancy tanks, but the boat sank by the stern, settling in an upright position but at a stern-down angle on the seabed. The twenty-six men sealed off by a watertight door in the flooded stern section were already dead.

During earlier tests the main induction valve, built into the top of the conning tower to supply the diesels with air, had been playing up. So during the diving procedure a close watch had been kept on the warning lights for this valve in the main control panel – red for open, green for closed. The green light came on. But the rate at which water had poured in made it clear that it was this big valve which had failed to close.

Naquin had a marker-buoy sent to the surface and distress rockets fired. The absence of a surfacing signal finally alerted Navy authorities, who sent the *Sculpin*, the previous boat commissioned in the same class, from Portsmouth to the stricken submarine's last reported position. Contact was made at 1 p.m., nearly five hours after the disastrous dive. The telephone line attached to the buoy broke, but not before the *Squalus* had given details of her condition. A small flotilla of rescue vessels converged on the spot, including the tender *Falcon* from the submarine facility at New London, Connecticut, 200 miles away. The tender carried one of five submarine rescue-chambers designed by Commander Allen McCann, who was called to the scene with Commander Charles Momsen, the leading expert in underwater escape.

Nearly twenty-four hours after locating the *Squalus*, the rescuers completed their delicate and difficult preparations in deteriorating weather and lowered the rescue-chamber on to the tilted hull. The temperature within had sunk to just above freezing, the air was foul and humidity was 100 per cent. Locked on to the escape hatch, the two divers in the chamber introduced fresh air through a hose from the surface and distributed hot drinks and food. Most of the thirty-three survivors were brought up slowly but safely in three lifts by the chamber; the fourth and last dive rescued seven crewmen and Lieutenant Naquin, who as skipper intended to be last off. The hulk was cleared by 8.15 p.m., only thirty-six hours after the accident.

Four months later, in September 1939, *Squalus* herself was raised to the surface, overhauled and relaunched as USS *Sailfish*, which served very well throughout the war. When she sank the Japanese light carrier *Chuyo* in December 1943 she gallantly stopped to pick up survivors. Among them were some men from *Sculpin*, taken prisoner when their boat was sunk by a Japanese destroyer the previous month.

Ten days after *Squalus* went down, the submarine HMS *Thetis* left the Cammell Laird yard at Birkenhead on the Mersey for diving trials in Liverpool Bay. Her first such trials had been in April, but problems with her diving and steering gear had sent her back to the yard. The boat was the third member of the ocean-going "T" class to be commissioned, displacing 1,330/1,585 tons, somewhat on the small side for her type so as to economise on treaty tonnages. Her captain was Guy Bolus and there were 102 other men aboard – her crew of fifty-two and fifty others, a serious overloading. The "passengers" included experts and technicians from the Navy and the builders.

At 1.40 p.m., when the boat was thirty-eight miles out of Liverpool, Bolus signalled his intent to dive for three hours. Watchers aboard the accompanying tug *Grebecock* noticed that she seemed reluctant to go under, sinking until almost awash, then coming to rest slightly bow-down for half an hour, then slowly levelling off and finally sinking out of sight at speed. Then her bow reappeared briefly behind a big gout of air before going down again. No signal was fired when she reached sixty feet, as had been arranged. The alarm was raised some three and a half hours after she had last been seen. Destroyers and smaller vessels, and RAF reconnaissance aircraft, were sent to the spot.

The *Thetis* had refused to go down quietly because at least four of her eight forward torpedo tubes were empty of water when they should have been full. Lieutenant F.G. Woods realised this and began a systematic check. The first four tubes were indeed found to be empty. The dial on the fifth indicated to Woods that the bow-cap was closed. When he opened the inboard loading-door, however, he was knocked off his feet by a mighty jet of sea water. The cap was wide open. The men in the torpedo compartment could not get the watertight door in the first bulkhead to shut because a nut jammed; they retreated to the second and closed it from the inboard side. But the boat had gone to the bottom by the bow and was stuck in the mud, 160 feet down off the north Wales coast.

Unfortunately the needles on the bow-cap indicator dials pointed to the right to show starboard tubes were closed and to the left for port tubes, a stupid and unnecessary design blunder. Woods had misread number five's as meaning closed when it actually meant open. Further, when the boat was painted internally, the tiny hole which let water into the built-in test-cock (for checking whether there was water in a tube) had been blocked by paint. Woods examined each of these before checking the doors and found them all to be showing "dry". The immediate cause of the disaster was therefore about one square millimetre of paint compounded by simple human error, all encouraged by inadequate attention to detail.

Several attempts to close the offending bow-cap from within by men with breathing apparatus failed. There were two escape hatches but each could be used only at half-hourly intervals by two men at a time; and much precious air would have been used up to operate them. Bolus decided to await rescue. But the would-be rescuers were looking in the wrong place because the *Grebecock* had anchored where *Thetis* went under – some four miles from where she struck bottom; and the RAF had misreported the position of her marker-buoy by seven miles.

But just before 8 a.m. on 2 June, the stern of the 250-feet-long *Thetis* was sighted, protruding from the surface at an angle of forty degrees some fourteen miles offshore, by the destroyer HMS *Brazen*. As Bolus sent two officers to the surface via one of the escape hatches, only twenty feet below, the destroyer dropped small charges into the water to reveal her presence.

Meanwhile, residual water from the escape compartment had fallen back into the boat, causing an electrical short circuit and a small fire, soon extinguished but not before it had reduced the already seriously diminished oxygen supply even further. Just two more men, a sailor and a fitter, got out via the after escape hatch. Indecisiveness and ignorance among the small fleet of rescuers, lack of a sense of urgency and central direction, of heavy cutting gear and specialised equipment, fear of the treacherous local tides and finally a misguided and botched attempt to raise the stern even further – the cable snapped and *Thetis* disappeared altogether – meant that the other ninety-nine were asphyxiated. There was no response when hammers beat out the message "come out" in Morse code on the hull. Forty-eight hours after she went down, twice as long as anyone was likely to survive, the Admiralty officially abandoned hope for those left in *Thetis*. Public indignation over the very high loss of life was compounded by the American triumph with the *Squalus* only days earlier.

Thetis too was raised, refurbished and recommissioned as HMS *Thunderbolt* in April 1940. As such she also proved less fortunate than her American contemporary. After brave service in the Mediterranean, including giving the Italians a taste of their own medicine by delivering British "human torpedoes" to sink a cruiser in the Sicilian harbour of Palermo, she set out from Malta to make a night attack on an Axis convoy in March 1943. She sank with all hands when depth-charged by an Italian escort.

Thunderbolt, ex-*Thetis*, was one of thirteen T-class boats lost in the Mediterranean during the Second World War. Among their many successes worldwide, thirteen of the class sank thirteen enemy submarines.

As the major powers gave up the faltering attempts to disarm, the Axis powers armed themselves to the teeth. The pace was set in the Far East by Japan's adventurism in China; in Europe it was set by Hitler. In March 1936 he sent troops into the demilitarised Rhineland. In 1937 he began building the "Siegfried Line" on his side of the Rhine and concluded the Rome-Berlin Axis with Mussolini. He annexed Austria in 1938 and also took personal command of the Wehrmacht (German armed forces). In September he concluded the Munich Agreement with the British and French appeasers, acquiring the Sudetenland from Czechoslovakia (together with the latter's defence line). The Royal Navy mobilised amid general fears of war, showing that appeasement was dead. Britain and France guaranteed Poland's borders against aggression, a promise they could never hope to keep. Hitler overran the rest of Czechoslovakia and took Memel in the Baltic from Lithuania. On 23 August 1939 Germany and the Soviet Union signed their infinitely cynical non-aggression pact. Nine days later the German Army began the dismemberment of Poland. Britain and France declared war on Germany on 3 September. By then, thirty-nine German submarines were in position round the coasts of the British Isles. This time the U-boats would go into action on day one.

ACT II: 1939–45

Scene i: Germany versus Britain

LIEUTENANT FRITZ-JULIUS LEMP, captain of the German Navy's *U30*, did Britain an unintended favour on the first day of the second war between the two countries. Hindsight shows that, by sinking a passenger liner without warning, he silenced the new generation of waverers at the Admiralty who had refused to learn the principal lesson in naval strategy from the First World War – convoy.

It was none the less a brutal act and a shock to the world. The British Navy, heartened on the outbreak of war as it had once been depressed by Winston Churchill's occupation of his old job as First Lord of the Admiralty, signalled cryptically that day to all its ships: TOTAL GERMANY. Shortly afterwards the German Navy signalled: OPEN HOSTILITIES WITH ENGLAND AT ONCE. Lemp picked it up some 250 miles north-west of Ireland, where he was slowly patrolling to and fro on the surface. *U30* was one of ten boats of type VIIA, completed in 1936–7, displacing 626/745 tons, with a maximum speed of sixteen knots (eight submerged). The boat was an Igewit design derived from the "UBIII" class of 1918, with ranges of 4,300 miles at twelve knots and ninety at four knots underwater. She carried sixty-seven tons of diesel oil, four bow and one stern torpedo tubes, eleven twenty-one-inch torpedoes, an eighty-eight-millimetre deck-gun and a twenty-millimetre anti-aircraft gun. The crew on this early example of the medium-sized workhorse in the second U-boat fleet mustered forty-four, as was commonly the case on the two dozen type VIIB and 558 VIIC that were to follow.

As dusk fell *U30* sighted a big ship sailing westward on a precautionary zigzag course, approaching the boat. The vessel was obviously a passenger liner of medium size (large by any other standard). Lemp, a professional sailor of twenty-six, decided at once to submerge for an attack at periscope depth, positioning his boat at right angles and to the south of the ship's mean course so as to hit her amidships on the port side.

Captain James Cook of the Donaldson Line had taken the SS *Athenia*, a sixteen-year-old ship of 13,581 gross register-tons, out of Glasgow on 2 September, calling at Liverpool and Belfast for more passengers before setting off for Montreal, Canada. At noon on the 3rd, after the ship left the Northern Irish capital, he told his 1,103 passengers and 350 crew that Britain and France, their ultimatum to Hitler to withdraw from Poland having expired at 11 a.m., were at war with Germany. The radio room had been on special alert for such a message, and most passengers, including more than 300 United States citizens, were aboard to get away from Europe. Cook confidently asserted the unarmed ship's immunity under international law from submarine attack. The Hitler regime had put Germany's signature on the special protocol to the 1936 London Naval Treaty outlawing unrestricted submarine warfare and given assurances to the same effect on signing the Anglo-German Naval Agreement of 1935. The Nazis had also availed themselves of their conditional right under that pact to build up to 100 per cent of British submarine strength, as they had by September 1939.

Lemp's sealed orders, opened when he received the signal of war with Britain, told him not to attack any French vessel (because Hitler hoped to drive a diplomatic wedge between the French and the British) and to observe prize rules. The German naval command knew that many British merchantmen would soon disqualify themselves from such courtesies by fitting guns to their pre-strengthened main decks. Admiral Raeder wanted to declare the waters round the British Isles a zone for unrestricted warfare as in the First World War, especially as Britain had once again adopted its time-honoured stratagem against a western European enemy – blockade. But Hitler, thinking ahead to his planned invasion of "the main enemy", Russia, hoped for an early settlement with Britain and France. He also wanted to avoid antagonising the United States.

Lemp fired a torpedo through all these considerations. It hit the *Athenia* squarely on the port flank abaft of amidships, sending up a huge column of water and smashing the bulkhead between boiler and engine-rooms. Stairways between lower and main decks were demolished, trapping most of the 118 people who died with the *Athenia*. She listed thirty degrees to port but then settled in the water, enabling all lifeboats to be launched and an orderly abandonment to take place.

Having disobeyed orders, Lemp did nothing to help his illicit victim. He surfaced half a mile away and fired two shells over her superstructure in an apparent attempt to bring down her wireless aerials. These were working overtime, repeatedly transmitting the "SSS" signal of attack by submarine and giving the ship's position. Despite Lemp's attempts to jam, Malin Head radio at the north-west tip of Ireland picked it up at

8.59 p.m. A small fleet headed for the spot, including three British destroyers with Asdic. They, neutral Norwegian, Swedish and American merchantmen picked up the 1,335 survivors. Twenty-eight Americans had been killed; the "Lusitania factor", which had played such a fateful part in propelling the United States into the First World War, was thus at work from the very beginning of the Second.

Because of the transatlantic time difference, reports appeared in the American press linking the Athenia with the spread of Hitler's war from Poland across the Rhine and the North Sea. It was the most dramatic reminder of the horrors of unrestricted submarine warfare. The news was brought to Churchill, still settling into his office at the Admiralty, just after 10.30 p.m. He was furious. The death-throes of the abandoned Athenia would last until dawn the next day, but the Admiralty wasted no time in striking the first propaganda blow, announcing that the ship had been torpedoed by a U-boat. As American naval attachés, consular officers and reporters rushed to Ireland to interview survivors, the news agencies splashed the story all over the American media.

Captain Karl Dönitz, Führer der Unterseeboote, reacted with emotions not much different from Churchill's when the news reached him twelve hours later, thanks to Naval Intelligence monitoring of British radio. Lemp was now obeying orders, keeping wireless silence. When Hitler was told later on the 4th he issued a Führer order: "Passenger ships shall not be attacked until further notice even if escorted." This was transmitted repeatedly to all warships before midnight, about eight hours after a German public broadcast asserted that the Athenia must have been sunk in error by a British mine or warship.

This feeble effort was succeeded by much more virulent counter-propaganda. When Dr Joseph Goebbels's propaganda ministry discovered that British destroyers had reached the scene quickly, the Germans claimed that they had sunk the liner on Churchill's orders to influence neutral opinion against Germany. Both sides were patently aware of the Lusitania factor, even though ten times more people had been killed in that earlier sinking. The British destroyer commander at the scene said at the time that he had been sent not only to search for survivors (and U-boats) but also "in view of the probable political importance of the sinking". On 22 September Goebbels himself went on radio to accuse Churchill of having the ship blown up and sending the three destroyers to finish her off, simulating "a new Lusitania". It was to be a year before the US government officially accepted the British version.

When Lemp arrived home on 27 September he confirmed to his less than delighted superiors that he had sunk the Athenia. Admiral Raeder had him and his crew sworn to silence on pain of extreme punishment. The log of the *U30* was altered to erase any reference to the sinking, and the War Diary of the U-Boat Command credited the boat only with her two more modest victims, a steamer of 4,425 tons on the 11th and another of 5,200 tons on the 14th, sunk in the same area.

The sinking of the *Athenia* was important for two reasons. Despite the best efforts of German propaganda, it swung important elements of neutral opinion against Hitler by reviving the *Lusitania* factor. More importantly still, the Admiralty deduced (wrongly) that Germany was already committed to unrestricted submarine warfare (the U-boats were freed of the last restraints only in August 1940). This understandable error lent urgency to British efforts to establish a comprehensive convoy system. Churchill himself had been out of the Admiralty for two years by the time of the U-boat crisis in 1917, so perhaps it is not surprising that he was lukewarm on convoy. His attitude played into the hands of its opponents, with tragic results soon to be demonstrated. He accepted convoy as a necessary evil without appreciating its unique advantages for counter-attack. Meanwhile the loss of the *Athenia* was an unmistakable reminder to the world: the U-boats were back.

The first convoy sailed one day before Britain declared war. On 2 September the Royal Navy escorted a group of ships out of Gibraltar bound for Cape Town, South Africa. At that time and for some months thereafter, despite Lemp the Admiralty regarded surface ships as the greater threat. Although the German fleet was a fraction of the British (and of the Kaiser's), Raeder's deployment of his handful of first-class major warships made them a much greater threat than the High Seas Fleet had been. Instead of holding them back for a set-piece battle, he used them against commerce, especially the transatlantic main artery, on which the British war effort would depend. At his disposal in 1939 – five years sooner than Hitler's "earliest possible" date for war against Britain – were eight heavy ships: the two battlecruisers *Scharnhorst* and *Gneisenau*, the three pocket battleships *Admiral Graf Spee*, *Admiral Scheer* and *Lützow* (formerly *Deutschland*) – all of outstanding quality – plus three exceptionally large cruisers, *Admiral Hipper*, *Blücher* and *Prinz Eugen*. The latter trio was not a successful design, being too big and too short in range, as well as mechanically unreliable. But the Royal Navy possessed only one ship capable of keeping up with the battlecruisers at thirty-two knots – the twenty-one-year-old *Hood* – and only two others that were both faster and more heavily armed than the pocket battleships. Already launched but still being fitted out were two super-battleships, *Bismarck* and *Tirpitz*, much larger and more powerful than any British capital ship extant or on order.

All this meant that the British and French had to position their biggest warships round the Atlantic in groups, each large enough to overcome any one of the largest German vessels, and also capable of combining should the Germans send out a pair. The British had three battlecruisers and twelve battleships, all of First World War vintage except for two of the latter, launched in 1925. Five more battleships were under construction when war broke out. None of the countries of the British Commonwealth and Empire, which had loyally declared war alongside Britain, possessed a capital ship. Only the French could help police the Atlantic, where they deployed their *Force de Raid* of two battlecruisers, an aircraft-carrier, three cruisers and ten destroyers (withdrawn when France fell in June 1940). The French Navy's chief concern was as ever the Mediterranean.

Scapa Flow was once again the main base of the core of the British Navy, now styled the Home Fleet: five battleships, two battlecruisers, two carriers, twelve cruisers, seventeen destroyers and seven large minesweepers. Two submarine flotillas were based at Dundee in Eastern Scotland (ten boats) and Blyth in north-east England (six). There was one other home-based strategic formation, the Channel Force of two battleships, two carriers, three cruisers and nine destroyers, based in the Solent on the English south coast. The country was covered by six shore-based naval commands, of which the most important, as nerve-centre of the crucial struggle to keep the Atlantic routes open, was Western Approaches Command, taking in south-west English waters and the Irish Sea. It was based initially in Plymouth. The strongest of the six overseas commands was the Mediterranean, with three battleships, a carrier and seven cruisers. There were also commands for the North Atlantic, based in Gibraltar; the South Atlantic, including the South American Division (Freetown, Sierra Leone); America and West Indies (Bermuda); China (Hong Kong); and East Indies (Singapore). The last three were all but denuded. Australia provided six cruisers, New Zealand two, and Canada six destroyers.

The Royal Navy had six carriers in service; like their 232 combat aircraft they were mostly obsolescent. The Fleet Air Arm also had 191 training aircraft at four shore-based naval air stations. RAF Coastal Command had three groups, a total of seventeen squadrons, under the operational control of the Admiralty (which explains why the command was the Cinderella of the RAF for aircraft and equipment, supplied by the Air Ministry). Its 1939 mainstay, the Anson bomber, did not have enough range to fly to Norway and back, across Germany's exit into the

North Atlantic. The last sixty miles had to be covered by submarines. Coastal Command had no fighters or heavy bombers and the airborne depth-charge had yet to be invented. An already overstretched RAF Fighter Command was ordered in summer 1939 to provide four squadrons to protect shipping in home waters, but could not deploy them until a year later, after huge losses within miles of the ports.

If the RAF was laggardly in its support for the hard-pressed Navy, the relationship between the Luftwaffe and the Kriegsmarine was worse. Göring regarded everything that flew as rightfully his (as did his opposite number, Trenchard; the difference was that Göring almost always got his way) and Raeder failed to acquire an independent naval air arm (or a single carrier, although two were started). After four years of wrangling they came to an agreement early in 1939 whereby the Navy acquired operational control of all squadrons assigned to it. Raeder thought he had won a major victory, until Göring starved the naval squadrons of aircraft (whose production he controlled) and formed his own parallel maritime units. Bomber Group 40, consisting of thirty Focke-Wulf FW 200 "Kondor" long-range aircraft, was earmarked for deployment by the Navy in the event of war, but the planes did not become available until summer 1940. Until then the Navy had just two reconnaissance squadrons of medium-range aircraft, also targeted by Göring for takeover. Like the British and the French, the Germans had grossly neglected naval aviation.

As for the German Navy itself, the outbreak of war saw to it that Hitler and Raeder's "Z-plan" for a battlefleet capable of tackling Britain's by 1944 was consigned to the wastepaper-basket. The bulk of the fleet in 1939 was divided among two principal commands. C-in-C West, based in Wilhelmshaven to cover the North Sea and adjoining waters, controlled the two battlecruisers, one pocket battleship, one heavy and one light cruiser and supporting vessels plus the First Submarine Flotilla of nine type II coastal boats. The High Command on the Tirpitzufer in Berlin directly controlled the other two pocket battleships and three flotillas of ocean-going submarines (nearly three dozen boats in all).

Britain possessed almost four times as many Asdic-equipped escorts when the war began as Germany had U-boats. These odds seemed favourable enough to a tactically inept Churchill for the creation of hunting groups to search out the U-boats "like cavalry divisions" instead of concentrating every available warship on escorting the precious convoys. Much more significant than the three-to-one "superiority" in destroyers alone over U-boats was the ratio of merchantmen to all escorts, a daunting twenty to one.

Britain's strategic situation in 1939 resembled that of 1914 insofar as it was importing fifty-five million tons of goods per year: all its oil, half its food and raw materials for industry. The Merchant Navy had about 3,000 ocean-going vessels and 1,000 larger coastal ships totalling 21,000,000 tons; some 2,500 British ships were at sea at any given time. These numbers were rather smaller than in 1914, but the average ship was more than twice as large (and its cargo commensurately more valuable), at 5,250 tons compared with 2,300. The most precious type of merchant ship (apart from troopships and military freighters) was the oil tanker, uniquely vulnerable to attack. The Royal and Merchant Navies, the RAF and Army, and great swathes of the economy depended wholly or significantly on imported petroleum products, a new Achilles' heel for Britain that had hardly existed in the previous war, when coal was still king.

Another difference between 1939 and 1914 was the early British success in closing the Channel to the Germans for the duration. Dover Command sowed a thick barrage of mines, though not before one U-boat had passed the Strait. But in October 1939 two were lost to the mines while another ran aground and was abandoned. The Germans gave up. But they also sowed mines in British waters by U-boat, fast destroyer or converted merchantman. When the Luftwaffe refused to divert bombers to this task, the Navy was forced to use its handful of seaplanes, whose pilots were not trained for bombing. The result was that in November two of Germany's limited stock of 1,500 new and top-secret magnetic mines were dropped in soft mud in the Thames estuary, enabling brave technicians to discover their secrets. But by the end of the year mines had claimed 250,000 tons of British shipping; the Germans had sown 22,000 contact mines. An early British submarine success came in December, when HMS *Salmon* seriously damaged two of Germany's six light cruisers – *Nürnberg* and *Leipzig* – by torpedoes while they were covering a minelaying raid off the north-east coast of England.

Churchill allowed the Navy to deploy its priceless carriers in his misbegotten hunting groups. On 14 September the newest, *Ark Royal*, 22,000 tons, was patrolling off the Hebrides islands west of Scotland when Gerhard Glattes in *U39* just missed her with a salvo of torpedoes. The boat, a type IXA long-range submarine displacing 1,032/1,153 tons, was sunk and her crew captured by the accompanying destroyers. The euphoria was premature. Three days later Otto Schuhart was on his way home in *U29*, well pleased with his haul of three oil tankers totalling more than 19,00 tons, when he sighted Britain's oldest carrier, HMS *Courageous* (Captain W.T. Makeig-Jones, RN), 22,500 tons, ineffectually looking for U-boats in the waters west of Ireland with only two destroyers in company. So he hit her with a salvo of three torpedoes at 2,500 metres after two hours of manoeuvring under water. The converted battlecruiser, launched in 1916, sank in a quarter of an hour, with the loss of half her crew, 519 men. Schuhart evaded a four-hour destroyer hunt and returned to Wilhelmshaven as the German Navy's first war hero, to be personally decorated by Hitler on the quayside. The Admiralty was as depressed as the U-Boat Command was delighted. But these reactions were as nothing compared with those of both sides less than four weeks later.

Günther Prien of U47 was the first U-boat captain of the war to sink a merchantman – the British SS *Bosnia*, 2,407 tons – off the north coast of Spain on 5 September. It was the first of many "firsts" in a short but illustrious submariner's career. The son of a middle-class Leipzig family which fell on hard times in the great inflation of 1923, Prien, born in 1909, went to sea at fourteen as a cabin boy and soon became an officer. Bitter over being consigned to the scrapheap in the Depression, he joined the Nazi Party in 1932 and one year later joined the Navy below decks. Obvious officer material, he became a cadet and got his commission in the renascent submarine service. He took command in 1938 of the new U47, a type VIIB, somewhat larger than a VIIA with a displacement of 753/857 tons and a range fifty per cent greater – 6,500 miles at twelve knots. Her top speed of seventeen knots was one higher than the VIIA's but the armament was exactly the same, as was the safe maximum diving depth of 100 metres.

Sighting the *Bosnia* while surfaced, he fired a shot across her bow. The ship gallantly refused to stop and began signalling for help. Prien shelled her in earnest and soon set her ablaze. He made certain the crew were safe in their boats as a Norwegian ship showed over the horizon; he asked her captain to look after them before torpedoing the hulk and leaving the scene.

Prien sank another victim by gunfire and torpedo on the 6th, and the third and last of his first patrol by torpedo alone on the 7th. Both were British steamers and both were dispatched with punctilious attention to prize rules. Back in Wilhelmshaven awaiting a new mission while U47 was being serviced, Prien called at the officers' mess on Sunday, 1 October, only to be summoned to Dönitz's office. The submarine chief had been mulling over a special mission which Germany's first U-boat fleet had twice attempted in vain, at the beginning and the end of the Great War: to strike a blow at the heart of the enemy fleet in its main anchorage – Scapa Flow. Like so many other early German moves in the new war, Dönitz's concern was to overturn the results of the old (the invasion of Poland to regain Danzig being the first example). He also wanted to win more recognition for his command; the spectacular sinking of an aircraft-carrier had not made up for the embarrassing destruction of an unarmed liner and the newly promoted commodore wanted to show what the boats could do.

Over a chart of the Orkney Islands in the Plot Room at submarine headquarters Dönitz made it clear that this was a dangerous enterprise and therefore Prien had a free choice whether to go or not. But could he please answer by Tuesday? And if it was No, it would of course not be held against him ... But Dönitz knew his man; Prien jumped at the chance, without offering his crew of forty-three men the same choice. The attack was worked out with special attention to the complicated tides in and around the Flow. The moonless night of 13 October was chosen. At that time, before Italian prisoners of war built the Churchill Causeway linking the islands on the eastern side, there were seven entrances to the Flow: four to the east, two to the north-west and the main one to the south. Defences existed at all seven, but, despite prewar reminders to the Admiralty, they were not yet up to wartime standard by the forty-first day of the war. There was a profusion of blockships, booms, nets, hydrophones, mines, cables and guard-boats; but a German air reconnaissance had revealed the existence of a gap fifty feet wide at the northernmost channel on the eastern side, Kirk Sound, between the principal island of Mainland and the islet of Lamb Holm. Cables obstructed only half the entrance, leaving enough space for a submarine to squeeze through.

U47 left Wilhelmshaven on 8 October and crept across the North Sea, keeping to the surface as submarines always did except when diving was unavoidable. The crew, ignorant of the boat's orders, began to wonder why their aggressive martinet of a captain was taking such pains to avoid finding ships to attack, submerging whenever there was the slightest risk of being seen. Having approached in the dark to within sight of Kirk Sound, Prien took a good look through binoculars, submerged and withdrew. He then told his men what they were about to do. In a rare display of black humour Prien told them that anyone who did not wish to come was free to leave.

Meanwhile naval planes had repeated their high-level reconnaissance of the Flow on the 11th and 12th, reporting the presence of a plethora of fat targets: one carrier, five capital ships and ten cruisers. The absence of all but one of these the next day was blamed by Dönitz on the unavoidable reconnaissance flights. The real culprit was the naval command in Berlin, which sent the *Gneisenau*, escorted by a light cruiser and nine destroyers, in a sweep towards Norway on the 7th. This was partly to distract attention from the presence in the broad Atlantic of two pocket battleships and partly to lure the British Home Fleet (Admiral Sir Charles Forbes) to sea and expose his ships to attack by submarine and aircraft.

Sailors love nicknames, and they had christened Forbes "Wrong-way Charlie" for failing to find the German Navy in six weeks of war. He did it again on this occasion; but with the incomplete defences of Scapa Flow on his mind he dispersed his forces when he gave up the search on 9 October. The only capital ship to return to Scapa and stay there was the elderly battleship *Royal Oak*, which had barely managed twenty-one knots during the search. She took up her customary anchorage alongside the 1914 seaplane-carrier *Pegasus* at the southern end of Scapa Bay in the north-eastern corner of the Flow. The only other major ship in the great anchorage was the brand-new cruiser *Belfast*. An aircraft-carrier and a battlecruiser had come on the 11th and gone on the 12th, when three other cruisers set out for the Northern Patrol, guarding the waters between Shetland and Norway. Forbes's sometimes derided caution undoubtedly saved the Navy even worse embarrassment when Prien struck.

Just before daybreak on the 13th *U47* submerged for the day, settling on the bottom at about 300 feet well out to sea eastward of Orkney. Rest and silence were ordered for some twelve hours until "breakfast" at 4 p.m., still submerged. Preparations were now completed, including the attachment of explosive charges to various vital points in case it became necessary to scuttle.

At dusk *U47* surfaced and began her cautious approach to Kirk Sound. Four hours later, almost within sight of the chosen entrance, *U47* was forced to dive to avoid a steamer. Prien's plan was to enter the Sound just before midnight, on the surface, because the water was too shallow and fast-moving to permit a submerged entry. He was relying on surprise to get him through on the incoming tide but was taken aback by its strength. The boat was almost flung against the anchor chains partly blocking the Sound and the helmsman had to struggle to avoid grounding on the open side of the channel, to port. At 12.27 a.m. on 14 October *U47* burst into Scapa Flow.

There may have been no moon, but the unpredictable "northern lights" were more than enough to reveal to Prien on his little bridge that the anchorage was disappointingly empty. There was nothing ahead or to port so he turned to starboard, heading northward up the chain of islands on the eastern side. He thought he could see two capital ships, which he identified as *Royal Oak* (correctly) and, partly visible behind her, the battlecruiser *Repulse* (incorrectly: he must have taken *Pegasus* with her high side, flat top and seaplane-hoist for the long nose and forward turret of the temporarily absent battlecruiser, well out of harm's way in dry dock at Rosyth in the Firth of Forth, far to the south).

Approaching to the optimum range of 3,000 metres, he ordered all four forward tubes fired in succession. Number four jammed but one of the salvo of three was heard to explode after three and a half minutes. While the tubes were being reloaded he put about to fire his single stern tube, which missed. Turning again he fired three more, all of which detonated in quick succession in less than three minutes. This is how the scene was described in a cod "autobiography" produced by the propaganda ministry for which Prien was only partly responsible:

Then something unimaginable happened, which nobody who saw it would ever forget as long as he lived. Over there a curtain of water arose. It was as if the sea suddenly stood on end. Dull thumps sounded in quick succession, like an artillery barrage in a battle, and merged into a single, earsplitting crash – gouts of flame surged upward, blue, yellow, red. The sky disappeared behind this infernal firework [display]. Black shadows flew like giant birds through the flames, splashing into the water ... They were huge fragments from the masts, the bridge, the funnels. We must have made a direct hit on a magazine, and this time the death-dealing ammunition rent the body of its own ship.

I called below: "She's finished!"

Seconds of silence. And then a yelling, a single, animal cry in which the frightful tension of the past twenty-four hours released itself. A cry as if the boat, this great steel beast, were screaming on its own account. "Silence!" I yelled – and the boat was still.

To their own astonishment, the Germans were able to turn round and escape the way they had come. The eastward ride through Kirk Sound was much slower; the fierce tide was now running against them and at times they were barely able to make headway against it. Within an hour of the last explosion U47 was well clear. For the record we may note that on the next night the battered SS Neuchâtel arrived in the Flow, in compliance with an Admiralty order dated 10 July 1939. She had come to end her days as a blockship – across the entrance to Kirk Sound.

The first torpedo struck HMS Royal Oak, veteran of the Battle of Jutland, on the starboard bow with a muffled crump at 1.04 a.m., blowing a hole fifty feet wide and three plates high, above the waterline. The 29,000-ton dreadnought lurched and her great anchor chains roared into the water. Captain William Benn, RN, ordered an inspection and concluded, bizarrely perhaps, that there had been a spontaneous explosion in the paint locker at the forepeak. The wound looked much worse than it was and nobody had been injured. He ordered routine damage-control measures, sealing off the area by closing watertight doors. Many of his 1,257 men thought they had been bombed and took shelter below the armoured main deck, which greatly increased the eventual loss of life.

Twelve minutes later three torpedoes struck the ship amidships and below the waterline in quick succession, setting off a sympathetic explosion in a magazine. The veteran's back was broken; she turned turtle and sank in thirteen minutes, at 1.29. Rear-Admiral H.E.C. Blagrove, commanding the ship's division, went down with her after helping to save as many men as he could. Captain Benn was blown overboard and survived, with 424 of his men; 833 died.

In the ensuing pandemonium, destroyers and other small ships dashed about, firing at anything that moved, sometimes including each other. Prien meanwhile was back in the North Sea, cheerfully signalling: "Mission accomplished as ordered."

A Board of Inquiry into the loss of the *Royal Oak*, to this day an official war grave in Scapa Flow, gathered on 18 October under the chairmanship of Admiral the Honourable Sir Reginald Aylmer Ranfurly Plunkett-Ernle-Erle-Drax, KCB, DSO, RN. On 24 October it concluded, uncontroversially, that the battleship had been sunk in a torpedo attack by a U-boat. It recommended that the defences of Scapa Flow be completed forthwith. Admiral Sir William French, flag officer commanding Orkney and Shetland, was elected scapegoat by the Admiralty (the real culprit on the British side) and dismissed. But Churchill was generous enough to stand up in parliament and describe Prien's stunning attack as "a remarkable exploit of professional skill and daring". There had been nothing like it since 1667, when the Dutch Navy raided the River Medway in south-east England and Admiral M.A. de Ruyter set fire to several men-of-war, towing the English feet flagship to Holland.

Prien's derring-do had no direct strategic significance, beyond driving the Admiralty to make good its sin of omission at Scapa Flow, which was regarded as properly defended only in March 1940. His victim had been too slow to be of much use, except as a convoy escort against surface raiders. Only one more battleship was built by the British during the war in addition to the five on order in 1939. Hindsight suggests that Schuhart's destruction of the carrier *Courageous* was a greater blow to the British – or would have been if either side had understood the potential of naval aviation (in general, and in particular for defending convoys) at this stage of the war. But the battleship was then still the ultimate symbol of British power, and to have one sunk in the principal anchorage of His Majesty's fleet was a shattering psychological blow for

Britain and a huge propaganda victory for Germany.

Humiliation was piled on humiliation when the Admiralty, heavily criticised in the British press, ordered the Home Fleet to disperse to various secondary Scottish anchorages, as in 1914, until the gaps in the defences of Scapa were plugged. An indirect extra result of the raid therefore was the serious damage, done by German mines laid by other U-boats round Scotland, to the battleship *Nelson* off Loch Ewe (*U33*) and the cruiser *Belfast* off the Firth of Forth (*U31*) in November; the latter's back was broken and both were laid up for many months. Only when the war was over did the British discover that *U56* (Wilhelm Zahn), a type II coastal boat, had got the *Nelson*, her sister-ship *Rodney* and the battlecruiser *Hood*, Britain's largest warship and flagship of the entire Royal Navy, in her sights on 30 October off the Firth of Forth. Zahn fired three torpedoes at the *Nelson*, scoring two hits; neither warhead exploded and the formation did not notice.

Prien's stroke had a dramatic effect on morale on both sides. On his boat's arrival unscathed in Wilhelmshaven just before noon on 17 October, Raeder and Dönitz (instantly promoted to rear-admiral) were on the quayside to greet the crew, every one of whom received an Iron Cross, second class (Prien got the first class) on the spot. They went on to Kiel for new uniforms and then flew to Berlin, to be driven through the streets in triumph on their way to meet Hitler, who invested Prien with the Knight's Cross of the Iron Cross. The "Bull of Scapa Flow" as he was now known (a bull was painted on the conning tower of *U47*) gave notably unbullish, restrained interviews to press, radio and news-reels. The captain's busy day ended in a visit to the theatre with Goebbels, who joyously garnered a seven-course meal of propaganda from what remains the most famous raid in the history of submarines.

The first good news from the Royal Navy after these and other setbacks came, as it had done in the First World War, from the South Atlantic, where three outgunned British cruisers of the South American Division had driven the pocket battleship *Admiral Graf Spee* to scuttle herself (and her captain, Hans Langsdorff, to commit suicide) after the Battle of the River Plate at Christmas. This was an important reduction in the threat posed by German surface units to convoys as well as a much-needed boost to British morale – Hitler's first-ever military setback.

Nine weeks later British destroyers added a dramatic postscript to the story when they slighted Norway's neutrality by dashing into the Jøssingfjord in the south-west of the country. There they boarded the German tanker *Altmark*, which had served the *Graf Spee* as support-ship and brutally primitive mobile prison for 299 British seamen taken

from her victims. They were freed in a hail of small-arms fire. The ship
was stripped of all arms but, out of belated respect for Norway, not sunk.

Norway was much on the minds of the opposed naval and military
staffs as spring 1940 approached. In winter when the Baltic was iced up,
the Swedish iron ore vital to the German war effort was sent by rail
across Norway to its northern port of Narvik, whence it was shipped
down the Inner Leads, the long chain of islands off Norway's convoluted
Atlantic coastline, and then past Danish Jutland to Germany. The
Norwegian coast itself, with so many deep fjords capable of accommodating entire squadrons, was of strategic interest to both sides because
of its obvious significance for Atlantic naval operations, not least for
submarines.

Each side therefore drew up plans to invade should the other show
signs of doing so. As usual in such contexts, the Germans were thorough
and ruthless while the British were vague and bumbling. The Home
Fleet moved back to Scapa Flow in March, complete with two dummy
battleships to confuse the Luftwaffe. Three squadrons of Hurricane
fighters and seven times more heavy anti-aircraft guns than before
joined the hulk of SS *Neuchâtel* in strengthening the defences. The first
sortie of the Home Fleet was in distant support of Operation Wilfred
(gentle name for a soft idea) to lay mines at choke-points inside the
Inner Leads near Narvik and Trondheim against the ore-carriers. "Plan
R4" was also drawn up at the Admiralty for occupying those two ports,
plus Bergen and Stavanger in southern Norway, if the Germans retaliated. Since Norway was virtually in Germany's front yard but hundreds
of miles from Britain, it seems less than wise for the British to have
chosen to be hanged for a lamb called Wilfred rather than the sheep of
a full-blown pre-emptive strike. If they were going to breach Norwegian
neutrality they might as well get the most out of it: the British showed
no sign of understanding what they were up against with Hitler.

The even more innocuously named destroyer HMS *Glowworm*
(Lieutenant-Commander G.B. Roope) covered herself in glory by
ramming the German heavy cruiser *Hipper* and tearing a 120-foot gash
in her side near Trondheim on 6 April. The lone destroyer had become
detached in bad weather as the opposing forces groped their way towards
the inevitable confrontation over Norway. Having taken on a monster
ten times her own size, *Glowworm* was blown out of the water for her
impertinence. Roope was awarded a posthumous Victoria Cross.

The *Hipper* and her destroyers were one of six strong German naval
groups discovered by British intelligence to be at sea in the first week of
April. Forbes took the Home Fleet in the wrong direction, into the
North Atlantic looking for the *Scharnhorst* and *Gneisenau* which were

rumoured to be out. The troopships in Scottish ports on standby to invade Norway were stripped of their escorts in support of Forbes, a move which completely undermined Plan R4.

Meanwhile almost all the ships the German Navy possessed had been organised into task forces for the seizure of Copenhagen and Oslo, the Danish and Norwegian capitals, and four key Norwegian ports. On 8 April the gallant Free Polish submarine *Orzel* (eagle), a new, nineteen knot, ocean-going boat built in Holland and operating with the Royal Navy, sank a German transport. Norwegian-ships picked up the survivors, who revealed that they had been on their way to "protect" Bergen from the British. None the less that port and Trondheim were taken without difficulty by the Germans on the same day, 8 April. Only the coastal artillery at Bergen inflicted significant damage on the invaders, hitting one light cruiser, *Bremse*, and leaving another, *Königsberg*, dead in the water. On the 10th, British naval aircraft came over and sank the latter, the first fleet warship ever to be sunk by air attack in wartime. Kristiansand fell after a few hours of fighting ashore.

The Germans however did not have it all their own way at Oslo. The new heavy cruiser *Blücher* led the pocket battleship *Lützow* and escorts to seize the city from the Oslofjord. With impeccable German thoroughness the flagship carried not only naval and military staffs but also all the trappings of an occupation government: administrators, filing cabinets, extra uniforms and rubber stamps. Eighteen miles south of her objective, at the narrowest point of the approach, the *Blücher* came under fire on both sides from the guns (made in Germany by Krupp) of the coastal artillery at 4.20 a.m. on the 9th. Torpedoes from tubes ashore finished the job and the *Blücher* sank in two hours with heavy loss of life. The *Lützow* led the German withdrawal. But with a resilience quite remarkable in the circumstances, the Germans stopped ten miles down the coast and landed troops to advance on the capital from the south. The Luftwaffe dropped bombs and airborne troops. Oslo duly fell – twelve hours behind schedule. But in that vital half-day the government, the gold reserves and the royal family were evacuated to the north. The Germans also took Narvik with a group of ten destroyers.

At about the same time HMS *Renown* with her escorting destroyers (Vice-Admiral W.J. Whitworth) sighted both German battlecruisers, commanded by Vice-Admiral Günther Lütjens. They had better armour and speed, but she unhesitatingly opened fire on them in appalling weather. At the cost of two non-vital hits from the Germans' total of eighteen eleven-inch guns, the twenty-four-year-old British battlecruiser landed three heavy shells from her six fifteen-inchers on the *Gneisenau*, which lost one turret and her gunnery-control system. The

weather parted the two forces after a few minutes as the British sent
every large ship they could muster into their doomed bid for Norway.
Because British aircraft were as yet forbidden to bomb towns out of
gentlemanly fear of civilian casualties, Coastal Command was not
allowed to attack Stavanger airfield. The Luftwaffe promptly exploited
this to establish local air superiority against the Home Fleet.

Five small British destroyers under Captain B.A.W. Warburton-Lee
were detached by Whitworth to counter-attack Narvik, where they sank
two out of ten much larger German destroyers, including the flotilla
leader, damaged three others and sank five German freighters. The
Germans sank two of the five British destroyers and badly damaged a
third, which got away and helped the two survivors to sink an ammunition ship as they withdrew. Warburton-Lee was awarded a posthumous
VC. As the main German naval units withdrew, shielded from air attack
by the weather, two British submarines intervened usefully: *Truant*
crippled the light cruiser *Karlsruhe*, which had to be scuttled; and *Spear-
fish* put the pocket battleship *Lützow* out of action for a year with a
single torpedo.

On 12 April Forbes arrived off Narvik with the carrier *Furious*, the
battleship *Warspite* and escorts, to try to dislodge the Germans. The
carrier's planes were all but useless in the conditions, so *Warspite*, her
appetite whetted by her spotter-plane's prompt sighting and sinking of
U64, swept into the Vestfjord flying Whitworth's flag with nine
destroyers in company, sinking a German destroyer which thought she
was lying in ambush on the way in. Seven more large German destroyers
were sunk in the ensuing action, at the cost of two British destroyers
damaged. For lack of troops Whitworth was unable to exploit the opportunity he had created, despite a constant flow of confusing and ill-
informed orders direct from the Admiralty, where Churchill, as ever,
could not resist interfering in tactical matters. On 15 April the British
had a rare piece of luck: destroyers attacked *U49*, which sank in shallow
water; from it was recovered a copy of Dönitz's plan for the deployment
of twenty-eight U-boats in the current Operation *Weserübung* against
Denmark and Norway.

But the Germans, having taken Denmark without a fight and delivered
six infantry divisions from the south, were firmly ensconced at each end
of Norway and could not be dislodged. Suffice it to say here that too few
British, French and Polish troops did land, too late, in northern Norway,
but having come hurriedly and belatedly to the fray and unable to wrest
air superiority from the Luftwaffe, the Allies had to mount a messy
and difficult withdrawal at the end of a disastrous exercise in military
incompetence. The cruiser *Glasgow* managed to take off the royals,

the politicians and the gold from the port of Molde. But the brilliant evacuation by the end of May of 30,000 troops – the first of several – cost only one French and one British destroyer sunk.

Vice-Admiral Wilhelm Marschall, German fleet commander, sent the two battlecruisers and the patched-up *Hipper* to try to disrupt the withdrawal. On 8 June this powerful force sighted the carrier *Glorious*, sister-ship of the *Courageous*. The old flat-top, ineptly commanded by the ex-submariner Captain Guy D'Oyly Hughes, carried not only her own elderly fighters but also the last planes evacuated from Narvik; even more reason why he should have had aircraft on constant patrol over his ship and her two escorting destroyers. But he took no such precaution; what is more, when attacked he did not attempt to launch planes, behaving as if he were in command of a helpless cargo ship. The destroyers resisted valiantly but one was sunk in minutes. The other, HMS *Acasta*, charged the *Scharnhorst* and sent a torpedo squarely into her stern before joining *Glorious* on the bottom.

The battlecruiser was thus added to the long list of German naval casualties sustained in the operation. This chaotic struggle for Norway gave Raeder and Dönitz a huge coastline from which to dominate the North Atlantic with U-boats and surface ships (once the many repairs had been completed). The bulk of Hitler's fleet might be *hors de combat*; but that most un-naval person clearly regarded this as a small price to pay for Norway, its coast and his iron-ore supply.

Once again totalitarian ruthlessness on Hitler's part had triumphed over irresolution among his enemies; once again British naval and military leadership, not excluding Churchill, had proved wanting, as at the beginning of the previous war. In the first May of the First World War Churchill had paid the price, being ousted from the Admiralty; in the first May of the Second he left the Admiralty again – for number ten Downing Street. Prime Minister Neville Chamberlain resigned on 10 May after a passionate debate in the House of Commons. More important by far than Churchill's shortcomings was his claim to "speak for Britain", earned in the thirties when he was one of the few opposing appeasement and Hitler.

To help offset the German seizure of Norway and Denmark, Britain occupied the Danish Faroe Islands, between Shetland and Norway, and Iceland. But on the very day that Churchill took over the reins in London as a result of the Norwegian fiasco, the Germans struck again, unleashing 134 divisions against the Netherlands, Belgium, Luxembourg and France. This "Blitzkrieg" brutally ended the Phoney War of not very masterly inactivity. For the British the loss of the Norwegian coast was bad enough; enemy acquisition by the end of June 1940 of the coast of

France, with its excellent submarine bases, was a disaster for Britain which came very close to being total. Operation Dynamo rescued a third of a million British and French troops from Dunkirk, and Operation Aerial another 200,000 from ports further south; but they had to leave their equipment behind. For the time being Britain had no Army; only the Royal Navy and the Royal Air Force remained in the game against Hitler, who decided not to press home his advantage by an invasion (for which he temporarily had no Navy). Fortunately, low cloud and incompetence prevented Göring from making good his promise to destroy the remnants of the British Expeditionary Force as it waited on the beach for rescue by destroyers and flotillas of small boats. Hitler also held back at Dunkirk in the hope of persuading Britain to settle before he turned east.

The British were now down to forty-three serviceable destroyers with another fifty-one under repair. A similar total of these most important vessels had been lost in the war so far, largely in the botched Norwegian operations and the miraculous evacuation of France, just as the U-boat arm acquired enormous new strategic advantages.

Unbeknown to the British, however, this service, which threatened their interests more than any other, was all but paralysed by a technical problem which had come to a head during the Norwegian campaign. On 13 April *U48* got in range of the battleship *Warspite*, fired a salvo of four torpedoes and achieved nothing. Two days later Prien in *U47* took aim at a "wall of ships" and fired four "eels" to no effect. His second salvo yielded no result beyond an explosion against a distant rock, which brought destroyers about his ears. The occasional earlier complaint about torpedo performance had been arrogantly ascribed by staff officers to "nerves" or errors by submarine skippers and technicians. But now the world's most famous submariner, Günther Prien, took up the matter in a furious memorandum to Dönitz in which he wrote: "I cannot be expected to fight with a dummy rifle again." Nobody could accuse Prien of lack of nerve or incompetence. He was pushing at an open door, since Dönitz himself had calculated in January 1940 that a third of a million tons more shipping might already have been sunk but for poor German torpedo performance.

Shipping losses – British, French and chartered neutral – from all causes came to 755,000 tons (221 ships) in the first four months of the war to the end of December 1939. In the North Atlantic forty-seven ships (249,000 tons) were lost to U-boats, surface raiders, mines and aircraft; efficient torpedoes would have more than doubled the U-boats' contribution. Gerhard Glattes of *U39*, the first destroyed by the British, was betrayed by prematurely exploding torpedoes when he attacked the *Ark Royal*. Dönitz probably had the details, as submarine officers had a simple code for use in letters home from prisoner-of-war camp whereby they could send information about how they had been captured. Johannes Franz of *U27*, destroyed off north-west Scotland on 20 September, reported that he had fired three torpedoes, all of which had gone off too soon, giving him away. By the time his coded message got through, Dönitz had received one report after another from captains who got home, complaining of boatloads of torpedoes detonating prematurely or not at all. In his War Diary the U-boat chief noted on 31 October that "at least thirty per cent of torpedoes are duds."

The main problem lay with the detonators. The G7a (air-powered) and G7e (electric) torpedoes could be fitted with one of two detonators as the skipper saw fit: the MZ (magnetic) and the AZ (contact). The MZ, a First World War invention developed between the wars, was intended to set off the warhead at optimum distance from a ship's hull using the victim's own magnetic field. It was mainly intended to break the back of an armoured warship by blast. The AZ was essentially an elaborate percussion cap which exploded the warhead when it hit its target; the trigger was a little twin-bladed screw on the nose of the missile. This old-fashioned "pistol" was meant for "soft-skinned" targets such as merchant ships. In Norwegian waters the hypersensitive MZ (Magnet-Zünder) was distracted not only by proximity to the North Pole but also by lodes just below the seabed of the iron ore so plentiful in the region, by underwater volcanic rock, natural variations in the earth's magnetic field and even by sunspots.

The AZ (Abklopf-Zünder – percussion detonator) failed because the blades of the screw were too short, which meant they would not trigger the charge unless the torpedo struck its target at an angle close to ninety degrees. And if the section of the hull struck was curved rather than flat, the trigger might still not work. The cure was to lengthen the blades. In fact the Germans were quickly able to copy the reliable contact-detonators they found aboard HMS *Seal*, a large British minelaying submarine they captured in the Skaggerak on 5 May 1940, when she went dead in the water on hitting a mine. Lieutenant-Commander R. Lonsdale, RN, who had wounded men aboard and no scuttling charges, ran up the white flag and surrendered to a circling Luftwaffe seaplane. Lieutenant Günther Mehrens took him aboard and a German ship came to tow the prize away (Lonsdale was honourably acquitted after the war of needlessly surrendering his boat).

There was also a problem with the torpedoes themselves. They had never been tried in wartime conditions, when they had to be carried about for long periods in variable temperatures and depths. It took two years to discover (January 1942) that the chamber for the hydrostatic valve, which controlled the missile's horizontal steering fins by reacting to pressure, was not airtight. It was therefore vulnerable to changes in airpressure such as occur in submarines when diving, changing depth or surfacing. The higher the pressure in the chamber, the deeper the torpedo ran. Thus German torpedoes tended to run under their targets. This would not have mattered so much had the magnetic detonators been reliable, a fault which was not cured until December 1942. Until then the U-boats' principal weapon represented no improvement at all on their predecessors' torpedoes in the previous war. Analysis of three dozen German submarine attacks by thirty-one boats in the specially testing circumstances of the Norwegian campaign suggested that twenty which failed would have succeeded in damaging or sinking their targets had the torpedoes worked properly. Until the contact-pistol was improved, Prien's summary of the position in his post-Norway report remained valid: "to all intents and purposes the U-boats were without a weapon," at any rate against warships on the open sea.

Investigations by Vice-Admiral Oskar Kummetz, appointed by Raeder to replace the dismissed Vice-Admiral Götting as head of the Torpedo Inspectorate at the end of 1939, eventually identified bureaucratic inertia as the root cause of the crisis. Experiments in 1936–7 had revealed the deep-running tendency. An extra "depth-spring" was fitted to the balance apparatus and seemed to correct the fault, although it was only tried twice before it was fitted generally. But competition from other branches of the Wehrmacht meant such springs could not be produced in numbers until early 1939. Also in 1937, Max Valentiner, erstwhile ace and hammer of the Mediterranean, told the naval command that experiments with magnetic pistols in 1917–18 had shown them to be erratic. But he was loftily assured that things were much better now than in his day. Trials of torpedoes by German warships during the Spanish Civil War produced similar failures, but nothing serious was done. Rear-Admiral Oskar Wehr, head of the Torpedo Experimental Institute near Kiel, was dismissed, court-martialled and imprisoned for six months with two of his assistants. The sentence, mild by the standards of Hitler's Germany, suggests he was a scapegoat for general complacency and lack of alertness in the naval command, including Dönitz, who could hardly have been unaware of prewar failures and warnings (his memoirs gloss over the point).

None the less, by the end of May 1940 the U-boats alone, at a cost of two dozen of their number, had sunk 241 ships totalling 853,000 tons. Given their small numbers and their treacherous armament, this was a remarkable achievement, and an ominous one for the British.

For their part they had already discovered, inevitably, that Asdic was neither a miracle-worker nor God's gift to the anti-submarine warrior. It will be remembered that the device, in a dome under the ship's hull, transmitted a sonic beam and received as an echo the famous "ping" whose strength and frequency indicated the bearing and range of the detected object. Unfortunately this was more likely to be a shoal of fish, a wreck or the seabed than a U-boat. Operators needed a sixth sense to distinguish between a submarine's echo and all the rest. The ship using Asdic had to limit her speed to some sixteen to eighteen knots to enable the operator to pick out the echoes from the ship's own noise. Finally, Asdic could not detect a submarine on the surface, or even underwater at very close range, which meant that the ASW ship went "deaf" just as she came on to drop depth-charges. This could give a U-boat as much as two minutes to twist and turn out of harm's way, between loss of contact by the attacker and detonation of his depth-charges (the attacker had to pass over the enemy's estimated position before being able to drop his charges from the stern). The Royal Navy had experimented with Asdic on "non-intervention" patrols during the Spanish Civil War and, like the Germans with their torpedoes, glossed over the short-comings. Only in April 1940 did the Admiralty order Asdic watches round the clock instead of merely in daylight, abandoning the prewar assumption that the Germans would attack submerged by day in view of incontrovertible evidence that they struck on the surface at night. They might usefully have studied *Die U-bootswaffe* (the submarine weapon) published by Dönitz just before the outbreak of war, in which he stated his preference for such tactics.

All the same the Germans, who had concentrated on passive detection between the wars, believed for some time that Asdic was a super-hydro-phone of all but miraculous capability rather than an echo-ranger. U-boat crews wore soft-soled footwear and practised elaborate silence routines when enemy warships were about. They found that lying on the bottom (if possible) or going as deep as they dared helped them to escape. Depth-charges were detonated by a preset water pressure and for some time British ships set them to explode too soon, before developing a technique of dropping a "pattern" of charges set to go off at a variety of depths. The RAF did not acquire airborne depth-charges until summer 1940, and then only on the insistence of Coastal Command, against the inclinations of the Air Ministry. The prewar anti-ship bomb, never realistically tested, proved all but useless against surface ships, and totally so against a diving or submerged submarine. Nor did the British possess a bomb-sight of the necessary high degree of accuracy. It was fortunate that the *Nürnberg* was a sitting target when they attacked it. Until the acoustic torpedo was invented later in the war, aerial torpedoes were useless against submarines.

Both sides, if for diametrically opposed reasons, pursued an idea left over from the First World War: the merchantman with concealed armament. The British briefly resurrected the Q-ship in her original role as a decoy for U-boats, sending eight into the North Atlantic from December 1939 to March 1940. A ruse which had only limited success but had encouraged attack without warning when first tried stood little chance of fooling the alumni of the U-boat school. None of the decoys sighted a submarine but two were sunk by submerged attacks in the Western Approaches and the rest caused disruption to their own side because of the secrecy surrounding their deployment. An Admiralty enquiry in summer 1940 put paid to the idea. The Germans had used disguised commerce-raiders until 1918 with some success, and converted ten fast merchantmen for a repeat performance. The first and most successful, *Atlantis*, sailed on 31 March 1940, adding to the stress on the British surface fleet just as the U-boats withdrew to concentrate on Norwegian and western European operations until the end of May.

The fall of France a month later and its division between occupation zone and pro-Nazi Vichy gave Dönitz the whole of the long French Atlantic coastline down to the Pyrenees. On the other side of that barrier lay Franco's Fascist Spain, a sympathetic neutral (though not sympathetic enough to join the Axis in combat after the Civil War). The French coast enabled the U-boats to base themselves 400 miles further out into the Atlantic than before whereas the British lacked the westernmost bases of the earlier conflict, now in independent Ireland.

Faced with this problem and the apparently imminent invasion, the British under Churchill found the iron resolution hitherto missing from their prosecution of the war. As France's defensive effort crumbled, A. V. Alexander, Churchill's successor at the Admiralty, and Admiral Sir Dudley Pound, the First Sea Lord and Chief of Naval Staff, flew to Bordeaux, whither the French government had fled, for talks with Admiral Jean Darlan, the naval C-in-C. They entreated him to order the French fleet to sail out of reach of the Axis, whether to the French West Indies, British, Canadian or neutral American ports. All he would promise was that the Axis would not be allowed to use the French Navy. The British found this as comforting as the two dictators' promise not to use it against Britain if France surrendered. Only two elderly battleships, four destroyers, seven submarines and a few small craft joined Free French forces in Britain.

The Admiralty detached a strong "Force H" from the Home Fleet to replace the French Atlantic contribution against the German surface ships. Vice-Admiral Sir James Somerville was given the battlecruiser *Hood*, the carrier *Ark Royal*, two battleships, a cruiser and four destroyers and based himself at Gibraltar.

The core of the French fleet – two modern battlecruisers, two battleships, a seaplane-carrier and six destroyers – was in the Algerian port of Mers-el-Kebir, with seven more destroyers and four submarines at the nearby port of Oran. On 3 July 1940 Somerville initiated Operation Catapult and drew up his powerful squadron off Mers-el-Kebir. He offered Admiral Marcel Gensoul, the fleet commander, the choice of joining Britain, internment, sailing to the West Indies or scuttling on the spot. Sadly the French admiral decided the British were bluffing. Somerville was not. The battlecruiser *Strasbourg* and five destroyers managed to escape to Toulon. Every other ship was sunk or crippled in a shocking stroke which at least convinced the rest of the world that the British were serious. Four days later a Force H detachment damaged *Richelieu* without sinking her. The French battlefleet was swept from the board.

Meanwhile the convoy system was settling into a routine which was soon to be seriously tested by Dönitz: on 23 June 1940, just two days after the German armistice with France, a convoy of trucks known as the *Torpedozug* (torpedo-train) physically removed U-boat headquarters, its equipment and munitions from Wilhelmshaven to Paris, whence it would soon move again to Kernevel, near Lorient on the south Brittany coast.

The coastal convoy network which started on 6 September 1939 assembled outward-bound groups of transatlantic shipping in the Thames estuary and sailed them clockwise, escorted by warships, round the south coast of England, collecting more from Southampton, Plymouth and Falmouth on the way. These convoys bore the prefix OA. Others, styled OB, started from Liverpool and sailed down the Irish Sea, collecting more ships from the Welsh ports and Bristol. The two streams converged off Land's End and sailed westward, detaching a sub-convoy bound for Gibraltar (OG) as they passed the Scilly Isles. The transatlantic convoy would be escorted by a few warships, sometimes including a battleship, to longitude 12 degrees 30 minutes west, where the escort would leave; the ships sailed on together for another day before dispersing to their various North American destinations, while the escorts would put about to escort an inbound convoy.

The first of these to sail was SL 1 from Sierra Leone, the British West

African colony, on 14 September. HX 1, first of a long and crucial series, left Halifax, Nova Scotia, two days later, picking up ships from other North America ports and sailing in company to an escort pick-up-point. HXF 1, a fast convoy from the same port, sailed three days after that. HG 1 left Gibraltar for Britain on 26 September. Ships which could not sustain a speed of nine knots and those able to sail faster than fifteen travelled as "independently routed ships" (IRS).

These parameters were too narrow, representing a false economy in assembly times on the one hand ("better late than never" should have been the watchword) and an insufficient margin of safety against the U-boats, capable of eighteen knots surfaced, on the other. Fast liners could safely be left to sail alone, most notably the six grey-painted "monsters": the Cunarders *Queen Elizabeth* and *Queen Mary* of more than 80,000 tons each, two other outsize British ships plus one French and one Dutch super-liner, each capable of up to thirty knots. These were invaluable as troopships, able to embark an entire division.

Overall, in the first four months of the war to the end of 1939, 5,756 individual sailings had been made in convoy while only four convoyed ships were sunk by U-boats. All the other victims were unescorted, whether stragglers (slow-running ships), rompers (fast runners), detached from their convoy for some other reason or IRS. Once again the U-boats were choosing the easiest targets, and there were more than enough slow ships sailing alone to keep attacks on convoys rare until well into the conflict, making a high score possible for the predators.

Britain began systematic import reduction and substitution from the beginning, to curb the demand for shipping while creating the extra capacity for munitions from the United States. Imports were cut by some twenty per cent to forty-five million tons in the first instance and oil products were rationed at once. Rationing of other items followed as it became necessary.

The British Merchant Navy, which numbered 160,000 volunteers in 1939, including 4,500 masters, 13,000 officers and 20,000 engineers, could carry only three-quarters of the country's imports, leaving the rest to neutral shipping (not American, as US ships were not allowed to sail into war zones).

The Admiralty had revived its Trade Division in 1936, and in the following year appointed a Shipping Defence Advisory Committee and liaison officers to instruct the Merchant Navy in defence measures. By September 1939, 10,000 officers had been trained, 2,000 of them in gunnery, while 1,500 seamen had been taught to serve guns. About 1,000 ships had reinforced decks. In 1937 Paymaster Rear-Admiral Sir

Eldon Manisty was recalled, to tour the world setting up a Naval Control Service (NCS). This was in place six months before hostilities began. Each significant port had its own NCS officer, a serving naval man; in the main ports outside the Commonwealth and Empire there was a Consular Shipping Adviser (usually a former naval officer). They reported to the Admiralty daily on shipping movements.

Almost as dead as "Trade" in the dying years of peace was the Naval Intelligence Division (NID), revived after its failure during the Abyssinian crisis of 1936. Room 40 was but a memory, albeit a strong one for those still in the service who had worked there. Its legacy was the postwar Government Code and Cipher School (GC & CS), a small organisation for breaking foreign and protecting British ciphers which, like the Secret Intelligence Service or MI6, came under the control of the Foreign Office. It began in central London and moved to Bletchley Park in Buckinghamshire, well outside the capital. Its chief was Commander Alistair Denniston, formerly of Room 40, and it had sections geared to the needs of the three armed services and devoted to individual "target" countries, including Germany, Japan and the Soviet Union.

In 1937 Rear-Admiral James Troup, the new Director of Naval Intelligence, appointed Paymaster Lieutenant-Commander Norman Denning to head a new Operational Intelligence Centre (OIC) in NID. He spent a month at the GC & CS, forging a link which was to play a central role in the conduct of the war. OIC's function was to collect and redistribute naval intelligence from all sources. It won its spurs in the Spanish Civil War, when it kept track of all naval and mercantile shipping in Spanish waters on a single chart. This was the inspiration for the Submarine Tracking Room in the wartime OIC. Denning successfully pressed for the rapid extension of Britain's radio listening posts, of which there were just five: two in Britain, one in Malta and two in the Far East. The GC & CS sought to penetrate foreign radio transmissions picked up by listening posts or "Y-stations". The third component of a truly formidable British wartime signals-intelligence (sigint) apparatus, hugely expanded from First World War examples, was radio direction-finding (RDF; not to be confused with radar, originally known by these letters in Britain). This established the position of ships by triangulation, using their radio signals, picked up from two or more angles, as coordinates. A more accurate refinement of this, high-frequency direction-finding (HF/DF, or "huff-duff" in naval slang), was installed on convoy escorts from early in the war. It helped to locate U-boats by monitoring their high-frequency transmissions, favoured by the Germans because they thought the British relied exclusively on medium-wave transmissions for direction purposes, as during the Spanish war. The accuracy of such interceptions decreased as distance increased, which the Germans discovered when they compared the interception log of HMS *Seal* with the positions of their own ships at the times recorded.

Lieutenant-Commander Peter Kemp, invalided out of the service after the loss of a leg, was recalled by Denning to run the direction-finding service throughout the war. The OIC was expanded in the Munich crisis, when a new Operations War Room was set up, alongside a Trade Plot showing the position of all merchant shipping, and a War Registry to look after communicating with shipping (controlled by the Admiralty for the duration). Secure telephone and teleprinter lines connected OIC with GC & CS, naval and RAF commands in an exemplary network of intra- and inter-service communication. The Americans recognised its excellence and copied it in due course.

The Admiralty set up the Defensively Equipped Merchant Ship (DEMS) organisation three months before the war. Its role was to find and install old naval guns, anti-aircraft and machine-guns in the merchant fleet, and the men to operate them, for 5,500 vessels. By the end of 1940 some 3,400 ships had been armed. Self-defence on merchant ships eventually absorbed nearly 190,000 men from Merchant Navy, Royal Navy and Marines and even the Army, which earmarked 14,000 men for the Maritime Regiment of the Royal Artillery for the purpose.

On the German side, operational naval intelligence was known as the *Beobachtungsdienst* (observation service), which also relied heavily on sigint. Its most sophisticated branch was *xB-dienst*, which worked on foreign naval codes and ciphers. Wilhelm Tranow made important inroads into British cryptography in the Spanish days of mutual eavesdropping. The Royal Navy used manual ciphers while the Germans, like the Americans, the Japanese and the RAF, favoured mechanised ones. The Germans chose the "Enigma" encipherment machine, to which we shall return. The *B-dienst* also tracked enemy shipping by direction-finding.

Captain Wilhelm Canaris, before attaining flag rank and taking over command of the *Abwehr* (Wehrmacht intelligence) in 1935, reconstituted the First World War *Etappendienst*, a worldwide "staging service" for German surface raiders, disguised raiders, blockade-runners and support ships run by naval officers and agents in key ports. One of its jobs was to collect information on shipping, mirroring the work of the British NCS.

Dönitz maintained the obverse of the British Trade Plot and Submarine Tracking Room at his headquarters. A Situation Room (*die Lage*) in the Operations Department, run by Captain (later Rear-Admiral)

Eberhard Godt, Dönitz's able and unjustly forgotten deputy throughout the war, provided a panorama of the current position at sea, showing convoys, naval units and U-boats. Next door was the "Museum", which provided an up-to-the-minute analysis of operations, trends at sea and enemy conduct in graphs, tables and diagrams built on intelligence from all sources. To keep in the closest possible touch with the situation at sea, Dönitz himself read every patrol report and debriefed every U-boat skipper on his return unless prevented by other duties. Another manifestation of his concern for subordinates, a hallmark of the great commander, was the stream of signals to boats at sea, whether directing them to targets or forwarding urgent personal messages: Prien was told of the birth of his daughter by a message announcing the arrival of "a U-boat without periscope". No force had ever been to war on the basis of such a volume of signals; this garrulity was to be an Achilles' heel.

The American interpretation of the word "neutral" as applied to itself in 1939 was, not surprisingly, the cause of considerable irritation to the belligerents, if rather more so to the Axis powers than their enemies. The sympathetic Roosevelt administration seemed at first to be hamstrung in what it could do to aid Britain and France, and Britain alone in the eighteen months between the fall of France and America's appearance on the field of battle. There was the Johnson Act of 1934, banning new loans to nations which failed to pay off old debts – such as France and Britain, unable to meet vast obligations incurred in the First World War. The powerful isolationist tendency backed this law in the hope of forcing the defaulters to pay up. They were unable to do so, which meant that they found it almost impossible at first to obtain American munitions when war broke out.

In 1935 came the first of a series of Neutrality Acts. Collectively they denied loans and credits to belligerents; strictly limited the carriage of munitions in American ships, which were also forbidden to carry armament for self-defence if trading with belligerents; gave the President discretion to bar the latter from US ports; and imposed "cash and carry only" on purchases of any American goods by belligerents. Other laws modified American neutrality by authorising the arming of merchant ships after all and by letting them carry goods to belligerents' ports, presumably to avoid damaging US trade. The President was also authorised to declare combat and neutral sea zones in the western hemisphere.

His main political reference in determining America's interventions in the war in Europe, decisive long before it became a combatant, was isolationism. This tendency cut across party lines and held that the US should avoid entanglements outside its hemisphere. He needed the isolationists' support for his New Deal projects; their influence was therefore at its peak in his first term, 1933–7. Thereafter Roosevelt devoted much energy (and questionable political tactics) to undermining them so as to be able to use the American economy as a life-support for the British war effort. The Anglo-American relationship was truly special in those dark days, founded upon and culminating in the unique friendship between Roosevelt and Churchill, nourished by a broad stream of letters, telegrams, telephone calls and summit meetings. The connection was initiated by the American leader when Churchill was appointed to the Admiralty; Roosevelt wanted to be in touch with the one major figure in the British government who had most vehemently opposed appeasement in the thirties. Churchill's open appeal to America to "give us the tools and we will finish the job" was answered, for the time being, by Roosevelt's public promise of "all aid short of war".

Neutrality or no, there had been secret staff talks between British and American officers in May 1939, when it had been agreed that the US Navy would cover the western Atlantic in the event of war. When it came, the United States persuaded the Organisation of American States to declare this huge expanse of ocean a Neutrality Zone. To police the zone, closed to belligerents unless they possessed territory within it, as Britain and France conveniently did, the US Navy formed a strong Atlantic Squadron (soon upgraded to Fleet) with five battleships and nine cruisers. This meant that shipping was safe from U-boats and needed no escort in the western half of the Atlantic, an enormous help to the Royal Navy, which also enjoyed the use of Canadian ports such as Halifax for replenishment.

British gold and dollar reserves amounted in September 1939 to just over £1,000 million. There was virtually no prospect of adding to them by exports and every chance of their vanishing in months as Britain ordered ships, planes, tanks, guns and other munitions, taking over orders placed by the French before their defeat. Even in those days, when the pound was worth five dollars, such a sum would not last long on a "cash and carry only" basis. So Roosevelt told his lawyers to find loopholes.

As Britain braced itself for invasion after the fall of France, the omens at sea were darkening. In June 1940, when the U-boats returned to attacking commerce, 585,000 tons of British, Allied and neutral shipping were sunk worldwide. This was twice as bad as May, the worst month of the war so far (and the only one in the entire war when losses to aircraft exceeded those to U-boats – by a factor of three, thanks to the

Norwegian and western European campaigns). The U-boats alone sank almost 250,000 tons in June. The total shipping loss to enemy action in ten months amounted to about 2,250,000 tons, equivalent to eleven per cent of the British merchant fleet and five per cent of all shipping available to Britain. Submarines claimed forty-eight per cent of this, even before they began to exploit their new French bases; mines got twenty-six per cent, aircraft thirteen, surface raiders six and miscellaneous or unknown causes the rest. At this stage Britain's capacity for building new ships was some 88,000 tons a month, or barely a third of the average loss rate so far.

The U-boats sank two carriers and 215 merchantmen. Of the latter, 193 were IRS and only twenty-two under escort. Twenty-four U-boats were destroyed, of which eleven were caught by convoy-escort forces, a miserable rate of return of two convoyed ships sunk for every U-boat lost to escorts. The ratio looked far better for the Germans in IRS sinkings, with fifteen ships sunk for each U-boat destroyed (only three were lost to hunting patrols, three to mines, two each to British submarines, air attacks and unknown causes and one by accident). But throughout the period there was an average of only six boats on the warpath at a time, the rest being on their way out or home, training or on other duties. The Germans started the war with fifty-seven boats and ended this first phase with fifty-one. The average lifespan of an operational U-boat was three months and the replacement rate was ten per cent less than the loss rate at this stage. Dönitz was impatient to inaugurate pack tactics against the convoys but lacked the boats to do it.

A couple of experiments had already convinced him, however, that there was no point in sending a flotilla commander to sea on such missions because of the difficulties of communication between boats. It was much more efficient to home one or more individual boats onto targets and control them direct from headquarters by wireless. Here was a rich vein of sigint for the British to work; even richer if only they could decipher as well as intercept it.

The German occupation of French ports meant that type II coastal boats with their limited range could be deployed all the way round the British Isles while the ocean-going boats were as much as 450 miles, or getting on for two days, closer to their most fertile fields of operation.

The British were now firmly impaled on the horns of a terrible dilemma: to deploy the fleet, especially the few destroyers, against invasion or against the U-boat threat. The only way they could strike back at Germany was by bombing, which meant that RAF Bomber Command enjoyed absolute priority for longer-range aircraft while

Coastal Command was denied the handful it desperately needed for
maritime reconnaissance.

For the first time since Napoleon an enemy controlled the far side of
the "English" Channel, now effectively closed to both parties. Great
guns were already lobbing shells across the twenty-one-mile waterway;
the Luftwaffe could use short-range planes against coastal convoys and
the Germans based their fast, light E-boats in occupied Dutch ports for
raids on British North Sea traffic. The British were forced to shift as
much coastal shipping as possible from their east to their west coast,
while ocean convoys switched from the south to the north of Ireland
(from the Western to the North-Western Approaches). The Home Fleet,
all but stripped of destroyers, moved from Scapa Flow to the Firth of
Forth to be that much closer to potential invasion points in south-east
England, without abandoning the watch for major German ships as they
returned to duty from the repair yards after Norway. British cruisers
were distributed down the east coast to guard against invasion. Western
Approaches Command, which ran transatlantic convoy escort, was also
largely denuded of destroyers. Disguised raiders such as *Atlantis* added
to Admiralty headaches by spreading out across the world in pursuit of
British shipping.

Two British survivors of such an attack managed to reach a remote
West Indian island on 18 July; the British C-in-C, Americas, and West
Indies, Admiral Sir Charles Kennedy-Purvis, reacted by banning all IRS
sailings. Unfortunately the ban was local and temporary; had it been
worldwide and permanent much grief would have been avoided and
huge savings in shipping and cargoes made. This was even more desirable
now because the Italian declaration of war on 10 June and naval pre-
occupations elsewhere had closed the Mediterranean to British shipping.
It had to use the Cape route round South Africa instead of the Suez
Canal for voyages to and from the Far East and Australasia, a detour
almost equal to half the circumference of the earth, hugely costly in
time, fuel and numbers of ships at sea at any one time (150 extra if the
rate of delivery was to be maintained). Already a disguised raider had
sown mines off Cape Agulhas, South Africa, the southernmost point of
the continent, in May.

The immediate issue between Britain and Germany was whether the
Luftwaffe could offset German naval inferiority by wresting control of
the airspace over the south-east of England, the planned invasion area,
from the RAF: the scene was set for the Battle of Britain. In July Hitler
issued his directive for the invasion, and on 1 August another for
weakening the RAF by attacking its bases and the aviation industry.
The chain of radar stations on the English south and east coasts and

RAF Fighter Command, which used them as its eyes, was the front line between Hitler and Buckingham Palace. On 17 August he declared a total blockade of British waters, in which all ships, including neutrals, were subject to unrestricted submarine warfare and attack without warning by all other available means. The war zone coincided with the area barred to American ships by US neutrality law; this was no time to provoke the Americans. Tag X (D-Day) was set for 15 September.

As the burgeoning Atlantic campaign moved westward towards mid-ocean, the German torpedo crisis was checked, if not overcome. Commander Viktor Oehrn brought U37 back to Wilhelmshaven on 9 June after a triumphant patrol: he sank ten ships with a total tonnage of 41,200 and damaged another of 9,500 tons in five weeks in the Western Approaches. He used guns or scuttling charges to sink six of his victims under prize rules and had no luck with the modified magnetic pistols, but sank four with the copied British contact pistols; morale rose when word spread among the flotillas.

As the siege of Britain began in earnest a myth was born of how the country "stood alone" against the Fascist hordes. In European terms it certainly did, and there can be no denying that it held the line for democracy until the United States joined the fray.

But alongside the British stood the Commonwealth and Empire, from which important reinforcements of soldiers, airmen and sailors came to share the burden. In the context of the second transatlantic U-boat campaign it has to be recognised that Britain could not have kept the lifeline open without the usually unsung contribution of the Royal Canadian Navy. The Canadians have seldom been given credit for their unglamorous and sometimes tragic contribution to winning the Atlantic campaign because their Navy came first under British and then American operational control and acquired its first independent command only after the crisis was past.

The RCN, founded in 1910, boasted two old cruisers in 1914 (one for each coast, Atlantic and Pacific) and mustered 9,000 men in 1918. In 1922 it had shrivelled to one destroyer and two armed trawlers per coast amid jokes about "Canada's two-ocean Navy". In the Slump it was nearly abolished to save money. But in 1939 it started the war with six modern, British-built destroyers and eleven other sea-going vessels (minesweepers and patrol-boats), 2,000 regular sailors and 1,700 in reserve. By September 1940 the RCN numbered 10,000 and in 1944 it reached its peak strength of 95,705, with 378 warships. This represents a forty-eight-fold increase in personnel, compared with twenty-five for the US Navy, fourteen for the Australian and eight for the British. Such a huge expansion was bound to generate acute growing pains.

As in 1914, Canada, having declared war on Germany one week after the British (10 September 1939), sent one Army division to Britain immediately (it was soon to be expanded to a corps). It offered its prairies as a granary for Britain; its ports as a refuge for evacuees, the Royal Navy and, should the need arise, for government and royal family; its industrial, docking, repair and military training facilities; its shipyards; and the trained pilots of the Royal Canadian Air Force. It also acted as a staging post for forwarding American munitions and industrial manufactures overland to its ports for onward shipment to Britain.

W.L. Mackenzie King, the Liberal Prime Minister who served twenty-two years in the post, decided at the outset that Canada's main contribution would be focused on its Navy and Air Force rather than the Army (whose contribution nevertheless was considerable). For all its vast size Canada was and is a small country demographically, and he saw opportunities to expand its industrial and technological base by concentrating on the less manpower-intensive, more technical services and their sophisticated equipment. So he rejected British advice to turn to America for Canada's shipbuilding needs and ordered sixty-four corvettes and twenty-four "Bangor" minesweepers from the country's own small yards. More orders followed. The British eventually built four more big destroyers for Canada, which assigned ten of its corvettes to the Royal Navy as soon as they were ready.

Canadian yards also took on a first order of ninety standardised freighters of the "Liberty ship" type, also built in huge numbers in the United States. Canada began the war with a merchant fleet of only thirty-seven ships of more than 2,000 tons. The Ottawa government created the Park Steamship Company to run the home-built ships; by the end of the war it owned 175. The Canadians also joined the DEMS scheme, arming 713 merchantmen, and added to the British network of stations eavesdropping on enemy wireless. Three Canadian Pacific liners were converted into armed merchant cruisers. The Canadians started building their own destroyers during the war and generously sent all seven then in their service to Britain in the invasion scare of summer 1940. It was the prewar staffwork of Captain R.H. Oland, RCN, that made it possible to send the first convoy from Halifax to Britain, HX 1, six days after Canada declared war. Captain Eric Brand, RN, arrived at Naval Service Headquarters in Ottawa from Britain in June 1939 to serve "on loan" as Canada's Director of Naval Intelligence throughout the war, setting up a Canadian OIC to support Britain's. Brand also commanded the Convoy and Routeing Section at NSHQ.

The Canadian and United States Navies initiated serious contacts in

May 1940, when the possibility of a British defeat was at its most acute. A Major Goulet of the United States Marine Corps came from Washington to Ottawa to see Captain Brand, in whose papers their extraordinary conversation is recorded. The Americans were worried about Newfoundland, now a Canadian province but then an independently administered British colony, and the part of North America closest to Britain. The entire island, with its suddenly crucial main port of St John's, lay eastward of sixty degrees west, the boundary of the Pan-American Neutrality Zone (the only important Canadian port east of that line was Sydney, Cape Breton, at the eastern end of Nova Scotia province, already in increasing use as a support for Halifax). Canada, though naturally interested in Newfoundland, had no rights or responsibilities in its defence.

Goulet, an officer of comparatively low rank, turned out to be the bearer of a most portentous message at this nadir in British fortunes: "I've been told to tell you unofficially that if any British ships are in trouble they would be welcome in American ports." Brand replied: "Well, that's an historic statement – I can't thank you enough."

Brand's papers also show that Canada had earmarked Gaspé Bay, New Brunswick, in the Gulf of St Lawrence, as a "spare bedroom" for the British fleet in the event of a successful German invasion, "the finest harbour in the world, I think, for anchoring a lot of ships: deep water, ten fathoms, easy entrance, beautiful shelter . . ."

Five days after becoming Prime Minister, Winston Churchill had "looked at the books" and told Roosevelt that Britain was about to run out of liquid funds and would therefore be unable to comply with the "cash and carry" proviso. On 15 May 1940 he asked to borrow fifty American destroyers. The President played for time and angered Churchill by tactlessly expressing his concern that the British fleet might fall into German hands. At the same time Roosevelt exploited concern, not to say near panic, about Britain's fate to announce a vast armament programme. Hesitation in Congress in spring to approve extra defence expenditure of $2 billion made way in summer for eagerness to approve $10.5 billion in new spending. More ships were authorised at a stroke than had been funded throughout the inter-war years in $5.3 billion-worth of extra naval expenditure; 50,000 aircraft were to be built; aided by conscription and mobilising the National Guard, the US Army was authorised to expand to 100 divisions.

Roosevelt had decided to run for an unprecedented third term and was still wary about isolationism; the emphasis was therefore on defending the western hemisphere against the dictators. On 17 August 1940

Roosevelt met Mackenzie King at Ogdensburg on the New York State side of the St Lawrence Seaway shared with Canada. They set up a Permanent Joint Board of Defense with orders to draw up a "Plan Black"; what to do in the event of Britain's defeat.

Meanwhile the lawyers had found loopholes in the neutrality laws: the administration was free to do what it liked with *surplus* munitions. Shiploads of infantry weapons left over from 1918 were therefore sent to Britain. Then they found that while the President was not free to give Churchill the destroyers he was pleading for, he could barter them. So on 13 August he offered Churchill fifty First World War coal-burning "tin cans" in exchange for US military facilities on British islands in the western hemisphere, from Newfoundland to the West Indies. This fifty per cent increase in the Royal Navy's stock of destroyers (seven went to Canada) was finally confirmed on 2 September in the "destroyers-for-bases deal". The ships with their four tall funnels needed modernisation but proved remarkably robust when they joined the fleet.

Mindful of the vital American shipbuilding contribution to the frustration of the U-boats in 1917–18, the British early in 1940 cast about for a successor to the "Hog Islander" off-the-peg freighter. They chose a much enlarged version of the tramp-steamer originally built by the Sands Company of Sunderland in north-east England in 1879, a simple, sturdy, coal-burning ship of 10,800 tons with triple-expansion engines, capable of ten knots and initially costing $1.8 million apiece. The Canadians also built to this design, which had to be adapted to American engineering norms. The first British order in America was for sixty "Liberty ships", which originally needed one million man-hours each to construct. The first keel was laid at the Todd-Bath yard at South Portland, Maine.

The British sent a Technical Mission to Washington in August 1940 in the hope of bartering their latest military technologies for further American aid. Their trump card was radar – *RA*dio *D*irection *A*nd *R*anging. The Americans were sceptical at first, knowing from shipping losses that Asdic/sonar was not all it was cracked up to be. But British work on ASV – anti-surface-vessel – radar, which foreshadowed that priceless supplement to Asdic, a radar of high enough frequency to detect the conning towers of surfaced submarines, did impress the US Navy, which promptly arranged for American manufacturers to produce sets based on British models for both countries. The Americans also acknowledged that intensive British training had improved the yield from Asdic. In October 1940 the administration agreed to let the British in on all its defence technology except the Norden bomb-sight and a new mine, in exchange for British secrets. At this stage radar had proved itself in the Battle of Britain, won in September, when Hitler called off the invasion.

But the British had no means of knowing that this was off the agenda. The American Christmas present which transformed their fortunes was confided by Roosevelt to Churchill on 17 December and made public in one of his famous radio "fireside chats" on 29 December. Using the analogy of helping a neighbour by lending him a hose to put out a fire, the President, confident after winning his third term, declared America to be "the great arsenal of democracy". Work began at once on the "Lend-Lease Bill". Its number in the House of Representatives was 1776, the date of the Declaration of Independence from Britain, as the far from moribund isolationist tendency was quick to point out. The President would acquire the right to "sell, transfer title to, exchange, lease, lend or otherwise dispose of" goods to any country vital to American security. It was signed into law on 11 March 1941; Roosevelt was at last free to supply "all aid short of war". Congress voted the first Lend-Lease budget of $7 billion two weeks later; the total involved in Lend-Lease to all Allies by the end of the war reached $48 billion. It may well have been enlightened self-interest, but it was also open-handed, unstinted and a war-winning factor.

Britain received about one-third of this enormous total, of which only about one-fifth was ever repaid by "reverse Lend-Lease" or in cash. The scale of American generosity became clear after the war when Washington not only wrote off the rest but also instituted Marshall Aid for European reconstruction. The Americans may have been exaggerating when they claimed in 1918 to have saved Europe by their belated intervention in the First World War; there can be no doubt that their money and their industry ensured victory in the Second.

The triangular alliance which fought the Atlantic campaign against the U-boats was forged in the first three months of 1941, when "American-British Conversations", collectively known as ABC-1, were held in Washington between the military staffs. Australian, Canadian and New Zealand advisers were in touch with the British delegation but took no part in the talks themselves, which worried the Canadians a great deal. They won their point in November 1941, when American-Canadian arrangements were incorporated into the ABC-1 structure at talks entitled ABC-22.

The assumption in these discussions was that the United States would become a belligerent and that the alliance would also fight Japan. The most important strategic decision of the war, to be confirmed later by the political leaders, was taken in principle at ABC-1: "Germany first".

The Canadians found themselves in the unenviable position of coming under Admiralty orders in the North Atlantic and of neutral Washington elsewhere. They were also worried that "destroyers for bases" gave the US Navy air and ship facilities in Newfoundland. Britain, however, handed St John's, the island's main naval base, to Canada in May 1941. The Canadians ensured that their local naval commander always out-ranked the local American one and that their naval presence was larger. Once the Americans were embroiled in the Pacific there was no contest. The RCN was called upon to place five destroyers and fifteen corvettes under US command in the Atlantic and the rest of its mushrooming fleet under British command in the north and east. Each of the three North Atlantic powers had military missions in the capitals of the other two.

One of many ways in which Canada supported Britain was in taking part in the Children's Overseas Resettlement Scheme. The Dutch liner *Volendam*, 15,400 tons, was damaged but not sunk by a torpedo on 30 August 1940, thirteen days after Hitler declared unrestricted submarine warfare round Britain; fortunately all 321 British children aboard, on their way to sit out the war in Canada, were saved. But on 18 September, the liner *City of Benares*, with ninety migrant children among her 400 or so passengers, was sunk while acting as the commodore's ship of an unprotected "convoy" in the gap between the western extremity of the British escort provision and the American Neutrality Zone, 600 miles west of Ireland. Heinrich Bleichrodt in *U48* sank the 11,100-ton ship, which was unable to launch most of her lifeboats; about 300 passengers went down with her, including seventy-seven of the children. The remaining thirteen were found alive among fewer than 100 survivors by aircraft a week later and picked up by destroyers. Their poignant story had a greater impact in Britain than any other sinking, even the loss of the *Athenia*. The resettlement scheme was suspended.

Confident that Hitler would not gratuitously seek to acquire an enemy as powerful as the United States, the Americans now proceeded to stretch the definition of "neutrality" beyond the laws of lexicography. Ten large Coastguard cutters were added to the fifty destroyers, whose obviously American profiles gave them virtual immunity, except in British waters, for fear of an "incident". The next American contribution was a move into escorting convoys, from 1 April 1941. Admiral Harold R. Stark, USN, Chief of Naval Operations, drew a Support Force from the Atlantic Fleet (Admiral Ernest J. King) and its Neutrality Patrol. The force was headed by Rear-Admiral Arthur LeRoy Bristol, USN, with headquarters at Norfolk, Virginia. The Americans financed naval and air bases respect-ively for the force at Gareloch and Loch Ryan in Scotland and at Londonderry and Lough Erne in Northern Ireland, at a cost of $50 million. A similar sum was set aside, in the US Navy's July 1940 shipbuilding budget of $4 billion, for escorts and related vessels; the rest went on 1,325,000 tons of large warships and 100,000 tons in auxiliary ships, as part of the commitment to a "two-ocean Navy". Even the fully mobilised industries of the United States could not achieve this aim for two years; it is debatable whether it was ever attained, as will become clear.

The massive American build-up and commitment to Britain could not prevent the German submarine service from referring to the second nine months of the war as *die glückliche Zeit*, "the happy time". As in the previous conflict, a handful of "aces" pushed up the U-boats' score on remarkably destructive individual patrols. The basic qualification for "ace" status, signified by a Knight's Cross at the successful captain's collar, was 50,000 tons sunk. The highly advantageous new U-boat bases and the enemy destroyer shortage, plus a superabundance of IRS, offered an embarrassment of targets. Even though the U-boats were at the peak of their individual efficiency and convoys were at their least protected in this period, often making do with just one escort, IRS sunk were twice as numerous as convoyed ships destroyed. There was still only an average of six boats at a time hunting merchantmen. October 1940 became the worst month of the war for shipping so far, when U-boats alone accounted for 352,000 tons, or nearly 59,000 tons per boat at sea, a score unmatched before or after. Yet in February 1941 the number of operational boats available fell to just twenty-one; Dönitz had switched maximum available resources to training just as deliveries of new boats were delayed by competing demands from other branches of the Wehrmacht. Twenty-six Italian submarines gathered at Bordeaux by November 1940 but generally proved to be more of a liability than an asset, built with the Mediterranean rather than the rough Atlantic in mind. By summer 1941 there were only ten at Bordeaux, usually left out of German planning and contributing very little to the total Axis submarine score.

The first ace, inevitably, was Günther Prien, who qualified by sinking seven ships in two weeks (three on one day) of June 1940, bringing his total to 66,600 tons even before the U-boats moved to France. Six of the haul were from two convoys in the Bay of Biscay and the Western Approaches. An eighth victim fell to his last torpedo on 2 July, as he turned back to Wilhelmshaven, and resulted in an unlooked-for tragedy.

In his sights on 2 July, still in the Western Approaches, was a 15,500-ton westbound passenger liner he easily identified as the *Arandora Star*. He may have been able to make out British Army uniforms on her deck, as she had 254 troops as well as a crew of 174 seamen aboard. The sad fact was that she was carrying 1,250 enemy aliens, mostly Italian, from Britain to internment in Canada: the troops were guarding them. He hit her amidships and she sank with the loss of 821 lives. Seven hours later the Canadian destroyer HMCS *St Laurent* arrived and managed to cram 857 survivors aboard. Prien's Knight's Cross for the Scapa Flow exploit was upgraded by the addition of oak leaves, though not for this.

Also flourishing in his deadly way in this "happy time" was the highest-scoring U-boat ace of the Second World War, Otto Kretschmer, who destroyed 238,000 tons in a year and a half (and won oak leaves and swords to attach to his Knight's Cross). Born in Silesia in 1912, he joined the Navy at eighteen and rose to command a coastal submarine, *U23*, by 1937. Shortly before war broke out he was promoted *Kapitänleutnant*, as ever the normal rank for a U-boat skipper, and sank 21,000 tons of shipping as well as a British destroyer by February 1940. He did this with twenty-three torpedoes, of which fifteen misfired, for reasons already described. In April he took the new *U99*, a type VIIB ocean-going boat, to sea for training, and then for her first war patrol in June, during which he more than doubled his score before docking at Lorient on the French coast.

In August 1940 "Silent Otto", as he was known (he was laconic both in person and in his use of wireless), began to be trumpeted by German propaganda as "the wolf in the Atlantic". When he received his Knight's Cross from Raeder, the quayside parade was remarkable for featuring an entire U-boat crew dressed, *faute de mieux*, in captured British Army uniforms: Kretschmer had risked his career before the war by protesting against Prussian "bull", which was largely eliminated from the U-boat arm as a result. But he refused to lend his name to a hyperinflated "autobiography" of the kind foisted upon a naive Prien.

He was a member of the first operational "wolf-pack", mustered in September 1940 against the two eastbound convoys SC 2 (slow, from Halifax) and HX 72 – Dönitz's answer to the growing strength and cohesion of enemy escorts after their overstretched summer. Kretschmer's tactical policy was to fire one torpedo per target at as near to point-blank range as he could get, by night and on the surface. Sometimes he would surface inside a convoy. He won his oak leaves in November by sinking two armed merchant cruisers and two other large ships.

After a long refit, *U99* left Lorient for her eighth war patrol, the talismanic gold-coloured horseshoe still attached to her conning tower. The haul on one voyage of 62,000 tons of shipping which ensued would have been enough to earn Kretschmer "ace" status all by itself; as it was, it merely increased his overall score by a third. But it was also the last but one voyage of *U99*.

Another leading ace of the day was Joachim Schepke in *U100*, who sank seven ships totalling over 50,000 tons from one convoy – HX 72 – in four hours, by attacking it from within: he sank the second ship in three successive columns in fifteen minutes. Kretschmer got two in a similar attack on HX 72 which, like SC 2, had first been sighted by Prien.

These three aces were supported by such as Bleichrodt and Engelbert Endrass, Prien's first lieutenant or executive officer at Scapa Flow, now commanding *U46* and an ace on his own account. They led the new "wolf-packs", a term employed by the media of both sides, in a huge cull of shipping which reached its peak on 18 and 19 October, the two worst days for shipping losses of the entire war. A huge mêlée developed round convoys SC 7 and HX 79, in which thirty-seven ships out of a total of seventy-nine were sunk despite the presence of fourteen escorts; Prien got seven, Endrass six, Kretschmer five, Bleichrodt four, Schepke three (plus two damaged) . . .

This depressing débâcle led the British to realise that quantity of escorts was not the whole answer to the wolf-pack. More and more warships were being sent back to the convoys when the invasion scare began to subside. But individual escorts would detach themselves, sometimes for days on end, to help a straggler or a stricken ship or to hunt for survivors, dangerously weakening the protection for the rest.

The "Senior Officer, Escort" was exactly that, the highest-ranking skipper present, sometimes a mere lieutenant-commander. He was expected to supervise a mixed collection of escorts as well as the convoy commodore, often a retired Navy captain or flag officer and responsible for keeping the convoy itself together. The coordinated pack of submarines would have to be countered by the coordinated escort group. In July 1940 Vice-Admiral Gilbert Stephenson, recalled from retirement as a convoy commodore, was made Commodore, Western Isles, and took charge of training escorts smaller than destroyers (mainly corvettes) at Tobermory on the Scottish island of Mull. Other schools were set up in western Scotland. Eight escort groups, usually commanded by a captain, RN, were formed in October 1940 by Western Approaches Command; group training took place off south-west Scotland, Liverpool and Northern Ireland. A tactical training centre for escort officers was opened in Liverpool, Britain's principal convoy port.

Western Approaches Command itself was relocated on 7 February 1941 from Plymouth to Liverpool, reflecting the protective shift in the easterly terminus of the main convoy route from south to north of

Ireland. Ten days later Admiral Sir Percy Noble became C-in-C in succession to Admiral Sir Martin Dunbar-Nasmith, who became C-in-C, Plymouth. Number 15 Group, Coastal Command (Air Vice-Marshal J.M. Robb), made the same transfer. Derby House in Liverpool concealed the underground bunker cum operations room which became the main Area Combined Headquarters for the fight against the U-boats, with its own duplicate of the London Trade Plot and direct, secure communications with OIC and Air Ministry in London. In April 1941 complete operational control of Coastal Command officially passed to the Admiralty; the Air Ministry remained responsible only for training, equipment and administration.

Such was the final shape of the command structure which fought out what Churchill called "the Battle of the Atlantic", a campaign which lasted as long as the war and was more important for Britain's survival than any other. Neither the RAF victory in the Battle of Britain which staved off a German invasion in autumn 1940 nor the Allied invasion of Normandy in summer 1944 would have been possible but for the war matériel shipped across the Atlantic.

As more warships became available for escort, the British pushed the western protection limit for convoys to nineteen degrees west; but the U-boats, thanks to their French bases, could operate for weeks at a time as far as twenty-five degrees west in the "gap" between the escort from Halifax and that from Britain. Cover in the gap was often limited to one of the forty-six armed merchant cruisers (AMC) converted at the beginning of the war. Their usefulness was limited to dealing with daylight U-boat attacks under prize rules, obsolete after a year of war. They were useless against submerged or night attacks by U-boat or any by German surface raiders, which rejoined the Atlantic struggle after refits towards the end of 1940. Six AMCs were sunk by U-boats in summer 1940 alone, and several more, such as *Rawalpindi* and *Jervis Bay*, in gallant but hopeless fights with immensely superior German heavy ships. The AMCs were mostly converted to troopships, a much more appropriate role, from the end of 1940.

The "happy time" lasted from July to November 1940, during which period just eight U-boats were sunk for the loss of 144 IRS and seventy-three ships in convoy. The victims included the *Empress of Britain* which, at 42,300 tons, earned the sad distinction of being (and remaining) the largest ship ever sunk by submarine. Another melancholy record was achieved by one of the lost boats, *U31*, a rare type VIIA, which managed to get herself sunk twice. The first time was in shallow water to RAF bombing off the German North Sea coast in March 1940, whereupon she was raised, refitted and recommissioned. The second was permanent with the loss of all hands, when she was depth-charged by the destroyer HMS *Antelope* on 2 November in the North Atlantic while trying to attack a convoy. No further U-boat was sunk by enemy action for more than four months, but the next one was to be a triumph indeed.

The lull in U-boat losses reflected a lull in their activity. Their score in November of 147,000 tons was less than half of October's, although German mines, surface raiders and aircraft took the overall total to 386,000 tons, just 57,000 tons fewer than October. The total for December was 350,000, including a stronger submarine contribution of 213,000. In January the figures were 320,000 tons (127,000) and in February 1941 403,000 tons were lost of which submarines got 197,000. The U-boats and their crews were tiring in bad winter weather; in September 1940, the first anniversary of the war, Dönitz had exactly the same number, fifty-seven, operational as a year earlier (though the first serious reinforcements were about to arrive after expanded construction and training). At the same time the British were becoming more proficient in evasive routeing based on sigint, and were slowly building up the quantity and quality of their escorts.

When Dönitz renewed his offensive its main thrust was further to the north and west than before, in the waters south of Iceland. He had observed that the British were using more northerly routes. Once again Prien's *U47* led the assault, sighting westbound OB 293 about 200 miles south-east of Iceland on 6 March 1941. When three more boats – Kretschmer in *U99*, Joachim Matz in *U70* and Commander Hans Eckerman in the minelaying UA (originally intended for Turkey) – reached the scene, they formed a pack. Headquarters at Lorient sent them into the attack, opening an unprecedented series of running battles between U-boats and convoys which cost both sides dear.

Kretschmer started the proceedings just after midnight with a pass across the bows of the convoy, sailing as usual in several parallel rows. He knocked out a tanker, which sank, and a 21,000-ton Norwegian whaling factory-ship, which stayed afloat. But as he went into the attack on the surface those on the bridge saw the conning tower of the submarine wreathed in St Elmo's fire. This spontaneous discharge of static electricity is a traditional omen of sinking among superstitious sailors.

Matz was next to fire a "browning" salvo (a sweeping shot at a mass target on the analogy of firing a shotgun at a flock of birds). He damaged a British freighter. His second victim, the Dutch tanker *Mijdrecht*, was hit but managed to stay afloat and ram *U70*, which was damaged.

The leader of the escort group, Commander J.M. Rowland, RN, in the destroyer HMS *Wolverine*, with another such and two corvettes, began a five-hour Asdic search during which over 100 depth-charges were dropped. *U70*, already leaking badly, suddenly went out of control, descending to 650 feet (150 more than the specified maximum). The crew raced backwards and forwards along the hull in their efforts to stabilise the boat; as rivets popped, water poured in and the crowded interior became a shambles, Matz used his last reserves of battery power to drive the submarine to the surface, whereupon he gave the order to abandon. As British launches approached he coolly went back aboard to make sure *U70* would sink, just managing to get clear as she started to go down by the stern. Twenty of his crew went down with her while twenty-six went into captivity with Matz. Kretschmer managed to steal away.

Prien was still with the embattled convoy at 1 a.m. on the 8th, signalling for reinforcements, when *U47* was sighted on the surface by *Wolverine*. The two escorting destroyers took it in turns to drop patterns of ten depth-charges while the other used her Asdic, a deadly new tactic coming into general use at this time. After four hours "a loud clattering sound like crockery breaking" was heard by the *Wolverine*'s hydrophone operator and *U47* popped up to the surface very close to the escort leader before sinking out of sight. A minute or so later the British hunters saw an eerily silent, rapidly spreading orange glow beneath the surface as the *U47* exploded, as if the "Bull of Scapa Flow" had actually burst through the very gates of hell. Prien, aged thirty-one, the world's most renowned submariner, was lost with all forty-six of his crew. His final score was a British battleship and 161,000 tons of merchant shipping – but nothing from OB 293.

Kretschmer was still on the prowl on 15 March when Lemp (he of the *Athenia*), now commanding *U110*, a type VIIC, sighted and reported the heavily laden, eastbound HX 122 some 300 miles north-west of Scotland – forty-one ships zigzagging in unison at eight knots. Kretschmer, Schepke and two other boats joined Lemp in a wolf-pack of five, which now took on the Fifth Escort Group headed by Commander Donald Macintyre, RN, in the destroyer *Walker*, with three others and two corvettes in company. Macintyre, soon to be promoted captain, was one of the best escort leaders, but Kretschmer sank four tankers and two freighters from inside the convoy in little more than an hour and withdrew, having run out of torpedoes.

Walker sighted *U100* outside the convoy and dropped a pattern of ten depth-charges as the submarine dived. Schepke kept control of his damaged boat as it returned to the surface, whereupon the destroyer

Vanoc (Commander J.G.W. Deneys, RN) scored a historic first: she located the boat's conning tower with her brand-new type 286 ASV (anti-surface-vessel radar) and swung round to ram. The destroyer rode over the U-boat with a rending of metal. Six Germans were saved from the water as Schepke went down with forty other men and his boat.

At this moment the Asdic operator on *Walker* persuaded Macintyre that he had a fresh and different contact. After half an hour of hunting, Macintyre's pattern of six depth-charges sent *U99* plunging to 700 feet, where she should have imploded. Kretschmer expended all his compressed air to blow the main ballast tanks and the boat shot back to the surface. He struggled to keep afloat under *Walker*'s gunfire long enough to enable his abandonment order to be carried out. The radioman sent: "Two destroyers – depth-charges – 50,000 tons sunk – imprisonment – Kretschmer" as a signaller on deck flashed to Macintyre: "Captain to captain: please save my men drifting in your direction. I am sinking." Macintyre ceased fire, had lights lit and nets lowered. Although the boat with the golden horseshoe had gone, her crew (except for one petty officer) and her captain survived the war in captivity. So did their boat's record as the most successful German submarine of the war, having accounted for forty-four merchantmen of 266,000 tons and a destroyer.

Presented with the unique opportunity of questioning the leading U-boat ace, Macintyre and his officers, some of whom had been led by propaganda to expect a raving Nazi, were profoundly impressed by the reserved, polite and impeccably professional commander. "I sincerely hoped that there were not too many like him," a British staff officer noted. Kretschmer was imprisoned in Canada and was awarded the swords to his Knight's Cross while in captivity. He managed to fine-tune the system of coded messages in letters home to such an extent that he was able to summon a U-boat to the mouth of the St Lawrence to pick up escaped prisoners (recaptured before they could make the rendezvous).

The loss to Germany of two of her most celebrated aces in half an hour drove the Nazi propagandists to frenzied, Wagnerian outpourings of official mourning and naturally gave great comfort to the British and their hard-pressed Navy. In all, the escorts had sunk five boats in fifteen days (a humble trawler sank *U551* between the Faroes and Iceland on 23 March). But the British had to wait another two months before they learned that one of the five was Günther Prien's *U47*, the most heartening success of them all because of her captain's unique reputation.

The German propaganda machine found it exceptionally difficult to cope with this loss. Having raised Prien to the status of super-hero the propagandists, overestimating the effect of their work, feared the result for morale of revealing that he had died. It was quite normal for U-boat headquarters to take a week or even longer to conclude that a submarine had been lost, because wireless silence was the norm except for operational necessity (such as reporting a convoy and calling for reinforcements, when loquacity took over). But the Supreme Command of the Wehrmacht needed seventy-six days to pluck up the courage to mention Prien's disappearance, in its daily bulletin of 23 May.

The SD, the security service of the SS which also monitored public opinion, noted public anxiety about Prien in a secret report dated 28 April. Dönitz disliked this suppression of the death of his favourite skipper and on 24 May paid his own tribute in an order of the day to the submarine service. By this time rumours were rife: one said that Prien and his entire crew had been sent to concentration camp for mutiny; somehow Prien's fierce protest about dud torpedoes had become known and his disappearance was linked with this. The rumours were still alive after the war, when some claimed to have seen papers relating to his court-martial, or even the man himself in a camp at Torgau on the Elbe early in 1945.

The elimination of the top U-boat aces led Churchill to conclude prematurely that Britain had turned the corner against the main enemy at sea, a mistake he made more than once in the First World War. But the country had lost 5,471,000 tons of shipping so far, of which 3,174,000 had been sunk by submarines. The total haul of U-boats sunk was only thirty-six, a margin overwhelmingly in Germany's favour. Even so the SD was reduced to claiming vaguely in April 1941 that the British had developed an unspecified "secret weapon".

So they had, in a way: radar, the most important technological advance of the war, was slowly beginning to appear on the escorts. Asdic in expert hands was proving extremely useful, even more so when escorts hunted in pairs. Radio detection was almost a science. Teamwork promised better results against the wolf-packs, as did the steadily increasing use of maritime air patrols. There was no single magic answer to the U-boat, nor would there be; but if there was one contribution which counted more than any other single factor on the British side, it was intelligence.

Scene ii: Diversions

INTELLIGENCE, as we have begun to see, was the guiding hand in the second U-boat siege of Britain and in the strategy of the defence. It played a much bigger role on both sides in the second campaign than in the first, thanks to a quarter of a century of growth in the technologies of wireless, aviation and proto-electronics.

On the German side, the B-dienst had sharpened its skills in the Abyssinian crisis, when it eavesdropped on British ships from Italian listening posts, and during the Spanish Civil War. Most of the main belligerents in the Second World War had been on hand in some way: the totalitarian regimes fighting with one side or the other and the European democracies keeping up the façade of non-intervention. The xB-dienst made damaging penetration of British naval codes, still in use in 1939 and beyond. The Germans could intercept messages exchanged among warships, merchant ships, convoys and ports – the basis of *die Lage*, the plot at U-boat headquarters. The capture of the British HMS *Seal* in May 1940 with much of her secret paperwork intact had been as much of a heavenly gift to the B-dienst as to the Torpedo Inspectorate. Describing some of these successes, Captain Stephen Roskill, the official British historian of the Second World War at sea, says on page 208 of his second volume (published in 1956): "The reader should not, of course, assume that we British were meanwhile idle in achieving the opposite purpose." Here, for all to see, was the conscientious recorder's revelation that the British broke German ciphers during the war. None the less it was only in 1974 that the "Ultra" triumph described below and its enormous scale were revealed to an astonished world.

When war came, the xB-dienst employed 700 people on cryptanalysis. The German weakness in this area was that Naval Intelligence was one of seven German organisations in the field whereas the British had one, the Government Code and Cipher School, which grew to employ no fewer than 10,000 people at its peak.

Regardless of inter-service rivalries, reconnaissance by Luftwaffe and naval planes of Britain, its surrounding waters, ports and shipping was regular, thorough and fruitful. The British neglected this important source of information until the war began, whereupon they found they lacked specialised aircraft. Existing types such as the Hudson medium bomber and the Spitfire fighter had to be adapted to photographic reconnaissance, which became a British speciality in due course. In January 1941 a Central Interpretation Unit was created to monitor photo-reconnaissance from all sources, including No 1 Reconnaissance Unit of Coastal Command, and distribute the resulting analyses.

The GC & CS in particular and British intelligence in general, understaffed and underfunded though they were until war broke out, made remarkable progress against the codes and ciphers of potential enemies in the 1930s, including Japan. Where the GC & CS fell down was on the obverse of its offensive role in attacking enemy ciphers: defending Britain's. This helped the xB-dienst during the early and middle stages of the war.

Central to the enormous British effort against enemy ciphers was the ugly and rambling Victorian mansion at Bletchley Park and the excrescences of Nissen huts and other temporary buildings it sprouted as demand for space grew. This headquarters of the GC & CS was the setting for a classically British spontaneous growth, an anarchic institution operated on a shoestring by a group of eccentrics.

Its principal target was the German "Enigma" electro-mechanical encipherment machine used by all three main branches of the Wehrmacht. Externally the machine was a flat hardwood box not two feet long and one foot wide with a conventional typewriter keyboard on top, and behind it a panel of electric lights lettered in the same way. When the operator held down a key, one of the lights would go on. Connecting the two was an asymmetrical and variable wiring system consisting of a "plug-board" on which pairs of letters could be connected with each other at random (or left unconnected); three, and on later naval versions, four interchangeable wheels, each with twenty-six settings and twenty-six contacts; and a "reflector" containing one more set of thirteen asymmetrical wired connections between pairs of letters. The wheels worked like those in a mechanical adding machine: the twenty-sixth "click" of the first wheel would make the second advance by one click and the twenty-sixth click of the second would advance the third by one. In its simplest version the Enigma machine, named after Elgar's "Enigma Variations", offered, for each letter of a message, encipherment possibilities totalling twenty-six to the power of six. By the addition of a choice of any three, or even four, wheels out of eight, and of a rotating ring attached to each wheel so that the setting of the wheel itself was encoded, some 150 million million million substitutions for each letter became possible. To decipher a message, all the recipient had to do was ensure his machine had the same initial plug-board and wheel settings as the sender's and tap out the message on his keyboard, whereupon the plain language would be revealed by the panel of lights.

This product of nineteenth-century technology, invented in the 1920s for commercial purposes, contained no technological secret; indeed the original German patents were on file in London and the British and Americans between the wars developed comparable machines which all their forces (except the Royal Navy) used during it. Polish and then French intelligence opened the attack on Enigma and managed by cryptanalysis of its output to construct a functional replica of it without ever seeing one. The Poles invented a machine they called a "bomba" (because it ticked) to work its way through all the possible settings of an Enigma wheel; thus six bombas were needed to cope with an Enigma using any three out of a range of six wheels. This remarkable mathematical feat gave the British a good start in attacking the real secret of Enigma: the settings of the wheels when the operator began the encipherment process. These settings were changed in accordance with a top-secret pattern distributed at intervals in advance to all participants in a network (such as an Army or Air Force group, or all warships at sea including U-boats).

It fell to the outstanding mathematician Alan Turing at GC & CS to build the British "bombe" (the name was adopted from the French), capable of working its way through all the possible settings for an Enigma which could permutate any three wheels (later four) from eight in any order and change the permutation (to say nothing of the plug-board and the ring settings) daily. The first was delivered in May 1940; before that the classical scholars, mathematicians, chess champions and congenital crossword-puzzlers who went to war at Bletchley made remarkable progress by a combination of lateral thinking and guesswork. At the end of 1939 they at last deciphered a German Army message after two months' work. In February 1940 the aptly named minesweeper HMS *Gleaner* sank *U33* as she was laying mines off the Clyde and relieved the captured survivors of three Enigma wheels. In March Bletchley Park deciphered a series of Luftwaffe test messages. In April the British captured the German patrol-boat *VP2623* at Narvik, and with her enough Enigma paperwork to enable GC & CS to decipher the traffic from six days of April by the end of May, the first break into naval cipher.

On 1 May the Germans dropped the predetermined wheel settings and let the individual operator make his own choice before encipherment. This meant, however, that he had to tell his correspondents what setting he had used so they could decipher his message. This was done in the first three letters of the transmission. For added security he then reset the wheels for the message itself, transmitting that information by means of another three letters, repeated once. Each message therefore began with an "indicator" of nine letters, on which the British attack was focused once their significance was realised. On 22 May a message sent under the old predetermined system was repeated with the new random one, a lapse which eventually helped the British to achieve a long-term breakthrough into the naval ciphers, the most difficult Enigma traffic. Their campaign against it leapt forward in March 1941, when a commando raid on the Norwegian Lofoten Islands captured the German armed trawler *Krebs*. Enough Enigma "software" was recovered to enable Bletchley Park to decipher the whole of the previous month's traffic in the important cipher used for German ships at sea. This proved to be the penultimate stage in the campaign to crack German signals fast enough to be of operational value.

The final element was provided, fittingly perhaps if involuntarily, by no less than Fritz-Julius Lemp, now in command of *U110*. Attacking the westbound OB 318 in mid-Atlantic at two minutes to noon on 9 May 1941, Lemp sank two freighters in quick succession from periscope depth, ahead and to starboard of the convoy. The corvette *Aubretia* of the Third Escort Group (Commander A.J. Baker-Cresswell in the destroyer *Bulldog*) got a brief Asdic contact and dropped depth-charges, whereupon the damaged *U110* broke the surface. After a confused action the Germans abandoned ship; Lemp appears to have died trying to ensure his boat was scuttled. Some of his crew died in the water; those rescued were confined below, out of sight, as Sub-Lieutenant David Balme, RN, took a boarding party of eight specially trained ratings on to the U-boat. Their task was to strip her of anything of potential intelligence value at once, in case she sank under tow to Scapa Flow (as indeed she did). Not only was Lemp's entire Enigma software found, together with valuable signalling material, the machine itself was taken intact, its wheels and plug-board in the latest settings. It took Bletchley Park about two weeks to convert the trickle of naval decrypts into a flood with the aid of this priceless capture. Roskill gave the clash two lines in his first volume, published in 1954: "In the North Atlantic, convoy OB 318 was intercepted early in May and lost five ships, but its escort retaliated by sinking *U110*." The honoured historian found out more after publishing his second volume and felt it his duty to correct the record in a separate monograph, *The Secret Capture* (1959).

He revealed that Lemp's boat had been boarded and her secrets taken to Britain. But he could not reveal that the *Bulldog* had brought home an Enigma. Instead he included a passage describing the two packing-cases in which Lemp's legacy was stored for handing over to intelligence officers up from London, and their reaction on looking inside: "What! This...? And this...? We've waited a long time for one of these!" That is as near as he could go to revealing that "one of these" was an Enigma. On the evening of the delivery the First Sea Lord, Admiral Sir Dudley Pound, sent his congratulations to Baker-Cresswell; and when an officer from his group was being decorated by King George VI for his part in the OB 318 action, the monarch remarked that the operation in which he had gained it was "the most important single event in the whole war at sea".

By far the greatest value of this kind of intelligence, whether in the context of this narrative or of the war as a whole, lay in the power it gave to OIC to divert shipping out of harm's way. Because the effects of preventive measures cannot be calculated the benefit is un-quantifiable, but it must have run to millions of tons of ships and cargo.

Decrypts might well reveal to British commanders where the enemy was and even what he was about to do, but unless they were in a position to deliver enough force to the right place in time there was little they could do until the later stages of the war. Hence the high-grade intelligence was sometimes of little or no immediate operational value. This was a source of constant irritation to Churchill, who insisted on adding to his enormous workload by reading Bletchley decrypts each night. But his keen interest in the work of GC & CS led him to visit it in autumn 1941, and to order an immediate and positive response to a written complaint from Alan Turing about persistent bureaucratic refusals to meet Bletchley Park's then modest needs for extra personnel. Turing's was the brain around which almost the entire Bletchley effort was built; to help its invaluable work even further he built the world's first programmable digital computer, "Colossus", to speed up the tedious checking procedures of cryptanalysis. A few who knew of his unique contribution to the second defeat of the U-boats, and therefore to victory, said he deserved an earldom; he had to rest content with the relatively modest OBE (Order of the British Empire). He was allowed to keep it when convicted after the war of practising homosexuality, then illegal in Britain. Turing killed himself by taking cyanide two years later. He was forty-one.

The information garnered by GC & CS was paraphrased and summarised for forwarding to OIC and the most senior military and naval commanders. Material from this source was flagged by the codeword "Ultra" from June 1941, when the output of Bletchley Park began to increase exponentially. Sometimes Ultra material could not be used because it could only have come from deciphered Enigma traffic, a fact which an alert German eavesdropper might have noticed.

As naval Ultra began to come on stream at the end of May, the Royal Canadian Navy closed the mid-ocean gap in the surface-escort system, which had so helped the U-boats. Commodore L.W. Murray, RCN, arrived at St John's to command, under the tutelage of C-in-C, Western Approaches, the freshly created Newfoundland Force of mostly Canadian and some British destroyers and corvettes. Eastbound convoys, more valuable because fully laden, were from June entrusted to five escorts in turn, all the way across. A local escort would conduct the ships from Halifax (fast convoys) or Sydney, Cape Breton, (slow) to a "Western Ocean Meeting Point" (WESTOMP). From there the Newfoundland Force would cover them to the Mid-Ocean Meeting Point (MOMP) at thirty-five degrees west. A British escort group from Iceland took over from there to eighteen degrees west, the eastern EOMP. The last ocean leg was overseen by an escort from Western Approaches until a local escort took over in coastal waters. The British Third Battle Squadron (usually two capital ships plus acolytes) was withdrawn from Halifax to home waters after the sinking of the battlecruiser HMS *Hood* by the super-battleship *Bismarck*, and the destruction of the latter by the bulk of the Royal Navy, in the Battle of the North Atlantic in May 1941.

The upper speed limit on ships required to travel in convoy, lowered to thirteen knots in a false economy of November 1940, was restored to fifteen in June, cutting the numbers of ever-vulnerable IRS. Since ocean-going U-boats, their ranks swelling with the larger and more comfortable type IX submarines, cruised at ten to twelve knots, a ship ploughing along at little more than thirteen could hardly be said to be safe. The type IX was built in seven versions, with displacements varying between 1,032 and 1,616 tons surfaced; 194 were constructed, the earliest with a range of 10,500 miles and the last with three times that – so much endurance that it became the attitude of the crew (enhanced by relative spaciousness and comfort) rather than the capacity of the fuel tanks which determined the duration of patrols.

End-to-end escort was introduced on the Gibraltar route on 10 July and the Sierra Leone route four days later. The westward shift of the U-boats in the North Atlantic, which forced the British to introduce end-to-end cover, also, ironically, gave the Admiralty more sea-room to divert convoys away from danger with the aid of Ultra and HF/DF; there were more U-boats, but in a much larger operational area. After a wolf-pack of eight boats sank half the twenty-two ships in slow, eastbound convoy SC 26 in April for the loss of just one submarine, convoys were diverted northward and escort cover extended westward (pending end-to-end).

One reason for the northward shift of the main convoy route in spring was to improve air cover, now available from Britain in the north-east, Gibraltar in the south-east, Canadian bases in the north-west and Iceland in the north. The Canadian Air Force was given nine American long-range Catalina flying boats (one of the great aeronautical workhorses of the war) by Britain, which had acquired them under Lend-Lease. Allowing for aircraft availability, prevailing winds and other factors, the Canadian planes could patrol up to 600 miles eastward, the Iceland aircraft 400 miles southward and British and Gibraltar-based patrols up to 750 miles westward. The ranges of the aircraft types available for maritime patrols left a gap some 300 miles in diameter in the central North Atlantic, south of Greenland and out of reach of shorebased air cover, a fact duly noted by Dönitz as his flotillas grew in numbers and endurance. The unnecessarily protracted existence of the "air gap" almost gave him victory, as will be seen.

Just as the British reorganised themselves, so did their enemy. For the first time since December 1940 the Germans tried submerged attack by day (no help to Lemp, as we noted) instead of on the surface at night, especially if the xB-dienst enabled a pack to lay an ambush ahead of a convoy. The change in tactics, which was positively advantageous to efficient Asdic operators, was soon reversed. Ironically, the U-boat Command decided (the enemy usually preferring to write his own script) to shift the focus of its attacks southwards to the warmer waters of the equatorial Atlantic just as the North Atlantic convoys were shifting northwards. In the area between the Azores and West Africa, Commander Günter Hessler in *U107* notched up a record for the Second World War: fourteen ships totalling 86,700 tons sunk in a single patrol over the end of May and the beginning of June. Hessler was Dönitz's son-in-law, later became his staff captain (operations) and immediately after the war wrote an invaluable insider history of the U-boat campaign at the behest of the Allies.

The initiative still rested with the U-boats, which in May 1941 were sinking four times as many IRS as ships in convoy. In the second nine-month period of the war, to March 1941, they accounted for some fifty-five per cent of a total loss of shipping worldwide of 5.2 million tons, sixty per cent more than in the preceding nine-month period, leaving a total shipping stock of thirty-five million tons available to Britain, including its own, Allied and neutral bottoms. Just over one million tons of new shipping were built, leaving a net loss of over four million. German surface raiders accounted for twenty-two per cent, aircraft fifteen and mines seven. Dönitz, having shifted the axis of his attack from north-south in the eastern Atlantic to east-west across the central North Atlantic, had accumulated 113 boats, of which thirty-two were operational and eighty-one were in training; fifty-four were ocean-going, twice as many as he had when the war began. There were now at least ten boats instead of six on war patrol at any one time, with similar numbers outward and homeward-bound. The average operational life of a U-boat had risen from three to four months; thirteen boats were lost in the period, including those of the top aces, but forty-one new submarines were delivered. The British escort crisis was however slowly easing, thanks to American and Canadian help: the Germans now had to face 375 Allied ocean escorts (240 of them destroyers), an increase in nine months of 140, or sixty per cent. That this was nowhere near enough is shown by the rising trend in losses to a still limited force of U-boats. But from April British warships were allowed to call at American yards for repair and refit, while the Americans opened airbases in Bermuda and Greenland and brazenly moved the eastern boundary of their Neutrality Zone from sixty to twenty-six degrees west. Admiral Bristol at Norfolk, Virginia, now had five squadrons of Catalinas to patrol the zone, as well as three flotillas of destroyers. One, USS *Niblack*, on 11 April became the first American ship to fire a shot in a war the United States had as yet no intention of joining: having recovered the survivors from a torpedoed freighter she got a sonar contact and dropped depth-charges, without result.

In May 1941, as both sides tried new tactics, the successful intervention of the first six operational type IX boats helped the Germans to sink fifty-eight ships, a rise of one-third over April. More than half this total went to the type IXs in the tropical Atlantic. The British strengthened their command at Freetown, Sierra Leone, as best they could, but Dönitz was not about to abandon the main hunting ground in the North Atlantic, as the bloody tussles over OB 318 and HX 126 made clear.

The finds aboard *U110* and British naval raids on two German weather-ships in Greenland waters in May and June 1941 had helped Bletchley Park and Naval Intelligence to develop a broad and detailed picture of the entire U-boat operation as run from Kernevel near Lorient. The decrypts now pouring out of Bletchley Park by teleprinter to the Admiralty were evaluated by the Submarine Tracking Room (STR), run by Commander (later Captain) Rodger Winn, RNVR, who developed a near-telepathic ability to read the mind of Godt, Dönitz's head of operations.

Winn joined OIC as a civilian assistant aged thirty-five when war broke out. The forensic skills of a first-class barrister helped him to impress Rear-Admiral John Godfrey, Director of Naval Intelligence and a veteran of Room 40. Despite a limp and a twisted back, legacies of boyhood poliomyelitis, and poor eyesight, Winn was commissioned into the reserve as a full commander at the end of 1940 and given charge of the STR, in succession to Paymaster-Captain W. Thring who had done the same job in the previous war and was now exhausted. Winn's powerful shoulders and arms lent him the air of a Shakespearean Richard III as he pored over a chart, plotting global moves against his archenemy Dönitz. He also brought wit, charm and swift intelligence allied with common sense to a workload second to none in the British war effort. Rodger Winn's importance to Naval Intelligence was analogous to that of Alan Turing (now chief consultant) at Bletchley Park, which provided the information used by Winn to orchestrate the convoys and their escorts.

Perhaps it was instinct which led Dönitz and his staff at this turning point in the fortunes of British intelligence to introduce new wireless restrictions. Enquiries by the submarine command and the B-dienst, prompted by the loss of the aces in spring and the subsequent comparative elusiveness of the convoys, yielded no clue to the mounting successes of the GC & CS. The Germans concluded that the British were developing a detailed picture of U-boat dispositions and tactics from direction-finding and traffic analysis; to the end of the war it was inconceivable to the Germans that anyone could have broken into Enigma. When the truth came out in 1974, Dönitz was staggered.

On 9 June 1941 Standing Order 243 imposed wireless silence on U-boats at sea unless engaged with the enemy, or if a signal was necessary for tactical reasons or in response to a special request from headquarters. New wireless channels and frequent changes between them were introduced, together with a new system of coded references to the lettered grid-chart of the Atlantic issued to all U-boats, new codebooks and new security measures such as double encipherment of grid references. All this made it particularly difficult for the STR to locate individual boats, which were now addressed by the surnames of their commanders rather than their numbers. None the less the British managed to build up a detailed picture of U-boat operations from the radio output of submarines and headquarters regardless of difficulties with individual signals. Interruptions or delays in the flow from Bletchley Park never henceforward reduced OIC to blind impotence, despite serious setbacks from time to time: when all else failed, Winn's finely tuned instinct often filled the gap.

Also from June 1941, Ultra's output was shared with the American and Canadian naval commands. One example of the potential value of judicious use of Ultra, which was not to be exploited unless the British were able to pretend they had got the information from other sources, came at the end of that month. The STR worked out, from intercepts by the Y-stations decrypted by the GC & CS, that no fewer than ten U-boats were gathering to attack convoy HX 133. Western Approaches therefore, on the strength of its confidence in the STR, boldly reduced the escorts of two other convoys to a minimum and assembled a group of thirteen. Even so, five merchantmen were sunk, as were two of the attackers.

On 20 June 1941 *U203* (Rolf Mützelberg) sighted a battleship and destroyers zigzagging in the Denmark Strait between Greenland and Iceland, ten miles or so east of longitude twenty-six west and therefore outside the American zone. Despite having identified the big ship as USS *Texas*, Mützelberg pursued the formation for 140 miles trying to get in range before he gave up. The American sonar did not register his impertinent but ultimately impotent presence. When Raeder mentioned this to Hitler the next day, the dictator had one of his notorious tantrums and forbade any activity that might provoke the Americans for the immediate future. On 22 June Hitler transformed the nature of the Second World War by launching Operation Barbarossa – the invasion of the Soviet Union. At such a moment he was less keen than ever to become involved in hostilities with the United States; he had correctly read Roosevelt's strategy as to avoid combat as long as possible, however much aid he might be giving to Britain. He doubtless hoped that the Japanese would soon tie down the Americans, diverting their attention to the Pacific.

None the less it was the biggest error of his career to open a second front in the east without closing the one he was contesting with the British in the west. Britain and the United States immediately offered aid and supplies to Stalin, with enormous implications for the already strained transatlantic route, Allied shipping stocks and war production –

Admiral Karl Dönitz debriefs a returning crew (top). The leading U-boat ace of the Second World War, Commander Otto Kretschmer, is glimpsed ashore (left) and the war's leading U-boat hunter, Captain "Johnnie" Walker, is seen on his bridge (above).

An Allied tanker (above) succumbs to a torpedo.
A U-boat (below) succumbs to Allied air-attack.
The war-winning Liberator (inset) sets out to close the air-gap.

The revolutionary German "electro-boats", the coastal type XXI (above) and the ocean-going type XXIII, which came six months too late to turn the tables against the Allies.

USS *Nautilus*, the world's first nuclear submarine, at sea (above); and Britain's nuclear HMS *Valiant* laid bare.

Admiral Hyman G. Rickover, father of nuclear submarines, with two modern examples: USS *Georgia*, a "Trident" missile-boat coming to the surface, and USS *Nevada* in dock with her missile tubes uncovered.

Britain's first nuclear submarine, HMS *Dreadnought* (above); and the world's only diesel-powered class armed with ballistic nuclear missiles, a Soviet "Golf II" type.

The biggest submarine ever built: a vast Soviet "Typhoon" – Leonid Brezhnev's answer to "Trident".

and concomitant opportunities for the Wehrmacht, with its strong Norwegian positions, including airbases, harbours for surface ships and of course the U-boats. The British soon noticed easements in their strategic position as large Luftwaffe elements left the Western for the Eastern Front and German surface units concentrated in the Baltic.

Aid for the Soviet Union, as called for in the Anglo-Soviet mutual assistance pact signed in Moscow on 12 July 1941, entailed opening a new convoy route from Britain via Iceland to Murmansk, the only western Russian port that could stay open all year. Raeder had urged its capture on an uncomprehending Hitler. The Russians grimly beat off a belated German thrust at the harbour overland. The new route brought the Home Fleet, now commanded by Admiral Sir John Tovey, back into the convoy business, in which it had played no part since the collapse of the Allied Norwegian expedition in spring 1940. The British would deliver goods supplied by the United States, or from their own stocks which would eventually have to be replenished by the Americans. At the end of July the Home Fleet's two carriers and escorting forces carried out an inconclusive raid on German-occupied ports in Finland and northern Norway, during which the minelayer *Adventurer* was successfully detached to Archangel, near Murmansk, with a cargo of mines, the first maritime delivery of munitions to Russia.

Meanwhile American attitudes towards the Axis were stiffening. An American freighter, the *Robin Moor*, was sunk by *U69* (Jost Metzler) on 21 May just outside the zone boundary, not far from where the *Bismarck* had strayed over the line while passing the Denmark Strait only days earlier. Roosevelt reacted by bending the boundary to take in Iceland and ordering the US Marines to relieve the Anglo-Canadian garrison there. In June he had Axis assets in the United States frozen and Italian and German consulates closed. Some 4,400 Marines of the neutral United States took *de facto* possession of Iceland on 7 July.

The first Anglo-American summit of the war opened in secret at Argentia, Newfoundland, on 9 August. Roosevelt said he was "going fishing" and transferred to a cruiser at sea, while Churchill stole aboard a battleship and sailed the convoy route. Roosevelt was as chary as ever of declaring war but offered to take over the Canada-Iceland segment of the northerly convoy route, which represented a saving of fifty escorts to the British and Canadians. The leaders also discussed aid to Russia. The first numbered "convoy" from Russia to Britain, styled QP 1, consisted of one aircraft-freighter returning empty and left on 28 September, escorted by the heavy force which had brought it; the first convoy bound for Murmansk, designated PQ 1, left Hvalfjord in Iceland the next day, covered by a cruiser, an escort group and two extra destroyers.

The main political result of the Argentia conference, apart from cementing a personal relationship hitherto sustained solely by telex and telephone contacts, was the "Atlantic Charter", an early version of the yet to be formalised Allied war aims and the origin of the United Nations Declaration.

Summer 1941 provided the U-boats with a comparatively meagre harvest on the transatlantic route. The worst month of the war thus far was April, when the daunting total of 688,000 tons was sunk by all causes. The special factor at work in the month was hectic activity in the Mediterranean (see below). In May the total haul was 511,000, in June 432,000 and July 121,000 tons. The U-boats themselves accounted for 325,000 tons in April (less than half, unusually) but in August sank just 80,000 tons. Ultra, the reduction of the Luftwaffe in the west and better escort helped to explain this dip in the hitherto inexorably rising trend. But it worked to the disadvantage of hard-pressed RAF Coastal Command. Britain took delivery of its first twenty B24 "Liberator" bombers from Consolidated Aviation in June. It was the British who had spotted the potential of this unjustly neglected, four-engined plane because of its unusual range. It could outfly any other bomber then in service and carry a payload of twenty-four depth-charges. Coastal's new C-in-C, Air Marshal Sir Philip Joubert, appointed in June, managed to reserve half of the B24s, enough for a squadron (the others were kept for special duties). Modified by the addition of extra fuel tanks and ASV radar, these planes went into service in September. They were the only Allied wartime type capable of covering the mid-Atlantic "air gap" from land. Almost at once half of his dozen was taken away by the Air Ministry as Coastal Command went to the back of an increasingly clamorous queue, behind not only the US Navy and Army air forces but also Bomber Command, whose C-in-C, Air Chief Marshal Sir Arthur "Bomber" Harris, was besotted with launching the first 1,000-bomber raid on Germany.

But it was a humble Hudson, the medium-range bomber on which Coastal Command was forced mainly to rely at this stage, which won a remarkable duel with a U-boat on 27 August. Squadron-Leader J. Thompson was on patrol about 100 miles south of Iceland when he saw U570 (the high number was disinformation) moving slowly on the surface. Commander Hans Rahmlow was on his third day at sea on the type VIIC's maiden patrol. Thompson swooped and dropped four depth-charges, turned and raked the submarine with his machine-guns. The crew poured out of the conning tower and Rahmlow ran up a white flag. Thompson threatened by signal-lamp to open fire again if any attempt was made to scuttle; Rahmlow replied by similar means that he was unable to do so and asked for rescue. A Catalina relieved the Hudson until an armed trawler arrived from Hvalfjord to take the boat in tow. Thus did *U570* become His Majesty's Submarine *Graph*, an invaluable aid in training and ASW and fair recompense for HMS *Seal*.

Did he but know it, Joubert's problems with Bomber Command were less serious than those of Dönitz in his dealings with Göring and the Luftwaffe. The submarine admiral's staff established a reasonable working relationship with Bomber Group 40 and its two squadrons, each of fifteen Kondor long-range bombers (based at the French airbase at Mérignac near Bordeaux from July 1940), but the group remained firmly under Luftwaffe control. Later in the year they were given a second base at Stavanger in southern Norway. This enormously increased their operational reach: instead of flying 1,000 miles out across the Atlantic and back, they could make maximum use of their 2,000-mile endurance by flying one-way trips further out to sea – if they could be sure of good landing weather in Norway. In their first full month of operations they sank 53,000 tons of shipping; in November 1940 they got 66,000 tons. They were also able to home U-boats on to targets, a most promising stratagem, from which the British were eventually saved by Göring's obduracy.

Dönitz fondly imagined he had scored a victory over the Reichs-marschall, the world's only six-star general, in January 1941, when he persuaded Hitler to place Group 40 under his operational command while Göring was on holiday. A month later Göring invited Dönitz aboard his personal armoured train and tried to persuade him to give the Kondors back. Dönitz made his excuses and left, without dinner. But he was outranked; Göring, having failed to persuade, overruled the Navy and took the group back. At least its new commander, Lieutenant-Colonel Martin Harlinghausen, was a former naval officer who understood the Navy's needs. But the Kondor force was not built up or reinforced and gradually faded out of the struggle over the convoys, to the enormous relief of the British and their allies.

Dönitz was not displeased when Hitler issued his War Directive number twenty-three on 6 February 1941. This was rare for openly admitting that he had been wrong to discount the effect on the British war effort of shipping losses imposed by the Navy and the Luftwaffe. He looked forward to even more of the same when extra submarines became operational later in the year and foreshadowed detailed new orders for closer air-sea cooperation.

As if in reply, Churchill exactly one month later produced the directive for which he coined the term "Battle of the Atlantic", calling for all-out counter-attack against the U-boats and the Kondors, bombing their yards and bases and also reorganising the British ports. A standing Battle of the Atlantic Committee was set up, to meet every day, report to the Prime Minister every week and to oversee measures against congestion, whether in the shipyards or the docks. Ernest Bevin, Britain's leading trade unionist and socialist member of the War Cabinet as Minister of Labour, for the duration of the war acquired dictatorial powers over the British workforce unprecedented in a democracy. Some 40,000 troops were taken out of uniform and sent to the docks to eliminate delays exacerbated by overcrowding and bombing.

Any fond imaginings on the British side that the U-boats had passed their peak were rudely swept away in September, when they sank 203,000 tons out of a total loss of 286,000. In the North Atlantic, three sinkings out of four took place in the air gap. Dönitz could now field thirty-five boats on war patrol at a time, and could therefore muster two or more packs simultaneously. This flexibility and strength became available to him just as the weakness of the Canadian Navy brought on by forced growth came to a head. That resulted in the decimation of, among others, slow convoy SC 42, which set out from Sydney, Cape Breton, on 30 August: sixty-four ships (convoys were rather larger than they used to be) carrying half a million tons of cargo, protected by the 24th Escort Group of just one destroyer and three corvettes, all Canadian.

The STR knew that a pack of no fewer than fourteen U-boats dubbed *Markgraf* (marcher earl) had gathered south of Iceland. The pack, as was the custom, was given a name which it kept only as long as it stayed together. The new German code for positions prevented the OIC from working out where it was. But the sighting report from *U85* (Lieutenant Eberhard Greber) was intercepted and deciphered. SC 42 was therefore diverted just south of Greenland, as far north as possible. But it was attacked by four *Markgraf* boats on the night of 9 September, losing eight ships sunk and one tanker damaged: one corvette was detached from the overstretched escort to tow this precious vessel to Iceland. The next night seven boats made a second attack, sinking another seven ships.

The Admiralty in desperation scoured the ocean for reinforcements and diverted two more Canadian corvettes, *Chambly* and *Moose Jaw*, from training. They caught up with the convoy from astern on 10 September and promptly picked up an Asdic contact. They dropped depth-charges and were amazed to see *U501* (Commander Hugo Förster) pop up to the surface alongside *Moose Jaw*. The corvette's four-inch gun jammed after one round so she tried to ram, but the angle was wrong. Hunter and hunted ran side by side as if locked together until the Canadians heard a German voice shouting orders from their own deck. It was Förster, who had nimbly jumped aboard without getting his feet wet. The Canadians swung away and turned to ram again, firing machine-guns to keep the Germans' heads down. The *Chambly* had meanwhile lowered a boat with a boarding party. The Canadians could not persuade the Germans to go back inside their boat, even at gunpoint, because they had set scuttling charges on Förster's shouted orders.

Having seen for themselves that this was the case, the boarders scrambled out again as the submarine slid below the surface, taking one Canadian and eleven of her own crew with her. Förster, who said later he had boarded the corvette to seek rescue, and thirty-five of his men were saved (Förster was tried in a British prisoner-of-war camp by a kangaroo court of German officers for allegedly deserting his command; he later committed suicide at another camp). The Canadians had sunk their first U-boat of the war, a great fillip for the strained RCN. Three more corvettes came to the aid of SC 42 and on the 11th the Second Escort Group of five destroyers from Iceland joined up. A second submarine from *Markgraf*, *U207*, and one more merchantman were lost in the last hours of the battle. The convoy, reduced by sixteen ships, a quarter of its number, reached Britain without further incident.

On 15 September the Americans announced that they would escort convoys from their continent to Iceland. They covered the fast (HX) eastbound convoys while the Canadians continued to take the slow ones from Sydney, Cape Breton. On the following day the United States Navy escorted HX 150 to Hvalfjord. But Admiral King, commanding the US Atlantic Fleet, refused a Canadian request for the loan of destroyers, even though the Americans were in overall command of escort in the north-western Atlantic. King argued that as the British and Canadians were providing the majority of the escorts it was up to them to find reinforcements. At the request of their other mentor, the Admiralty, the Canadians raised the strength of all six of their escort groups by two ships each to six, but could only provide one destroyer per group. The rest were corvettes of the 1939 design, which tended to ship water in rough weather: the British had adapted theirs, giving them more freeboard forward. The Canadian escort of SC 44 lost a corvette as well as four merchantmen to a wolf-pack, while the condition and performance of the RCN escort of SC 45 so alarmed a British ship's captain that he reported it to the Admiralty.

SC 48 brought grief in mid-October to all three navies in the North Atlantic. A heavy storm broke up the convoy itself and HMCS *Shediac*, a destroyer, lost touch, her radio tuned to the wrong channel for incoming signals. She searched for her own convoy for five whole days, without success. The ships she was supposed to be protecting met a German patrol-line not detected by STR; three of them were sunk in quick succession. Five American destroyers came to the aid of the Canadians. The British sent the destroyer *Broadwater* and the corvette *Gladiolus*. Both were sunk by U-boats keen to get at their charges, of which six were also sunk on 17 October. Joachim Preuss in *U568* sank the corvette; but forty minutes earlier he had killed the first eleven American sailors lost to enemy action in the war when he torpedoed the USS *Kearny*. The destroyer managed to reach Iceland on one engine, escorted by her sister-ship, USS *Greer* (which depth-charged a U-boat without success on 4 September). It was not until 30 October that the inevitable happened. Commander Erich Topp of *U552* sank the destroyer USS *Reuben James*, escorting HX 156, with a single torpedo; 115 American sailors were killed and forty-six survived. Although Roosevelt exploited these developments, a surprise to an American public which had no idea how heavily the US Navy was engaged in the North Atlantic, the administration forbore from asking Congress to exercise its exclusive privilege, of declaring war on Germany.

HX 156 lost no other ship; but SC 52, which set off around the same time, was the only convoy of the Second World War to return to its starting point for fear of submarines. The STR had picked up the gathering of the *Raubritter* (robber knight) pack; when it sank four ships at the rear of the convoy and after two more merchantmen, having been diverted a little too far north, ran aground on the Grand Banks, SC 52 was sent back to wait for a few days. This was doubtless a relief for its Canadian escort, because RCN ships were now being forced to spend an inhuman twenty-six days out of thirty at sea as they sailed further and further east to help out the British, who had been obliged to divert escorts to the Sierra Leone and Gibraltar routes. The official interval in port for escorts was twelve days, devoted partly to leave and partly to maintenance.

British escort commanders, including Donald Macintyre and Captain E.B.K. Stevens, seconded to command the Canadian destroyers at St John's, warned the American, British and Canadian authorities of the dangerous overstrain on RCN ships. The Canadians were so short of men that sailors sentenced to imprisonment were forced to serve their time at sea (by this time they would doubtless have preferred a dry, warm cell ashore). Even when they got a few days' shore-leave, it was as likely as not to be in Iceland, from autumn to spring nobody's idea of a holiday resort. The Admiralty eventually went so far as to apologise to Commodore Murray, the Canadian commander at St John's, while even the blistering Admiral King and his subordinate, Admiral Bristol, made an attempt to ease the burden. The Canadian sailors, forced to the limit of endurance, unjustly acquired a reputation for incompetence and inefficiency. Their historian, Marc Milner, uncompromisingly attributes this to recklessness and indifference to their plight among the Canadian Naval Staff, exclusively concerned with maximum expansion at any price.

Meanwhile, as submarine sinkings fell back, Dönitz was becoming suspicious. Complaining about the thin pickings harvested by the long patrol-lines he could now operate with three dozen boats at a time to call upon, he noted in his War Diary in November:

It cannot depend on chance ... It is possible that from some source or other the British obtain information on our concentrated formations and take diversionary measures which occasionally lead them into the path of detached boats. Their information might be gained:
  a) as the result of treachery...
  b) by decrypting our radio messages ... [which is] out of the question...
  c) by coordinating radio traffic analysis and sighting reports...
  d) by radar.

U-boats close together on a narrow front could mass more quickly into a pack, whereas if they formed a broad front with greater spaces between them they were more likely to get a sighting. Dönitz now decided he had enough boats to have it both ways. His belief in the invulnerability of Enigma undiminished, he decided to form a broad line consisting of widely spaced groups, in each of which the boats were close together.

But, as we shall see in the next chapter, the sharp increase in German submarine strength during 1941 did not give Dönitz as much scope in the Atlantic as he would have liked because he was frequently required to divert boats to what he saw as secondary fronts, in particular the Mediterranean. From his transfer to U-boats in 1917 to his death in 1981 he never departed from his belief that the war of attrition on the Anglo-American transatlantic trade route was the main issue. His only uncertainty as U-boat, and later Navy, supremo was whether to focus on tonnage or supply. It was quite clear that any ship destroyed was, ton for ton, an equal blow to the enemy regardless of where it was sunk; and no less clear that the loss of a fully laden vessel bound for Britain was a double blow because the cargo was lost with the ship. War on tonnage had to outstrip the enemy's shipbuilding capacity to succeed, whereas war on supply was a constant threat to the entire British war economy but offered half as many targets. In the end the Germans and their U-boat chief never quite attained the position of being able to make this choice, settling instead for the ships they could most conveniently deny to an increasingly elusive enemy, laden or unladen. Given the phenomenal expansion of American shipbuilding, begun before the US joined battle, the eventual outcome of a tonnage war was bound to be favourable to the Allies – if they could only deliver enough food, goods and munitions to keep Britain (and now Russia) going in the meantime.

Burgeoning German submarine strength led an Admiralty committee to conclude firmly – at last – in May 1941 that "we cannot afford to weaken our convoy escorts to provide the ships required for searching forces [i.e. hunting groups] until far greater strength is available." Four months later, as losses rose again in the Atlantic, the key issue for the British was maritime airpower. The U-boats, aided in mid-ocean by Kondors and operating out of range of Anglo-Canadian aircraft, had enough strength to try to punch a hole in the surface-escort screens in order to get at their mercantile charges. The first attempt to solve this problem was the CAM (catapult-armed merchantman), a freighter which carried both a cargo and a ramp over its bow, from which its one and only Hurricane fighter could be hurled into the air against a Kondor. The pilot had to ditch his fighter in the sea when he ran out of fuel, and hope to be picked up.

In a memorandum to the Admiralty, Air Chief Marshal Joubert expressed his anxiety about the air gap at the end of September and advanced his solution: the escort-carrier, a merchant ship converted to carry ASW planes and sail with convoys in the gap. The British had captured the modern German grain-carrier *Hannover* early in the war and converted her into the world's first MAC (merchant aircraft-carrier). Restyled HMS *Audacity*, she displaced 5,537 tons and was equipped with a strengthened deck and six aircraft, which were able to land on the MAC thanks to arrester-wires of the kind fitted on "real" carriers. Thriftily, MACs also carried reduced cargoes, as well as, questionably, the Red Ensign of the Merchant Navy (the aircrews and supporting personnel were from the Royal Navy).

Only bulk-carriers and tankers with their long, clear decks and rear superstructure were suitable for such conversion. Six of the former and four of the latter were purpose-built as MACs and nine existing tankers were converted, two to be operated by the Dutch Navy. At the same time, the British ordered full-blown escort-carriers from the United States under Lend-Lease. The first five were converted merchantmen and the remaining thirty-eight were purpose-built to a standard design. These little aircraft-carriers took no cargo and flew the White Ensign of the Royal Navy, mostly displacing 11,420 tons and accommodating up to two dozen ASW planes. But they did not become available until the Atlantic struggle was past its peak: the Americans were simultaneously equipping their own Navy with this useful new class, which was to play a major role in the Pacific campaign.

The career of the pioneering *Audacity* (Commander D.W. Mackendrick, RN) was spectacular but short, spent entirely on the route between Gibraltar and Britain. Her first convoy was OG 74, outward-bound to Gibraltar, in September 1941. In company were twenty-six freighters, a sloop and five corvettes. On the 20th Commander Johannn Mohr in *U124* sighted the convoy and sank two merchantmen late that evening. A rescue ship (a freighter also equipped to help others in trouble, increasingly deployed with convoys at this time) went to their aid and was sunk by a Kondor. But one of the six Martlet fighters from *Audacity* spotted *U201* (the ace Adalbert Schnee) and forced her to dive with bursts of machine-gun fire. Two more took off later and shot down another Kondor, the first aircraft to be destroyed from an escorting carrier. The tiny Martlet was not capable of destroying submarines, but its ability to find them and force them under, thus depriving them of the speed to keep up with the convoy, was valuable enough. Schnee caught up sufficiently to be able to sink three stragglers from OG 74 the next night.

Audacity raised her Kondor score to three, for the loss of one Martlet and its pilot, before joining up with homeward-bound convoy HG 76 of thirty-two ships on 14 December. This soon became the epicentre of a prolonged running battle, one of the hardest fought of the entire war. The escort group was the 36th, led by Commander (later Captain) F.J. Walker, RN, in the sloop HMS *Stork*.

"Johnnie" Walker was to become the most famous and accomplished escort leader of the war and had already refined his group's tactics. As an ASW specialist Walker was an extreme rarity in the service before 1939, and would almost certainly have left it but for the war. Eighteen months after it began he was given command of the 36th's two sloops and six corvettes. Dönitz was concentrating on the Mediterranean at this stage and the STR was aware of the presence of many U-boats on either side of the Strait of Gibraltar. Walker was therefore given not only two extra sloops and three corvettes but also three destroyers and *Audacity*, all in all the most powerful convoy escort so far. Swordfish naval aircraft from Gibraltar dropped depth-charges against two U-boats sighted on the first evening and forced a third to dive next morning. On the 17th the STR soon reported the gathering of a wolf-pack of five, styled *Seeräuber* (pirate), across his route.

Commander Arend Baumann made the first attack on HG 76 that morning in *U131* but was spotted by a Martlet and driven under. *Stork* led four other escorts in a sweep twenty miles west of the convoy and crippled the boat with a hail of depth-charges, forcing her first to dive deeply and then to bob to the surface as Baumann expended his last compressed air. Even so he managed to shoot down an attacking Martlet. Two of Walker's destroyers opened fire accurately at a range of seven miles, forcing Baumann to scuttle and abandon. *U434* (Wolfgang Heyda) suffered a similar fate the next day after severe harassment by two destroyers. Martlets drove off two Kondors; so far not one torpedo had been fired at the convoy while two U-boats had been lost. Two destroyers turned back to Gibraltar later that day.

But at dusk Lieutenant Dietrich Gengelbach in *U574* was picked up on an escort's Asdic. He surfaced for speed and got away from the underpowered corvette, firing a salvo of torpedoes at maximum range without a hit. In the early hours of the 19th Gengelbach was astern of the convoy when he sighted the destroyer HMS *Stanley*, whose magazine exploded when he torpedoed her. But Walker had picked up her contact report and raced to the spot, attacking as *U574* dived; Gengelbach was soon forced back to the surface. U-boat and sloop chased round on parallel circular courses, *Stork* on the outside but too close to be able to depress her main guns sufficiently: the gunners were reduced to swearing at the enemy. Having cleared the conning tower with machine-gun fire, Walker fell back on the oldest naval stratagem, ramming. *U574* turned turtle and sank, helped on her way to the bottom by a last pattern of depth-charges. Five of her crew and twenty-five from the *Stanley* were rescued by *Stork*. By this stage the convoy had lost just one merchantman to a stray torpedo. Two more Kondors appeared; one was shot down and the other driven off with damage. On the 19th a Martlet mortally wounded yet another Kondor at point-blank range, colliding with it as it went down and just managing to land on *Audacity*.

The last of the five original attackers, the ace Klaus Scholtz in *U108*, doggedly kept in touch with the convoy as Dönitz committed another five boats to the long battle. On the morning of the 20th the Martlets drove off a Kondor and in the afternoon they forced two U-boats, sighted ahead of HG 76, to dive. In the evening Engelbert Endrass attacked from the rear in *U567* and sank one ship. At the same time Gerhard Bigalk in *U751* infiltrated the ten-mile gap between the convoy's right flank and *Audacity*, manoeuvring independently and without escort, despite Mackendrick's request to Walker for protection. At 8.30 p.m. Bigalk fired a salvo of torpedoes and scored three hits which cut the miniature carrier in two, each part sinking separately with heavy casualties, including Mackendrick. Bigalk dived and was found by an escort's Asdic, but got away to boast about his exploit on German radio at Christmastime. Walker unjustly blamed himself for the loss of the *Audacity*, even though he had acted entirely correctly in giving priority to protecting the merchantmen in the unending struggle. Even he could not be everywhere at once.

Two hours after the dispatch of the carrier, Endrass returned to the attack and was promptly picked up by three escorts. Lieutenant-Commander H.R. White's sloop *Deptford* made the last depth-charge attack before giving up for the night and returning to the convoy. Minutes later the British heard a massive double underwater explosion; *U567* had manifestly met a fate similar to that of her captain's mentor, Prien of *U47*. *Deptford*'s delayed victory was marred by her subsequent collision with the stern of *Stork*, when two German prisoners were killed and the escort leader's Asdic was knocked out. Walker, facing another 700 miles of fraught passage to England without air cover and with a reduced surface escort, was thoroughly depressed. One more Kondor put in a brief appearance and homed four more U-boats on to HG 76.

But on the morning of 22 December, more than four days' sailing from Britain, a Coastal Command Liberator appeared and began circling protectively overhead for hour after hour. Then another took its place. They forced two German submarines to dive and lose touch, and attacked a third with depth-charges on the 23rd, to no effect. The exhausted convoy reached England without further incident on 27 December. The final score for the Germans was the small carrier and a destroyer plus two merchantmen out of thirty-two; but the British had sunk four U-boats, including a leading ace, and destroyed or damaged half a squadron of Kondors, in a battle over a single convoy. On balance victory belonged to the convoy. There were bigger and bloodier convoy battles before and after HG 76; but a more intense contest over one convoy is unlikely to emerge from the crowded annals of the Atlantic campaign.

If Liberators could now come 700 miles from Britain and remain on station over a convoy for hours on end, they could also close the air gap in mid-North Atlantic from bases in Iceland and/or Newfoundland. But the half-squadron currently available to Coastal Command was based in Britain, and the gap remained open. By frittering away the rest of

Britain's first consignment of Liberators on other tasks, the RAF in 1941–2 very nearly undid over the Atlantic the result of its most famous victory over Britain itself in 1940. Since the significance and value of maritime airpower against the U-boats was now fully proved by German and British deployments and understood by high-ranking professionals on both sides, it is not hindsight that leads to this conclusion. One of the main culprits was Churchill, whose pugnacious character led him to sympathise wholeheartedly with the *idée fixe* of "Bomber" Harris: the 1,000-plane raid by Bomber Command.

The Germans meanwhile were wrestling with a different restraint on effectiveness: the increasing problem of supplying U-boats and disguised surface raiders at sea. They went to enormous lengths to overcome it, making use of the remoter islands of the Portuguese Azores and the Spanish Canaries. From the beginning of the war two German oil tankers "interned" off Las Palmas out of sight of shore topped up U-boats by night – and themselves by day, with more oil brought by coastal tankers. Thanks to Ultra the British discovered the role of these ships and protested to Madrid. The tankers were moved into Las Palmas harbour in September 1941, but they quietly moved out again and resumed business before the end of the year.

The first vessel designated for U-boat supply was in mid-Atlantic by May 1941. During the summer the Royal Navy disposed of seven such ships, even though they maintained radio silence, sailing in circles at preselected positions known to U-boats. Those caught were found either en route to their stations or by a scout-plane from a passing warship. In October, for example, the *Kota Penang* was sunk by the cruiser HMS *Kenya* east of the Azores.

The Germans were forced to divert the disguised merchant raider *Atlantis* (Captain Bernhard Rogge) to supplying U-boats. This formidable vessel was the first and most successful of her category. She was on her way home after being at sea since March 1940, circumnavigating the globe to sink or capture twenty-two merchantmen totalling 146,000 tons, a record unmatched by any other surface raider, including conventional warships. The diversion had however to be signalled by wireless and was therefore discovered at Bletchley Park. The fate of *Atlantis*, whose scouting aircraft had broken down, was sealed.

The spotter-seaplane of the cruiser HMS *Devonshire* (Captain R.D. Oliver, RN) found her at the end of November. Oliver opened fire with his eight-inch guns at nine miles, just as Rogge was refuelling *U126*. Her captain, Ernst Bauer, was having breakfast on the raider at the time, and his boat crash-dived without him. Rogge, seriously outgunned, abandoned ship as the cruiser pounded her to destruction and 308 survivors took to the boats, including Bauer. The British did not pick them up, quite legitimately because they knew at least one U-boat was in the area. So it was left to Bauer, eventually rejoining his command from a lifeboat, to organise one of the most extraordinary rescues of the war.

He crammed fifty-five *Atlantis* men into his boat while another fifty-two clung to her minimal deck; 201 men were squashed into four lifeboats and two launches and taken westward under tow, fortunately in calm water, to the known position east of Brazil of the submarine supply-ship *Python*. The *Atlantis* men were doubtless hugely relieved to clamber aboard. The *Python* sailed for the waters around the Cape of Good Hope. At a position south of St Helena on 1 December, she was refuelling *U68* and *UA* when the *Devonshire's* sister-ship, HMS *Dorsetshire* (Captain A.W.S. Agar, VC, RN) opened fire from eight miles. Agar had also been alerted by Ultra and directed to the German rendezvous. The two boats dived but *U68* was badly out of trim; *UA* (Commander Hans Eckermann) counter-attacked with a salvo of five torpedoes but missed. Once again the Germans abandoned ship and the British departed without helping them because of the U-boats. This time 414 men were in the water; for the *Atlantis* survivors it was the second time in nine days. The two submarines returned to the scene, took aboard about 100 men each and towed the rest in lifeboats. A launch plied among the members of this slow-moving double procession, exchanging survivors between the submarines and the lifeboats so that they all got their share of fresh air and delivering hot food and drinks prepared in the miniature galleys of the U-boats. Incredible though it may seem, Eckermann briefly dropped his chain of lifeboats so that he could attack a passing oil tanker sailing alone. He missed and returned to his charges.

Dönitz, alarmed by the loss of supply-ships and enraged by being forced to abandon his patrols in the South Atlantic, sent two more U-boats to help the survivors. Commander Nicolai Clausen arrived in *U129* on 3 December; two days later Commander Johann Mohr caught up in *U124*, which had sunk the light cruiser *Dunedin* on 24 November as it hunted the *Atlantis*. The enlarged procession headed north undisturbed until the 14th, when four roomy Italian submarines arrived from Bordeaux to ease the overcrowding. The lifeboats could now be destroyed and the return of the eight submarines completed with dispatch. They proceeded independently to St Nazaire, arriving between Christmas Day and 29 December. Dönitz had already decided to abandon trying to replenish submarines by surface ship: his answer was to use U-boats to supply U-boats. The first of these "milch-cow" submarines was delivered in December 1941; we shall return to their work and their fate.

The combination of U-boats and need for munitions forced Britain to reduce annual food imports by ten per cent to thirteen million tons during 1941, although bread was never rationed. Overall, imports fell to thirty-three million tons, sixty per cent of their 1939 level. Ironically, food rationing greatly benefited the nation's health and self-reliance as volunteers worked on the land or dug allotments in their spare time. The fear of invasion had receded with the German Army and Luftwaffe into the vastness of Russia from June. The British Home Fleet sent submarines, aircraft-carriers and surface raiders to harass the Wehrmacht in the Russian north, making a material contribution to the frustration of the German attempt to capture Murmansk overland. But in general British attacks on German shipping, admittedly a much smaller and more readily defended target found almost exclusively in coastal waters controlled by the enemy, were notably less effective by whatever means than the German onslaught on British ships. Hitler was obsessed with holding on to Norway at all costs and therefore kept disproportionately large forces in that country, even after the invasion of the Soviet Union. They now included *Tirpitz*, the most powerful battleship ever built outside Japan, which was earmarked for northern waters as soon as her end-of-year sea-trials were completed.

British shipping losses to U-boats, undoubtedly Churchill's biggest wartime worry as he frequently admitted later, began to be alleviated in August 1941, when the SS *Ocean Vanguard* was launched – the first American "Liberty" ship, the standardised freighter of 10,800 tons, of which sixty had been ordered in 1940. Congress authorised the construction of 200 more in April 1941. One month later the United States agreed to build the first 100 of a new kind of ocean escort, a 1,500-ton American design to which the British gave the new-old classification of frigate; the Americans preferred the designation "destroyer escort". Hitherto the best the Anglo-Canadian shipbuilding effort could manage was eight new escorts per month.

As 1941 drew to a close Germany was still winning the tonnage war, sinking ships faster than their replacement rate. The U-boats were ably assisted by the xB-dienst which, in September, broke into British Naval Cipher number two, the Royal Navy's main one for internal traffic. In December the German cryptanalysts did even better by penetrating number three, used for communication among the American, British and Canadian Navies in the Atlantic. Although the B-dienst did not completely overcome enemy ciphers any more than its British counterpart, it garnered more than enough to be able to build up a comprehensive picture of convoy operation, mirroring the work of the British OIC. The Germans' most useful tactical source became the convoy sailing telegram sent by the British Naval Control Service Officer (Port Director in the US). This signal informed the ocean escort of exactly what shipping to expect, its destinations and course after all last-minute additions, subtractions and alterations, and the time the convoy set out. Another crucial source until the British battle squadron was withdrawn from Halifax during 1941 was its flag officer's daily noon situation-report, intercepted in the European late afternoon by some of the forty or so listening posts along the occupied or pro-Axis Atlantic littoral from the North Cape to Vigo. Because the form of the message never varied, the B-dienst, which had over 1,000 staff at the height of the conflict, was able to penetrate it very quickly, no matter what variant of cipher number two was used. The Germans also read the much simpler British and Allied Merchant Ship (BAMS) code with ease; Captain Heinz Bonatz, the B-dienst commander, had written a confidential book on British wireless procedure just before the war.

In the nine months before the United States came into the war the British lost more than 1.5 million tons of shipping to submarines alone. Two-thirds of the losses were among IRS. But German submarine losses rose by fifty per cent to about three per month as their monthly sinking rate fell by twenty-five per cent; 5,500 tons were sunk per month per U-boat at sea – a quarter of the rate achieved in the previous nine-month period. This decline, revealed only by postwar analysis, shows how effective Ultra and the STR were. It was masked at the time by the great leap in overall U-boat numbers (200 by the end of 1941) enabling Dönitz to keep twice as many boats at sea at a time, despite a massively expanded training programme in the Baltic (which inevitably diluted operational standards). Fewer sightings by both sides reduced the losses of both in proportional terms, and the operational "life-expectancy" of a U-boat more than doubled, to nine months. The Anglo-Canadians increased their surface escort forces by a third to about 500, but they were still losing eleven tons of shipping for every ten that they could build or "borrow" under Lend-Lease. British escorts had become much more efficient and their weaponry was improving apace. Second-generation radar was being introduced at this stage, capable of detecting surfaced submarines at 7,000 yards; the "Hedgehog" multiple mortar, which lobbed showers of miniature depth-charges ahead of an ASW ship, eased the problem of Asdic "blindness" at close range. Constant patrols over the Bay of Biscay by Coastal Command forced U-boats to travel underwater on departure and return to their French bases, reducing their operational time by increasing their transit time.

The other great strategic development of 1941 after Barbarossa was the Japanese attack on the Americans at Pearl Harbor on 7 December, which took the war across the Pacific and made it truly global, forcing the Americans to take up arms at last. Three days later the Japanese easily sank by air attack the two capital ships Britain had sent to the Far East to "deter" them. The Japanese did not warn their German allies of their intentions, returning the compliment for the German assault on Russia. In the short term Hitler's ensuing and rash declaration of war on the US improved the German Navy's position immensely: the entire Atlantic was thrown open to the U-boats, free at last to sink anything on sight without fretting about neutrality zones or flags. Fortunately for the Allied cause, the Red Army saved Moscow the day before Japan struck. Thanks to the Russo-Japanese Neutrality Pact of April 1941 – Japan's revenge for the Nazi-Soviet Pact of August 1939 – Marshal Zhukov was able to move his tanks and heavy artillery from the Soviet Far East to save the capital and inflict a bitterly miserable winter on the Wehrmacht.

December 1941 was not much more comfortable for the newly expanded alliance against the Axis. The US Navy was in disarray and the US Army and its Air Force unready. The American, British and Dutch colonies in the Far East were clearly doomed as the Japanese advanced southward on a broad front. Australia and New Zealand were under threat. And in the Mediterranean, British land, sea and air forces were on the defensive.

Before turning to the warmer waters of what Mussolini rashly called *Mare Nostrum* ("our sea"), let us take a look at how the German submariners fared ashore. Dönitz was a stern taskmaster in the iron Prussian tradition, but this did not prevent him, as we have glimpsed earlier, from following the golden rule of the successful commander: to do everything possible for the wellbeing of his men. One result was the exceptionally high morale the British noticed on the rare occasions when they captured U-boat personnel (a U-boat was usually already sunk in advance of her own destruction, which meant nobody survived; only when she was caught on the surface – or when her death-throes happened to bring her there – could the crew hope to escape).

The demand from Dönitz for absolute devotion to duty at sea was rewarded by the chance of "living like a god in France", as the U-boat men described it, between patrols. This heaven on earth was something to which the trainees in the Baltic looked forward and on which their instructors, or the crews of boats in northern waters, looked back longingly, hoping to return. Dönitz had his own railway train, on which crewmen were taken for home leave and brought back, together with spare parts and equipment for the boats. Home leave was as rare in the submarine arm as in any other force on either side, but local leave in one of the French bases was unique.

Submariners returning from sea could easily be detected ashore without radar. Pasty-face and reeking of diesel oil, to say nothing of imposed inattention to personal hygiene, bearded by custom born of necessity, they wore stained uniforms disfigured by oil and salt, their leather jackets and boots often covered in mould. The first stop ashore therefore was for a luxurious bath or shower and clean clothing. Then they would set out to spend their accumulated pay and allowances – roughly twice as high as the rest of the Navy's – on the returning sailor's traditional avocations ashore. The service laid on *U-bootsweiden* (U-boat meadows), rest-and-relaxation centres in first-class requisitioned hotels or châteaux inland. Those obliged to stay in port could go to the Cecilia Bar in Brest, the Astoria Bar in St Nazaire, the Maritza in La Baule (nicknamed *die Giftbude*, the poison-hut). In Lorient, close to an indulgent headquarters, there were the Hôtel Beau Séjour and the bar officially known to submariners as *Les Trois Soeurs* and unofficially as *die sechs Titten*, where a riotously good time could be had by all. Local French people, who had no choice in the matter, seemed prepared to tolerate the binges and accept the occupation francs of the boisterous young Germans, who fully understood the *carpe diem* principle. They could die tomorrow, and their roistering ashore had an undertone of desperation most directly comparable with the off-duty moments of RAF fighter pilots during the Battle of Britain, and bomber crews thereafter.

The British devoted a great deal of effort – in vain, even after the pendulum had swung against the U-boats – to attacking the morale of the enemy submariners. Garnering information from every possible source, including prisoners of war, spies in occupied France and sigint, a special section of Naval Intelligence operated the *Atlantiksender,* a "black" propaganda transmitter. Dönitz called it the Atlantic *Giftküche* (poison kitchen) and made it an offence for his men to listen to it. None the less they did, and were astute enough to recognise it for what it was: a backhanded compliment to their own success. Why else would a hard-pressed enemy devote so much time, talent and energy to such an exercise?

The idea came from Lieutenant-Commander Ian Fleming, RNVR, the future creator of the fictional superspy, James Bond, and drew such considerable contributors as Sefton Delmer, prewar Berlin correspondent of the London *Daily Express*. The station seemed to know everything. It reported submariners' parties ashore which had run out of control, dwelt on the imputed shortcomings of U-boat weaponry and equipment and boasted of the purported technical advantages of the Allies. Announcers even read out the results of sports events among the crews: Peter Cremer, ace commander of *U333*, wrote in his memoirs that the station reported on one occasion: "This afternoon Third Flotilla, La Rochelle, played Twelfth Flotilla, Bordeaux, and won 5:3." Even the names of the goalscorers were given. Ashore and at sea in the Bay of Biscay the German submariners listened to these outpourings with amazement and amusement – and carried on regardless.

The disparity in strength between Britain and such allies as it still had after the fall of France on the one hand, and the German-Italian Axis on the other, was most obviously laid bare in the Mediterranean in 1941. In this theatre the best and most strenuous efforts of the British armed forces were frustrated by a large handful of U-boats, the Luftwaffe and a tiny fraction of the German Army's total manpower at the time, with some assistance from Italy's Navy and Regia Aeronautica (Air Force) and none at all from its Army. For the Germans it was an irritating sideshow, a distraction from the real struggle in Russia, made necessary by the failures of Italian troops in North Africa and the Balkans; for the British it was the main front militarily until the invasion of Normandy in June 1944.

On 11 November 1940 the Royal Navy reasserted its supremacy in the Mediterranean for a while by laming the Italian battlefleet in port at Taranto with a new stratagem, an air-raid from a carrier. The precedent was carefully noted by the Imperial Japanese Navy. The British Army corps under Lieutenant-General Sir Richard O'Connor then inflicted a series of massive defeats on the Italians in North Africa, capturing Tobruk and Benghazi by early February 1941 and leaving the Italians with little more than a toehold round Tripoli in Libya. It was there that General Erwin Rommel landed in March, under orders from Hitler to stiffen Italian resistance with a new Afrika Korps of one infantry and two Panzer divisions which would soon follow (one per cent of the German Army). The Luftwaffe established itself in the new theatre with Fliegerkorps X, a mixed group of some 120 bombers, dive-bombers and fighters based initially in southern Italy and Sicily. The entire Luftflotte II (tactical Air Force) was to follow.

O'Connor was not allowed to finish his excellent work because the War Cabinet, against the advice of many commanders from all three services, had resolved to go to the aid of the Greek Army, which had valiantly smitten the invading Italians but now faced the Wehrmacht. This was a pity as the capture of Tripoli at that point, a racing certainty, would have saved the British Army nearly two years of unrelenting labour. The Germans were able to advance on Greece and Yugoslavia in April via the territory of Germany's new Balkan allies. The British Army in North Africa was disastrously stripped of battle-hardened Australian, New Zealand and British troops for a bungled intervention in Greece which became a retreat as soon as it started. The British Mediterranean Fleet, based at Alexandria in Egypt and supported by Somerville's Force H from Gibraltar, was massively engaged in escorting troop convoys, delivering supplies to North Africa and Greece, reinforcing Malta whenever it could, attacking Axis supply-lines and fighting the not inconsiderable residue of the Italian Navy, whose ships were nearly all faster than their British equivalents. The débâcle of the instant retreat from Greece was repeated in May and June in Crete.

For the British the whole affair was another Norway-cum-Dunkirk, doubtless made all the more bitter for Churchill, the prime mover, by recollections of Gallipoli. Ironically the "soft underbelly" approach, the traditional British stratagem of attacking a continental enemy at his weakest point, as executed by Wellington in Spain against Napoleon, had almost worked: O'Connor could have knocked the Italian Army out of the war but for the disastrously inept switch to Greece. Admiral Sir Andrew Cunningham, C-in-C in the Mediterranean, roundly defeated the Italian Navy a second time at the Battle of Cape Matapan (southern Greece) on 28 March, sinking three cruisers and two destroyers without loss but failing for lack of speed to finish off the Italian fleet flagship, the modern fast battleship *Vittorio Veneto*, with his superior firepower, after damaging her in an air-strike. The battle turned out to be the last fleet action in British history.

The submarine HMS *Truant* got a rare chance to work with the fleet in April 1941, when Cunningham took a heavy squadron – three battleships and a cruiser, covered by a carrier and destroyers – from Alexandria on the 18th to bombard Tripoli. Dispatched in advance, *Truant* sat on the surface in the night four miles off the Libyan port, shining a light out to sea as a guide for the gunners, who made a lot of noise but did not seriously affect the enemy's position. Meanwhile Rommel had begun what was to be an eight-month siege of Tobruk, which imposed yet another task on Cunningham, of keeping the garrison supplied; even so it fell to the Germans in December.

From February to May 1941 the British sank or otherwise stopped six supply-ships out of every ten on the Italy–Libya run, despite their setbacks elsewhere in the theatre. Malta underwent a prolonged siege and bombardment by air which made it untenable as a base for surface ships until late in October. From June 1941, when the Germans were firmly established in the Mediterranean, a complicated double campaign developed at sea, in which the British tried to cut the short, north–south Axis convoy route from Italy to North Africa while the Germans and Italians attempted to break the long, east–west Gibraltar–Malta–North Africa convoy line maintained by the British. Both sides used surface ships large and small, aircraft and submarines. But the RAF managed to sink two dozen ships totalling 102,000 tons while British submarines, playing the same role here as the U-boats in the Atlantic, accounted for fourteen totalling 75,000 tons. The leading British ace was Lieutenant-Commander M.D. Wanklyn in HMS *Upholder,* whose most spectacular feat was to sink in rapid succession the twin Italian liners *Neptunia* and *Oceania* (19,500 tons each) on 18 September, out of a three-ship, fast trooping convoy bound for Tripoli. He won the VC.

At this stage the British were stopping one ship in three bound for North Africa. When Force K, of two cruisers and two destroyers specially detached from Force H, arrived at Malta late in October and started work, the knockout rate rose to almost two out of three and then touched seven out of ten, including a 100 per cent score against a convoy of seven ships. The submarine *Utmost* crippled the Italian cruiser *Trieste* and a naval Swordfish aircraft seriously damaged her sister-ship, *Duca degli Abruzzi,* late in November. But maintaining the garrison in Tobruk alone cost the British twenty-five warships plus nine badly damaged, and five merchantmen sunk plus four crippled.

After the German invasion of the Soviet Union in June, relative Axis air strength began a slow decline as the British raised theirs; not only by convoy across the Mediterranean but also by deliveries overland from West Africa. A huge British naval and logistical effort built up the new Eighth Army of 100,000 men in North Africa and the fighting swung back and forth across the desert.

On 25 July 1941 Rommel visited Hitler in his headquarters, the "Wolf's Lair" in Rastenburg, East Prussia. He outlined his desperate supply position and called for a counter-attack on the British Mediterranean Fleet by a diversion of U-boats from the Atlantic. In mid-August Raeder, the naval C-in-C, ordered a constant presence of six to ten submarines in the Mediterranean. The first six passed the Strait of Gibraltar by the end of September; by early November the number rose to ten, despite objections from Dönitz, who had also been obliged to send extra boats to the eastern Baltic in vague and ultimately useless support of Operation Barbarossa. German determination to hold on in the Mediterranean was underlined by the arrival at this time of Luftflotte II.

Five days after Force K's total success against the Italian convoy, on

Friday 13 November, the modern British fleet carrier *Ark Royal* (Captain L.E.H. Maund, RN), attached to Force H, was returning to Gibraltar from the east with a battleship, a light carrier and a cruiser in company. The carrier had helped to fly thirty-seven Hurricanes and seven Blenheim medium bombers on to Malta. Ahead of her, alerted by the xB-dienst, lay *U81* (Fritz Guggenberger). It was 2.30 p.m. Coolly waiting until the carrier was 1,200 metres away, and ignoring her powerful escort (which had failed to detect either of the two U-boats in the vicinity), Guggenberger fired a salvo of four torpedoes from periscope depth, blowing a huge hole. Suddenly lightened, the U-boat almost broke the surface, but the crew raced forward to the bow torpedo-compartment and forced her nose down again; Guggenberger evaded the depth-charges. After a long struggle by rescue ships to save her, HMS *Ark Royal* rolled over and sank early the next morning, just twenty-five miles from Gibraltar. One man died. The subsequent British enquiry established a whole series of technical flaws which contributed to the sinking, all of which were eliminated on later British carriers.

The ship's cat, Oscar, was promptly banned from His Majesty's Navy. He was, after all, German, having been rescued from the wreckage of the *Bismarck* in May 1941 by the crew of the destroyer HMS *Cossack*, which was sunk in its turn by *U563* in October while escorting convoy HG 75 from Gibraltar. Most of the destroyer's crew had been rescued – with Oscar – and taken back to Gibraltar, where the animal was promptly promoted to ship's cat on the Royal Navy's hitherto most successful carrier. Oscar was banished to a seamen's home in Belfast, where he died peacefully in 1955. The home burnt down . . .

Back in the Mediterranean, twelve days after *U81*'s coup *U331* (Lieutenant Hans Diedrich von Tiesenhausen) was lurking off Alex-andria, Cunningham's main base, slowly patrolling underwater on the morning of 25 November. Hearing engine noises on the hydrophones, the Germans surfaced and raced northward. Early in the afternoon they sighted a squadron of three British battleships with escort. Tiesenhausen dived to periscope depth and managed to work his boat undetected into a position between the destroyer screen and the capital ships they were meant to be protecting. By the time the second of the three dreadnoughts was passing him, he was ready to fire a salvo of four. Three hit the starboard side of HMS *Barham* (Captain G.C. Cooke, RN) as the conning tower of *U331* bobbed above the surface; so close to the battle-ships that they could bring no guns to bear on the desperately diving U-boat. The stricken capital ship listed to starboard and sank when her magazines exploded. It was the first time in the war that a submarine had sunk a dreadnought on the open sea: the British concealed the disaster from the public for several months.

The Navy's suffering in the Mediterranean was still not complete for the year. On 14 December *U557* (Ottokar Paulshen) torpedoed and sank the light cruiser HMS *Galatea* thirty miles west of Alexandria. Mines sank another cruiser attached to Force K and damaged a third, leaving it with one. The British Mediterranean Fleet effectively ceased to exist when a fantastically brave attack by six Italian frogmen on three "chariots" or human torpedoes in Alexandria harbour left two battleships sitting on the shallow bottom. The British account at the end of the year showed one battleship sunk and four seriously damaged, one carrier sunk and two damaged, seven cruisers sunk and ten damaged, sixteen destroyers sunk and twelve damaged, five submarines sunk and three damaged. At the beginning of 1942, after all this sacrifice by the Royal Navy, the British Army stood on the same spot as it had at the beginning of 1941 – El Agheila in Libya, where O'Connor had broken off.

Nor was the German submarine assault on the Mediterranean without cost. Five U-boats were sunk in the vicinity of the Strait of Gibraltar in November and December: two by British corvettes, two by British aircraft and one by a Dutch submarine. Three more were so badly damaged by depth-charges from planes or ships that they had to limp back to their French bases. This represented a casualty rate of one-third of the two dozen boats Dönitz had been obliged to keep in the Mediterranean with effect from Hitler's order of 29 October, just after he had got back the eight boats diverted to the Baltic from June to September. Six more were still "defending Norway", and Dönitz was also forced to keep two more on station in the far North Atlantic to provide the Luftwaffe with weather reports. All this left thirty boats for the main task of attacking the 3,000-mile Anglo-American convoy route, a maximum of ten boats on patrol at a time. Hence the fall in Allied shipping losses in the Atlantic in this deceptively quiet period.

Dönitz was not afraid to protest. He wrote to Raeder in November:

The U-boat Commander is as before of the opinion that the main task of the U-boat war is attack. Only through attack does it have its effect against England, which can only welcome it if the U-boat war dies down. As a division of the U-boat arm is necessary and unavoidable on grounds of political strategy – viz. the Mediterranean – the laming of the U-boat war in the Atlantic through continual chipping away for secondary tasks should in my estimation be avoided at all costs ... in [Atlantic] reconnaissance, the absence of a single boat means fewer sighting reports for all and fewer chances to sight something. But sighting is the most serious problem of all in the U-boat war.

The only response to this appeal was an order on the 21st to withdraw all boats from the area between Britain and Iceland and send them to the waters on either side of Gibraltar. Thus the Atlantic was virtually denuded of U-boats as Hitler decided that the Mediterranean sideshow was to be promoted to the main naval theatre of war for the time being. The Naval Staff, ignoring all protests from Dönitz, wanted to prevent the remote possibility of a British landing in Morocco aimed at attacking Rommel in the rear (anticipating actual events by a whole year). The British were therefore given a very hard time in the Mediterranean; but the compensation of a prolonged breathing-space in the crucial Atlantic much more than made up for it. The switch of front by the U-boats was the reason why Johnnie Walker's convoy, HG 76, could be provided with such a lavish escort: the British were able to divert many escorts from their transatlantic to their Mediterranean routes.

Dönitz was under no illusion that the battle of HG 76 was a defeat. The loss of five submarines was a bigger blow than the sinking of two empty merchantmen, a destroyer and even a rudimentary escort-carrier, which had originally been take in prize from the Germans anyway. Some of his staff, including Godt, the operations chief, concluded that the U-boats were no longer capable of taking on the escort groups. Dönitz himself, who did not share the tendency of so many German war leaders to ignore realities, was less pessimistic all the same. He looked back on 1941 as a year of mixed fortunes which showed that Germany and its submarine service could take nothing for granted. He rightly saw the massive escort with HG 76 as an aberration rather than a new norm. The kind weather had worked in favour of the British in a way it did not in the North Atlantic, offering optimum conditions for hydrophones and Asdic, visibility and manoeuvre. Finally, the route the convoy took might be covered by British planes but the air gap in the middle of the North Atlantic was still there, crying out to be exploited. And rich new pickings awaited his captains in American waters, hitherto closed to them.

For the British, maintaining their position in the Mediterranean in 1942 in defiance of Axis air superiority (built up despite the competing demands of the Russian Front) was hugely costly for little enough return. It was hard to determine whether Malta, the little British archi-pelago in the middle of the ocean, was a useful base for operations against Axis shipping or a liability which could only be defended at enormous cost. In April constant bombardment forced the Royal Navy to withdraw its remaining handful of surface vessels from Malta to Alexandria until August. Only the submarines could remain, submerging or withdrawing during the day to evade the air attacks. In the same month the losses imposed by the British on Axis convoys to North Africa plummeted to one per cent. Saving the savagely battered island had become a matter of honour and political rather than military necessity for British leaders. They therefore sent sixty merchantmen laden with supplies into the Mediterranean to help Malta during 1942, of which exactly half arrived; twenty were sunk and ten turned back. In escorting these vessels Britain lost another carrier, three cruisers and nine destroyers while many more warships were damaged.

Much of the fighting in North Africa as the front swayed back and forth was for control of the airfields in the Cyrenaica region of Libya, from which the convoys of both sides, and Malta, could be attacked or defended. It was not until the end of August that Rommel was at last forced on the defensive by the Eighth Army, which thus put an end to the Axis threat to Egypt. This caused the Germans to abort their Operation Herkules for the capture of Malta. The main Battle of El Alamein in October saw a much enlarged and superior British Eighth Army under General Sir Bernard Montgomery inflict a decisive defeat on the Afrika Korps, still only three divisions strong and short of supplies, thanks not to the shrivelled British assault on supply-lines at sea but, as recent historical research has proved, to Italian logistical and Libyan physical bottlenecks on land. In that sense the monumental struggle for Malta was a diversion and a waste of time.

Any chance that Cunningham, without a single serviceable capital ship, would receive significant reinforcements was dashed by the Japanese onslaught in the Far East, which cost the British another two capital ships in its first week. Supremacy in the Mediterranean had passed to the Italian Navy, backed as it now was by German E-boats as well as U-boats and an entire tactical air force of the Luftwaffe. The British C-in-C was denied his own Coastal Command, although the RAF placed its mixed 201 Group, inadequately trained in the special skills needed for maritime work, at his disposal, if not under his command. Malta's air defence was in the hands of Air Marshal Sir Keith Park, the man who had led 11 Group, Fighter Command, as it bore the brunt of the Battle of Britain.

The first attempt of the year to get a convoy of three large freighters through to Valletta, Malta's main port, took place in February. Despite a strong guard of one cruiser and eight escort destroyers and a covering force of three more cruisers and eight fleet destroyers commanded by

Rear-Admiral Philip Vian, none got through. One was sunk, one scuttled and one crippled but towed into Tobruk.

Cunningham's last "big show" as Mediterranean chief before he was replaced by Admiral Sir Henry Harwood, the over-promoted victor of the River Plate, was Operation MG1, to cover convoy MW 10 of four ships from Alexandria to Malta in March. As escort Vian was given all the Mediterranean Fleet's remaining cruisers (four light) and destroyers (seventeen); one more in each category would sail from Malta to meet him west of Crete. Five submarines of the First Flotilla based at Alexandria were sent out as pickets against surface attack; but the main anticipated threat, as ever, was from the air. High-level Italian and low-level German attacks failed; but on 22 March the new Italian battleship *Littorio*, a pair of heavy cruisers and ten destroyers advanced towards the convoy. Frenetic activity by the aggressively led covering force drove them off twice with some damage, at a cost to the British of two destroyers and one cruiser moderately damaged; frantic but precise zigzagging by convoy and close escort frustrated German dive-bombing at a huge cost in anti-aircraft ammunition.

The RAF failed even to damage the retiring Italians; but the submarine *Urge* (Lieutenant-Commander Tomkinson) sank the Italian cruiser *Giovanni delle Bande Nere*, one of the frustrated attackers, on 1 April. *Urge* was one of the many coastal "U" class boats which formed the backbone of the Malta submarine force, made up of the First and later the Second and Tenth Flotillas. About a dozen of the class at a time were active in the Mediterranean from 1941 to 1944, supported by a few of other British types as well as Greek, Dutch, Polish and Yugoslav boats. The same day, Cunningham, undoubtedly the right man in the right job, was unaccountably transferred to head the important British Naval Mission in Washington. Neither demotion nor sinecure, this was none the less hardly the most appropriate appointment at this crucial stage for the country's best fighting admiral.

So desperate were the British to hold Malta that they turned to the Americans for help. The carrier USS *Wasp* (Captain J.W. Reeves, Jr, USN) of the US Atlantic Fleet went to the Clyde in mid-April and took aboard forty-seven Spitfires before being escorted into the Mediterranean by the battlecruiser HMS *Renown*, two British cruisers and a strong force of American and British destroyers. All but one of the planes were safely delivered by being launched from the carrier at a distance of well over 100 miles. The exercise was therefore repeated in May, with the elderly British carrier *Eagle* embarking another seventeen Spitfires to accompany the *Wasp*'s forty-seven. Sixty-one managed to land on Malta. The *Eagle* executed three more successful Spitfire deliveries after the *Wasp* returned to the Atlantic Fleet. The fast mine-layer *Manxman* made a clear run to Valletta in May with ammunition, aircraft parts and fighter-control equipment. This enabled Malta at last to mount an adequate air defence, including the ability to cover incoming convoys – if the Navy could bring them close enough.

In June convoys sailed simultaneously for Malta from Gibraltar and Alexandria. The former got two out of six merchantmen through; the latter lost five out of eleven and the remaining six were forced to turn back when the escort all but ran out of ammunition after constant air and surface attacks. The British submarine *Umbria* (Lieutenant S. Maydon) sank the Italian cruiser *Trento* on 15 June; but *U205* (Franz-Georg Reschke) sank the British cruiser *Hermione* in the early hours of the 16th during the prolonged air and sea battles which developed round this double convoy disaster. Four more British cruisers were damaged, four destroyers sunk and half a dozen damaged in the various actions. An RAF Wellington damaged the battleship *Littorio* with a torpedo, putting her out of action for the rest of the year. Harwood's stream of irresolute orders to Vian (Cunningham hardly ever interfered in this way) played an important part in the total failure of the convoy from Alexandria, the last from there until November.

As the baffled Eighth Army prepared to make a stand against Rommel at El Alamein, under three hours by tank from Alexandria, Harwood evacuated his headquarters there at the end of June, moving to Ismailia on the Suez Canal. He sent his remaining ships to Haifa in Palestine or Port Said in Egypt, losing the 14,650-ton submarine depot-ship *Medway* to *U372* (Heinz-Joachim Neumann) in the process, on the 30th.

In August the British made "one more heave" to resupply a desperate Malta in Operation Pedestal, cancelling a convoy to Russia in its favour. The cover for the fourteen merchantmen from the Clyde was vast: three fleet-carriers, two battleships, seven cruisers, two dozen destroyers and auxiliaries, all under the flag of Vice-Admiral E.N. Syfret, RN. They passed into the Mediterranean on 10 August and were under constant Luftwaffe surveillance from the 11th. At lunchtime *U73* (Lieutenant Helmut Rosenbaum) fired a salvo of torpedoes from periscope depth at HMS *Eagle* (Captain L. Mackintosh, RN) which took a huge hole in her port flank and sank in eight minutes, with the loss of some 260 men out of 1,160. That night a destroyer rammed and sank the Italian submarine *Dagabur*, crippling herself in the process. The first air attacks that afternoon had missed, but in the onslaught from Sardinia the next day by Italian and German aircraft, torpedo-bombers and fighters sank a freighter and bored a hole in the deck of the carrier *Victorious* with an unexploded bomb. Another destroyer knocked herself out by ramming and sinking a second Italian submarine, the *Cobalto*. The second raid of the day sank a destroyer and damaged the carrier *Indomitable*, which had to withdraw.

Rear-Admiral H.M. Burrough now took four cruisers and twelve destroyers on the last leg to Malta. In the most spectacular attack ever made by an Italian submarine, Lieutenant Renato Perrini in *Axum* destroyed the anti-aircraft cruiser *Cairo* and badly damaged the light cruiser *Nigeria* (Burrough's flagship) and the tanker *Ohio*. *Nigeria* turned back to Gibraltar; Burrough moved his flag to the destroyer *Ashanti*. The convoy was now without any ship capable of directing fighters, so the Spitfires from Malta withdrew for the time being. The day's third air-raid sank one merchantman and damaged another, while Lieutenant Sergio Puccini in the submarine *Alagi* sank a freighter and put a torpedo through the bow of the cruiser *Kenya*, which managed to keep her station. German and Italian motor-torpedo-boats harried the convoy after dark, so damaging the cruiser *Manchester* that she had to be scuttled, and sinking four merchantmen and damaging another, which sailed on. At dawn the planes came back to sink another freighter and inflict further damage on the *Ohio* and two other merchantmen. But the Italian heavy ships were deterred from joining in by Lieutenant Alastair Mars in the British submarine *Unbroken*: he seriously damaged one heavy and one light cruiser with his torpedoes north of Malta.

By the time the badly hammered ocean escort began to limp back to Gibraltar and the light escort from Malta came out (four minesweepers and seven launches), there were just five merchantmen left out of fourteen, two barely afloat and virtually reduced to hulks, including the powerless *Ohio*. On the evening of 13 August three ships slowly entered Valletta, one almost awash. A fourth limped in the next day. And on the 15th, Malta's national day, the destroyer *Penn* towed the indestructible *Ohio*, barely afloat after a third air-strike which miraculously failed to set her ablaze, into the harbour. She was welcomed by a wildly cheering crowd, and her master, Captain D.W. Mason of the Merchant Marine, was awarded the George Cross. Her cargo of petroleum and the 30,000 tons of supplies offloaded from the four other survivors of Pedestal just managed to keep Malta in the war until the strategic situation in the Mediterranean was transformed by Montgomery's victory at the end of October, and by the Anglo-American landing in Morocco (Operation Torch) in November.

Submarines played a decidedly more modest role on both sides in the Mediterranean in 1942 than they had in 1941. The British were hampered by Rommel's threat to Alexandria and the constant air bombardment of Malta, which made the island a dangerous base even for submersible boats, and by Axis airpower generally, which seriously inhibited them by day.

The Germans had been operating about ten boats in the eastern basin and up to fifteen around Gibraltar, approximately half on either side of the Strait. But on the day after Pearl Harbour Dönitz sought approval for the dispatch of twelve of the larger type IX boats to operate in the newly available American waters, where their qualities would come into their own as they had not always done in the often confined waters of the Mediterranean. Six such boats were already on their way there as reliefs or replacements; these were diverted to patrol off the Azores while the Naval Staff made up its mind. They were eventually sent westward on 2 January.

At the same time the number of boats on diversion from the Atlantic to the Mediterranean was reduced to six; of these, three were ordered into the western basin. Two managed the fraught passage; one gave up after two attempts and remained outside. The other three patrolled between the Azores and Gibraltar with orders to make their presence felt sufficiently to mask the overall reduction in U-boat commitment to the Mediterranean area. But their attempt to attack convoy HG 78 in mid-month was foiled by a powerful escort. Three boats were simply not enough to stretch the defence, and one was sunk. So was *U581* when she tried early in February to sink a British troopship, damaged earlier and driven to take refuge in the Azores by *U402*.

The very high score already run up meanwhile by the handful of boats operating in American waters, to be described later, led the German Naval Staff in February 1942 to wind down the Mediterranean operation. Had this been the only factor affecting Dönitz's deployment in the Atlantic, the Allied cause would have suffered even more shattering damage from shipping losses than it did. But Hitler was once again obsessed with the "threat" to Norway and demanded the diversion of twenty boats at a time to northern waters late in January. In the period from April to September 1942 Churchill did indeed consider a new Norwegian adventure to relieve the Russian convoys, also described below, but deferred to the opposition of his military leaders.

Back in the Mediterranean, the Axis surrender in North Africa on 12 May 1943 closed that campaign and cleared the way for the Allied invasion of Sicily on 10 July, followed by the invasion of the mainland and the Italian surrender early in September. Admiral Cunningham, who had returned from Washington to command the naval side of Operation Torch, was on hand to witness the surrender of the Italian fleet at Malta on 10 September, in a scene reminiscent of the German surrender in the Firth of Forth in 1918. Cunningham's former flagship *Warspite*, the gnarled old battleship which had fought at Jutland and attended the internment of the Kaiser's Fleet, led the British line superintending the exit from the war of the first of the three Axis powers to give up.

Italy declared war on Germany on 13 October and a bitter fight up the Italian peninsula ensued, with an indifferently led Allied attack running up against a superbly conducted German defence. From June 1940 until the Italian surrender the Royal Navy alone had forfeited 175 surface warships of all sizes in the Mediterranean, from one battleship and two carriers to motor launches, including forty-four precious destroyers. To these must be added the forty-one boats lost in the main British submarine campaign of the war. But in May 1944 two flotillas were still hard at work in the Mediterranean: the First, including ten British boats (eight "U" and two "S"), four Greek, one Dutch and one Yugoslav; and the Tenth, consisting of three "U" and one "T" class British boats.

The Allied domination of the Bay of Biscay made it very hard for U-boats to reach the Mediterranean. Only five managed to get through in the five months preceding the Italian surrender, not at all sufficient to replace German losses. Three left in July, the last to go from the French bases (abandoned at the beginning of August); all of them were caught and sunk by the RAF in the Bay. In the six months from September 1943 to February 1944 fourteen U-boats conducted patrols in the Mediterranean; in the ensuing quarter seven did so; both of the last two German boats on patrol in the Mediterranean in May were sunk by the 17th. Then there were none.

The reopening of the short and now safe Mediterranean route to the east significantly raised the shipping tonnage available to the Allies by ending diversions round the Cape of Good Hope. At the same time, massive military operations in the ocean itself from summer 1943 increased the demand for merchant shipping by a not dissimilar amount. But the famous "Force H" based at Gibraltar was disbanded on 14 October, its ships shared between the Home and Far Eastern Fleets. Cunningham went home on the 15th to succeed the stricken Pound as First Sea Lord while the reduced Mediterranean Fleet rebased itself, first at Algiers and then Naples.

Submarines stayed on at Malta to reconnoitre and act as beacons for the Mediterranean landings, and to hunt such German-controlled shipping as was still active in northern Aegean and Adriatic waters. Two were used clandestinely to supply British troops in the Dodecanese

Islands, which the Germans seized from the Italians and successfully defended in November against botched British operations. Another landing in Italy, at Anzio, took place in January with two British submarines once again showing the way for the invasion force. The landings went well; the subsequent German resistance proved as tough as ever and Rome did not fall until 6 June – D-Day in Normandy. On 15 August the last major amphibious operation in the Mediterranean, the invasion of southern France, passed off well; but the Germans hung on in northern Italy until April 1945.

Scene iii: America versus Japan

WHEN ADMIRAL CHESTER W. NIMITZ formally took command of the United States Pacific Fleet at Pearl Harbor on the last day of 1941 he had his flag as "CINCPAC" hoisted on USS *Grayling*. This act was a remarkable departure from naval tradition: such was the dominance of the "big gun" and its platform, the battleship, that nothing other than a dreadnought ship of the line would serve as the flagship of a senior admiral in one of the great navies.

But *Grayling* (SS 209) was a mere submarine, the 209th to join the United States Navy, one of twelve in the "T" class, then the most modern in American service. She measured 308 feet overall and carried a three-inch gun, four machine-guns and ten twenty-one-inch torpedo tubes, six forward and four aft. Twenty-four days after Pearl Harbor was ravaged by two air-strikes, mounted without declaration of war, from Admiral Nagumo's Mobile force of carriers, the Pacific Fleet had no functioning battleship to put under the feet of the unassuming Texan admiral. Fortunately its three carriers had not been in port when Nagumo struck on 7 December 1941.

Six hours later, Admiral Harold R. Stark, Chief of Naval Operations in Washington, issued the fleet order, "Execute unrestricted air and submarine warfare against Japan." Such, in eight words, was American naval strategy against Japan for the duration. The submarine arm of the United States Navy was the first branch of the American services to go on the attack and, with the exception of one or two defensive deployments in aid of the surface fleet, that is where it stayed. Lieutenant-Commander Elton W. Grenfell, USN, took the submarine *Gudgeon* out of Pearl Harbor on 11 December to reconnoitre the Japanese Inland Sea. During this opening patrol of the war the boat sank the Japanese submarine *I173* on 24 January 1942, 220 miles west of Midway Island, northwestern outpost of the US territory of Hawaii. This was the first time an American submarine had sunk an enemy warship (two dive-bombers

The Pacific

from the carrier *Enterprise* had sunk *I170* north of Hawaii on 10 December).

Stark's order for unrestricted submarine warfare infringed article 22 of the London Naval Treaty of 1930, which required submarines to follow prize rules. American (and Japanese) submarines were originally built as adjuncts to the battlefleet. Lack of combat experience in the First World War and the development of aircraft, depth-charges and sonar after it led the American submarine service to exercise extreme caution operationally. The standard mode of attack was from deep water by sonar. There was no question of attacking at periscope depth, not even at night, still less on the surface in darkness so successfully practised by the Germans in this war. But in good weather an aircraft could sight a submarine as deep as 125 feet in the Pacific. The culture of caution was reinforced by an order to remain submerged in all areas within 500 miles of an enemy airfield. The Pacific is by far the world's largest ocean, but such a restriction proved seriously inhibiting because of all the islands held by the Japanese or taken in the first few months of war. Since the older US boats lacked air-conditioning, this order was stifling in two senses. Further, promotion in the peacetime submarine arm had been slow, and many boats had captains of relatively advanced age, another factor which compounded the cautious approach.

So did the fact that they were poorly armed, worse than the boats of any other principal belligerent. The "S" boats still used the Mark X torpedo, a relic of 1917–18 which moved a 500-pound warhead just 3,500 yards at thirty-six knots, a speed many Japanese warships could match. Later boats used the Mark XIV, a twenty-one-inch missile developed in 1931 with a 640-pound warhead and ranges of 4,500 yards at forty-six knots and 9,000 at thirty-one. These short-range, underpowered torpedoes had not been tried in simulated wartime conditions; nor had their exploders (American for detonators or "pistols"). This made American torpedoes an even greater liability to their own side than their German counterparts. The Mark VI exploder, a closely guarded secret, purported to offer a skipper the choice of magnetic or contact detonation. Despite the difficulties endured by the Germans and the British with their torpedo detonators in more than two years of war, the Americans had not tested the Mark VI in battle conditions. Submariners soon discovered that the magnetic setting was useless. They also found that their torpedoes ran deep; this was because they had been tested only with lightweight dummy warheads.

The main advantage, a considerable one, enjoyed by American fleet boats after the old "S" class was the world's highest standard of submarine comfort, which brought high endurance. From about 1940 US submarines were generally better than German in size, speeds surfaced and submerged, manoeuvrability and emergency diving. Many of these qualities derived from the fact that the submarines had been designed with fleet work in mind, a role in which they were hardly ever used.

The "unrestricted warfare" order was in practice unlikely to lead even to an accidental breach of international law because the Navy and Army controlled every Japanese merchantman (*maru*). By this time they were all ferrying troops, military supplies or loot from captured territories. American legalism had been outraged by the surprise attack on Pearl Harbor which, however typical of Japanese tradition it might be, had driven a fleet of carriers through international convention. More or less simultaneous attacks took place on American possessions in the Philippines, Guam and Wake.

The Japanese also invaded British Malaya, off whose eastern shore on 10 December naval aircraft destroyed the British "Force Z" of one new battleship, *Prince of Wales*, and one battlecruiser, *Repulse*. After all their adverse experiences in the Mediterranean and elsewhere, the British had failed to provide this force with air cover, even though it was under constant threat from the world's strongest naval air arm with all its experience in China. The ignominious dismissal of the British from the war in the Pacific until the Americans had already won it was completed in the middle of February 1942, when the much-vaunted "Gibraltar of the Far East", Singapore, fell to Japan in the British Army's greatest humiliation ever.

The main objective of the Japanese in their extraordinary advance across an 8,000-mile oceanic front was the Dutch East Indies (now Indonesia) with its oil and minerals. This vast and rich archipelago, whose "mother-country", the Netherlands, was already occupied by the Germans, quickly fell island by island; a feeble, joint ABDA command (American, British, Dutch, Australian) with a ragbag of ships, planes and troops could not mount a concentrated defence and lost a series of land and sea battles.

The US Pacific Fleet possessed fourteen operational boats at the beginning of December 1941. Only three were ready for sea after the chaos of the air-raid when Stark's order was received. After *Gudgeon*, US submarines *Pollack* and *Plunger* set off for the Inland Sea on 13 and 14 December respectively. The first boat to fire a shot in anger did so from dry land – *Tautog*, in dry dock at Pearl at the time, claimed to have shot down a Japanese plane with her machine-guns.

Eight reinforcements arrived to join COMSUBPAC (commander, submarines, Pacific Fleet) from the west coast, and the Atlantic Fleet sent eleven "S" boats though the Panama Canal. The first newly built boats of the thirty-six to be added to the fleet during 1942 began to report for duty within weeks.

But it was one of the twenty-nine submarines attached to Admiral Thomas H. Hart's Asiatic Fleet, based in the Philippines when war came, that was the first American boat to sink a merchantman. Lieutenant-Commander C.C. Smith, USN, in *Swordfish*, sank the *Atsutasan Maru*, 8,700 tons, off Hainan Island south of China and west of the Philippines on 15 December 1941. Another *maru* fell victim to *S38*, one of six in the class serving under Hart, in Lingayen Gulf in the Philippines on 22 December during troop-landings – one of sadly few effective counter-strokes against the multiple Japanese invasions of the opening phase.

As the aggressors inexorably took control of the great south-east Asian archipelagoes, the Asiatic Fleet withdrew from Manila Bay at Christmas 1941. So did its ineffectual Task Force 3, the submarines. The boats were divided between two new commands, one based in the Dutch East Indies (until they were overrun in March) and the other at Darwin in northern Australia. When these bases had to be abandoned (Darwin was bombed by the Japanese) the two forces respectively based themselves for the rest of the war at Fremantle, western Australia, and Brisbane, in Queensland, on the other side of the island continent. Around these and the other remnants of the Asiatic Fleet was built the US Seventh Fleet, placed under General Douglas MacArthur, USA, in the command specially created for him, the South-West Pacific. This ranked equal to Nimitz's Pacific Command, a fact which rapidly became a crushing burden on the conduct of the war. The Australian-based submarines came under COMSUBSOWESPAC. There were frequent exchanges of boats between him and COMSUBPAC, who was responsible for the administration and maintenance of all submarines in the Pacific.

Although they failed to make any notable impression on Japanese dispositions during the all-conquering opening phase, Pacific and Asiatic Fleet boats ran secret missions to the Philippines, delivering munitions and collecting removable assets, including key people. This exciting work continued from early January 1942 until the fall of the last Philippine-American military position at Corregidor in May. Otherwise the American submarine campaign got off to a generally inauspicious start. The boats were not centrally controlled on the Dönitz model and they lacked support from reconnaissance and tactical intelligence, to say nothing of their poor striking power.

There being no cure for inexperience except experience, time would cure most of the problems; but the problems were serious. The Asiatic

Fleet/South-West Pacific operational area included much constricted water. The US Navy until this war had designed, developed and built, but failed realistically to test, its own torpedoes, derived from Whitehead models produced under licence. The caution bred into submarine officers, mentioned above, led staff officers far from the front to attribute the many torpedo failures to submarine commanders and technicians rather than to the weapon itself or its detonator.

The resurrected *Squalus*, now patrolling as *Sailfish*, had another unique experience in the Philippines in the first week of the war. Her captain, Commander Morton C. Mumma, Jr, was a martinet. When the boat came under Japanese depth-charge attack he panicked, but had the wit to order his executive officer (first lieutenant or "number one" in Britain) to have him confined to his own cabin. The boat got away. Ironically, Mumma was credited (erroneously) with sinking a destroyer on this patrol and was awarded the Navy Cross, the highest decoration in the Navy short of the Congressional Medal of Honor.

When the submarine USS *Sturgeon* attacked a convoy unloading troops at Balikpapan in Borneo on 23 January 1942 with a salvo of torpedoes, a series of satisfying explosions ensued. This prompted the signal to Asiatic Fleet headquarters: "*Sturgeon* no longer virgin." Unfortunately no enemy ship was hit, so the joyful ejaculation was premature.

On 9 March 1942, when Java, administrative and strategic head and heart of the Dutch East Indies, fell, completing the opening phase of conquest on Japan's southern front, Roosevelt wrote to Churchill with a plan to carve up the world. The United States would take the lead in the Pacific while Britain did so in the Indian Ocean and Mediterranean Sea; the two would share responsibility for the Atlantic. Britain reserved the right to return to the Pacific when it could. Australia and New Zealand, whose very survival depended on the struggle for the Pacific, were not consulted. From the ABC talks and the first wartime Anglo-American summit meeting at Argentia the Americans and the British remained consistent in their political commitment to "Germany first".

But for the US Navy Japan came first throughout the war, as its virtual abandonment of convoy escort and the stripping of its fleet in the Atlantic now made clear. The breathtaking build-up of the US fleets in the Pacific could leave no doubt on this score. And it was not until well into 1943 (but then by a rapidly growing margin) that the strength of the US Army in Europe and Africa surpassed its deployment in the Pacific. Only the Army Air force focused its main effort on Germany (without exactly neglecting Japan from 1944). Unable to resolve the claims of Army and Navy for supreme command in the Pacific, Roosevelt and his principal advisers gave the wrangling services one each: Mac-Arthur in the South-West Pacific and Nimitz in the Pacific (soon subdivided into North, Central and South Pacific Ocean Areas). MacArthur's command embraced his beloved Philippines, Borneo, New Guinea, Australia, some of the Solomon Islands and the Dutch East Indies (minus Sumatra, which went to the British South-East Asia Command). Nimitz essentially got the rest, a vast collection of islands including New Zealand, Fiji, Samoa and New Caledonia. The dividing line ran along longitude 159 degrees east.

This is not the place to explore the monstrously costly and ultimately unresolved internecine struggle between the two American services. But MacArthur's twin tactical submarine commands, based in eastern and western Australia, and the larger, strategic submarine force of the Pacific Fleet worked well together most of the time, as did their respective fleets. As noted, Nimitz had administrative and logistical control of every submarine in the ocean, and boats moved from one command to another as required.

Staggered by the huge scale of its own gains in less than four months, and by its own tiny losses, the Japanese junta cast about for a follow-up. Japan was poised, once war damage was repaired, to become economically self-sufficient, the overriding aim of the junta summed up in that ominous phrase, "Greater East Asia Co-Prosperity Sphere". Phase I of the Japanese war-plan was to have been followed by a purely con-solidatory Phase II; Phase III was to consist of aggressive defence of the assets gained until the United States lost the will to fight. But the triumph of Phase I seduced the junta into trying to improve on per-fection. They resolved to extend the newly secured defensive perimeter even further, to embrace the Aleutian Islands, Midway and Hawaii, Fiji, Samoa, New Caledonia, New Guinea ... The compromise eventually cobbled together after much argument – "Phase I, stage 2" – was a fundamental blunder which replicated the over-extension of the Allies in 1941. It was to cost Japan the war by presenting the Americans with early opportunities to counter-attack.

An inspiring example was Colonel James H. Doolittle's attack on Tokyo with Army bombers flown from American carriers on 25 April 1942, a "pinprick" which led to paroxysms of rage and general loss of face among the junta, provoking them into over-prolonging their aggression until it collided with the law of diminishing returns. The Japanese naval C-in-C, Admiral Yamamoto, planned a three-pronged strike against the Aleutians, US islands in the North Pacific off Alaska, against Midway and also Papua New Guinea (administered by Australia).

Before the war the Australians, British, Dutch and especially the Americans had made huge progress in attacking the daunting Japanese diplomatic, consular and naval (but not military) codes and ciphers, on which they secretly exchanged information as Japan's aggression mounted. Another way in which the Japanese resembled their German allies (apart from opportunism, racism, ruthlessness, military prowess and a taste for atrocities) was their complete faith in the invulnerability of their own communications, which were, after all, in Japanese. Changes to their naval cipher, made at intervals for security reasons, were therefore minor and not enough to defeat or deter Allied cryptanalysts, who were able to extract the sense of most messages in most grades of cipher within a reasonable time.

Thus Commander Joseph Rochefort, USN, the eccentric and highly gifted chief cryptanalyst at Pearl Harbor, got wind of the planned attacks on Papua and Midway in a brilliant demonstration of sustained deduction, inspiration and cunning. The result was two great sea battles, in which the United States Navy first halted and then reversed the hitherto irresistible advance of the Japanese Empire before the Pacific war was six months old.

The Battle of the Coral Sea (which lies between Australia and New Guinea) at the beginning of May was the first carrier clash ever, and the first naval battle in which the opposed ships (as distinct from their aircraft) never sighted each other. Like Jutland, it was a divided victory – tactical for Japan but strategic for the United States. The Americans lost one fleet-carrier sunk and a second seriously damaged out of a total available strength of four, plus an oiler and a destroyer sunk. The Japanese lost one light carrier, a destroyer and some small craft, with moderate damage to one fleet-carrier out of six. But they believed their own pilots who, like their colleagues everywhere, exaggerated the effect of their attacks in the heat of battle, and wrote off the entire American task force. Even so, the sinking of a fairly important fleet unit (the carrier *Shoho*) was Japan's first setback of the war, apparently enough to justify the deferment of a new attack on Papua, eventually cancelled altogether. But Japanese troops were landed as planned at Tulagi in the southern Solomons. The southward advance had been halted, even if Yamamoto himself regarded the Coral Sea clash as a minor hitch.

Submarines played no part in it; but both sides deployed them for their next encounter, the crucial Battle of Midway four weeks later. Nimitz gambled on Rochefort's bold prediction that the Japanese would attempt to take the island which, as its name implies, is in mid-ocean, and decided to set a trap. The main naval cryptanalytical unit, the Pacific section of Op-20-G in Washington (roughly equivalent to the British Operational Intelligence Centre), backed by Nimitz's chief, Admiral King, disagreed with Rochefort's interpretation, but Nimitz was prepared to risk his entire fleet on it.

By attacking one of the few outlying American possessions left in the Pacific, Yamamoto hoped to provoke a fleet action between his superior forces and the Americans. He got his wish, but on American terms, because they knew he was coming and were thirsting for revenge. The three weeks of repairs needed by USS *Yorktown* after the Coral Sea were completed in three days, raising Nimitz's available carrier force to three. Pitched against them were Admiral Nagumo's four, backed by the bulk of the Japanese fleet, which put out a forward screen or "advanced expeditionary force" of sixteen submarines. Rear-Admiral Raymond Spruance was to be in command of the American force at the height of the battle; it also included eight cruisers and fifteen destroyers. Nimitz, for the first and only time in the history of his command, made a defensive deployment of submarines, posting twelve to screen Midway, four to cover Pearl Harbor and three in reserve. Midway Island itself was enlisted as an unsinkable, fourth "aircraft-carrier" with ninety-two planes.

Two days of fighting early in June 1942 brought the total destruction of all four of Nagumo's fleet-carriers together with 225 aircraft and nearly all their pilots, plus one heavy cruiser sunk, another and a destroyer damaged. The Americans lost *Yorktown*, 151 planes (many of whose crews were rescued) and a destroyer.

The crippled and burning carrier HIJMS *Soryu* was given the *coup de grâce* by the American submarine *Nautilus* (Lieutenant-Commander W.H. Brookman, USN); he had missed a Japanese battleship earlier in the engagement and was depth-charged twice for his pains. The crippled and burning USS *Yorktown* was similarly dispatched by Lieutenant-Commander Tanabe, IJN, in *I168*, which also sank the destroyer USS *Hammann* as she lay alongside providing power for a last salvage attempt. The American submarine *Tambor* sighted a squadron of Japanese heavy cruisers near Midway Island; her periscope was sighted in turn and during the chase two of the cruisers collided at speed and were left to make their own way home. The pair were later attacked by American carrier planes; one was sunk and the other put out of action for two years.

The Japanese captured two of the Aleutian Islands, Attu and Kiska, a liability after their failure to seize Papua and Midway with the other prongs of their triple operation.

The Japanese submarine service consisted of sixty-four boats at the end of 1941, in three main categories: large (fleet and cruiser) "I" boats, medium and small "RO" (coastal) boats. There were also four inefficient minelayers, three very large aircraft-carrying boats and scores of two-man, two-torpedo midget submarines of questionable value. The main designs were derived from First World War German and British models, and the "I" boats had the respectable range of at least 10,000 miles. The underwater seaplane-carriers were built to attack the American west coast and the Panama Canal, by far the most obvious and promising strategic target for the submarines of America's enemy. But they were never deployed, and the Canal, the US Navy's vital link between east and west coasts and Atlantic and Pacific fleets, was, astonishingly, left in peace.

The German naval attaché in Tokyo, Vice-Admiral Paul Wenneker, soon gave way to despair in 1942 when his advice on the most advantageous deployment of submarines fell on deaf ears:

I suggested the desirability of attacking the route between Honolulu and the west coast because that would force the use of convoys and would force the withdrawal of many escorts from the western Pacific...

We arranged for one full Japanese submarine crew to be sent to Germany for training. They had, I think, very good training in German boats and in German attack methods, but unfortunately they were caught in the North Atlantic ... while returning [home].

This was all the more unfortunate in their frustrated ally's view because the Japanese from 1933 boasted far and away the best torpedoes in the world, the "Long Lance" series. The Japanese tested their torpedoes against real, if dispensable, warships and trained their technicians to the utmost.

Particular attention was also paid before the war in all branches of the service to night-fighting, for which the Imperial Navy acquired special night-glasses and rangefinders as well as searchlights and flares capable of lighting up, indeed dazzling, an enemy. These measures went a long way, at least in the early part of the Pacific war, to make up for the absence of radar and sonar, also explaining why Japanese ships so outperformed Allied vessels in the surface actions round the East Indies. The Japanese Navy's best "eyes" and arms were landbased aircraft of enormous range, including the Zero, finest fighter in the world of its day (1940), the "Betty" medium bomber and the "Nell" torpedo-bomber, all with ranges in excess of 1,300 miles.

All the stranger, therefore, that the submarine service was so backward in a Navy which in most other respects was the most formidable in the world. The reason is not hard to find, echoing early British attitudes to the weapon familiar to us. The Submarine Command (later styled the Sixth Fleet) reported to the Naval General Staff in Tokyo after Phase I: "We have discovered that it is very hard for submarines to attack warships and to blockade a well-guarded harbour. We believe that the principal targets of submarines should be merchant ships, not warships." This advice from below was dismissed with the customary contempt. Submarine skippers had been taught that their most important targets were enemy aircraft-carriers, followed by battleships and other warships in descending order of size. It was Lieutenant-Commander Kitamura's *I58* which first sighted and reported (but vainly attacked) Britain's naval task force off Malaya.

As if to show what might have been, a Japanese submarine bombarded the Californian coast near Los Angeles on 23 February 1942, causing a great deal of anxiety. But this was merely the first of a short series of isolated pinpricks against the west coast. Not even the 2,000-mile strategic route between such ports as San Francisco or San Diego and Pearl Harbor, used by warships and merchantmen alike, was subjected to submarine attack. Nor was the long supply route to the Soviet Union's Pacific coast (probably for fear of provoking Stalin) or any of the uniquely long American lines of communication to the various battlefronts, from places as far away as Australia, New Zealand and the continental United States. The only explanation available to this day is the opinion of the Japanese admirals, who were every bit as obtuse as the generals, that the submarine was a weakling's weapon which could justify its existence only by attacking other warships. How humiliating it must have been for them to be reduced later in the war to using submarines for clandestinely supplying beleaguered island garrisons. The Allies had every reason to be thankful that the Axis, a political rather than a military alliance, never got round to conducting coordinated submarine campaigns in Pacific and Atlantic simultaneously. The one such initiative came from the Germans, who based a flotilla of type IX long-range U-boats at Penang in Japanese-occupied Malaya in the latter part of 1942, for operations in the Indian Ocean. This was the principal threat to Allied shipping in the Far East from submarines during the war.

Twenty-four fleet boats were sent to sea by Japan before the multiple surprise attack with which it opened its war with the west, twenty of them to support the attack on Pearl Harbor. One – *I70* – was lost to planes from the returning carrier *Enterprise*, which launched a counter-attack. But by the end of the year, had they but known it, they had enjoyed what was to be their most fruitful month of the war. Eight merchant ships totalling 40,700 tons, six of them American, were sunk and seven totalling 47,500 damaged, all in Pacific waters north of the Equator. As we have seen, no attempt was made to disrupt the obvious and crucial reinforcement of the Pacific by the US Atlantic fleet via Panama.

But on 11 January 1942 Commander Inada's 2,243-ton *I6*, which carried a single seaplane, sighted the American flat-top *Saratoga* (Captain A.H. Douglas, USN) 500 miles south of Oahu. One torpedo of his very long-range salvo struck the 33,000-ton carrier on the port side, well below the waterline. The Americans detected neither torpedo-track nor submarine and were taken by surprise. Fortunately the victim had been built on the hull of a cancelled battlecruiser and was better armoured than any other type of carrier. Three compartments were flooded and six men killed, but after counter-flooding to right herself the ship managed to reach Pearl Harbor for the extensive repairs which kept her out of the great mid-year battles. She was hit again, on the other side, in the Solomon Islands area on 31 August 1942 by Commander Yokota's *I26*, but withstood this also, returning to the fray in November. Lieutenant-Commander Togami in *I172* forced the abandonment of an air-raid on Japanese-occupied Wake Island from the *Lexington*, sister-ship of *Saratoga*, by sinking her oiler south of Oahu on 23 January 1942.

The most remarkable single attack by any Japanese submariner was executed by Lieutenant-Commander Kinashi in *I19* on 15 September 1942. His boat, very large by the standards of all contemporary navies except his own, displaced 2,589 tons surfaced (3,654 submerged), measured 357 feet and had the remarkable speed of 23.5 knots surfaced (eight submerged). A crew of 101 operated her 5.5-inch gun, her floatplane with its launching catapult and her six torpedo tubes, for which she carried seventeen missiles.

At this stage of the war both sides were throwing everything they could muster into the escalating struggle for an island in the southern Solomons called Guadalcanal, a contest provoked by the Japanese landing at nearby Tulagi at the time of the Battle of Midway. On 15 September 1942 Admiral Richmond Kelly Turner's convoy of US Marine transports and troopships, with a heavy escort of two carriers, *Wasp* and *Hornet* (the only two then fit for battle in the Pacific Fleet), the battleship *North Carolina* (one of only two new dreadnoughts in the fleet) and destroyers, was on its way there from the New Hebrides. When it was about halfway across the Coral Sea, Kinashi got *Wasp* in his sights and fired a salvo of four torpedoes. Two struck the carrier, (21,000 tons) to starboard below the waterline, setting off her fuel stores and ammunition in a horrendous multiple explosion. The other two missiles hissed past the carrier, tearing a thirty-two-foot gash in the port side of the *North Carolina* (35,000 tons) and simultaneously blowing the bow off the destroyer *O'Brien* (1,570 tons), both of which were escorting *Hornet* six whole miles further away.

The Americans could not believe that torpedoes could travel so far and attributed the latter two hits to *I15*, known to be in the area at the time. But the Japanese record is clear: all four came from *I19*. The battleship shook off the damage, patching herself up and sailing to Pearl Harbor for repair with little loss of speed. The destroyer was towed to New Caledonia for patching up but broke in two on the way to Pearl and sank, without casualties. This unique Japanese submarine success left the Pacific Fleet with one serviceable carrier and one modern battleship. Even so, Admiral Turner completed his mission to deliver 4,000 more Marines to the US garrison on Guadalcanal, 100 miles from the scene of the attack.

The Japanese Navy deployed 190 submarines during the war, of which 129 were lost: seventy to warships, nineteen to submarines, eighteen to planes and twenty-two to miscellaneous causes, mainly accidents. They sank 184 merchantmen totalling 907,000 tons, plus two aircraft-carriers, two cruisers, ten destroyers and some smaller vessels including submarines. This represents a sinking rate of fewer than 5,000 tons (less than one average-sized merchantman) per submarine deployed, and just over 7,000 tons per boat lost, a rate which expresses in statistical terms the magnitude of the missed opportunity. This was no fault of the service since at least some commanders are known to have understood the possibilities they were not allowed to exploit. As Vice-Admiral Miwa, last chief of the submarine Sixth Fleet, explained to American interrogators after the war: "We wanted to attack the American fleet."

The Japanese had taken Tulagi, on the island of Florida east of Guadalcanal, to guard the left flank of their seaborne invasion of Port Moresby, capital of Papua New Guinea, to which the Battle of the Coral Sea put paid. To protect Tulagi they began to build an airstrip on Guadalcanal. The Japanese "strategy" was now to hang on to every scrap of territory they had taken, regardless of its value to them after Midway. The United States, unaware of this switch from offence to defence, was determined to protect its main ally in the Pacific, Australia, by rolling back the Japanese.

The Allied strategic objective at this stage was Rabaul on the island of New Britain in the Bismarck Archipelago, north-east of New Guinea. This had become the main Japanese air and naval base in the region since it fell to them on 23 January 1942. The first step was to drive the Japanese out of Tulagi; this was assigned to Nimitz (the boundary between his and MacArthur's commands was, by protracted negotiation, solemnly moved one degree of longitude to the west to allow the Pacific Fleet into the area!). The next stage was to be a double advance by MacArthur "up the Solomons ladder" and along the northern coast of New Guinea. Three Australian brigades held Port Moresby, against which the Japanese sent a column of 8,500 men overland. Despite a two-to-one numerical advantage the Allies took six months to end the threat.

The American assault on Guadalcanal with the First Marine Division was covered by a naval task force of fifty-seven warships, including (at first) three carriers, a battleship and eleven cruisers – the bulk of the Pacific Fleet, which put the Marines ashore on 7–8 August. Also on hand were six American submarines for reconnaissance. One of them, *S38* (Lieutenant-Commander H.G. Munson, USN) sighted the first Japanese reinforcement of six troopships and sank one; the rest were recalled to Rabaul by the local commander, Admiral Mikawa, who decided to attack the American invasion fleet with seven cruisers.

The ensuing Battle of Savo Island in the night of 8–9 August was the worst defeat in American naval history, with four cruisers (one Australian) sunk and one more, plus two destroyers, damaged with no loss to the Japanese. But once again Admiral Turner coolly completed the landing, made possible by the sacrifice of the cruisers. The Americans' naval consolation prize was won by *S44* (Lieutenant-Commander John R. Moore, USN), which sank the heavy cruiser *Kako* on 10 August with a salvo of four torpedoes as Mikawa's victorious squadron sailed back to Rabaul. Thanks largely to *S38*'s deterrent stroke at the start of this first of many heavy naval clashes off Guadalcanal, the Japanese, despite their overwhelming tactical victory, had been prevented from reinforcing; the Allied cruisers' fight to the death however helped the American landing to succeed.

Ten days after that the Pacific Fleet staged a unique diversion. The idea was to sow confusion among the Japanese by striking a blow far away from the new Solomons front (and 2,200 miles from Pearl Harbor). The objective was the island of Makin (now Butaritari) in the Gilbert Islands (now the independent state of Kiribati), which Nimitz knew from aerial reconnaissance to be lightly defended. In fact it was held by a single platoon of forty-seven men, led by a Sergeant-Major Kanemitsu.

The American invasion force consisted of 222 men from the 2nd Raider Battalion, US Marines, led by Lieutenant-Colonel Evans F.

Carlson, USMC. His second-in-command and executive officer was Major James Roosevelt, the President's son. What made the undertaking unique was the mode of transport: America's two largest submarines, *Nautilus* and *Argonaut*. Each displaced nearly 3,000 tons surfaced and over 4,000 submerged and normally had a complement of about ninety men. They could sail 18,000 miles at eight knots and each had a pair of mighty six-inch guns as well as torpedoes. In charge at sea was Commander John Haines, USN, captain of *Nautilus*. They left Pearl on 8 August.

Amid confusion caused by lack of knowledge of coastal and tidal conditions, seventeen motorised rubber boats (one of which became separated) had put the Marines ashore by dawn on the 17th. An American gunshot fired in error alerted the little garrison, which resolved in the Japanese manner to defend the only noteworthy installation, the radio station, to the last man. While bombarding shore positions, the *Nautilus* fortuitously sank two Japanese motor-boats bringing sixty reinforcements from other islands; but Kanemitsu's force was eventually doubled by the survivors, reducing the American advantage to rather less than three to one. Whenever Japanese bombers went over, the American submarines rather ponderously went under. The twelve men from the separated American dinghy were able to attack from the rear while the rest engaged the dug-in Japanese from the front.

As a short twilight fell over the island, the Marines' difficulties mounted when they tried to return to the submarines amid continuing Japanese air-strikes. The weak motors could not make headway against an angry surf; fewer than half of the raiding force reached the boats. By dark seventy Americans, one-third of the total, were still ashore. They panicked and decided to give themselves up – not a wise decision in view of the lethal punishment prescribed by the Japanese for such weakness – but could find nobody to accept their surrender. The confused action continued for two more days. Most of the "marooned" marines managed to get back aboard on the third night and the two submarines stole away, back to Hawaii and a heroes' welcome. Twenty-one Americans had been killed. Nine were captured and beheaded on the orders of Vice-Admiral Abe at Kwajalein in the Marshall Islands. Abe was hanged after the war.

This ill-conceived pinprick delivered by submarine had strategic consequences diametrically opposed to American intentions. The Japanese, instead of withdrawing outlying garrisons, proceeded to strengthen them all over the Pacific, which meant that future American landings were more strongly opposed. On the other hand, this penny-packet reinforcement of hundreds of islands reduced the numbers of Japanese defending the strategic objectives in the theatre, which were not many. But there were to be no more Makins; the original had been a shambles, even if it was passed off as a triumph.

The savage struggle for Guadalcanal became a total war of wills. It continued in four dimensions as the Americans defended their enclave, including the all-important captured airstrip, renamed Henderson Field (in honour of a fighter-commander lost defending Midway), on land, in the air, on the sea and under it. It was during these clashes in and around "the Slot", the waters enclosed by the Solomons, that the Japanese submarines sank one American carrier and damaged another (see above). In mid-November, as the Americans ferried in yet more marine reinforcements, the Japanese arrived with a superior naval squadron and the same intent, which led to the naval Battle of Guadalcanal. In the first phase the Americans lost two fighting admirals, two light cruisers and four destroyers and suffered widespread damage to other ships; the damaged cruiser USS *Juneau* was dispatched by Commander Yokota in *I26*, the boat which had put *Saratoga* out of action in August. As in other navies, a few bold Japanese submarine captains accounted for a disproportionate number of successes. The Japanese forfeited two destroyers; one battleship was damaged badly enough to be finished off by American planes after the first phase of the battle. By this time the waterway between Guadalcanal and Savo Islands was known to the Americans as Iron Bottom Sound because of all the ships sunk there. In the second phase the Americans lost five more destroyers but the Japanese were deprived of a second battleship, a heavy cruiser, another destroyer and a dozen transports. The American reinforcements were landed in full while the Japanese only managed to put a fraction of theirs ashore: a clear overall victory for the United States.

Japan was already feeling the pinch of what had become a war of attrition, in which their supplies of matériel were finite and shrinking while America, the "arsenal of democracy", could muster all but infinite resources. The Japanese war staffs now began to worry about the erosion of their precious merchant fleet. In a perfect world they would have like an extra 700,000 tons for the southern Solomons "auction" alone. On turning to the Germans for help they received the reply on 26 September 1942 that there were no ships to spare. The Army threatened to pull out of Burma, the British colony east of India which was the western extremity of the Japanese advance, unless 200,000 tons of shipping were added to the 1.04 million already allocated to it.

Japan started the war with a merchant fleet of about six million tons. The admirals anticipated a loss of 800,000 tons in one year of war in the Pacific but expected to cover this, and to spare, from captured shipping and new construction. The fundamental error made by the junta (and their allies in Europe) was their belief that the democracies would have no stomach for a long fight. None of the Axis powers therefore had a contingency plan for the long haul before going to war. Once the Anglo-Saxon powers (and the Soviet Communists) failed to succumb to *Blitzkrieg* in a few months, the Axis proved incapable of a war of attrition. Despite purporting to have learned the main lesson from Germany's defeat in 1918, neither Japan nor Germany achieved, by waging war, the autarky which would have enabled them to go on waging war until their enemies gave up. By the end of 1942, instead of producing a balance or a modest credit in merchant shipping, the Japanese showed a net loss of about 178,000 tons (1,123,000 tons sunk, 945,000 tons captured or built).

The dominant factor behind this adverse result was the initially hesitant American submarine offensive, which nevertheless accounted for 180 ships totalling some 725,000 tons during 1942. Postwar statistical analysis by the US Strategic Bombing Survey revealed that the Japanese loss rate in shipping passed their ability to replace it as early as April 1942, after only four months of war in the Pacific. The logistical turning point thus came two months before the strategic one at Midway. Had the Japanese found 300,000 tons more shipping for Guadalcanal in the earlier stages (before they had to reinforce by "Tokyo Express" destroyer-transports at night, or even by submarines) they would probably not have been forced to evacuate the island in February 1942.

As it was, by then 10,000 of them had died of starvation and a similar number from sickness, compared with 15,000 killed in action and 1,000 captured, out of a total of 36,000 ground troops engaged. The Americans lost 1,600 killed out of a total of 60,000 troops and Marines committed. American command of the air (and superior resources and logistics) during the day had trumped Japanese command of the sea at night. The parallel victory by 60,000 Australian and American troops in Papua, where many of the 20,000 Japanese invaders had also starved to death, had equally helped to prove at last (to everybody but the Japanese) that Japan's Army was not invincible, any more than its Navy. But in the background to these grotesque tussles over foetid and remote island territories, the submarine had already established itself as the nemesis of Japanese seapower. The Americans relied on stealth at sea as their principal naval stratagem until they could build up their surface fleet and airpower to overwhelm the Japanese.

The achievement of the submarines in what we may now see as their "learning curve" looks all the more remarkable in the light of the troubles experienced by the American service during 1942. As COM-SUBPAC's force built itself up to an eventual total of about 100 operational boats and COMSUBSOWESPAC assembled a total of some forty submarines at his two Australian bases, the latter's nine worn-out "S" boats were all withdrawn by September 1942, leaving twenty boats in Australia for the time being (Nimitz had fifty-nine at this stage, including eight "S" boats). After the battle which saved it, Midway became a forward submarine base, 1,100 miles closer to Japan than Pearl Harbor. So did Johnston Island, for boats on their way to Japan's mandated islands such as the Carolines. Boats of both commands were replenished and maintained at Pearl Harbor and there was frequent rotation of submarines between the two. MacArthur's boats would reconnoitre Japanese-occupied islands for Nimitz on their way to and from Pearl.

Patrols in Japanese home waters declined for a while as operational demands from the Solomons mounted. The new SJ radar sets, specially developed for submarines, were now being fitted to the boats, which were able to risk closer approaches and also minelaying off such Japanese strongpoints as Formosa, Truk (the great Japanese naval base in the Carolines) and in Tokyo Bay. After the victory in Guadalcanal, American submarine patrols increased rapidly, with many more boats due to join both Pacific commands during 1943. But the great American torpedo crisis touched upon earlier got worse in 1942 before it got better.

"Undoubtedly torpedo inferiority added months to the war and thus cost the US thousands of lives and billions of dollars of treasure," says the unpublished Submarine Operational History (SOH) of the US Navy in the Second World War. "The reason for this inferiority lies deep in the organisation of the US Government and the psychology of its people," it concedes.

The Navy's Torpedo Station at Newport, Rhode Island, had enjoyed a monopoly of torpedo construction from 1869 to 1940, when a second was opened at Alexandria, Virginia. Strict rules about rotation of assignments afloat and ashore meant that no American naval officer served more than thee years at a time at either station; thus there were hardly any torpedo experts inside the Navy and none outside it. The main objective in torpedo tests was to ensure that each $10,000 missile was recovered: fitted only with a lightweight dummy warhead, they were set to pass under their target. Everyone went home happy if the missile ran in a straight line, regardless of depth. "The war began with an entire generation of submarine personnel none of whom had ever seen or heard the detonation of a submarine torpedo," says the SOH.

The cosy torpedo monopoly did not rush to build up a stockpile as American involvement in the war loomed. Even at the beginning of 1942, total American torpedo-production capacity was sixty per month. When the Asiatic Fleet abandoned Manila Bay and left 233 missiles behind, nearly half the US Navy's total contemporary stock was lost. Submarines with their cautious captains were not only told to be sparing with torpedoes on war patrols but were, unforgivably, sent to sea with only a two-thirds load. This was a false economy worthy of the British at their worst: firing a pair instead of a salvo, or one rather than two, especially when the torpedoes were so unreliable, meant that more missiles were wasted than would otherwise have been the case. The final absurdity came when captains were commended, in wartime, for *not* firing their ammunition. In 1942 the United States manufactured 2,382 torpedoes and fired 2,010.

But private companies started to make torpedoes for planes and surface vessels soon after America went to war. A contract went to Westinghouse Corporation for the new Mark XVIII electric torpedo, intended for submarines also. The Mark XIV already in service was modified to run at its higher speed and shorter range only, and restyled the Mark XXIII.

Meanwhile complaints from skippers about dud torpedoes and detonators mounted to such an extent that they could no longer be complacently ascribed by the Navy's Bureau of Ordnance to nerves or incompetence. The main complaint was that the missiles ran deep and in a report echoing the rage of Günther Prien, Lieutenant J.W. Coe of USS *Skipjack* wrote in June 1942, after a patrol on which he nevertheless managed to sink four ships:

To make round trips of 8,500 miles into enemy waters, to gain attack position undetected within 800 yards of enemy ships, only to find that the torpedoes run deep and over half the time will fail to explode, seems to me to be an undesirable manner of gaining information which might be determined any morning within a few miles of a torpedo station in the presence of comparatively few hazards.

In response, Rear-Admiral Charles A. Lockwood, commander of MacArthur's submarine forces and soon to become COMSUBPAC under Nimitz, promptly ordered *Skipjack* to do just that, in the waters west of Fremantle, Western Australia. A Mark XIV was set to hit a net 850 yards away at ten feet below the surface. It hit at twenty-five. A second hit at eighteen feet. A third, set at zero feet struck at eleven, having bumped the bottom on the way. The Royal Navy had experienced the same problem for the same reason – in the First World War. Lockwood forwarded these depressing results to the Bureau of Ordnance on 22 June. A supporting report from COMSUBPAC arrived shortly afterwards. The Bureau wriggled in the age-old bureaucratic tradition. Admiral King had been observing the correspondence from afar with mounting fury and stepped in, commanding the Bureau to run proper tests on the Mark XIV and Mark XV (the destroyer variant). These confirmed the tendency to run ten feet deeper than set; from autumn 1942 a new torpedo depth-control accurate to within three feet was introduced.

The correction of one fault served only to expose another. Now there were more premature detonations, because the delicate mechanisms of the torpedoes and their untrustworthy detonators were upset by running through the more turbulent water close to the surface. Once this was corrected, the magnetic exploder in the Mark VI detonator was found to be hypersensitive (not unlike German experience), going off much too far away from its target. Submariners therefore opted, sometimes against orders, to use the contact pistol, whereupon the number of dud torpedoes which hit without exploding went up sharply. At one time commanders were allowed to deactivate the magnetic pistol in one Pacific command and forbidden to do so in the other.

It was not until October 1943 that the flaw in the contact pistol, caused by the simple fact that the firing pin did not always hit the primer hard enough to detonate it, was corrected. The defect was attested beyond dispute in an extraordinary front-line experiment by the submarine USS *Tinosa*, off Truk. Out of a salvo of six fired by the boat, two hit and crippled a tanker without sinking her. Commander Daspit coolly took advantage of his sitting target to fire nine more torpedoes from the optimum range of 875 yards at right angles. All nine hit; none detonated. Daspit took his last five missiles home in disgust. The Japanese towed their tanker into Truk and saved her and her cargo. The introduction of the improved explosive Torpex in February 1943 increased the effectiveness of such torpedoes as deigned to explode. The improvement in the contact pistol in October 1943 was officially held to mark the end of the torpedo crisis; but SOH statistics on their performance thereafter show that it was not really solved during the war. The persistence of the problem was masked by the very high sinking rate achieved by the American submarines in their peak year of 1944.

But for most of the first two years of their war, submariners often unjustly took the blame for dud torpedoes. The Bureau of Ordnance refused to cooperate with Westinghouse on electric torpedo production until ordered by King to do so. The result was the Mark XVIII, based partly on a captured German G7e missile, just as the Germans had been forced to copy features of British torpedoes in their own crisis.

So high was the mistrust of torpedoes in the submarine service that for many months electric "fish" were issued only to volunteer captains. In the peak year of 1944, just one in three fired was electric. Only in 1945 was the ratio reversed. This choice seems correct in retrospect, as the Mark XVIII was found after the war to have been the poorest performer. The Mark XXIII (simplified Mark XIV) performed best; and COMSUBPAC's boats consistently outperformed those of COMSUBSOWESPAC. Overall, the best submarine performance was delivered by Pacific Fleet boats armed with Mark XIVs. The Americans recorded a wartime hit rate of thirty-four per cent – less than half that of the Germans – and claimed one ship sunk for every eleven missiles fired.

Although submarine crews were hand-picked in all navies, their special reliance on the qualities of the captain conferred a unique burden of responsibility on that officer, who on the other hand had unique opportunities for exercising any initiative he might possess. In the first full year of war nearly one third of all US skippers were replaced for poor performance or unsuitability.

As the submarine campaign expanded the failure rate of captains fell to one in seven, still high. As the need for skippers grew, chiefly because of expansion but also thanks to unsuitability, their average age declined, a trend which did not please a conservative service run by elderly men (King was born in 1878, Nimitz in 1885, Halsey and Spruance, his alternating fleet commanders, in 1882 and 1886 respectively). In the German service, especially towards the end, skippers of twenty-two or twenty-one were not uncommonly in command of crews with an average age below twenty. In the American, a submarine captain was unusually young at twenty-seven. British submariners fell somewhere in between. And whereas the latter quite often came from the RNVR (reserve), the US Navy gave wartime commands to only seven USNR officers. A captain could not hide his inadequacy in the claustrophobic conditions of a submarine, where he had to take life-or-death decisions in uniquely public circumstances. At first captains seldom exercised the permitted option of attacking from periscope depth rather than by sonar, and German success with night attacks on the surface (the safe choice until improved radar reached the Allied escorts) passed the Americans by.

The weakness of their tactics was exposed by their boats' failure to delay the Japanese in the Philippines which, under prewar plans, should have held out until the battlefleet (in fact knocked out at Pearl) arrived. Tactics were no more effective in the East Indies, and no strategy existed for submarine deployment when war began. For example, Japan was well known to have no oil of its own, making it totally dependent on deliveries from overseas. Had this been identified as the Achilles' heel of the Empire in the immediate aftermath of Pearl Harbor, the war would have been shortened significantly. As it was, the American submariners, like the Japanese, regarded enemy carriers and capital ships as their main targets. The Japanese started the war with 575,000 tons in tankers and one year later, despite their overall shipping loss, had 686,000, thanks mainly to captures. Tanker losses to enemy action amounted to a mere 9,500 tons. At the end of 1943 the total afloat reached a peak of 873,000 tons, despite sinkings of 169,000. After the devastating sinkings in 1944, the peak year of the American submarine onslaught, the Japanese were left with only 200,000 tons in tankers, after losses totalling 755,000.

Overall, the Japanese merchant fleet amounted to 5.82 million tons at the end of 1942, 4.88 million in 1943, 2.72 million at the end of 1944 and 1.5 million at the surrender. Sinkings in those four years amounted to 1.12 million, 1.82 million, 3.89 million and 1.78 million tons respectively. Captures and construction totalled 945,000 tons in 1942, 878,000 in 1943, 1,735,000 in 1944 and 565,000 in 1945. American submarines alone accounted for fifty-five per cent of these huge losses, or some 4.75 million tons – more than 1,300 merchant ships plus eight carriers, a battleship and eleven cruisers. This represents a tonnage more than five times higher than total sinkings by Japanese submarines, even though American supply lines were far longer and their tally of shipping at sea much higher (and rising massively) once the drive across the Pacific began late in 1942.

If the gap between American and Japanese submarine performance was great, the difference between the ASW capability of each side was enormous. As in the Atlantic, American ships and aircraft in the Pacific deployed all the aids produced by Allied technical superiority in ASW. American innovations included sonar buoys and "MAD" – the magnetic anomaly detector which detected submerged submarines from the air by their steel content – while the British came up with the "Hedgehog", the forward-firing multiple ASW mortar, and the "Leigh Light", the airborne searchlight which pinpointed a surfaced enemy submarine at night like a rabbit in a headlamp beam. The Americans produced the best long-range maritime aircraft while the British developed the most refined radar, eventually capable of detecting a conning tower several miles away. Both the great western navies learned the lesson of convoy the hard way (the Americans rather late in the day, as the next chapter will make clear).

Japanese admirals, as we have noted, disdained the submarine and, like their pre-1917 British counterparts from whom they copied so much, they were even more dismissive of the fundamental ASW strategy of convoy. It was thus not until the end of 1943 that the Japanese Navy set up a First Escort Squadron of ten destroyers, eight coastal-defence ships, three minesweepers plus smaller vessels and "special gunboats" (small armed merchant cruisers). At the same time the 901st Naval Air Squadron based at Takao, Formosa, was earmarked for convoy air cover. These modest forces protected small convoys running between southern Japan, Formosa, the Philippines, Singapore, North Borneo and Palau in the Philippine Sea – Japan's conveniently short, interior lines of sea communication.

The naval squadron expanded into the First Escort Fleet in November 1944, commanded by Vice-Admiral Kishi, and the air squadron into an Air Flotilla (group). Kishi had about sixty escorts, including four of the last fleet destroyers left to Japan, forty-five cutters, four minesweepers, two sub-chasers (small ASW vessels) and converted merchantmen. The air group grew to a scratch collection of about 170 aircraft. Twenty specially adapted "Bettys" (christened "Lornas" by the Americans) joined the group in 1945; they had both radar and MAD, effective to 900 feet, which was much deeper than any submarine of the time could dive. But these purpose-built planes amounted to much too little, very much too late. Japanese ASW planes carried no guns; on detecting a submarine they dropped charges, reported by radio exclusively to their own headquarters, released a marker-buoy, circled over the area and signalled visually if a friendly ship appeared.

The naval aviation research station at Yokosuka developed two sizes of depth-charge, 250 kilograms (550 pounds) and sixty (132), from conventional bombs. Their fuses were primitive, being governed by timers rather than the adjustable hydrostatic (water-pressure) detonators used by the Allies since the First World War. The maximum setting of sixteen seconds caused a Japanese charge to explode at 250 feet. Early in the Pacific war they had been set to detonate much sooner, enabling American boats to dive out of danger. But one of the most stupid legislators ever to darken the doors of the House of Representatives, Congressman Andrew Jackson May, gave aid and comfort to the enemy after a tour of the front. He announced at a press conference that American submarines were doing just fine because the Japanese set their depth-charges to go off too soon. Vice-Admiral Lockwood, COM-SUBPAC, was beside himself with rage, calculating that this appalling leak cost ten boats and 800 American submariners' lives (the statistical basis for his calculation is unclear). The gaffe was as crass as the revelation in June 1942 by Colonel Robert R. McCormick's *Chicago Tribune* and associated publications that the Americans had broken into Japanese ciphers before the Coral Sea and Midway battles. The Japanese acted on May's tip but ignored McCormick's.

The Imperial General Headquarters (Navy) in Tokyo created an administrative Grand Escort Fleet to supervise escort work in local naval commands round the occupied territories, and also to protect the Army's entirely separate troop and supply convoys (the Army retained its own jealously guarded transport fleet; so did the Ministry of Transport, a pointless triplication). The command kept a plot of estimated enemy submarine positions based on reports from aircraft and ships, plus radio direction-finding ashore and afloat, at which the Japanese were more proficient than any other Navy. But all this was a pale shadow of the Allied effort in the Atlantic struggle. The massive American depredations during 1944 were overwhelmingly achieved against ships sailing independently; in May 1944, at the peak of the Japanese ASW effort, only one ship was lost in convoy but the Americans had an embarrassment of IRS to choose from.

Japanese escort forces claimed four or five US submarines sunk out of ten working the heavily used shipping lane between the Philippines and Formosa. The 901st air group may have accounted for about twenty American submarines. The pilots, as ever, were overcome by inflation and claimed 500. Their efforts with airborne torpedoes, which had worked at Pearl Harbor against surface ships, were abandoned: submarines could dive fast enough to evade them. The Japanese "curly" torpedo which spiralled downwards for four circuits lacked the sensitive magnetic detonator which might have made it deadly. Japanese radar development was late and primitive, so that its emissions were at least as useful to the enemy for detection purposes as to the operator. Only when the war was lost could Japanese radars detect submarines at twelve miles. Air and surface ASW patrols were neither coordinated nor even capable of communicating with each other by radio (both main western allies started the war with the same internal deficiency but corrected it, developing VHF – very high frequency – radio for such purposes). The American SOH may claim to be a record of "the world's best submarine force" – something which the shade of Dönitz would not be alone in challenging – but is objective enough to admit:

It would do very well however for all submariners to humbly ponder the fact that Japanese anti-submarine defences were not of the best. If our submarines had been confronted with Allied anti-submarine measures, the casualty list of the submarine force would have been much larger and the accomplishment of Allied submarines much less impressive.

In fact "Allied" submarines took no significant part in the Pacific campaign. The British concentrated on the Indian Ocean; one or two Dutch submarines put in an appearance in the waters round their Japanese-occupied colonies; Australia and New Zealand had none to deploy. But Australia provided a little-known facility at Sydney: an anti-submarine warfare school called HMAS *Rushcutter* (the Australians, like the British, pretended that their naval shore establishments were ships). Founded in November 1938, it was commanded by Captain Harvey Newcomb, a British ASW officer transferred to the Royal Australian Navy. The school trained 326 officers and 1,286 ratings for Pacific and Atlantic and also trained American, British, Dutch and French ASW personnel.

During 1943 the Americans began to wrest control of the sea, and the airspace over it, from the Japanese in the double advance by Nimitz and MacArthur. The capture of Rabaul was abandoned in favour of what Admiral King called a "whipsaw" strategy, a rationalisation of the American leadership's inability to choose between the two thrusts, switching from one to the other instead. MacArthur used the term "leapfrogging" or "hitting 'em where they ain't" for the stratagem of bypassing isolated enemy garrisons, which Nimitz seems to have thought of first. Rabaul and other enemy bases large and small were simply left to rot, the Japanese unable to supply or remove their troops except by submarine or other desperate expedient. This island-hopping approach undoubtedly accelerated both advances, especially in 1944. But it could not compensate for the loss of impetus due to two advances rather than one, because neither Navy nor Army could bring itself to cede supreme command to the other and Roosevelt, who alone might have settled the colossally expensive argument, ducked the issue.

Only after the surrender of Japan did his successor, President Harry S. Truman, finally name MacArthur as Supreme Commander, Allied Powers. The reduplication of the advance across the Pacific, something only the United States could have afforded, inevitably had a dragging effect in the European theatre. It also helps to explain why it took 1,166 days to expel the Japanese from territory they had conquered in 180. Once the war become one of attrition, of which the chief instrument was the submarine, there could be only one winner. The only question was how long it would take, to which the answer depended on the

Japanese will to fight. This was so extraordinarily strong that a truly desperate measure was taken to cut the Gordian knot.

Meanwhile, in 1943, the American sinking rate approached an average of one ship per submarine patrol – 335 sinkings on 350 missions. Almost a quarter of the tonnage sunk was made up of tankers, which however, as we have seen, was not enough. COMSUBPAC still specified as late as June 1943 that the priorities were enemy carriers, battleships, light carriers and cruisers, in that order. A commander of Nimitz's calibre ought to have overruled this on the basis of experience in the Atlantic. One would have expected his chief, Admiral King, to have such a blind spot because his Anglophobia led him into an almost fatal bungling of the convoy issue in the Atlantic (see next chapter); but Nimitz, who often disagreed with King, should have put tankers at the top of his submariners' list of priorities.

But these men were getting into their stride. It was in 1943 that the *Wahoo* became the most famous submarine in the Navy of a nation which conferred stardom on its heroes as no other. Lieutenant-Commander Dudley W. "Mush" Morton won both the Navy and Distinguished Service Crosses for his work from the Seventh Fleet base at Brisbane in Australia at the beginning of the year. Morton took command for the boat's third patrol in January and stole into Wewak harbour in New Guinea to disable a Japanese destroyer. On his return to the open sea he attacked a convoy, damaging a tanker and sinking two supply-ships and a troop-transport, surfacing afterwards to machine-gun the soldiers in the water. The boat got a heroes' welcome on arrival in Pearl Harbor in the first week in February and the legend of the *Wahoo* was officially born, as a morale-booster not only for the public but also for the submarine service, still distracted by torpedo problems.

Morton's next patrol in the Yellow Sea between Korea and China produced a numerical record for one patrol in the US service of nine ships sunk, in exceptionally dangerous and shallow waters at that. In May 1943 COMSUBPAC sent the *Wahoo* to the north-western Pacific where she sank three merchantmen. But even a commander as bold and cool as Morton was not immune to torpedo failure: he felt his score would have been six but for misfires. Now enjoying the kind of prestige achieved early in the war by Günther Prien, he bearded COMSUBPAC (Lockwood) in his office at Pearl Harbor to such effect that the magnetic exploder in the Mark IV detonator was at last officially condemned as unreliable. The order went out to all Pacific boats not to use it. But Seventh Fleet's COMSUBSOWESPAC at Fremantle continued to do so, which meant that boats passing from one command to the other used their detonators according to the whim of the relevant flag officer (or said nothing and made their own choice). But when Admiral Thomas C. Kinkaid left Nimitz's North Pacific Command to become C-in-C of the Seventh Fleet under MacArthur in November 1943, he ordered Rear-Admiral Ralph Christie (COMSUBSOWESPAC) to outlaw the magnetic exploder.

Wahoo disappeared in the Sea of Japan on Morton's fifth patrol in command, in October 1943. Using the new Mark XVIII electric torpedoes, he sank four ships totalling 13,300 tons, including a transport with more than 500 troops aboard. But on the 11th a Japanese naval plane sighted the boat near La Perouse Strait and depth-charged her to destruction. In all the Americans lost fifty-two submarines from all causes (forty-five to enemy action) during the war, overwhelmingly in the Pacific; 3,506 submariners went down with them.

When the Japanese admirals belatedly discovered convoy, the US Navy responded to this reprise of 1917 in the same way as Germany did in that year in the Mediterranean: they formed what they insisted on calling "wolf-packs." But they imitated what Dönitz had experienced in the First World War rather than the much bigger groups he assembled in the Second, for which the term was coined.

The official name for the new tactic was the "Coordinated Submarine Attack Group", usually of three boats, of which one served as "flagship" with the group commander aboard. The first order to form one went to Captain John P. Cromwell, USN, commanding SUBDIV (Submarine Division) 43 of the Pacific Fleet, in November 1943. He joined *Sculpin* (Commander Fred Connaway, USN) which, while still alone, sighted a Japanese convoy east of Truk in the Carolines on 19 November. Forced to the surface by depth-charges, *Sculpin* was mortally wounded by destroyer gunfire. Connaway had no choice but to abandon ship and scuttle. It was at this rather belated point that Cromwell realised he could not afford to risk being "interrogated" by Japanese intelligence officers. He was privy to Ultra and carried details in his head of the impending American attack on the Gilbert Islands: Operation Galvanic. With exceptional gallantry he decided to go down with the boat. After the war, when survivors of the crew returned from the rigours of a Japanese prison camp, they saw to it that he was awarded a posthumous Medal of Honor.

The first pack was formed in December by Captain Charles B. Momsen, USN, commander of SUBRON (Submarine Squadron) Two, from the boats *Cero*, *Shad* and *Grayling*. They used coded VHF communications (TBS radio, "talk between ships") on the surface only, because radio waves could not penetrate water (which is why the Germans directed their Atlantic packs from Lorient rather than making captains take the extra risk of surfacing to talk in the middle of a convoy battle). This first pack sank three ships of 23,500 tons and Momsen received the Navy Cross. His advice to Lockwood was that there was no need for a flotilla commander because the senior captain in the pack could be left to do the coordination on the spot, saving space and complications and reflecting German experience in the First World War. Momsen also thought that the Dönitz system of centralised control was likely to be more efficient, as the first American pack's main problem had indeed been communication between boats at sea. The poor performance of Japanese ASW was the main reason why no such tactic was needed in the US submarine offensive.

For their part, Japanese submarines were able only to deliver isolated blows to the advancing Americans during 1943. Their assault on the Gilbert Islands was overwhelming, involving for example an entire US Army division against one Japanese battalion on Makin; but on 24 November Lieutenant-Commander Tabata in *I175* sank the new escort-carrier USS *Liscombe* nearby with a single torpedo, sending a flaming column of fuel 1,000 feet into the air. *I176* sank the American submarine *Corvina*. The equivalent of a division of Americans attacked Tarawa, about 100 miles south of Makin, and met much stiffer resistance from nearly 7,000 Japanese, who inflicted casualties exceeding seventeen per cent (a bare two per cent of the defeated Japanese survived); Tarawa was classified as a disaster for the Americans by their media.

The Americans had learned what Japanese tenacity in defence could do, a sobering lesson indeed, but were well placed to attack the Pacific Command's next target, the Marshall Islands to the north. The Gilberts operation marked the parting of the ways for Nimitz and MacArthur, whose forces had been working together, if often at a distance, in the climb "up the Solomons ladder" and the simultaneous march across New Guinea which resulted in the isolation of Rabaul by Operation Cartwheel. But in attacking the Gilberts the Navy had gone back to a new starting line, 1,500 miles further from Tokyo, for an offensive it conducted without direct reference to MacArthur's efforts to the north and west. The Navy surged across sporadic Micronesia even though the best the Japanese could do from outside against its assault on the Gilberts was a brief raid by forty-six planes from the Marshalls. Had the Navy contented itself with securing Palau to guard MacArthur's flank in New Guinea and flung its huge resources into his advance, the war might have been shortened by a year. But the two commands had become fierce competitors for resources from home.

"There was no single agency which could coordinate both the Army and the Navy. Had there been someone ... who had the power to coordinate, I feel things would have gone much better. As it was, each branch tried to carry out operations of its own with insufficient understanding of the other ..." Ironically, these words of regret (uttered in 1945) come, not from one of the presiding minds in the American war effort, but from Captain Genda Minoru, IJN – the man who planned Pearl Harbor.

Having come so far in the history of the Pacific campaign, we can usefully conclude this self-contained story before returning to the Atlantic and the victory over the U-boats which determined the outcome of the entire war.

The American underwater offensive against Japan did not reach its peak until 1944, when the phenomenally expanded United States Navy also scored a series of overwhelming surface victories in the island-hopping advance towards Japan. The turning point for the Americans in the Pacific war had been their victory at Midway in June 1942. For the Japanese it came two whole years later when the Americans, heavily engaged in the opening phase of the Normandy invasion on the other side of the world, mounted an operation almost as large against the Marianas archipelago ten days later, on 16 June. The targets were the Japanese islands of Saipan and Tinian and the occupied American island of Guam. From Saipan the new American B29 "Superfortress" long-range bombers would strike Japan. The Japanese Navy tried to interfere but lost much of its remaining airpower for no return in the mid-June Battle of the Philippine Sea, known to the victorious Americans as "the Great Marianas Turkey-Shoot". Admiral Spruance of the Fifth Fleet and his carrier commander, Vice-Admiral Marc A. Mitscher, won this huge defensive air engagement without knowing the position of the enemy's fleet.

But two American submarines found it on 19 June: *Albacore* (Commander J.W. Blanchard, USN) hit the new carrier *Taiho*, which blew up and sank later; and Lieutenant-Commander Kossler's *Cavalla* sank the Pearl Harbor veteran, the carrier *Shokaku*, instantaneously with three torpedoes. Admiral Ozawa was left with six carriers but only thirty-five aircraft as he withdrew with his five battleships, thirteen cruisers and escorting destroyers. Saipan fell on 9 July, amid horrific scenes of mass death-leaps over cliffs by 8,000 Japanese non-combatants, to add to the 24,000 troops killed and 1,780 captured in the defence of the strategic island. Tinian was secured by 2 August, Guam to the south having come back under the Stars and Stripes on 29 July.

But it was Saipan which shocked the Japanese at all levels. The better to defend it against the anticipated American attack, General Tojo, the Prime Minister, had added the portfolio of Chief of the General Staff to his responsibilities. As a result of its loss he and his Cabinet fell on 18 July. But the real damage to Japan's ability to wage war was now being done by the American submarine service. A vivid portrait of its work was left by Commander Eugene B. Fluckey, captain of the *Barb*, one of the most successful boats with fifteen merchantmen and two warships sunk. During a mid-year patrol around the Kurile Islands north of Japan he sighted a convoy:

The first ship that came towards us was a large transport. We submerged upon sighting her, made our attack and sank her with three torpedo hits ... As this ship sank in a very graceful fashion, just slowly settling, still going ahead under full power, some landing craft floated off her which were filled full of Japanese Army personnel [who fired on *Barb* when it came up; the boat withdrew to sink another ship].

We returned to the scene of our crime, the last sinking, to pick up a prisoner to see if he could give us any information. It was a very gruesome picture ... The clouds at that time were settling down close to the water, it was just getting dark; the atmosphere was much like one you'd expect from Frankenstein. The people were screaming and groaning in the water. There were several survivors on rafts. The water at that time was very cold, about twenty-seven degrees [Fahrenheit]. These people were gradually freezing and dying. We took the most lively-looking specimen aboard, who was very anxious to come aboard ...

As we have seen, the Japanese response to the strangulation by the American submarines of their maritime arteries was hopelessly inadequate. From the end of 1944, however, the American submarine campaign collided with the law of diminishing returns and carrier planes overtook it as the principal eliminator of the residual Japanese merchant fleet. The boats' most destructive month was November, during which they accounted for fifty-six merchant ships of 214,000 tons, and eighteen warships of 125,900 tons. In the year as a whole the boats sank 603 ships totalling 2.7 million tons (eighty-eight ships and half a million tons more than in the previous two years combined). Japanese raw-material imports fell from 16.4 million tons in 1943 to ten million in 1944; the merchant fleet fell from 4.1 to two million tons over the same period. These losses came to less than half those endured by the Allies in the deadliest days of the U-boats, but the Japanese Merchant Navy amounted to rather less than half the British tonnage at the beginning of the war, and there were no hugely productive American yards to provide replacements.

American and Japanese analysts at the time and much later agreed that the imperial economy, undermined at sea and then flattened from the air, would have come to a full stop in spring 1946. It is therefore not unreasonable to suggest that an American submarine fleet with 100 more boats (a minor diversion of a colossal shipbuilding programme), concentrating on tankers and other merchantmen rather than warships, might have made the awesome weapon used to terminate the war with Japan unnecessary. As it was, the boats claimed fifty-seven per cent of Japanese shipping (including 201 warships) sunk. Putting in a strong finish, aircraft took thirty-three per cent. The rest went to surface ships and mines.

In terms of numbers of ships sunk the leading American ace was Commander Richard H. O'Kane in *Tang*, which destroyed two dozen ships of 94,000 tons. The boat was lost to one of the many dud torpedoes foisted on the service during the war: she succumbed to a missile she had fired herself. Nine survivors out of eighty-seven aboard, including O'Kane, also survived the barbaric Japanese prison camps; the commander was awarded the Medal of Honor, one of seven won by the submarine service. As in the Mediterranean, some boats were used in support of amphibious operations in the Pacific.

The American submarine arm accounted for one battleship, seven carriers, nine cruisers, about thirty destroyers and seven submarines. Their most spectacular victim was HIJMS *Shinano*, laid down as the third mega-battleship of the 70,000-ton Yamato class but converted into an armoured carrier after Midway. She set off from Yokosuka for her maiden voyage on 29 November 1944 and was sighted within hours by *Archerfish* (Commander J.F. Enright). Four out of six torpedoes fired struck home; the giant ship took seven hours to die.

The Japanese tanker fleet still mustered 700,000 tons in September; at the end of the year there were 200,000 left. The main reason for the sharp decline in American sinkings was clear: lack of targets on the open sea. To ensure fair shares for all boats of the targets available an intricate patrol system was created for Japanese waters. Patrol areas were subdivided into zones and each boat got her turn in every one. The areas were given highly American codenames such as "Convoy College" in which each zone got the name of an academic degree, or "Hit Parade"; the packs gave themselves names such as *Blakeley's Behemoths* or *Ed's Eradicators*.

The last throw of the Japanese submarine arm, which had let the Germans loose in the Indian Ocean in 1943 rather than raise its game against Allied merchant traffic, came on 29 July 1945. Taught to give absolute priority to enemy warships, an excited Commander Hasimoto, on a lonely patrol east of the Philippines in *I58*, thought he had an American battleship of the "Idaho" class in his sights – unescorted. In fact it was the heavy cruiser USS *Indianapolis*, 9,950 tons (Captain Charles B. McVay), which had been Spruance's flagship for his smashing victory at the Battle of the Philippine Sea in June 1944. The Americans thought that the Japanese Navy, including its seldom troublesome submarines, was finished by this time and took no ASW precautions. The cruiser was not zigzagging and had no sonar or escort, even though she had just delivered the detonator of the first atomic bomb to Tinian and was on her way to Leyte in the Philippines. Just before midnight Hasimoto fired six Long Lances, of which at least two struck home.

The 850 survivors who took to the water out of a crew of 1,199 had to wait eighty-four hours before being sighted by chance from a Catalina on 2 August: American warships were not expected to sink any more. By then only 316 were left alive. This slackness by the victorious US Navy is alarming enough; the observer is left wondering what would have happened had *I58* found the old cruiser *before* she made her delivery of the detonator for one of just two extant American A-bombs (there would not be a third until well after the war). The *Indianapolis* thus gained the melancholy distinction of being the last American warship to be sunk in the Second World War, the last victim of a submarine in the conflict – and the last success of the Imperial Japanese Navy.

Almost thirty-seven years were to pass before a submarine executed the next such sinking.

Scene iv: Defeat of the U-boat

THE HALF-YEAR in which the Americans, urged on by Admiral Ernest J. King, managed by a mixture of luck and resolve to stave off Japanese aggression in the Pacific, brought their British ally to the brink of defeat in the Atlantic, thanks to King's greatest blunder.

The U-boat veterans christened the period from January to June 1942 their "second happy time" as they inflicted massive damage on the Anglo-American lifeline across the North Atlantic. King, a man described by one of his daughters as the most even-tempered man in the Navy – "always in a rage" – was also a chronic Anglophobe. This led him to reject British advice based on the lessons of the First World War, painfully relearned in the Atlantic in the first twenty-eight months of the Second, about the crucial importance of escort for merchant shipping. As he milked the Atlantic Fleet of destroyers and other ships for the Pacific, King determined that there were nothing like enough warships for a proper escort system, and virtually abandoned merchant ships to their fate in American waters. The British principle, derived from hugely expensive experience, that any escort was better than none was blindly replaced by King's insistence that "inadequately escorted convoys are worse than none".

Dönitz launched Operation *Paukenschlag* ("drumbeat" or "thunderclap") against shipping off the American east coast. But the conflicting demands of Norway and the Mediterranean inspired in the U-boat commander a sense of frustration rather than of fulfilment. He was allowed at first a maximum of six long-range type IX boats at a time instead of the planned twelve; and his idea of deploying packs of type VIIs further north had to be scaled down, after the initial attack, to independent patrols as individual boats became available. The harsh winter in the Baltic disrupted training, which further reduced the number of operational boats.

The U-boat service was not ready to begin *Paukenschlag* until the

war with America was five weeks old, in mid-January 1942. By then
seven type VIIs and five XIs were in place from the Canadian St
Lawrence estuary to the north to Cape Hatteras, North Carolina, to the
south. Reinhard Hardegen in *U123*, a type IX, opened what was to be a
very lengthy account by sinking the 9,000-ton British merchantman
Cyclops 300 miles south of Cape Cod, Massachusetts, on 12 January.
This holder of the Knight's Cross with oak leaves sank six more freighters
and damaged a tanker inside a week. By the end of the month Dönitz
may have felt he was fighting with one hand behind his back; but
Americans were devastated by the loss of more than 200,000 tons
(thirty-five ships) in the coastal waters between Newfoundland and
Bermuda, 4,000 miles to the south. Many believed there were scores,
even hundreds, of U-boats off their coast. Another ten ships totalling
63,000 tons were sunk on the transatlantic route.

The second happy time soon acquired a second soubriquet: "the American turkey-shoot". Morale in the U-boat service rose to new peaks.
The type VIIC surpassed itself by operating at ranges well beyond
specification. This was achieved by storing diesel oil in tanks meant for
drinking and washing water, trimming and ballast, and in jerrycans
stuffed into every cranny on the outward voyage. One of the two
lavatories aboard had to be used as a food store on the way out. Drinking
water was carried in cans, making the crammed, 750-ton boats even
more uncomfortable. The ballast and trimming tanks not intended for
fuel would be emptied first on the way out so that sea water was back in
use by the time the operational area was reached. The boats took three
weeks to sail to and from it at their most economical speed and by the
shortest ("great circle") route, which the convoys were soon forced to
use also, thanks to serious tanker losses. Dönitz was simultaneously
proud and horrified when he heard of this dangerous dedication and
forbade it. The order was largely ignored.

A boat going to sea carried about one week's supply of fresh food.
Bread and potatoes soon acquired mildew in the humidity aboard, which
prevented any unprocessed food from lasting longer than a few days.
But certain staple German foods, such as dense rye bread, smoke-cured
and salted cold meats might have been invented for these conditions.
Salamis and smoked hams would be hung from pipes inside the boat.
But by halfway through a patrol the U-boat men were reduced to hard
tack (dry biscuits) for their dietary fibre, and canned food. As soon as a
can was opened, its content was imbued with the indescribable atmosphere of a submarine at sea, a mixture of stale air, condensation, fumes
from fuel and batteries and the bacterial cocktails emitted by unwashed
bodies and soiled clothing. Submariners generally came home with acne,

constipation and matted beards; shore personnel were invariably bowled over by the foul exudation from a returning boat. Those who had created the brew had long ceased to notice it but sometimes became dizzy when exposed to fresh air. All this was accentuated on the extra-long patrols of *Paukenschlag*.

The results were truly spectacular for the Germans and unbearably disheartening to the British after two and a half years of war. In the first quarter of 1942 the U-boats sank 216 vessels (1.25 million tons) in the North Atlantic, overwhelmingly in American waters. The Allied worldwide loss in this period, which included the main Japanese conquests, reached 1.93 million tons of which 1.34 million were due to submarines. These figures attest to the stupendous success made possible by the failure of the US Navy to escort shipping in its own waters. What was worse, fifty-seven per cent of sinkings were tankers. The Americans were undoing the grim labours of the British and Canadian navies in the Atlantic. They nursed ships most of the way across, only to see them fall victim to "a merry massacre" (the words of the US Navy's own historian) in American waters. A programme for building 810 extra escorts in American yards for all three North Atlantic navies was begun in March, over and above the 300 already under construction.

Vice-Admiral Adolphus Andrews, commanding the Eastern Sea Frontier (ESF – most of the east coast), was forced to go to war almost empty-handed. The Americans knew there was no enemy plane capable of reaching the continental United States from either side and that a Channel only twenty miles wide had kept Britain safe from invasion for nine centuries. Commanders such as King chose to ignore the fact that U-boats had managed to put in a brief appearance in American waters towards the end of the First World War.

The Federal Building on Church Street in downtown Manhattan was partly commandeered to serve as an (initially very pale) American reflection of Western Approaches' Liverpool bunker, from which naval-escort and air forces were directed to protect shipping. But Andrews had just twenty small vessels and 103 aircraft at his disposal, most of which were useless for ASW purposes. Army Air Force crews were untrained in work at sea and their radios could not communicate with ships. Andrews complained to King at New Year, 1942. King sympathised but did almost nothing about it. His British opposite number, Admiral Pound, offered ten corvettes and two dozen ASW trawlers to ESF. These were gratefully accepted in an ironic reversal of roles. Coastal Command reluctantly stumped up a squadron of ASW planes to fly from a base in Rhode Island, but not until June 1942.

As the situation in American waters slid rapidly into a major crisis by March, Pound appealed to King for convoy, as did Churchill to Roosevelt. King ignored the efforts of Captain G.E. Creasy, RN, the Admiralty's Director of ASW, to get hard-won British lessons across, and stubbornly ran the gamut of all the Admiralty's blunders from 1914 to 1917, not forgetting Q-ships.

From mid-February US Atlantic Fleet destroyers did *ad hoc* escort duties in ESF for a few days at a time after serving ocean convoys. The British eventually slowed the convoy cycle so as to release two escort groups for US waters; but a handful of U-boats which would barely have been enough for a pack against a convoy continued their "merry massacre" unabashed.

In fact King was not blind to the value of convoy. He merely believed that a weak escort was worse than none. Most American naval commanders, including Andrews, agreed. As merchant seamen began to revolt in New York harbour against sailing without protection, the Americans were reduced to desperate expedients. Inland waterways were used whenever possible; ships were told to sail coastwise in marked lanes by day and put into port at night – the "bucket brigade" system, as Andrews styled it, recalling how fires used to be fought by chains of buckets. Such ASW vessels as existed patrolled the marked lanes (shades of 1916!) concentrating against every (usually false) U-boat sighting. This left the Germans free to attack everywhere else, aided by the fact that ships sailed in straight lines from one marker-buoy to the next. The "Hooligan Navy" (official title: the Corsair Fleet) was set up by the Coastguard to muster privately owned boats as ASW pickets fifty miles out to sea. Ernest Hemingway briefly joined it in his yacht, with machine-gun, hunting rifle, pistol and grenades. The main result was a fusillade of false sightings which continually diverted the already exiguous ASW forces. The Civil Air Patrol of private fliers did rather better and was eventually conscripted *en bloc* by the Army Air Force. The three Q-ships sent out were all shot up by U-boats. There was no attempt to black out the east coast, so that U-boats at night had a wondrous backdrop of light behind their targets.

The sinking of the destroyer USS *Jacob Jones* in ESF waters on 28 February, on temporary detachment from the Atlantic Fleet, led to the continuous attachment to ESF of a daily average of two destroyers from the fleet on a hand-to-mouth basis. Her sister-ship *Dickerson* was crippled in error by the American merchantman SS *Liberator* (7,720 tons) on 18 March; the latter's punishment was to be sunk the next day by *U332* (Johannes Liebe). By this time Andrews, on King's orders, was well advanced in planning for convoys – once there were "enough" escorts available. The Air Ministry now diverted fifteen US-built aircraft to the ESF, a change of heart closely akin to a panic measure.

By spring 1942 Dönitz had extended his onslaught southward into the next two Sea Frontiers, the Gulf and the Caribbean, even though the number of boats at his disposal had not significantly risen. Hitler was still obsessed with Norway, but Operation *Neuland* or part two of *Paukenschlag* opened as early as 16 February, when Werner Hartenstein boldly ignited the oil refinery at Aruba, Netherlands Antilles, in *U156*. Three other boats sank a total of seven tankers near the blazing facility, a devastating stroke against the Allied fuel supply. By March another ten ships, mostly tankers, were sunk in the same area; hit-and-run raids in the West Indies, the Bahamas and the Gulf of Mexico followed. Dönitz mounted the odd attack on the main route at the same time, to deter the British from switching forces to the east coast.

On 24 February for example, ON 67 actually enjoyed the luxury of an American ocean escort as it approached Newfoundland from England; this did not deter a rare wolf-pack from sinking six of its ships. In the United States, land of plenty, rationing was introduced. Rubber and petroleum were followed by, of all things, coffee. In Britain the fortunes of war were as negative as they had been in mid-1940. As Singapore teetered on the brink of capture and another British Army struggled in North Africa, brilliant German staffwork achieved the Royal Navy's greatest humiliation for three centuries by sailing the battlecruisers *Scharnhorst* and *Gneisenau* plus the heavy cruiser *Prinz Eugen* from Brest in France to home ports up the "English" Channel in daylight. But the British submarine *Trident* (Commander G.M. Sladen, RN) soon torpedoed and crippled *Prinz Eugen* off Trondheim.

The worst setback for the British was a closely guarded secret: naval Ultra dried up as the German Navy, more security-conscious than any other enemy service, introduced a fourth wheel into its Enigma machines and gave the submarine arm a tough new cipher of its own, codenamed Triton. In anticipation of a fourth wheel, work had started on a quadruple "bombe" at Bletchley in December 1941. Britain had not previously revealed to the Americans how it was penetrating German ciphers, so they knew nothing of bombes and could not help immediately in their production. It was to be ten and a half months before Triton was penetrated. As an illustration of the scale of the problem, we may note that it took six triple bombes seventeen days to decipher a brief Triton message of 14 March 1942 – announcing the promotion of Dönitz to full admiral. It was fortunate that the loss of U-boat Ultra coincided with the second happy time: Ultra could not have made up for the lack of cerebral intelligence in the US Navy Command.

In February the xB-dienst completed its attack on British naval cipher number three, used for communication among the three North Atlantic Navies until June 1943. In March the Germans salvaged a copy of the new Merchant Ship Code, due to come into effect in April, from a sinking freighter. The handful of *Paukenschlag* boats were also helped by transmissions on the emergency wavelength (600 metres, medium wave). Ships rushing to the position of the distressed vessel were not infrequently joined by a U-boat which caused even more distress.

To increase the effectiveness of his exiguous forces in the Atlantic, Admiral Dönitz introduced the *Milchkuh* (milch-cow) or tanker-submarine in mid-March 1942. The first was *UA*, now adapted to refuel type VIIs, which needed it most. A new, purpose-built type XIV was developed in 1941 and the first, *U459*, put to sea on 28 March. Five more followed within weeks; in all twenty were built. The new type, slow at fourteen knots and armed with only four torpedoes, was large by German standards, displacing 1,688/1,932 tons and capable of carrying 432 tons of diesel plus parts and stores; more than enough to replenish four type VIIs completely, except for minitions. In one week of April *U459* was able to top up eight U-boats, sometimes two at a time. The experience was described memorably by Heinz Schaeffer, the future captain of *U977*:

... some of the engine-room staff went forward and aft to open the fuelling valves and clear the way for the supply-hose. Icy cold though it was, these men wore only bathing trunks, the belt to which they were lashed biting into their flesh. At times one or other of them would even be washed overboard and only be hauled in again with a good deal of effort ...

We were cruising parallel to the supply boat, perhaps ninety yards away. A line was fired over us by pistol, and this was followed by the hose and a towing-wire. We breathed again as the precious fluid began to flow in. Altogether we took in twenty tons of it, not to speak of bread, potatoes, vegetables and other food in watertight sacks. The whole thing went off perfectly, though it was our first experience.

Another U-boat called up, wanting to be victualled too ... we both dived, first the supply boat, then ourselves ... with lines, hose and wire left in place, and so we cruised for three hours on end at a depth of twenty-five fathoms. It was a fantastic conception: we were embarking diesel oil under water for the first time in history.

In March 1942 shipping losses reached an alarming 834,164 tons world-wide, of which 538,000 were lost to submarines and 534,000 in the North Atlantic (overwhelmingly off the United States east coast). This echo of April 1917 ended an abysmal quarter for the Allies, during which some 250 ships had been lost close to the shore of North America.

Rear-Admiral John Godfrey, RN, Director of Naval Intelligence, sent Rodger Winn, head of the Submarine Tracking Room, to Washington to plead the cause of convoy and persuade the Americans to copy the Operational Intelligence Centre. Winn, using all his skills as an advocate, fought his case up to the highest instance, COMINCH himself. To his astonishment King accepted his arguments on STR and OIC without demur and promptly set up a new Atlantic Section in "Op-20-G" (operational intelligence) at Naval Operations headquarters, under Commander Kenneth A. Knowles, USN. The two commanders, both to be promoted captain, soon established one of the most intimate and successful Anglo-American collaborations of the war.

Early in April 1942 King accepted proposals from his three east-coast Sea Frontier commanders for a coastal convoy system from mid-May. Dönitz, now able to field eighteen boats at a time in the area, soon (but coincidentally) shifted his attention further south. Only fourteen ships were lost out of an Atlantic total of 123 in Eastern Sea Frontier waters in May; but the tanker crisis grew alarmingly.

The Germans stayed ahead of the game by unerringly shifting the focus of their attack to one weak point after another. Worldwide shipping losses fell to 674,000 tons (432,000 to submarines, 391,000 in the North Atlantic) in April 1942, rose again in May to 705,000 tons (607,000 and 576,000). In June they reached what was to prove the worst monthly total of the entire war, exactly thirty-two tons more than in March: 834,196 tons sunk, 700,000 by submarines, 624,000 tons in the North Atlantic.

On 19 June General George C. Marshall, Chief of Staff of the US Army, took on his naval opposite number, Admiral Ernest J. King, in a letter demanding action to staunch the huge shipping losses, which "threaten our war effort". On the 21st King loftily replied that he had always been in favour of convoy. He could not resist attacking the British for failing to devote enough effort to bombing U-boat yards and bases and went on: "Escort is not just *one* way of handling the submarine menace; it is the *only* way that gives any promise of success [King's emphases] ... We must get every ship that sails the seas under constant close protection."

The days of the German aces' second happy time were at last numbered. In July 1942 shipping losses worldwide fell by a quarter, to 618,000 tons. In the same month, thanks to a mighty leap in American production, the total of new shipping launched passed, if only just, the total sunk, for the first time in the Second World War. The British had strained every nerve to reach an annual building rate of 1.25 million tons, but Roosevelt himself ordered the Director of the War Shipping Administration, Vice-Admiral Emory S. Land, USN, to organise the construction of 750 freighters in 1942 and twice that number in 1943. By summer 1942 a "Liberty" off-the-peg ship which had taken six months to build at the start of the programme took barely three months, thanks to the introduction of assembly-line methods. The all-time record was set in November 1942, when the SS *Robert E. Peary* was completed in four days and fifteen hours at the Richmond, California, yard of the Kaiser Corporation.

Ironically, in the same pivotal July, despite a steadily rising Allied submarine destruction rate, Dönitz at last commanded more than 300 U-boats (331), the number he would have liked at the beginning of a war with Britain. But, unbeknown to him, Dönitz had already lost the tonnage war, of which he had written in his War Diary in April:

... the enemy merchant navies are a collective factor. It is therefore immaterial where any one ship is sunk, for it must ultimately be replaced by new construction. Shipbuilding and arms production are centred in the United States ... By attacking the supply traffic – particularly the oil – in the US zone, I am striking at the root of the evil, for here the sinking of each ship is not only a loss to the enemy but also deals a blow at the source of his shipbuilding and war production. Without shipping [Britain] cannot be used for an attack on Europe...

By spring 1942 the Canadians supervised shipping in the north-western Atlantic, the Americans the western and the British the eastern sector. The British were now providing fifty, the Canadians forty-eight and the Americans just two per cent of transatlantic escort vessels; the "American" groups had only one or two US ships each. Canadian groups had to be thinned out to find ships to protect convoys between Halifax and Boston. Even so, as soon as coastal cover was in place the Germans moved southward, proving King wrong in his belief that weak escort was worse than nothing.

But as the Allies struggled to close the gaps in their anti-submarine defences, the Germans were not monopolising the fortunes of war after all. The remission in the great torpedo crisis was followed by a relapse. Lorient noticed from performance analysis in mid-year that the sinking rate was "only" fifty per cent (how envious Nimitz would have been!); 806 missiles had been expended to sink 404 ships. Dönitz assessed this record as poorer than 1918 performance. But the new FAT (*Feder-Apparat Torpedo* – spring apparatus) was successfully tried in the middle of 1942; it ran straight on launch and then veered, according to setting, to left or right in a series of loops. Ultra revealed the development of the FAT to the British during 1941, but not its technology. The Allies wrongly assumed it was an acoustic torpedo, and thus by a happy accident had not only developed counter-measures by the time the Germans did introduce one, but also built their own acoustic weapon.

Meanwhile the sinkings continued. The Allies without Ultra took six months to discover the existence of the milch-cows, which enabled Dönitz's men to find rich pickings as far south as Brazil; the eighteen U-boats on hand were briefly supported by four Italian submarines in the latter phase of *Paukenschlag*, which was formally concluded on 19 July – the most destructive phase of the Second World War U-boat campaign.

Elsewhere, the Allies expanded their ASW training on both sides of the Atlantic. Captain Gilbert Roberts, RN, ran the Tactical School in Liverpool from January 1942. The Canadians worked out a course in night attacks which was copied by the Americans and the British. Lieutenant-Commander E.F. McDaniel, USN, opened a "Sub-chaser Center" in Miami known as McDaniel's Academy, for training escort crews. Captain W.D. Baker, USN, founded the Atlantic Fleet's ASW school in Boston in February 1942.

How the British and German naval commands might have smiled had each been privy to the main concern of the other in the middle of 1942. It was exactly the same.

Admiral Sir John Tovey of the Home Fleet called on the Board of Admiralty to resign *en bloc* in a letter dated 28 May 1942. Summarising it in his quarterly report for April–June, Tovey reminded their Lordships of what he had vainly told them:

... the whole strategy of the war was governed by sea communication ... the Navy could no longer carry out its much increased task without adequate air support; that support had not been forthcoming ... [RAF Bomber Command] had for long enjoyed absolute priority ... Whatever the result of bombing of cities might be, it could not of itself win the war, whereas the failure of our sea communications would assuredly lose it ...

It was difficult to believe that the population of Cologne would notice much difference between a raid of 1,000 bombers and one by 750 ...

I informed [their Lordships] that in my opinion the situation at sea was now so grave that the time had come for a stand to be made, even if this led to their Lordships taking the extreme step of resignation.

On the other side of the water Admiral Karl Dönitz, commanding U-boats, wrote in his War Diary on 11 June:

That there should be no air protection for a damaged and defenceless U-boat is deplorable, and must have a depressing effect on the crews. Even a few heavy fighters or modern bombers would suffice to keep off enemy aircraft. At least they could escort a damaged U-boat until she came under the protection of our minesweepers and patrol vessels ... There being no defence in the Bay of Biscay against Sunderland [flying boats] and heavy bombers, the RAF can do what it likes.

The British admiral was demanding long-range Liberators for the air gap south of Greenland. The German was complaining about the shift of Luftwaffe strength from France to Russia, which enabled Coastal Command to dominate the Bay of Biscay, through which the U-boats had to pass at the beginning and end of each patrol. Dönitz knew that the Luftwaffe was still causing trouble for British shipping with fighters from Dutch and Norwegian airfields attacking obsolescent Coastal Command escorts over convoys. The Germans could not know that Coastal Command was waging a campaign of its own for more effective planes, alongside Tovey's efforts to close the Greenland air gap, and the Admiralty's to get air reinforcements for the Mediterranean and Indian Ocean.

The Air Ministry in general and Bomber Command in particular insisted on absolute priority for the bombardment of German cities. In April the Admiralty and Coastal Command extracted four extra bomber squadrons for North-Western Approaches and the Bay of Biscay, and in May the RAF sanctioned constant air patrols over the Bay – the origins of Dönitz's worries in June. Dönitz ordered all boats to stay under in the Bay as the British introduced their Leigh Light to pinpoint submarines detected by aircraft radar at night.

So insistent had the German admirals' complaints about lack of maritime airpower become by March 1942 that Hitler was briefly moved to order the resumption of work on a German aircraft-carrier and the conversion of merchantmen to escort-carriers, decrees soon subverted by Göring. In June Hitler stopped all work on carriers. Germany has never had one to this day. Dönitz bearded Göring in his East Prussian headquarters in order to divert one squadron of twenty-four Junkers Ju 88 long-range fighter-bombers against British air patrols.

The Americans, too, sank into inter-service rivalry over airpower at sea, complicated by the voracious demands of a naval war on two fronts. The Pacific enjoyed *de facto* priority no matter what was said at Allied summit conferences. In the Atlantic, King gave priority to the Atlantic Fleet's squadrons over the Sea Frontier Commands and the Coastguard. Army's First Bomber Command, a group of eighty-four planes, was diverted to aid the Navy with longer-range patrols, although its pilots started with no experience of maritime work. In July 1942 the Atlantic Fleet's new Commander, Patrol Wings (Atlantic), had three wings of aircraft at Argentia, Newfoundland, and Norfolk, Virginia, to cover the coast from Florida northwards, now stringently blacked out, against the U-boats.

Admiral Tovey's main concern during this period was with the convoys to Russia and the threat presented by the German super-dreadnought *Tirpitz* (in the far north since January 1942) and supporting ships to the Russian (and transatlantic) convoys. The main damage on the Murmansk run, however, was done by the Luftwaffe from its Norwegian bases, sometimes supported by German destroyers or occasionally by U-boats. The correct tactic for a convoy faced with a major surface attack was to disperse; but against submarine and air attacks the right thing to do was to stay together to maximise the effectiveness of escort and anti-aircraft defences. That left the question of what to do when faced with all three at the same time, a dilemma which overwhelmed the notorious, Russia-bound convoy PQ 17. Several convoys in both directions had been battered by German destroyers, aircraft and submarines, but no capital ship had attacked them, although one or two hesitant forays had been made (enabling the submarine HMS *Trident* to knock out the *Prinz Eugen*). The British saw to it that the *Tirpitz* would have no refuge in France should she come out into the broad Atlantic like her sister, the *Bismarck*.

In the successful if bloody "St Nazaire raid" on the Brittany coast at the end of March, British sailors in small vessels and Army commandos destroyed the huge lock there, which had doubled as a dry dock prewar for the great liner *Normandie*. This was the only facility outside Germany able to accommodate the *Tirpitz*. The raid had the inconvenient side effect for Dönitz of an order from Hitler on 29 March to evacuate Lorient and move to Paris immediately.

As the British planned convoy PQ 17, the Germans under Grand Admiral Raeder worked on Operation *Rösselsprung* (knight's move in chess) against it. The "knight" was *Tirpitz*, supported by the two pocket battleships, one heavy cruiser and a dozen destroyers. This formidable group was to make a thrust east of Bear Island while aircraft and U-boats were to probe west of that Norwegian possession. The British ordered their covering force of four cruisers to stay west of the island if the German big ships were reported at sea. Distant cover to the south was provided by the Home Fleet as usual; Coastal Command was allowed to fly cover from Russian bases. The convoy escort group of six ships was led by Commander J.E. Broome, RN, in the destroyer *Keppel*. Four extra escorts, three rescue ships, two anti-aircraft ships and two submarines, one oiler, minesweepers and trawlers were also with the convoy, which consisted of thirty-three ships and set sail from Iceland on 27 June.

It was sighted by German planes and submarines on 1 July. The U-boats fired torpedoes but missed, thanks to a smart emergency turn by Commodore J.C.K. Dowding, RNR, in charge of the merchantmen, and deterrent moves by Broome's escort. The covering cruisers were forty miles to the north. The escort also drove off an attack by nine Heinkel He 111 torpedo-bombers without loss. On the night of 3–4 July PQ 17 passed to the north of Bear Island. In the evening two dozen Heinkels damaged three ships, two of which had to be scuttled. The other, a tanker, turned back and reached safety. One ship had been lost to a lone torpedo-bomber earlier in the day.

Unfortunately the RAF had been unable to locate any German heavy ships; none was in port at Trondheim and Narvik was closed in by bad weather. The Germans had indeed put to sea but were not by any means committed to an attack. At the Admiralty tension soared. Admiral Pound came down to OIC and asked its chief, Captain Norman Denning: "Can you assure me that the *Tirpitz* is still in Altenfjord?" Denning could not prove his belief that the monster was not at sea. At 9.36 p.m. on 4 July Pound, certain without a shred of positive evidence that the German heavy ships were out, ordered: "Convoy is to scatter." The decision should have been left to the commanders on the spot; but the Admiralty had never been good at delegating since the invention of wireless, and this blind interference from London led to a massacre.

By noon on 5 July the Luftwaffe and the U-boats had sunk six merchantmen; Heinz Bielfeld in *U703* got the seventh, the SS *River Afton*, 5,479 tons, Commodore Dowding's ship. He was among the few survivors. Later in the afternoon a tanker and a minesweeper were destroyed; that day's German score was twelve ships sunk. The escort and the covering cruisers, having abandoned the merchantmen, were perplexed to find no sign of a German surface attack. It was only on the morning of the 6th, when Hitler was satisfied it was safe, that *Tirpitz* came out of the Altenfjord – only to return when it was clear that the British had already scattered their convoy. The final, shocking tally for PQ 17 was twelve merchantmen and a rescue ship sunk by the Luftwaffe and ten merchantmen by U-boats. Eleven merchant vessels and two rescue ships reached Russia: one third of the richly laden convoy. Nearly 100,000 tons of munitions were lost.

The Americans blamed the British for abandoning the convoy without due cause and remained bitter about the disaster for the rest of the war. Pound had been right to anticipate a surface attack (aborted only because the convoy had scattered before it could be pressed home) but wrong to pre-empt the tactical decision to scatter. Rear-Admiral L.H.K. Hamilton, commanding the covering cruisers, had been ordered to avoid an action with German ships if they included *Tirpitz*. The order was crystal clear and should have sufficed. Pound, a chronically sick man, died in October 1943 of a stroke probably brought on by overwork. Nobody would have been surprised had the characters "PQ 17" been found engraved on his heart.

In the first seven months of 1942, submarines sank 3,556,000 tons out of a worldwide loss of Allied shipping of 4,765,000 tons; 3,319,000 were sunk in the North Atlantic. But on 27 July, after the most sustained and concentrated period of destruction of shipping by the U-boats, their commander-in-chief went on German radio to make one of the most remarkable broadcasts of the war. He told the German people, unfamiliar with such bluntness, that U-boat losses would mount as harder times lay ahead. It was his answer to the soaring propaganda inspired by the easy pickings off the American coast, now properly defended and therefore all but abandoned by the Germans eight days earlier. The British deduced that Dönitz was about to return to the main convoy route, despite the universality of surface escorts, and would choose the weakest spot in the Allied defences: the air gap south of Greenland. Shorter runs to and from this latest operational area, 1,000 miles closer to home, meant many more boats could be concentrated in it.

The Admiralty, thwarted by the Air Ministry, was still looking for a way to plug the gap, nicknamed "the Devil's Gorge" in the German service and "Torpedo Junction" in the Allied navies. There was a second zone out of reach of Allied planes around the Azores, owned by neutral Portugal, to which both sides referred as the Black Gap or Pit. The area was a favoured rendezvous for U-boats and milch-cows.

To discourage concentration by the enemy, Dönitz kept some boats in the Gulf of Mexico-Caribbean area, sinking fifteen more ships by the end of August, at a cost of three boats. The Germans then moved their profitable diversion further south, to the area between Trinidad and the Orinoco estuary. They caught 375,000 tons in the quarter ending with October, by which time the Interlocking Convoy System had embraced the area and Brazil had joined the Allies, giving them firm control of the "waist" of the Atlantic between South America and Africa.

The slogging matches between wolf-packs and escort groups resumed in the main air gap as before, but the most unusual incident of the second half of 1942, as the Atlantic campaign approached its climax, began south of the Equator in the waters north of Ascension Island on the night of 12 September. It was very nearly the death of Dönitz.

Commander Werner Hartenstein in *U156*, a type IXC, sighted a large, grey-camouflaged liner with guns on her main deck – a legitimate target therefore. There were 2,600 troops aboard this unaccompanied ship, a 19,700-tonner called *Laconia*. Unfortunately, 1,800 of them were Italian prisoners of war captured in North Africa and on their way to internment in North America. Hartenstein had no means of knowing this in advance and put a torpedo into her side. He then made amends.

He resolved to organise a rescue, and began transmitting on the international maritime emergency wavelength in English. He reported he had picked up 193 men, gave the position and promised not to attack any rescuer unless attacked himself. He also reported to his own headquarters. Dönitz ordered the milch-cow and the three other operational boats he had sent to join Hartenstein in pack *Eisbär* (polar bear) for a South Atlantic sweep, as well as two more distant U-boats and an Italian submarine, to help him. By this time Hartenstein had more than 200 extra people aboard below, another seventy clinging to his deck in a fortunately calm sea, four lifeboats in tow and a huge, improvised Red Cross flag hanging off the bridge. The rest of *Eisbär* headed for the Cape of Good Hope as a diversion, leaving the two other German and one Italian submarines to help with the rescue. So far it was a close copy of the *Python-Atlantis* rescue nearly two years before.

Then a US Navy Liberator bomber from Ascension came over on the morning of the 16th and reported to base. Ordered to attack, it made two passes and dropped four depth-charges, capsizing one lifeboat. Hartenstein cleared his boat by cramming as many "passengers" as possible into the lifeboats or on life-rafts. Ordered by headquarters to abandon the rescue, he did so, an hour after the air attack. His two supporters, *U506* and *U507*, also type IXCs, carried on until lunchtime on the 17th, when Dönitz ordered them to put all non-Italians on the lifeboats and rafts (or in the sea clinging to their ratlines) and be ready to dive at any time. At this point a Catalina came over and dropped an inaccurate pattern of depth-charges. The Vichy authorities in the Ivory Coast, then a French colony, had sent two rescue ships which met the two U-boats that evening. About half of those aboard the *Laconia* before she sank – 800 British and Poles and just 450 Italians – were saved in this extraordinary saga.

Dönitz was beside himself. "Uncle Karl's boys" had been within their rights to attack the liner but had shown compassion when they discovered the consequences, only to be bombed not once but twice by the enemy. At 7.24 p.m. German time that night he fired off a new standing order to all U-boats by radio, here quoted in full:

1) All attempts at rescuing members of ships that have sunk, including attempts to pick up persons swimming, or to place them in lifeboats, or attempts to right capsized boats, or to supply provisions or water, are to cease. The rescue of survivors contradicts the elementary necessity of war for the destruction of enemy ships and crews.
2) The order for the capture of captains and chief engineers remains in force.
3) Survivors are to be picked up only in cases where their interrogation would be of value to the U-boats.
4) Be severe. Remember that in his bombing attacks on German cities the enemy has no regard for women and children.

This was one of the main elements in the case against Dönitz at Nuremberg. The prosecution said it violated the London Protocol of 1936, outlawing unrestricted submarine warfare, which Germany had signed (although Hitler went back on it in 1939). The defence argued that the safety of the submarine took precedence over rescue and that ASW aircraft made rescue impossible. Admiral Nimitz honestly conceded in a written submission: "As a general rule, United States submarines did not rescue enemy survivors if by so doing the vessels were exposed to unnecessary or additional risk, or if the submarines were hindered from the execution of further tasks." The judges ruled that the order was not a licence to kill but was ambiguous and therefore reprehensible. Dönitz escaped the death sentence and got ten years' imprisonment.

The harsh struggle over the Russian convoys continued, with proportionally higher losses than in the North Atlantic, until the route was suspended in November 1943. The reason was Operation Torch, the US Army landing (covered by the Royal Navy) in north-west Africa on 8 November 1942, just after General Montgomery's decisive defeat of Rommel at El Alamein. To provide shipping for this major undertaking, the Gibraltar and Sierra Leone as well as the Murmansk routes were effectively closed down; the Atlantic was stripped of all possible escorts; and a plan to use extra escorts in reserve groups able to dash to the aid of any threatened convoy had to be deferred.

The defence in the Atlantic campaign was therefore put under renewed strain just as it overcame the disastrous effects of *Paukenschlag*. The Germans were expecting to have to fight harder for victims on the main convoy route but were relieved to find the going easier than they expected. The absence of Ultra and the need to economise on everything – shipping, fuel, escorts, munitions – for Torch, and to make up for grievous losses earlier in the year, made Allied adherence to the great circle route a benefit to the U-boats. Dönitz had plenty of boats to send to the Mediterranean as well, to help the Afrika Korps; and when the Americans were established ashore their demands for supplies mushroomed, necessitating even more convoys. Torch also caused a six-month delay in the mid-ocean deployment of the new escort-carriers now being delivered. Meanwhile the only two squadrons of VLR Liberator bombers not in the Pacific or over Germany were, on Admiral King's insistence, based in Morocco for Torch rather than patrolling the air gap through which all non-Torch Atlantic convoys had to pass.

All this lay behind the record month for the war in specifically U-boat destructiveness: 729,000 tons in November 1942, out of a total for the month of 808,000 worldwide (509,000 in the North Atlantic). The all-time record loss in the South Atlantic of 161,000 tons had been achieved in the previous month. Allied shipping losses in this period in British home waters and to mines, aircraft and surface raiders fell to negligible levels. But the U-boat was now the unchallenged principal threat to the Allied war effort as bigger packs engaged in sprawling battles, sometimes with two convoys at a time. In August and September the U-boats sighted one-third of sixty-three transatlantic convoys, and of this one-third they attacked one-third, i.e. seven, sinking a total of forty-three ships.

The Canadians, who covered the slow convoys while the British escorted the faster ones, had a particularly bleak time: the weaknesses caused by forced expansion described earlier were compounded by shortage of the latest radar, slightly older and less well-equipped ships. After losing seven ships sunk and four damaged plus one destroyer sunk from westbound ONS 127, the Canadian escort group C4 went on to lose fifteen merchantmen from eastbound SC 107 in this period. Only one U-boat was lost out of a pack of seventeen in the latter fight (to a Canadian plane).

As Churchill's "Battle of the Atlantic" ground on to its bloody climax, the Prime Minister decided to bring in a new broom to command the main British ASW effort at Western Approaches. The entirely worthy Admiral Sir Percy Noble, in charge since February 1941, was replaced on 19 November 1942 by Admiral Sir Max Horton, Flag Officer (Submarines) since 1940. Noble went to Washington as head of the British Naval Mission. Horton was a much more colourful figure and had the good luck to be in command when victory came; but the achievements of 1943 were built on Noble's work – which would have brought victory in 1942 but for competing demands on scarce resources.

The arrival of Horton, autocratic and intolerant of fools as ever, galvanised the gloomy bunker and its staff of more than 1,000. One man who knew how to deal with him and had the moral courage (and superior wisdom) to do it was Rodger Winn in the Submarine Tracking Room. Horton attacked him at a fortnightly meeting of the new Anti-U-boat Warfare Committee (set up by Churchill in November 1942), after yet another convoy had been decimated. Winn remained calm and politely challenged the new Western Approaches C-in-C to do better. Half an hour later Horton was in Winn's seat at the STR with all the information before him that the Room had possessed at the time. As the peppery admiral struggled to digest the mound of conflicting and incomplete information, Winn struck: "The chief of staff at Western Approaches in Liverpool is waiting urgently ..." Horton had the grace to concede defeat and trusted Winn implicitly thereafter.

The spread of the Interlocking Convoy System drove the U-boats into the South Atlantic, where their record score, in October 1942, of 148,000 tons sunk included three other liners apart from the *Laconia*. The type IXD2 U-boat with its phenomenal range of 23,700 miles at twelve knots enabled the Germans to move round the Cape into the Indian Ocean in the following month, without benefit of milch-cow at first, to claim 127,000 tons with half a dozen of this rare variant (only thirty were built). The milch-cow flotilla lost two of its members late in 1942 but seven were at sea in December; operational strength rose to a peak of nine boats for the climactic spring of 1943.

The displacements of latter-day types VII and IX rose by up to fifteen per cent as their hulls were strengthened to enable them to dive as deep as 300 metres in an emergency. From August 1942 boats were issued with the Metox radar detector or *Biscayakreuz* (Biscay cross).

From July the U-boats had been crossing the Bay surfaced by day because the danger of being detected by aircraft radar at night was greater. Relatively heavy anti-aircraft guns were fitted in pairs on a "bandstand" at the after end of conning towers. A primitive radar was fitted to the U-boats themselves from summer 1942, but the Germans were seriously behind in this field, and a submarine's low profile minimised the range of any scanner. The FAT torpedo raised the scoring rate from fifty to seventy-five per cent. Development was still continuing on the complicated *Zaunkönig* (wren) acoustic torpedo. Dönitz also sought a replacement for the discontinued Kondor aircraft, to work with the U-boats in areas reachable by Allied planes. His appeal for a couple of dozen of the new Heinkel He 177 long-range (1,375 miles radius) bombers collided ineffectually once again with Göring's intransigence.

All he got was a squadron of two dozen Junker Ju 88Cvi heavy fighters for inshore cover in the Bay; by the end of October, however, the "Bay Offensive" had dwindled to regular, small-scale patrols.

A series of hurricanes in December 1942 "limited" shipping losses in the North Atlantic to 262,000 tons out of a worldwide total of 349,000 (331,000 to submarines). But the final suppression of the U-boat threat still appeared to the Allies to be receding into the future at the end of a terrible year. Although monthly shipbuilding started to overtake losses in July, the result for the year as a whole was still a net decline in shipping stock of 750,000 tons, while in the war so far the U-boats had sunk 1,160 ships of 6,266,000 tons out of a global total of 7,791,000. Eighty-seven German and twenty-two Italian submarines had been destroyed, but the Germans had 393 on their books at the end of the year, 144 more than twelve months earlier; 212 were operational, eighty-four simultaneously in the Atlantic. The one good item of news for the Allies at this fraught time came on 14 December: naval Ultra was back. Before $U559$ (Hans Heidtmann) sank off Port Said in the Mediterranean, the British who had fatally wounded her managed to get aboard and snatch the latest German short-signal codebook, which helped Bletchley Park to break into the new cipher at last.

The Home Fleet resumed Russian convoys in mid-December under the new designation JW 51A and B. The latter section of a two-part convoy to Murmansk, sighted and reported by a U-boat, was attacked in a mighty gale by the heavy cruiser *Hipper*, pocket battleship *Lützow* and six destroyers in the Battle of the Barents Sea at the end of the month. At the cost of one minesweeper and one destroyer sunk and one destroyer and one merchant ship damaged, an inferior but skilfully handled British force of cruisers and escorts sank a German destroyer, damaged the *Hipper* and safely delivered all the freighters in the convoy. The *Hipper* took no further part in the war.

Nor, as a result of her botched foray, did Grand-Admiral Erich Raeder, Commander-in-Chief of the German Navy for fourteen years and now aged sixty-seven. He stood stony-faced on the carpet at Hitler's headquarters at Rastenburg in East Prussia on 6 January as the Führer indulged for ninety minutes in one of his contrived rages. It ended in an order to scrap all the remaining heavy ships. Raeder, denied the opportunity to defend himself, withdrew to write a memorandum arguing that such an act would present the enemy with a colossal naval victory free of charge. When this fell on blind eyes, Raeder resigned on 30 January. Considering his limited resources in 1939 and the interference from Hitler, which prevented him from making the best use of the surface fleet and the U-boats, Raeder's performance had been very sound. Even Hitler could not reject Raeder's recommendation for his own successor. His parting shot was: "Please protect the Navy and my successor against Göring." Raeder was convicted at Nuremberg and sentenced to life imprisonment but released on health grounds in 1955. He died in 1960.

The new *Oberbefehlshaber der Kriegsmarine* at the age of fifty-one was the freshly promoted Grand-Admiral Karl Dönitz – his reward for leading the most cost-effective branch of the entire Wehrmacht, the only arm still on the offensive and capable of a strategic victory. As so often happens when someone resigns on an issue of principle, the new incumbent won the case whose rejection had led to his predecessor's downfall. Dönitz managed to persuade Hitler that if he wanted the big ships' guns to be used for the defence of Norway, they might as well be delivered still attached to their hulls. The residual fleet remained in being. Dönitz retained direct command of submarines for the rest of the war, delegating day-to-day responsibility to the U-boat operational chief, Admiral Godt.

Back on some kind of form, Ultra warned the new-designation, all-tanker convoy TM 1 (Trinidad to Mediterranean) on 3 January 1943 that a pack styled *Delphin* (dolphin) of six U-boats was lying in wait between the Azores and Madeira for Torch traffic. As this was a military convoy it was keeping wireless silence. Commander R.C. Boyle in the destroyer HMS *Havelock*, leading escort group B5, decided to ignore an order to divert southwards after dark because he needed the calmer weather promised by his current course to refuel. This was a mistake, because *U514* (Hans-Jürgen Auffermann), on passage between the Cape Verde Islands and Trinidad, happened to sight TM 1 and report it. Meanwhile Ultra fell silent, as it was prone to do in the tussle with four-wheel Enigma even after the breakthrough, until the 9th. Auffermann's radio was playing up so he made a lone attack in the late evening and sank one of the nine tankers. In evading B5 he lost touch and earned a rebuke from headquarters, but Dönitz gambled that the target would not change course and left *Delphin* in place.

On 8 January the pack, now ten, made contact. First Günther Selbicke in *U436* and than Herbert Schneider in *U522* scored two hits each, laming four tankers. Commander Hans-Joachim Hesse in *U442* crippled a fifth. In the course of the 9th the Germans were able to return and finish off all five, reducing the convoy to three; *U436* and *U571* were damaged by the escort and withdrew. Fritz Schneewind in *U511* got an unexpected bonus on the 10th in the shape of an IRS which happened to be in the vicinity, which he sank. Schneider, aided by *U620* (Heinz

Stein), struck again and sank his third victim that night. Dönitz spurred on his eight undamaged boats to a first 100 per cent score against a convoy, but was thwarted by an RAF Sunderland flying-boat from Gibraltar, where the last two tankers arrived unharmed on the 14th. It was still a record: 55,000 tons of shipping, over 100,000 tons of oil and seventy-seven per cent of the vessels in a convoy destroyed.

Churchill and Roosevelt, meeting on the 14th at Casablanca, Morocco, to celebrate the success of Torch, once again gave the defeat of the U-boats top priority, delaying the invasion of north-west Europe which the Americans (and the plaintive Russians) wanted above all other things. More escorts (sixty-five) and end-to-end air cover were agreed. But General Dwight D. Eisenhower hung on to his two North African squadrons of VLR Liberator IIIs; the escort-carriers remained in the Mediterranean covering his forces; and Admiral King saw no need to divert planes from the Pacific, which was still his main preoccupation.

Ultra was working at about fifty per cent of its pre-fourth-wheel efficiency but the great circle route was abandoned in favour of the old ruse of diversion. This was not as effective as before because there were more convoys, and many more U-boats to spot them. Ultra was able to reveal that Dönitz was preparing a new and intense Atlantic onslaught: he opened a second command radio-channel to be able to orchestrate two wolf-pack attacks simultaneously.

Admiralty calculations late in 1942 showed that eighty per cent of ships lost in convoy were under Canadian escort. So when the RCN asked for fourteen extra destroyers, Horton sent British vessels to "stiffen" the Canadian groups; their captains, uncoincidentally, were senior to any Canadian officer present. Then three of the four Canadian groups were transferred to the less arduous Gibraltar run, leaving only C3, the most efficient, in the North Atlantic for the start of the decisive round. The rest returned at the end of March 1943, by which time the Greenland air gap had at last been closed. The British thus grabbed most of the glory; but Admiral Sir Percy Noble, C-in-C of Western Approaches in 1941–2 told the truth when he said, later in the war: "The Canadian Navy solved the problem of the Atlantic convoys."

Before the metaphorical storm there was a lull, caused largely by real storms in the Atlantic. In January 1943 the Allied shipping loss sank to its lowest level since November 1941 at 261,000 tons (203,000 tons to submarines). Just one North Atlantic convoy lost one ship, although the U-boats still found nineteen IRS to sink. Meanwhile the number of boats simultaneously operational in the crucial area passed the 100 mark. Dönitz was therefore able to assemble a pack of twenty against the eastbound SC 118 in the first week of February. The British escort group B2, led by Lieutenant-Commander Proudfoot was a scratch force of nine ships not yet worked into a team; but two American destroyers and a Coastguard cutter came from Iceland to help. The escort got its retaliation in first, by sinking U187, but the Germans sank two stragglers by the evening of the 6th, when the Americans arrived.

Commander Siegfried Baron von Forstner in U402 lived up to his Wagnerian name by sending six ships to the bottom in two remarkably dogged attacks that night, becoming an instant ace. Two more ships were sunk by others; the French corvette Lobelia sank U609 (Klaus Rudloff). Forstner kept up the pressure despite being forced to submerge no fewer than seven times by air patrols, sinking his seventh and last victim the next night and earning the Knight's Cross. An RAF Liberator from Londonderry sank U624 as she surfaced to report progress. The final score was thirteen ships sunk plus two stragglers, for three submarines sunk and two badly damaged, in a four-day struggle in which fifteen U-boats were detected and attacked.

The other great battle in February, when U-boat strength on station in the North Atlantic peaked at 120, centred on the westbound ON 166, rare for being escorted by the American-led group A3 under Captain Paul R. Heineman, USN, in the Coastguard cutter Spencer. This multinational but well-trained group included another US cutter and five corvettes, four Canadian and one British, and was nicknamed, in US Navy fashion, "Heineman's Harriers". A Polish destroyer joined later. There were sixty-three merchantmen in company. Seventeen U-boats lay in wait and the first victim in the battle was one of them, U225, depth-charged by Spencer. But the Germans soon got the upper hand and sank fourteen freighters over five days (21–25 February) in the air gap.

One more U-boat was sunk in uniquely bizarre circumstances: U606 (Lieutenant Hans Döhler) had helped to sink three merchantmen but was depth-charged by two escorts as she dived. The main hatch in the conning tower was not fully closed and the boat plunged to 750 feet as water poured in. When all the remaining compressed air aboard was used to blow the tanks, the boat shot to the surface and was quickly rammed by the cutter USS Campbell, which was so badly damaged that she had to be towed away. On the stricken submarine the first officer and the engineer appeared on deck clutching sparkling wine and German sausage, followed by ten crewmen who joined them in an eccentric picnic. As incredulous sailors on the decks of the approaching escorts watched, one of the sailors took the opportunity of slapping the face of the first officer, a hated disciplinarian. Thereupon all were flung into the water as the U-boat suddenly went down again, taking the other thirty-eight aboard, including the no less unpopular skipper, to the bottom. The slaphappy picnickers were rescued by the escorts. Continuing bad weather affected the performance of both sides, limiting the German haul in the North Atlantic to 289,000 tons out of a worldwide total of 403,000 (359,000 to submarines).

The climax of the Atlantic campaign came in the fortnight between 6 and 20 March 1943, in the form of a gigantic multiple struggle between four big, eastbound, laden convoys – SC 121, HX 228, SC 122 and HX 229 totalling 202 merchantmen – and six wolf-packs embracing a shifting collection of about forty U-boats. SC 121, broken up by a mighty storm, lost a quarter of its ships, thirteen in all, despite the best efforts of "Heineman's Harriers". No U-boat was caught despite frequent appearances by Allied aircraft from the 9th. HX 228 consisted of sixty ships and was subjected to a series of attacks from 10 to 14 March. The British group B3, supported by the new American A6 group, led by the first escort-carrier to take part in the Atlantic campaign, USS *Bogue*, kept losses down to four ships, plus one escort; the Germans forfeited two boats. The *Bogue* could not fly her planes in the appalling weather and had to take refuge in the middle of the convoy. The Germans relied entirely on the new FAT torpedoes but the thirteen U-boats taking part were unable to deliver an impressive score. Their fourth and last merchant victim was sunk by Lieutenant Albert Langfeld in *U444*. The boat was sighted by HMS *Harvester* (Commander A.A. Tait, RN, Senior Officer, Escort), rammed and sunk. The destroyer was so badly damaged that she presented an easy target to Hermann Eckhardt's *U432*, which sent her to the bottom with her captain. Next on the scene was the French corvette *Aconit* (Capitaine de corvette Levasseur). She dropped a pattern of depth-charges, forcing the submarine to the surface, then opened fire with her single four-inch gun and finished the job by ramming.

This double battle, involving many of the same U-boats, was a mere appetiser for the greatest convoy clash of the war, centred upon convoys SC 122 and HX 229, bound for Britain on the main route a week later. SC 122, consisting of fifty slower merchantmen, left New York on 5 March under the protection of B5 (Commander Boyle in *Havelock*, lately escort of the unlucky TM 1). Boyle was supported by one US destroyer, a British frigate, five British corvettes and a trawler. HX 229 left three days later with forty ships escorted by B4, minus its regular leader and temporarily led by Lieutenant-Commander G.J. Luther, RNVR, of the destroyer *Volunteer*, who was new both to the group and to convoy work. Three more destroyers and two corvettes were in company.

Two packs of eight and eighteen boats were sent to form a parallel line across the path of SC 122, while a third pack of eleven was mustered against HX 229. The B-dienst was working overtime, and very effectively, to plot the convoys and inform the boats via U-boat headquarters; but HX 229A, a supplementary convoy formed at the last minute to relieve pressure on New York harbour, caused confusion among German intelligence officers and the British OIC was able to divert it out of danger altogether. More confusion was caused by wolf-pack *Stürmer*, just formed with eighteen boats from earlier packs: the boat at one end made contact with SC 122 while the boat at the other reported HX 229. It took Dönitz's staff some hours to work out that the line was in touch with two separate enemy formations.

When this was clear, the boats on hand were reorganised and redistributed among three packs to tackle both convoys and their escorts simultaneously over the five days from the 16th to the 20th. So intense was this massive imbroglio, spread across hundreds of square miles of ocean, that several escorts had to withdraw temporarily for lack of fuel. In the end twenty-two of the ninety merchantmen in the two formations were sunk, an all-time record of 146,000 tons for one convoy action; one destroyer was sent to the bottom and the one trawler on hand foundered in bad weather. But of the thirty-eight boats which attacked SC 122 and HX 229, just one was sunk, by a Sunderland.

The Germans were publicly jubilant; the British were privately devastated. The Admiralty began to doubt the value of Ultra because it was more difficult to divert shipping out of trouble with so many U-boats at sea. Some staff officers reverted to the perennial heresy of opposition to convoy, because no less than two-thirds of all losses in March had been in or near convoys (seventy-two out of 108). IRS losses fell to twenty-two; but that represented seventy-nine per cent of the twenty-eight which had set sail alone, whereas convoy losses amounted to four per cent of 1,800 ships, proportionally only one eighteenth of the IRS loss-rate. The U-boats still preferred lone ships. The other losses were rompers or stragglers separated from their convoys.

If things were therefore not as bad as they seemed to innumerate British admirals, they were rather worse than they seemed for the apparently victorious Germans. The trained minds at OIC thought they could discern, from the unprecedented mass of wireless traffic generated by the March convoy battles, a new note of irresolution among submarine skippers – and one of desperation at their headquarters. The U-boats could have inflicted even more damage in the last phase of their onslaught; but it was the stream of complaints about interference by enemy aircraft that caused U-boat command to call off the operation. This intrusion had been achieved by aircraft flying at the very limit of their range, in weather so poor that the escort-carrier on hand could not operate her planes at all.

But the Allied problem was solved at last, even as the crisis of the battle loomed. The most vital convoy conference of the war opened in Washington on 1 March on as discordant a note as it is possible to imagine: Admiral King announced his intention of withdrawing residual American ships from the main, northerly transatlantic route to the more southerly ones. His sop to the British was the escort-carrier *Bogue's* support group, to supplement the five such teams being formed by the British as a "fire brigade" to help convoys under attack. The Canadians were at last to have their own supreme command: Admiral L.W. Murray, RCN, as Commander-in-Chief, Canadian North-West Atlantic, from May. The conference also agreed to supply the RCAF with its first twenty VLR Liberators for the air gap.

King and the US Army still refused to transfer such planes from the Pacific or North Africa; Bomber Command was no less stubborn. It took a direct order from Roosevelt towards the end of March, backed by an unenthusiastic Churchill, to break the logjam in the airmen's minds. The American Navy would provide sixty Liberators for the North Atlantic and the Army Air Force seventy-five; the RAF would divert 120 from the bombing of Germany. Bomber Harris reacted as if his command were being demobilised, but the air gap was sealed at last, and with it the outcome of the second U-boat campaign in the Atlantic as well as the war as a whole. When the decision to close it was finally taken, the immediate need was for Liberators in Newfoundland until the Canadians were ready to operate theirs. Coastal Command had only twenty-three in operation while King controlled 112, mostly in the Pacific with a few in the Caribbean. Like the British, the American Navy had acquired operational control of Air Force ASW aircraft (in June 1942). King insisted that the Army Air Force should close the air gap. The unit which tipped the balance in the Battle of the Atlantic was therefore No 6 Antisubmarine Squadron, USAAF, which started flying from Newfoundland in April.

The Allies lost 693,000 tons of shipping in March 1943, of which 627,000 tons were sunk by the U-boats (their second-best month ever after the peak of the previous November) and 476,000 in the North Atlantic. In the last five months of 1942 fifty-one U-boats, or about half the new production, were sunk by Allied ships and planes; in the first quarter of

1943, thirty-five were destroyed. On 26 February Dönitz persuaded Hitler to keep the big ships intact and to allow him to demobilise 40,000 skilled workers from the Wehrmacht to step up the submarine construction programme. He extracted a promise of air support which Göring had no intention of honouring, and concluded a private arrangement with Albert Speer, the Minister for Armaments, to ensure continuous supplies of raw materials for the submarine programme.

So sharply did convoy sightings fall away after November 1942 that Dönitz once again suspected a leak. Vice-Admiral Erhard Maertens, then chief of the B-dienst, whose decrypts of diversion signals showed the Allies knew where the U-boats were, was ordered to mount an enquiry as security was tightened even further. In the end the Germans concluded that the Allies had a super-sensitive detection device, probably a new radar. In February 1943 a British bomber shot down over Rotterdam yielded an intact H2S centimetric radar set, which the Germans rightly guessed would be in use at sea in a maritime version. New detectors – first *Naxos*, then *Hagenuk* – were developed to sense it; the latter device gave no detectable emissions of its own, unlike *Naxos* or *Metox*.

The next pair of homeward-bound convoys, SC 123, and HX 230 at the end of March, were almost eerily quiet. The *Bogue* support group covered them both in the air gap and only one straggler was sunk. The reinforcements from the Home Fleet, now that Russian convoys were suspended, formed Britain's five new support groups, one of which was centred on Britain's first escort-carrier, HMS *Biter*. April was as quiet for both sides as the last ten days of March. Fifteen U-boats and thirty-nine merchantmen totalling 235,000 tons were sunk in the North Atlantic out of a worldwide total of 345,000 tons (328,000 to submarines). Bad weather had much to do with these results. Dönitz also tried his favourite diversion, a switch of attention to the mid-ocean African routes. TS 37 (Takoradi, Gold Coast – now Ghana – to Sierra Leone) was sighted by Werner Henke in *U515*, who gave himself away by reporting it. The escort was weak – one corvette and three trawlers – and asked a passing RAF patrol by signal lamp (evading counter-eavesdropping by the U-boat) to fetch help. Three destroyers came down from Freetown, but by then Henke had sunk seven ships unsupported in the night of 30 April–1 May. He set a record by sinking five of them in five minutes.

The largest wolf-pack ever assembled, *Fink* (finch), of forty submarines, lay in wait in two long lines for the forty-three ships of eastbound ONS 5 at the end of April, in atrocious weather south of Greenland. The first ship was sunk on the 29th and the first U-boat on

4 May; that night seven more ships were lost, but the escorts damaged and drove off seven submarines and sank one. On the 5th the Germans made no score but the escorts sank one U-boat in the evening. Overnight three more ships and two U-boats went to the bottom. When a support group arrived to help, the sixth and last U-boat of the battle was destroyed. This gave a final account of one submarine sunk for every two merchantmen; three more submarines had been lost in the area, one to an air patrol and two in a collision during one of the mass attacks. This was a clear victory for the defenders. When the surviving U-boats and others moved south against SC 129 and HX 239 they lost three of their number in exchange for three merchantmen.

Also in May, SC 130, covered by Commander Peter Gretton's B7 escort group, backed by the first of the new support groups, became a triumphal procession. Gretton, one of the best escort commanders, told the commodore of the forty-five freighters, Captain Forsythe, that he did not wish to be delayed as he had an important appointment to keep – his wedding. Forsythe said he had an engagement only slightly less important – a round of golf on the same day – and would do his best to press on. The escorts sank five submarines from four different packs, including *U954*, in which Sub-Lieutenant Peter Dönitz, aged twenty, younger son of the C-in-C, went down with all his comrades. The convoy arrived on time without a scratch and its two commanders kept their appointments. All four other convoys against which Dönitz assembled packs during May completed their crossings unscathed, although the Germans lost six more boats in vain attacks on them.

The position in the Atlantic had been transformed out of all recognition in less than eight weeks, thanks to the first VLR Liberators and escort-carriers appearing in the air gap. The statistics sum it up clearly: the Germans forfeited thirty-eight U-boats to enemy action in May 1943 alone (five more were lost in accidents); Allied shipping losses fell to 299,000 tons in May worldwide (164,000 in the North Atlantic out of 265,000 to submarines). The operational U-boat fleet meanwhile reached its peak strength of 240 on 1 April; it was to fall back to 207 in only three months. The closure of the air gap was accompanied in April by a renewal of the Bay Offensive with the much deadlier centimetric radar. The sea-change in the strategic position in the Atlantic was clear beyond doubt to both sides by the end of May. Karl Dönitz signalled to his captains at sea:

The struggle for our victory, becoming ever more hard and bitter, leads me to reveal to you in all clarity the seriousness of our situation at this moment and of our future ... Only you can fight the enemy offensively and beat him. The

German nation has long felt that our arm is the sharpest and most decisive and that the outcome of the war depends on the success or failure of the Battle of the Atlantic.

At the same time Max Horton signalled to all escorts:

In the last two months the Battle of the Atlantic has undergone a decisive change in our favour ... All escort groups, support groups, escort-carriers and their machines as well as the aircraft from the various air commands have contributed to this great success ... The climax of the battle has been sur-mounted.

On 24 May 1943 the U-boat Command withdrew its boats from the North Atlantic to the "Black Pit" south of the Azores. A few remained on patrol in the otherwise abandoned waters to send out artificial radio traffic from ghost flotillas, making sure that the Allied escort effort could not relax. As far as Dönitz was concerned the withdrawal was temporary. A Germany which had already flown the world's first jet aircraft (Me262), the first ballistic missile (V2) and the first cruise missile (V1) by Christmas 1942 could hardly be written off.

Nor could the U-boat service, however much it was now on the defensive. The Allies exploited Ultra to detect and destroy the ten milch-cows in service. The new US Tenth Fleet, a purely administrative organisation created by Admiral King to run the American ASW effort in the Atlantic, deployed escort-carriers against them while British Coastal Command and Johnnie Walker's group worked in tandem to find and sink them on the strength of Bletchley's decryptions. In June and July the Germans lost fifty-four boats, forty-four to aircraft and six on one day (30 July). The Bay Offensive had reached its peak, along with Allied sinkings of six milch-cows and attacks on a pack of ten type IXDs (*Monsun*) en route to wage war on shipping in the Indian Ocean. On 20 July Dönitz was still telling his captains to "stay up and fight" in the Bay; he had *U441* (Götz von Hartmann) fitted with eight rapid-fire anti-aircraft guns and a high-angle semi-automatic cannon as a "trap" for Allied planes.

They dealt with it by concentrating against the flak-boat and killing half the crew before a rare flight of Ju 88s arrived to drive the British off, enabling the battered boat to limp back to base. On 2 August Dönitz abandoned "stay up and fight". He was also forced to use type IX operational boats to supply type VIIs stranded far from home by the loss of the milch-cows. Three of these were soon caught in the act of refuelling; one more purpose-built milch-cow was sunk by the British

and two damaged, leaving just one operational at the end of August. By
June 1944 there was only one type XIV left – in the Indian Ocean. It
never came back.

Professor Hellmuth Walter had produced a small experimental submarine as early as 1940, capable of the fantastic speed of twenty-three
knots underwater, where it was partly powered by hydrogen peroxide.
Technical difficulties proved insurmountable; but a compromise design
led to a new generation of *Elektro-U-boote*, on which serious work
began with Hitler's blessing in September 1942.

The Type XXI was the ocean-going version, displacing 1,621/1,819
tons and capable of 15.6 knots surfaced but 17.2 submerged. It had six
twenty-one-inch torpedo tubes and twenty-three torpedoes, relying on
large banks of the latest lightweight batteries and a revolutionary
rounded hull, derived from the shape of the big sea-mammals, for its
high maximum submerged speed. Its range underwater was a remarkable 285 miles at six knots. The type XXIII was the coastal model,
displacing 234/258 tons and capable of 9.7 knots surfaced but 12.5
submerged (range 175 miles at four knots). Every submarine designed
after the Second World War copied Walter's hydrodynamic borrowings
from whales and dolphins.

Meanwhile the old VIIC warhorse was given a last lease of precarious
life by a device which now demanded attention, although it had literally
been lying around unused since 1927. Its Dutch inventor, *Kaptein-
luitenant* J.J. Wichers, called it a *snuiver* (sniffer). It was a rigid double
tube of two concentric pipes, one inside the other, about the same length
as a periscope, which folded down into a recess on deck when not in
use. At the top was a cap containing a valve which closed the tube
automatically underwater. When the Germans occupied the main Royal
Netherlands Navy base at Den Helder in north-west Holland in May
1940, they found two almost complete submarines fitted with this device.
Four operational *snuiver*-boats had gone to England. The German and
British navies took no notice of this invention at the time; but in 1943
necessity prompted an unknown German staff officer to remember it.

The principle was simple: when vertical, the inner pipe expelled
exhaust from the diesels while the outer pipe sucked in air. This meant
that the submarine could run underwater at periscope depth on its
diesels. Batteries could also be charged underwater by the same method.
The cap of the *Schnorchel* (snorter), as the Germans called it, was too
small to be detected by metric or centimetric radar and more likely to
be spotted in daylight by its exhaust-trail than its own minimal bulk. It
was an obvious means of increasing the survivability of types VII

and IX. The device brought the conventionally powered, submersible torpedo-boat as close to being a real submarine as possible. Allied sailors succumbed to "schnorkelitis" when the device became known – an affliction very similar to the "periscopitis" of the First World War – leading to many false alarms and much waste of ammunition.

Other difficulties experienced by the Germans, until they got used to the schnorkel, included noise. Running the diesels underwater made the boat deaf, so they were switched off three times an hour to enable the hydrophone operators to listen for ships' engines. But one engine could be used to drive the boat while the other charged the batteries. Three hours' schnorkelling made possible an entire day's silent slow running on accumulated battery power. The schnorkel could also be used to air the boat without surfacing (consummate skill was needed for this risky procedure): the valve would be closed briefly with the diesels running, which would rapidly reduce the air pressure inside the hull; when the valve was reopened, fresh air would be sucked in at once. Overlong closure would cause the crew to gasp for breath and their eyes to bulge. It is suspected that at least two U-boats were lost to faulty or mishandled schnorkels.

Their development and installation was coordinated by a group of scientists brought together by Dönitz in summer 1943 to review all technical aspects of the now faltering U-boat campaign. Hitler's confidence in *Blitzkrieg* had led him to ban all long-term research as superfluous early in the war, and the fact that Göring was nominally responsible for scientific research did nothing for the flow of new ideas. So the U-boats had to wait until 1944 for their Gema eighty-centimetre radar sets. *Hohentwiel* was adapted from a Luftwaffe radar; its forty-three-centimetre wavelength enabled it to detect planes at six miles. The Germans almost superstitiously blamed radar for increasing Allied detection of U-boats even at vast distances (radar to this day cannot see over the horizon). In August 1943 a captured RAF pilot did his bit for disinformation by solemnly confirming that the British could pick up emissions from German *Metox* radar-detectors at ninety miles, and therefore hardly ever had to use their own radars. On 14 August the use of *Metox* was banned. *New Wanze* (bug) detectors began to be fitted instead from the same month; their emissions were low. The *Naxos* detector was the first to pick up Allied centimetric emissions; this was succeeded by the *Fliege* (fly) in 1944, and later in the year by the *Mücke* (gnat), which could detect the latest three-centimetre radar. Thus was the infant sub-science of "electronic counter-measures", which began with radio-jamming before the First World War, taken several steps forward in a matter of months.

The acoustic torpedo, for use mainly against warships, was issued in the technologically significant month of August 1943. Henceforward U-boats went to sea with three types of missile: the acoustic for escorts plus the G7e electrical and the FAT "curly" for merchantmen. Also supplied to submarines at this experimental time was the *Aphrodite*, essentially an outsize condom (hence the name?) festooned with metal foil, to be released filled with gas as a decoy for Allied detection devices; it was soon succeeded by a more sophisticated version called *Thetis* (a large stockpile of these, as well as of conventional condoms, was found on a U-boat salvaged in the Kattegat in 1993). A *Pillenwerfer* (pill-thrower) was fitted to U-boats to release the *Bold* gas-bubble which was intended, not very successfully, to mislead Allied sonars. *Alberich* was also introduced to the same end – a rubber coating for submarines intended to absorb Asdic (the Japanese tried the same idea against radar) – an early foray into today's "stealth" technology which came too late in 1944 to make much difference.

The Allies however were ready for acoustic torpedoes because Ultra interceptions misled them into thinking that the FAT was such a device. The British and Americans immediately started work on Fido, their own version, introduced at sea at about the same time. The Americans invented the Foxer, a simple noisemaker towed by a warship to distract the acoustic *Zaunkönig* torpedo. The British came up with the Squid, a mortar which fired three full-sized depth-charges at a time ahead of a ship (the Hedgehog fired much smaller charges) while the Americans perfected their MAD (magnetic-anomaly detector). Catalinas fitted with it, known as Madcats, also carried backward-firing air-to-surface rockets so that they lost no time by having to circle for an attack on a target found by MAD. Both sides were using forward-firing, air-to-surface rockets at sea.

The most important of all these inventions was undoubtedly the schnorkel, which all but restored to the U-boat the invisibility taken from it by Allied airborne radar. It was not enough to turn the tables; but it sustained the residual U-boat threat sufficiently to tie down massive fleets of ASW escorts until the end of the war. Another few months of war in Europe could well have seen scores of "electro-boats" running rings round the escorts, making a huge new Allied outlay on fast warships and advanced technology necessary, and raising the possibility of using the atomic bomb to extirpate a revitalised U-boat campaign. It was probably fortunate for Germany, therefore, that the Allied air forces delayed, and their armies stopped, construction of the new boats before more than a handful had been sent to sea, while Ultra shortened the European war by an unquantifiable but clearly significant period. The best efforts of Hellmuth Walter, Karl Dönitz and Albert Speer made it a very close-run thing indeed. It is ironic to reflect that "Bomber" Harris and his American contemporary, General Carl Spaatz, may have achieved enough in the end to save the German ports from a fate even worse than relentless bombardment by high explosive.

Perhaps the most symbolic statistic of 1943 affecting the U-boat campaign was recorded at the end of October, when the total tonnage of new construction passed the total of Allied shipping sunk worldwide in four years of war. It would have taken a large number of new-generation U-boats to affect this strategic advantage.

The Home Fleet's main headache remained the "fleet in being" represented by the *Tirpitz*, lurking in her northern fastness of Altenfjord, and her companions, including the *Scharnhorst* and the *Lützow*. The British decided to eliminate this threat by stealth, and developed the "X-craft" midget submarine for the purpose. The battleship was completely immobilised in September 1943 for six months, with her three main engines knocked out. Hitler was furious; the Germans were left with just one capital ship in Norway, the *Scharnhorst*; and the Home Fleet could take a more relaxed view of the imminent renewal of Russian convoys. RAF Lancaster bombers armed with the six-ton Tallboy bomb sank the *Tirpitz* near Tromsø on 15 November 1944. The *Lützow* had been recalled to Germany in September 1943. The untroubled resumption of the Russian convoys at the beginning of November 1943 tempted the *Scharnhorst* and her five destroyers to sea at Christmas. Superior covering forces from the Home Fleet, commanded by Admiral Sir Bruce Fraser since May, cornered her near convoy JW 55B. She and the battleship *Duke of York* then fought the last big-gun engagement in the history of either Navy; the German battlecruiser slowly sank with the loss of all but thirty-six of her crew.

The performance of the U-boats plunged into a trough in August 1943, when they sank a mere four ships in the Atlantic totalling 26,000 tons (two each in north and south) and one craft of nineteen tons in British waters. Sinkings in the Mediterranean and Indian Ocean took the worldwide total to 120,000 tons. At the end of the month Dönitz assembled twenty-eight boats and a milch-cow from France, Norway and Germany into a pack hopefully named *Leuthen* (Frederick the Great's victory in the Seven Years' War) to go after the convoys again. By 18 September it lay across the tracks of convoys ONS 18 (slow) and ON 202.

On the 19th, when a Canadian Liberator sank *U341*, OIC combined the two into one convoy of sixty-six. But early on the 20th Paul-

Friedrich Otto in *U270* fired a *Zaunkönig* in combat for the first time and blew off the stern of the frigate HMS *Lagan*. Later in the day a Coastal Command torpedo-bomber dropped the first operational Fido and sank *U338* (Manfred Kinzel), a leader in the great battle of SC 122 and HX 229. The end of bad weather brought Allied air reinforcements on the 24th and the Germans withdrew, having sunk six merchant ships and three escorts, and badly damaging a fourth, for the loss of three boats. In six autumn weeks twenty-three U-boats were sunk by planes and on 16 November Dönitz ordered the second retreat from the North Atlantic in six months.

Since the earlier withdrawal, no more type VIIs or IXs had been ordered as the Germans impatiently awaited the new submarines. At the same time the British at last deduced that their naval cipher number three must have been broken and in June 1943 introduced number five, which was never penetrated. The U-boats withdrew to the Western Approaches and the Gibraltar area. But history did not repeat itself. Now a reluctant Göring allowed long-range He 177s to scout for targets for the U-boats. But this was in the teeth of Allied air superiority; and the pilots had no experience of maritime work. The U-boats submerged to crawl to and from operational areas along the coast of the Bay, surfacing only in neutral Spanish waters.

In January 1944 Dönitz assembled twenty-two boats west of Ireland. Six were sunk in a *tour de force* by Johnnie Walker's 2nd Escort Group of five sloops. The last was *U264* (Hartwig Looks), the first U-boat to take a schnorkel on a war patrol. He and his crew were rescued and profitably interrogated. So were the scientists and technicians saved from the wreck of *U406*, destroyed by the 10th Escort Group; they had gone to sea to test the latest radar detectors. The Germans' only consolation prizes for the loss of eleven boats, or fifty per cent, were the destruction of two RAF planes and a hit by *U256* (Lieutenant Wilhelm Brauel) with a *Zaunkönig* on the stern of one of Walker's sloops, HMS *Woodpecker*, which later sank under tow with no loss of life. When Walker returned to Liverpool at the end of February his ships were given a triumphal welcome.

The last big pack was given the portentous name of *Preussen* – Prussia – sixteen boats gathered west of Ireland at the end of February. By 22 March seven of them had been sunk for the loss of a sloop and a corvette as the convoys sailed to and fro unharmed. This harsh attrition was marked by two exceptional displays of high morale by the Germans. Three sloops of the 1st Escort Group hunted one U-boat – Rolf Manke's *U358* – for thirty-eight hours, a record for the entire war. Even so, after thirty-seven hours underwater, the boat managed to sink one of her tormentors, HMS *Gould*. It was only when *U358* was at last forced to come up for air an hour later that the other two sank her. When an RCAF Sunderland attacked *U625* on 10 March, her captain, Hans Benker, decided to "stay up and fight". The Canadians forced him to dive by gunfire and then dropped depth-charges. To their amazement the boat surfaced again and dashingly signalled by lamp, in English, "Fine bombing", before going down for the last time. A few men jumped clear but were never found. On 22 March Dönitz ordered another withdrawal, from the eastern Atlantic and the now hopeless campaign against the convoys. The score for the first quarter of 1944 was thirty-six submarines lost in the Atlantic and three merchantmen sunk out of 3,360 convoyed. By May there were just two U-boats in the North Atlantic, to provide weather reports as the Germans awaited the Allied invasion of France. The Canadians now called the once lethal North Atlantic convoy route "the milk-run".

The packs were beaten but individual boats did not give up. West of the Cape Verde Islands the Americans sank one of the last milch-cows, *U488*, on 26 April. Her would-be client, *U66* (Lieutenant Gerhard Seehausen), got away but was found on 6 May by the destroyer USS *Buckley*. An unequal gunfight ensued and the Americans rammed the submarine in the stern, setting it on fire. As the crew leapt aboard the destroyer to save themselves, Commander Abel, the American captain, gave the time-honoured but almost extinct order, "Prepare to repel boarders", and a desperate hand-to-hand struggle followed. Thirty-six Germans survived.

One of the ships which had hunted *U66* was the escort-carrier USS *Block Island*, 8,600 tons, and her group. One of her planes detected *U549* (Detlev Krankenhagen) and another hunt began. Perhaps driven to distraction by the relentless pinging of the sonars and the blast of the depth-charges all through the night, Krankenhagen decided to defy the huge odds against him by firing two acoustic and three electric torpedoes at his pursuers on the morning of 29 May. The latter all hit the *Block Island*, which sank very quickly. One *Zaunkönig* seriously damaged the destroyer USS *Barr* while the other missed. The rest of the group sank *U549* by depth-charge.

The battered group was replaced by Captain Daniel Gallery, USN, in the escort-carrier *Guadalcanal* with destroyers. His crew called him Captain Ahab because of his ambition to capture a U-boat and bring it home, a task for which he obsessively trained his men. When *U505*, a type IXC commanded by Lieutenant Harald Lange, was detected in the Azores area, the American sailors dubbed it Moby Dick and the chase was on. Gallery's destroyers located the boat by sonar, forced it to the surface by judicious depth-charging, sent a boarding party and captured the boat intact. It now stands outside the Museum of Science and Industry in Chicago.

After D-Day in Normandy on 6 June 1944, on which the scattered U-boats made almost no impression, the schnorkel came into general use and Dönitz restricted most of his boats to the relatively shallow waters round Britain. The wheel had turned full circle and the U-boats were back in the waters where they had scored their earliest successes. There they could evade Asdic by lying on the wreck-strewn bottom for twenty-four hours or more, after a few hours of schnorkel operation to clear the air and charge batteries. The new stealth also starved Bletchley Park of intercepts and reduced the value of HF/DF.

Ultra had misleadingly revealed a stream of early complaints about the schnorkel; Allied intelligence did not pick up the more favourable reports written by captains on their return to base. The schnorkel was therefore underestimated by the Allies. Nine days after D-Day, three schnorkel boats (*U621*, *U764* and *U767*) stole into the Channel, sank an American landing ship and two British warships and got away, despite the enormous invasion armada still in place. U-boats got to Guernsey in the German-occupied British Channel Islands on 21 June. On the 25th Lieutenant Heinz Sieder in *U984* damaged a frigate, evaded detection for four days and then scored four crippling hits on separate American supply-ships a few miles from Portsmouth, home of the Royal Navy, using his schnorkel to escape.

Ernst Cordes in *U763* was able to avoid the consequences of a unique error: he sank a freighter on 5 July, fired five torpedoes at a military convoy and missed, but escaped a massive hunt to take refuge at what he initially thought was the Channel Island of Alderney. It was in fact Spithead Bay near Portsmouth. His schnorkel saved him as he crept out to sea, firing a torpedo at a passing destroyer (it missed) before docking undamaged at Brest on 14 July. His War Diary reveals how unpleasant life on a U-boat had become:

It is nearly thirty hours since the boat was last aired. The first cases of vomiting occur and I issue each man with a potash cartridge [air-filter from an escape-hood]. Breathing becomes distressed. The enemy search group is still active . . . during the thirty hours of pursuit, 252 depth-charges were counted in the near vicinity, sixty-one at medium range and fifty-one at long range.

Even the U-boat men noticed the unspeakable stench created by these long periods of submersion, relieved in high summer only by furtive schnorkel sessions in the few hours of true darkness available. Natural and man-made waste had to be kept aboard for disposal via a torpedo tube when the opportunity arose. By August 1944 Allied bombing had become so intense that the U-boats found it difficult to operate even from their bomb-proof pens in France. Dönitz therefore ordered another withdrawal, to Norway, submerged and via the waters west of the British Isles, after four years in France. Between D-Day and this last retreat the U-boats had sunk five warships, twelve merchantmen and four landing-craft at a cost of twenty of their number. The latter total exactly matched the personal score of Johnnie Walker, who died suddenly ashore at the end of July from a stroke, at forty-eight. His obsequies in Liverpool were like a state funeral.

From Norway the U-boats doggedly returned to haunt British waters. Western Approaches was rocked by *U482*'s destructive patrol over the end of August and the beginning of September: Hartmut Count von Matuschka sank a corvette and four merchantmen from a convoy in the North-Western Approaches on the very doorstep of Liverpool. He sailed 2,500 miles out of 2,729 underwater and got back to Trondheim in Norway unharmed. Shortly afterwards Lieutenant R. Stollmann completed fifty days submerged (but achieved nothing else during his ordeal). In September the Allies sank only two U-boats and damaged two. In November shipping losses briefly surged upwards again, for the last time, to 135,000 tons – 86,000 in British waters, 59,000 to submarines. Vigilance was still essential: *U486* (Reserve-Lieutenant Gerhard Meyer) sank the American transport *Leopoldville* with the loss of 819 troops in the Channel on Christmas Eve. In the last four months of 1944 U-boats sank sixteen ships in British waters. Even in the last full month of the European war, April 1945, 73,000 tons were sunk by U-boat.

A jarring note amid Allied anticipation of the defeat of Hitler's Germany at New Year 1945 was sounded by A.V. Alexander, First Lord of the Admiralty. The schnorkel had made the U-boats very hard to find, he said; and he warned of the new generation of U-boats to come. American penetration of Japanese diplomatic cipher ("Purple") had extracted, from reports to Tokyo by the embassy in Berlin, the contribution expected from the new boats. Despite prefabricated construction inland as well as at the coast, the programme was seriously disrupted by Allied bombing of factories, canals and ports.

On 25 February Lieutenant Fridtjof Heckel was at sea in *U2322* off eastern Scotland when he sighted the modest British cargo ship *Engholm*, 1,317 tons, and sank her. His boat, a coastal type XXIII, was the first "electro-boat" to claim a victim. Warships in the vicinity gave chase but were startled by the boat's swift underwater escape.

In March Dönitz scraped together half a dozen type VIIC boats with schnorkels for a last pack, *Seewolf*, and sent it to the United States east coast. As Ultra picked up the reprise of messages from a bygone era and HF/DF tracked the boats' progress, there was panic in America. German agents spread false rumours that they were carrying V2 rockets such as had recently rained down on London. The US Navy assembled four escort-carrier groups with twenty destroyers and sank four U-boats, at a cost of one destroyer sunk and another damaged; the other two escaped, to surrender after the war.

On 30 April Hitler killed himself, having named Dönitz as his successor – the apotheosis of the U-boat chief whose submarines had inflicted more material damage on the Allied cause than any other arm of the Wehrmacht. Collectively they represented the second most cost-effective force ever deployed in the history of warfare (the most effective being the much smaller U-boat fleet of the First World War, which destroyed nearly as much shipping).

On the same day *U2511* left Bergen in Norway for a last raid on the Caribbean. Commander Adalbert Schnee, ace holder of the Knight's Cross with oak leaves, was trying out his third command, the first of only two type XXIs to go to sea before the war ended. Off the north of Scotland on 2 May he was detected by British ships but led them a merry dance as he swept away at high speed underwater. On 4 May he picked up the news of the German surrender in north-west Europe and the accompanying order to cease fire. At the time he had a British cruiser in his sights. He made a dummy attack and fled undetected.

On 7 May 1945 a Catalina of Coastal Command sank *U320* between the Shetland Isles and Norway. It was the last "kill" of the war in Europe. But the last shot in the Battle of the Atlantic, the central campaign of the entire conflict, was fired by *Kapitänleutnant* Heinrich Schroeteler, commanding *U1023*, a type VIIC with schnorkel, at the Norwegian minesweeper *NYMS 382*, which sank. It was 7.52 p.m. on 7 May 1945, the last full day of war with Germany. Schroeteler had been underwater and missed the 4 May order to cease fire. So had his colleague, Lieutenant Emil Klusmeier in *U2336*, a new type XXIII, who sank two small tramp steamers off the Firth of Forth, probably a little earlier on the same day.

Before ending the history of submarines in the Second World War with a summary of the main struggle, we have the worst marine casualty on record to consider. That too was the work of a submarine, a Soviet boat, in the last months of the war in Europe.

The Soviet submarine arm achieved even less in the Second World War than in 1914–17, partly because it was in thrall to the Red Army and was used defensively, partly because its opportunities were even more severely restricted in narrow Black Sea, sub-Arctic and Baltic waters. The Germans and their reluctant allies, the Finns, for example, were ensconced on both sides of the Gulf of Finland almost from the beginning.

The Pacific Fleet was inactive but never encompassed less than half of Soviet naval strength (as insurance against Japan); it sent vessels to reinforce the other fleets. Although the fighting round the Soviet shores of the Black Sea was as fierce as round the Baltic, very little has emerged about Soviet submarine activity there. The movements of two "brigades" of boats (forty-four submarines were present, though probably only one in four was operational, in the Black Sea in June 1941) were governed by Army needs as usual. The Germans could avail themselves of the small, allied Romanian Navy, but their armies dominated the Soviet Black Sea coast for much of the war. The Russians seldom had more than one submarine at sea at a time in 1941–2 and none at all on two days out of three. The Germans counted eleven merchantmen sunk but claimed to have destroyed ten submarines in 1942. At the end of the war the Soviets claimed 217 vessels of 317,522 tons sunk, of which submarines got seventy-two (105,000 tons); but they probably lost twenty-eight boats in the Black Sea.

The small Northern Fleet was founded in 1933 and in 1941 included a "brigade" of fifteen submarines in three divisions (three "K" class, six "Shch" and six "Malodki" coastals). They seldom strayed far from home, insofar as they went to sea at all in the early days. The Russians claimed forty-five merchant ships (45,000 tons) sunk in 1942, but the Germans counted half that. The Northern Fleet lost nine submarines in that year. The Russians claimed to have sunk 120,000 tons of German shipping by mine, plane and submarine and conceded German sinkings of Allied shipping totalling 184,475 tons in northern waters in 1943–4. The British sent three small "U" class boats to help out in 1944; one of them was lost on the way north.

In the Baltic the Russians claimed that thirty-five submarines (out of an initial total on paper of sixty-five) sank forty merchantmen and a few small warships. The Germans, also on the defensive in Baltic waters, claimed to have sunk twenty-six merchantmen totalling 52,500 tons and damaged eight (34,000 tons), for the loss of ten U-boats and seven more damaged. They also reported 1,738 mercantile sailings (over five million tons). So limited was the Soviet submarine threat that the Germans seldom felt the need for convoys. Overall, the Soviet submarine service probably started the war with 218 boats, added another fifty-four, lost 109 and sank 160 merchant ships totalling 402,437 tons.

Of the latter, 25,484 tons were represented by a single vessel, the *Wilhelm Gustloff*, built as a cruise ship but in January 1945 pressed into service as a refugee transport for Germans fleeing the Red Army's advance. Dönitz flung every vessel he could find into this vast evacuation, Operation Hannibal, from liners to U-boats, and between 23 January and 8 May 1945 brought 2,022,602 across the Baltic to west German ports. On 30 January at Gotenhafen (now Polish Gdynia) the *Gustloff* crammed about 8,000 people aboard including submariners, troops, wounded men and civilian refugees. This represented more than four times her maximum peacetime load. The big liner, converted into a hospital ship in 1939, had spent the war in harbour, serving as a barracks for the U-boat crews under training in Gotenhafen.

Even with all this extra traffic, the twenty-four active submarines of the Soviet Baltic Fleet carried out only twenty-seven patrols between 1 January and 8 May 1945. One of them was *S13* (Commander Alexander Marinesko), a "Stalinetz" class boat which had won the Red Banner for sinking two transports. Marinesko sighted the *Gustloff* soon after she had left Gotenhafen, and hit her with three torpedoes. Because nobody knew how many had boarded her, nobody knows how many went down with her. Fewer than 1,000 were rescued; 6,050 had been counted on, but some 2,000 more may have scrambled aboard in the chaos before she sailed. The dead therefore numbered about 7,000: nearly six *Lusitania* disasters, nearly five *Titanics* in one catastrophe, the worst in the history of shipping. It was done by a lone submarine, first cousin of the type VII U-boat, designed by the German engineers of IvS.

For the second Atlantic campaign and its offshoots, Germany constructed 1,162 U-boats, of which 830 went to war; 784 were lost, 696 to enemy action; 226 were scuttled and 156 surrendered. Two fled to Argentina. The rest were seized by the Allies and destroyed or shared out. Of the 40,900 men who served in Hitler's U-boats 25,870 died (sixty-three per cent).

The Allies lost 2,828 ships of their own or hired from neutrals, a total of 14,687,231 tons, to submarines, two-thirds of all Allied shipping losses worldwide; 2,452 vessels totalling 12.8 million tons were lost in the Atlantic. So were 175 warships, mostly British. The British Merchant Navy lost 30,248 men, the Royal Navy 73,642 (both mostly in the Atlantic). Coastal Command lost 5,866 men and 1,777 planes. The Royal Canadian Navy lost 1,965 men.

Japan lost 130 submarines, Italy eighty-five, Britain seventy-five and the United States fifty-two. The US Navy started the war with 111 boats and added 177. Some 16,000 American submariners went on war patrol, of whom twenty-two per cent or under 4,000 were killed. None the less this was the highest percentage in any major branch of the United States forces. American submarines sank twenty-three ships for every boat lost (the British were second with 9.3:1; the Germans managed 20.5 before August 1942 but only 1.7 thereafter, for a wartime average of 3.6. The Soviet ratio was 1.5).

EPILOGUE: AFTER 1945

The Nuclear Age

On 14 May 1945, six days after the unconditional surrender of the Reich, the type XB minelaying submarine U234, 1,763 tons, surfaced off the coast of New England, not so far from the main American submarine base at Groton, Connecticut, and surrendered to ships of the United States Navy. She had left Kiel, on Germany's Baltic coast, on 25 March. Considering what she was carrying, Captain Johann Fehler's boat was well named.

The radioactive, metallic element uranium has three isotopes (atomic variants): U238, U235 and U234. In some of U234's thirty minelaying tubes was a total of 560 kilograms of uranium oxide, the mineral from which U235 is extracted for use in nuclear reactors and bombs. This was intended to be part of Adolf Hitler's farewell gift to his Japanese ally. What happened to the uranium oxide does not appear to be recorded; but it is known that 1,200 tons of uranium ore from the Congo, seized by the Wehrmacht in Belgium in 1940 and recovered by the United States Army in central Germany early in 1945, were needed for the extraction of the small quantity of uranium-235 required for the second American atomic bomb, to be dropped on Nagasaki: a ton of ore produces a tiny amount. It is therefore highly likely that U234's cargo reached Japan after all, but by other means.

The interest of the United States Navy in matters nuclear antedated the Second World War by at least six months. In March 1939 Dr George Pegram of Columbia University suggested to Rear-Admiral Harold G. Brown, chief of the Bureau of Steam Engineering, that the Navy consider the practical application of uranium fission. Naval research scientists soon anticipated using nuclear energy to create steam to drive submarine turbines, in much the same way as the element in an electric kettle heats water.

From the very beginning of the concept of the nuclear-powered submarine a return to steam was envisaged. The submarine's reactor would produce so much energy that the boat would also be able to produce its own oxygen. The result would be nothing less than the first true submarine, capable of staying underwater for as long as its nuclear fuel lasted (or as long as its crew could stand the strain). So far in this book, although the term submarine has been employed in accordance with contemporary usage, we have really been concerned with submersibles.

Preliminary research was authorised; but after Pearl Harbor all fissile material was reserved for the US Army's "Manhattan Project" for making the first atom bomb. But work continued on uranium enrichment in the Navy from 1941: enrichment promised a substantial reduction in the size of the reactor, enabling it to fit in a submarine.

Interest grew late in 1944, when the Allies were aware of German progress in submarines with high underwater speeds. They were working hard on counter-measures, including upgrading and adapting extant submarines with streamlining and better propulsion so they could be used for ASW training. These "Guppy" (greater underwater propulsive power) conversions of wartime boats continued after the war in the American, British and French navies until new hydrodynamic designs drawing on German examples were developed: USS *Tang*, HMS *Porpoise* and the French "Narval" classes. The Dutch Navy was also interested in nuclear propulsion for submarines, but never built any because the Americans would not supply the technology. None the less the Dutch made great progress in hull design.

Dr Philip Abelson of the Naval Research Laboratory wanted to copy the Walter experimental type XXVI, the first modern design to dispense with dual propulsion (which achieved twenty-three knots submerged but never overcame its technical problems, even in Allied postwar imitations). Abelson proposed substituting a steam turbine powered by a nuclear reactor for the German boat's gas turbine powered by diesel oil, supplemented by air on the surface but hydrogen peroxide when submerged.

But the main impetus for the most revolutionary development in the history of the man-of-war came from a passed-over US Navy captain called Hyman G. Rickover, a former submariner who had spent the war running the electrical section of the Bureau of Ships. Early in 1946 the US Atomic Energy Commission sanctioned the construction by Westinghouse of an atomic pile at Oak Ridge, Tennessee. Rickover joined the project on behalf of the Navy in May. Shortly afterwards he unearthed Abelson's report on the idea of an adapted "Walter", which the scientist thought could be built in two years and might stay underwater for years without surfacing or refuelling; he also thought it could launch V2-type rockets with atomic warheads.

Rickover's first report to the Bureau of Ships late in 1947 recommended accelerating the reactor programme for submarine purposes. It was rejected; but Rickover stayed on at the bureau. From his tiny office he embarked on winning converts for nuclear propulsion. One of the most important was Admiral Nimitz, now Chief of Naval Operations, who made Rickover head of the new Nuclear Power Division in the Bureau of Ships in 1949. One of his main problems was resistance from the Atomic Energy Commission. But he persuaded it to make him chief of its Naval Reactors branch. His two posts smoothed the path of liaison and cooperation between AEC and USN – in a crisis he could always send a memorandum to himself!

Rickover, born in 1900, was what is politely known as a "character", and less politely as a fire-eating bully. He kept a special chair in his office for subordinate visitors with its front legs shorter than its back legs, forcing the occupant to brace his own legs to stay in place; it was positioned so that the sun shone in his eyes as Rickover fired disconcerting questions.

But sometimes only this kind of driving intolerance of fools can overcome the bureaucratic inertia which so often obstructs technical breakthroughs. Rickover was also capable of strokes of genius in organisation and simplification, not only in the bureaucratic sphere (such as his "two hats" ruse to reconcile AEC and USN). Arguably the cleverest idea in developing the world's first nuclear-powered vessel was Rickover's decision to build the reactor twice over. Work began in the desert at AEC's installation at Arco, Idaho, some 600 miles from the sea, on Submarine Thermal Reactor (STR) number one, cooled by pressurised water. The heat from the core of the reactor was absorbed by this constantly recycled water and transferred to the boiler water sealed in the steam-generation system powering the turbines; the steam was condensed after use and recycled back to the boilers. The water in one circuit was kept completely separate from the water in the other.

STR II was constructed one step behind STR I as the problems were ironed out. To ensure that the reactor would fit in a submarine, STR I was built inside a real hull, prefabricated at the Electric Boat Company's yard at Groton and brought 2,500 miles overland in sections. To save time and money, an adapted "Guppy" design was used; the sea-going prototype with STR II was built at Groton. From the beginning this was to be an operational boat with torpedoes. The unprecedented construction method, far from being wasteful, probably saved five years in development time.

The naval contract for the first nuclear submarine was awarded to Electric Boat (now a subsidiary of the General Dynamics Corporation) on 21 August 1951. The name was announced four months later: what else could it be but the most famous in the history of submarines: *Nautilus*. President Harry S. Truman laid the keel on 14 June 1952.

At the same time, General Electric was working on a Submarine Intermediate Reactor (SIR) which used liquid sodium instead of pressurised water as coolant-cum-heat-exchanger. Rickover thought this might be better than pressurised water. The same method was used: landbased SIR I was constructed in a hull at West Milton, New York, while SIR II was built into the future USS *Seawolf*, completed in 1957. There were rather more technical hitches than with the pressurised water reactor, which was therefore preferred for all later boats.

In July 1952 Rickover received the Gold Star to put up alongside the Legion of Merit for his war work. On the very next day, to the outrage of the press, he was passed over for rear-admiral for the second time, which meant he would be obliged to retire in 1953. But the long-deferred promotion came in that year; in 1958 he rose to his final rank of vice-admiral and remained on the active list until 1964 (two years longer than normally permitted); and then he was allowed to stay on indefinitely as an adviser, as befitted one of the greatest innovators in naval history.

STR I went critical at Arco at the end of March 1953 and was nursed up to full power three months later. Several technical faults developed on a mock run equivalent to 2,500 sea-miles in eighty-six hours, an average "speed" of twenty-nine knots; but an iron-nerved Rickover refused to allow a shutdown (although it was throttled back three times). STR II was launched with *Nautilus* on 21 January 1954 by President Eisenhower's wife, after one year, seven months and one week under construction. It was a feat to set alongside the year-and-a-day gestation of HMS *Dreadnought*. The boat, which cost $29 million without her propulsion plant and $100 million in all, is 323 feet long, displaces 3,674 tons surfaced (4,092 submerged) and could deliver eighteen knots on the surface and twenty-three underwater (the present tense is used because she is open to the public at the Submarine Museum at Groton). She bears the number 571 and the then new classification SSN (submarine, nuclear). She ranks alongside the greatest feats of the United States space programme as a technological achievement. Commissioned into the Navy on 30 September 1954, she made her first brief run at full power on 3 January 1955: two days behind the schedule laid down in 1950! Two weeks after that her captain, Commander Eugene Wilkinson, sent the historic signal: "Under way on nuclear power."

The boat had six torpedo tubes, air-conditioning, a juke box, a library with 600 books, a mess which could seat thirty-six enlisted men at a time (or become a cinema for fifty in five minutes), a laundry, and the unheard-of luxury of one bunk per man for a crew of 100. Although *Nautilus* was considerably smaller than the largest submarines built by Japan during the war, the absence of electric motors and their large batteries enabled the builders to provide palatial accommodation. The extra facilities, which included a soda fountain and ice-cream, anticipated very long periods underwater. Air-conditioning provided a steady temperature of about seventy degrees Fahrenheit (21° C).

The air was originally kept fresh by bottles of oxygen and a "scrubber" (air purifier) but this was soon superseded by the extraction of oxygen from sea water by electrolysis powered by the reactor. The "total submarine" had arrived, capable of more than twenty knots underwater "for ever" between annual refuellings. The radiation shielding was so thorough that the crew were exposed to less radiation aboard than ashore, from background radiation in the new nuclear age. As an extra precaution mercury thermometers, chloro-fluorocarbons (CFCs) in aerosols or cooling systems and oil-based paints were banned, as all of these would produce toxic gases in intense heat. Here at last was true stealth at sea; capable of diving to more than 400 feet, *Nautilus* need never betray herself to ships, aircraft or even "spy in the sky" satellites.

The *Nautilus* made history by virtue of the technical leap implicit in her construction. Under her second skipper, Commander William R. Anderson, she did it again in summer 1958, by sailing from the Pacific to the Atlantic under the Arctic ice-cap on her second attempt. She reached the geographic North Pole on 3 August and surfaced in a gap in the ice to send another historic signal: "*Nautilus* 90 north."

The strategic implications for the Cold War, which had begun immediately after the Second World War, were staggering. Just as *Nautilus* was directly descended from German types, so the first American rockets were derived from the German V2, whose design team under Wernher von Braun was hard at work for the United States. In the early 1950s General Dynamics produced a "Strike-Submarine Missile Weapons Study" at the behest of the Navy, showing that a submarine-launched, nuclear-tipped rocket was entirely feasible. In 1955 the Department of Defense ordered Army and Navy to collaborate on developing a missile with a range of 1,500 miles. One result was the Navy's Strategic Systems Project Office, whose technical director was Captain Levering Smith, the rocket engineer who became the brain behind Polaris, Poseidon and today's Trident. He "retired" as a rear-admiral but, like Rickover, remained in harness, as head of the SSPO.

After shortlived experiments with non-nuclear rockets such as "Regulus", the US Navy abandoned the joint "Jupiter" project with the Army: the missile was too large. In January 1957 the Navy started work on Polaris, a sufficiently small, solid-fuel missile twenty-eight feet long, weighing fourteen tons and capable of accurate delivery at up to 1,200 miles, thanks to its advanced version of the "Ship Inertial Navigation System". Like a torpedo's guidance system, this was built round the gyroscope; and the missile, though expelled vertically rather than horizontally from the boat, was also launched by compressed air (later gas, then steam from the propulsion system) until clear of the water, whereupon rocket propulsion took over. Polaris was first test-fired successfully in April 1956.

But how was this terrifying new weapon to be deployed when a boat twice the displacement of *Nautilus* was needed to carry sixteen Polaris missiles?

By the late fifties the American nuclear submarine programme was advancing apace. The hull shape was now based not on the type XXI but on the experimental USS *Albacore* which, though conventionally powered, delivered a stunning thirty-three knots submerged (twenty-five surfaced) with her revolutionary hydrodynamic outline.

At Groton the nuclear boat *Scorpion* was taking shape. In another bold technological leap, the 252-foot vessel was cut in half, the bow and stern sections separated and a new mid-section complete with sixteen launching tubes, fire-control and navigational systems inserted. The result was 382 feet long, renamed USS *George Washington* (SSBN 598 – submarine, ballistic, nuclear) and launched on 9 June 1959. The first Polaris deterrent patrol set out very publicly from Charleston, South Carolina, on 15 November 1960. A naval band blew a loud farewell: a deterrent must be known to exist if it is to deter. After the trumpeted start of that patrol of sixty-six days, departures were secret. The second Polaris boat, *Patrick Henry*, was at sea before the end of the year. In 1961 the new Kennedy administration turned a rush into a gallop, resolving on a force of twenty-nine Polaris boats and demanding improvements in the missile's warhead and range. Polaris-A2 with a range of 1,500 miles was already being tested and went to sea in 1962; A3 would cover 2,500 miles and was deployed in 1964.

The latter was sold to the British for their first ballistic nuclear submarines, under an agreement reached between President Kennedy and Prime Minister Harold Macmillan in December 1962. The first British nuclear boat, the non-ballistic HMS *Dreadnought*, commissioned in 1963, was effectively the seventh in a class of six. To save time and trouble the British, having failed to match American technological brilliance, were allowed to buy a reactor similar to those in the six boats of the "Skipjack" class, although they did alter the hull design considerably. By 1994 the British tactical nuclear submarine fleet (SSNs) consisted of seven "Trafalgar" class, five "Swiftsure" and one "Valiant", all equipped with the Mark 24 heavy torpedo and the Harpoon (US) underwater-launched, anti-ship missile.

The first of four British ballistic-missile (Polaris) boats, HMS *Resolution*, was launched in 1966 with an American-designed, midships missile section and made her first deterrent patrol in June 1968. By 1994 this force was down to two boats, with a third undergoing a prolonged and indeterminate refit. The second-generation British "independent" nuclear deterrent, being developed at time of writing, will when complete also consist of four nuclear submarines, with American-designed missile sections and Trident-2 missiles as used by the US Navy. The first two boats, *Vanguard* and *Victorious*, were the most advanced of their category in the world.

Ironically, their missiles, with a range of rather more than the admitted 4,600 statute miles, made the latest SSBNs built to go with them all but unnecessary. Just as the Cold War subsided at the end of the 1980s, a Trident submarine became capable of hitting almost any target in the northern hemisphere from American waters. The Americans therefore abandoned their forward SSBN bases in Scotland and Spain in 1992. To keep its place at the "top table" a financially embarrassed Britain persisted with its £12 billion Trident programme. Its official excuse was the spread of nuclear weapons – to which this overblown programme was no mean contribution. Unstated was a widespread fear of the post-Soviet instability in Russia, with its 27,000 warheads. Such uncomfortable facts as the failure of the nuclear deterrent to deter Galtieri's Argentina or Saddam Hussein's Iraq (see below) were officially ignored.

But Britain will probably continue as a major nuclear power so long as the French retain theirs. The French, like the Dutch, tried but at first failed to persuade the Americans to part with nuclear-submarine technology and ploughed their own furrow. Rediscovering their ingenuity in submarine construction, the French built their own force of initially five SSBNs and their missiles, based at the colossal, German-built submarine pens at Brest. But in recent years it has emerged that the system was built with secret American technological assistance. Only after launching their SSBN programme did the French turn to building the world's smallest SSNs, the "Rubis" class, displacing only 2,385/2,670 tons apiece, which argues remarkable progress in reducing reactor size. These six boats could carry a submarine variant of the notoriously deadly "Exocet" anti-ship missile as well as acoustic homing and wire-guided torpedoes. They could also deploy two mines among a total mix of fourteen weapons. Three were earmarked for Lorient on the Atlantic coast and three for Toulon in the Mediterranean. A serious setback to the programme came in March 1994, when the captain and nine sailors died in a steam leak on the *Emeraude* in the western Mediterranean. No radiation leak was reported, and the boat got back to Toulon.

When the Cold War ended the United States possessed thirty-four ballistic nuclear submarines accounting for forty-five per cent of national strategic nuclear forces (bombers took twenty per cent and landbased missiles thirty-five). As the bombers and landbased forces were drastically reduced under Strategic Arms Reduction treaties (START), SSBNs were set to retain their supremacy in a much reduced American nuclear arsenal. By 1997 there were to be eighteen boats of the "Ohio" class, the biggest submarines ever built outside the Soviet Union, displacing 16,600 tons surfaced and 18,700 submerged. They travelled at rather more than twenty knots submerged and could dive to about 1,000 feet. Each carried twenty-four Tridents with up to eight warheads per missile (multiple, independently targeted re-entry vehicles or MIRVs). Numbers of warheads were to be reduced as "Ohios" fitted with Trident-1 were upgraded to carry Trident-2. Even this reduced deterrent looks like a stupefying demonstration of overkill. Nine boats were to be in the Atlantic and nine in the Pacific, and each boat was to have two crews to extract maximum use from them: two-thirds of the force were intended to be available at any time, with the remaining third undergoing short- or long-term refit.

The "Ohios" were named after states, as American battleships had been. The backbone of the post-Cold War American attack-submarine fleet was to be the "Los Angeles" class, the most numerous in the world with a planned total of sixty-two. The first, SSN 688, completed in 1976, gave her name to the series, all of whose members were named after cities, as cruisers used to be – except one, SSN 709, alias USS *Hyman G. Rickover*. These boats displaced 6,080/6,900 tons and measured 360 feet with a diameter of thirty-three feet. They were said to be capable of diving to at least 1,500 feet and travelling at submerged speeds well in excess of thirty knots. The improved "Los Angeles" class (with diving planes at the bow to increase icebreaking ability, rather than on the "sail") began with the fortieth, SSN 751 or USS *San Juan*. Most of the class, old or new, could eventually carry twelve Tomahawk vertically launched cruise missiles as well as Mark 48 torpedoes and Harpoon anti-

ship missiles. Most of them could also lay highly sophisticated mines,
including the SLMM (submarine-launched mobile mine), fired from a
torpedo tube, activated and left to lie in wait for hostile ships or submarines; and the CAPTOR (encapsulated torpedo) anti-submarine
mine, which is anchored to the seabed and automatically fires an acoustic
Mark 46 torpedo at a passing hostile submarine. The same four twenty-
one-inch torpedo tubes installed amidships could launch any of the
weapons carried by the "Los Angeles" boats, including Tomahawks if
necessary. The class was the most complicated and sophisticated general-
purpose submarine so far commissioned, but this was reflected by daunting and escalating costs: the first was priced at $221 million; ten years
later they cost three times as much.

The era of the billion-dollar boat arrived with a new attack class:
"Seawolf", the first of which was due for completion in 1996 and the
second (and last; originally there were to have been twenty-nine) was
authorised by Congress in 1992. Half as big again as the "Los Angeles",
they were intended to carry a mix of some fifty missiles, all launchable
from eight of the new twenty-six-inch-diameter tubes sited amidships,
as well as the very latest electronics and electronic counter-measures.

After the Cold War the main preoccupation of American submariners,
understandably, was to justify the retention of such a stupendously
expensive fleet.

As with the atomic and then the hydrogen bomb (but not with the
rocket, the satellite or the manned spacecraft) the Soviet Union followed
the lead of the United States and built nuclear submarines. After trying
out a pressurised water reactor in the icebreaker Lenin, the Russians laid
the keel of their first nuclear submarine in 1957. The Leninsky Kom-
somol was commissioned in April 1958. The United States had eight
nuclear boats in five classes with six different reactors five years after
the first was commissioned. That was in 1959, when Nikita Khrushchev,
the Soviet leader, told President Eisenhower he had nuclear boats twice
as fast as America's. The Russians had twenty-four by 1963, five years
into their programme. All apparently used the same type of reactor,
designated HEN by NATO, and there were three categories: SSN,
SSBN and SSGN (guided missile or "cruise"). In charge of the Soviet
fleet during this period of transition, not only to nuclear power but also
into an ocean-going Navy capable of operating in strength anywhere,
was Admiral Sergei Gorshkov, who stands alongside Admirals Fisher,
RN, and Rickover, USN, as a technical innovator.

The principal tactical target of the postwar Soviet submarine fleet,
which rapidly regained its place as the world's largest after the war,

was the American aircraft-carrier which had overpowered Russia's old enemy, Japan, in the Pacific. From the 1960s American ballistic submarines were allotted at least equal priority. Four German type XXIs had been taken into the Soviet fleet for experiments; they influenced the design of the "Whiskey" and "Zulu" classes. It should be noted that such designations are NATO's; the Soviets notoriously volunteered no military information except as propaganda. Before Khrushchev and Gorshkov, Soviet postwar naval strategy was indistinguishable from prewar: guarding the coasts in depth in support of the Red Army. Stalin died in 1953 without developing the "big Navy" he had dreamed of, but the fleet had begun protracted experiments with ship- and submarine-launched missiles developed from the German V1 flying bomb and V2 rocket, just like the Americans. German technicians were recruited in large numbers by the Soviet Union also. "Whiskeys" and "Zulus" were adapted for missile tests. In 1958 NATO surveillance aircraft, ships and submarines identified the "Golf" class, conventionally powered but the first to carry Sark ballistic missiles.

HEN is an acronym for Hotel, Echo and November, NATO's code-names for the first three Soviet nuclear classes, completed between 1958 and 1964. The nine "Hotel" missile boats were the largest, displacing about 5,000/6,000 tons and capable of diving to 1,000 feet. They carried Sarks. Surface speed was twenty and underwater twenty-five knots. The "Echo I" class of five carried Shaddock (anti-ship and/or anti-land) missiles. They displaced about 4,500/5,500 tons but at 375 feet were only two feet shorter than the "Hotels", indicating progress with weight-reduction. Performance was slightly better. The fifteen "Novembers" were Russia's first SSNs, capable of perhaps twenty-eight knots underwater. They displaced 4,600/5,300 tons and carried thirty-two torpedoes or sixty-four mines, launched from ten tubes.

Unlike the Americans, who soon put all their eggs in the nuclear basket, the Russians went on developing new classes of diesel-electric boats in tandem with the nuclear types: "Golf" with "Hotel", "Foxtrot" and "Romeo" alongside "November", "Juliet" with "Echo I" (all these NATO names derive from the embarrassingly inappropriate international phonetic alphabet, most of which was used up for this purpose).

Although the Soviet Union deployed the world's first missile-launching submarines, they were not to be compared to the first American SSBNs with Polaris (1960), a strategic weapon which worried the Soviet naval command. To counter it, and in response to American displays of surface naval power (most notably in the Cuban missile crisis of 1962), the Soviet Navy turned its back on tradition and its own coastline to set sail on the broad ocean, building four carriers and three nuclear-powered cruisers – one-third of respective American strengths. In doing so it was following in the wake of its own submarines, which had been detected from 1948 all over the world, reconnoitring foreign coasts, naval units and installations as well as nuclear tests. Soviet boats had been based in the Adriatic from soon after the war until Albania broke off relations in 1961, even though a permanent Mediterranean surface squadron arrived from the Black Sea only in 1964. Long-range reconnaissance planes and unlikely "trawlers" groaning under the weight of scanners and antennae appeared everywhere in a classic manifestation of the vacuum-cleaner approach to intelligence gathering. The days of coastal defence in depth were gone as Admiral Gorshkov showed the hammer and sickle in all the oceans.

The Soviet submarine service may have been four years behind the United States in developing nuclear boats but was at least ten years behind technologically. As compared with Germany before the war, so with America after it: Soviet quality might lag but quantity would not be wanting. As the Russians strove to build more boats and to close the technology gap, they also built up their air forces (as well as the landbased Strategic Rocket Forces from 1959, run by the Army, as ever the USSR's senior service). The resulting strain on a crippled economy was probably the main reason for the politico-economic collapse of Communism from 1989, which left the United States, unenviably, as sole superpower – and the world's leading debtor.

The second generation of Soviet nuclear boats began to appear in the mid-sixties, representing a considerable advance and a measurable narrowing of the technology gap. The first of some forty-nine "Victor" class SSNs was built in 1965 and displaced 4,300/5,100 tons, being capable of up to thirty knots underwater. Sixteen "Victor I" were followed by seven "Victor II" and twenty-six "Victor III" boats by 1990, each sub-class incorporating technical improvements to Russia's most numerous hunter-killer submarine. It carried thirty-two torpedoes or sixty-four mines and SS-N-15 rocket-powered nuclear depth-charges for ASW (the American equivalent of this, long since abandoned, was SUBROC).

Alongside the "Victors" was developed the "Yankee" class of thirty-four SSBNs, each carrying sixteen ballistic missiles (riskily powered by liquid fuel, rather than the solid propellant favoured by the Americans). The class, built between 1966 and 1974, already displaced 8,000/9,600 tons to accommodate the much larger Soviet missiles (bigger because of the volume of their fuel) and were 426 feet long, capable of about thirty knots and of diving to 1,300 feet. The contemporaneous "Charlie I"

SSGN class of twelve was about half the size and carried eight cruise-type, long-range anti-ship or anti-land missiles. The improved "Charlie II" appeared in 1972, although only six were added to the fleet in the ensuing nine years. All eighteen also carried mines and/or torpedoes but their chief target was the aircraft-carrier or modernised battleship at the heart of each US Navy battlegroup.

Despite the rapid expansion of its nuclear fleet, the Soviet submarine service kept much older classes in service in large numbers (the Americans commissioned their "last" diesel boat in 1959 but interestingly took it out of mothballs in 1993 for "ASW experiments"). Of the 296 Soviet operational boats in 1971, sixty-six were nuclear-powered; of the 257 available in 1980, 107 were nuclear. The total strength of the submarine fleet amounted to 380 in 1967 and 360 in 1986; the Russian Federation retained 250 in 1993.

In 1971 the Soviets introduced the world's largest extant diesel submarine, the first of the "Tango" class of twenty boats, displacing 3,000/3,700 tons and especially notable for quietness. Within the superpower arms race there was a submarine race; and within that there was a fierce competition in quiet running, a field in which the British became specialists. Most of the "Tangos" were still in service on the break-up of the Soviet Union. They were capable of twenty knots surfaced and sixteen submerged, armed with anti-ship missiles and torpedoes and covered with an "anechoic" (sound-absorbent) coating.

After the single, apparently experimental "Papa" SSGN, built in 1970 and never repeated, the Soviet Navy gave western analysts a headache by very slowly building no fewer than six "Alpha" SSNs, very small by Soviet nuclear standards at 2,800/3,700 tons, from the mid-seventies to the mid-eighties, having laid down the prototype possibly as early as 1967. The "Alphas" were thought to be made of titanium alloy, very expensive but with the immense advantages of extraordinary strength (making dives to 3,000 feet and more possible) and lack of magnetism, to deceive magnetic anomaly detectors (MAD, still a principal means of detection for ASW aircraft). But all six were withdrawn from service by 1992 as part of a drastic economy drive in the Russian Navy, suggesting that they were either extremely expensive to maintain or technically troublesome, or both. The Russians withdrew from the Mediterranean and Indian Ocean as they retired old vessels and slashed manpower, time at sea and ships under construction. Ballistic submarine numbers were also dramatically reduced, as in the United States, by compliance with START.

From the early seventies the "Yankees" began to be displaced by an improved version of themselves which the west codenamed "Delta". This important class of more than forty SSBNs was constructed in four sub-classes until the late 1980s. The earliest displaced "only" 9,000/ 11,750 tons while the half-dozen "Delta IVs" ran to 11,200/14,500 as technical improvements were incorporated, notably in electronics and ballistic missiles: those on the latest boats in the class could travel 6,000 statute miles. At the same time, the overall construction rate slowed down and boats were kept in service longer, probably to save money and possibly in anticipation of the technological breakthrough described below. In the mid-eighties some operational Soviet submarines were a quarter of a century old, but the newer the type, the smaller the technology gap, which had been cut to rather less than three years by the time Mikhail Gorbachev ceased to preside over a Soviet Union.

A major factor – probably the main one – in closing the gap was one of the worst known security leaks in the history of the United States: the spy-ring run by John Anthony Walker, Jr, a US Navy chief warrant officer, from 1968 to 1985. It included his brother and his son and its motive was money. The ring sold innumerable naval secrets, relating to surface ships as well as submarines, ciphers, communications, electronics, weaponry, construction and quiet running, enabling the Russians not only to catch up but also to counter US Navy deployments in wartime. A Soviet defector told the Americans that if there had been a war during the "Walker" heyday, the Russians would probably have won it. The whole disastrous affair, which ended when the ringleaders were imprisoned for life in 1985 for treason, cost untold billions in renewed American efforts to recover the technical lead which had offset Soviet numerical superiority. For the American defence industries it was not an ill wind.

The ominously quiet, Soviet "Akula" (meaning shark) SSN design of the early seventies, first detected at sea in 1987, was bitterly nicknamed "the Walker class" by Americans in the know, who regarded it as the most advanced attack submarine in the world at the time. In outline, with its long, comparatively low-lying, rounded sail it looked very similar to the "Alpha" but was much larger. It displaced 8,000/10,000 tons and was 360 feet long with a speed underwater of an estimated thirty-two knots. The post-Walker experimental "Mike" and operational "Sierra" (SSN) types were added to the alphabet soup at around the same time. The American response was meant to be the "Seawolf" mentioned above; but each would cost $2 billion at 1991 prices, and even "mass production" (e.g. thirty) would not take the price per boat below $1.3 billion. The Americans' displeasure on their discovery at around the same time that a Japanese company had illegally sold the Soviet

Union the metallurgical technology for making super-quiet propellers can be imagined.

In 1979 the Soviet Union added "Oscar" to NATO's alphabet: a vast boat displacing 11,500 tons on the surface and 15,400 submerged, the largest ever built by then. Capable none the less of thirty-three knots underwater, it was the latest SSGN (anti-ship and land cruise missile) type, also equipped with ASW missiles and torpedoes. After the first two, the hulls became even bigger, displacing 17,600 tons submerged to accommodate weaponry improvements in the "Oscar II" boats. Nine of these giants were in the Russian order of battle in 1992.

But the greatest monster of them all was the "Typhoon" class, which started building in 1977 and first appeared in the fleet in 1982. This submarine is by a very large margin the biggest ever constructed, at least 18,500 tons on the surface and 25,500 submerged (a larger displacement than the bulkiest surface ships in the Royal Navy, the three "Invincible" carriers). The six "Typhoons", 560 feet long and eighty feet across, are half as big again as the largest American boats, the "Ohios", and represent the response of the hard-line Soviet leader, Leonid Brezhnev, in 1974 to the American decision to develop the Trident missile. Armed with twenty SS-N-20 ("Sturgeon" to NATO) solid-fuel ballistic missiles with multiple warheads in tubes forward of the sail, and an array of torpedoes and missiles for self-defence, the "Typhoons" did not need to leave home waters to strike targets anywhere in North America. These underwater colossi consisted of an outer hull shaped like an airship with a flattened upper surface, containing two main parallel pressure hulls, each with a complete propulsion system (reactor, turbine and propeller-shaft). Amidships and beneath the sail was a third, small pressure hull containing the command and information centre. A cross-section of the boat at this point would resemble a grotesque enlargement of the interesting Dutch "Dolfijn" triple-hulled type, developed in the 1950s. The "Typhoon"'s stern featured both vertical and horizontal steering planes and there was a pair of retractable horizontal planes near the rounded bow, suggesting that the boat was designed to break through the polar ice, if necessary, to fire its missiles.

These were the first Soviet submarines to be given two crews of 150 men each, on the western pattern, to maximise their operational time. They were built at Severodvinsk in the Soviet far north-west and based nearby at purpose-built pens, cut out of solid rock at Gremikha on the Kola Peninsula, as part of the Northern Fleet, principal formation of the Navy. Hindsight suggests they may have been the biggest and most expensive white elephants ever built. Their size puzzled analysts: it may just have been the traditional Russian taste for bigness for its own sake, reflecting the world's largest state. Or the "Typhoon" could have been supplied with elaborate air-defence systems and weapons, or special facilities for prolonged submersion (one report claimed there was a seawater swimming-pool for the crew). Maximum speed (perhaps twenty-five knots submerged) did not appear to be a priority for these underwater monsters, whose main characteristic was "survivability" in a nuclear exchange. For all the adventurous probes on and under the surface of the world's oceans in the Gorshkov era and after, the Soviet Navy always kept six ships and submarines out of seven close to home in accordance with tradition. Its much reduced Russian heir economised by virtually abandoning distant operations. The still only lightly explored and understood ocean deeps are referred to as "inner space"; the Russians, who in the Soviet days routinely built extremely large stations for outer space, seem with the "Typhoon" to have built the ultimate inner-space station.

In 1979 the "Kilo" diesel class made its bow, displacing 2,500/3,200 tons and notably smaller than its predecessor, "Tango", though still large for a conventional type. There were twenty-one in the fleet by 1992, alongside seventy-seven other diesel-electrics (ten experimental), fifty-nine SSNs, thirty-six SSGNs and fifty-five SSBNs. The latter included six "Typhoons", forty-three "Deltas" and six "Yankees"; the SSNs eight "Akulas", three "Sierras" and forty-eight "Victors".

China, the world's fifth power to develop nuclear weapons, was also the fifth to acquire nuclear attack and ballistic submarines. Submarine development after the Communist takeover in 1949 depended on Soviet technology, but in the 1960s, after the two powers fell out, the Chinese proved entirely capable of making their own way into the nuclear age. They launched their first SSN of the "Han" class in 1972 and twenty years later deployed five. About 300 feet long, they displaced some 4,500 tons submerged and could reach thirty knots underwater on power supplied by a pressurised water reactor. The "Xia" class of ballistic-missile boats followed, displacing 7,000 tons submerged and carrying twelve missiles with a range of about 2,000 nautical miles, comparable with latter-day Polaris. The first was completed in 1987; six years later there was still only one known to be operational out of a planned force of at least three. Since the Chinese appear to have developed the boats and their propulsion, their missiles and warheads in virtual isolation, their progress in nuclear submarines has to be seen as a remarkable, if sterile, technological achievement for a nation and an economy staggering under the weight of the world's largest population.

As military and naval technology advanced on all fronts simultaneously after the Second World War, the submarine came to predominate in naval strategy. Nuclear power made the true submarine possible at last. Rapidly growing understanding of underwater acoustics and the multi-layered nature of deep waters offered new possibilities for concealment and detection alike. Electronics helped here, and also with the capabilities of underwater weapons, whether mines, torpedoes, anti-ship, cruise or ballistic missiles. Boats could detect targets and each other at tens, then scores of miles and in some conditions more; their non-ballistic missiles could be homed on maritime and even underwater targets more than 100 miles away. Elaborate "arrays" of sensors and antennae were extended from the sails (or fins; the "conning tower" was long gone) or else from special pods on the hull to enable the submarine to detect and listen to its enemies or handle radio signals from beneath the surface. At the same time, progress with "quietness" increased stealth at sea and made the boat harder to find and evade.

The western deployment of ballistic-missile submarines in the remotest areas of the Atlantic and Pacific was matched by Soviet deployments within striking distance of North America. Hunter-killer or attack submarines meanwhile practised seeking these strategic boats (and each other) in such fraught waters as the Denmark Strait between Greenland and Iceland, with their underwater "mountain ranges" offering opportunities for concealment and ambush alike. Hypersensitive, passive sonar detectors on the seabed and ASW ship and aircraft patrols worked together to detect the passage of the other superpower's submarines. Three Soviet nuclear submarines are known to have collided with American surface warships. One was involved in a crash with an American "Los Angeles" nuclear boat (*Baton Rouge*) underwater in February 1992, off the Kola Peninsula, home of the Northern Fleet and its submarines. This was by no means the first time a NATO submarine was caught in Russian territorial waters: conventional British boats were almost lost there at least twice on spy missions. Neither superpower advertised these nerve-racking contretemps and details are scanty.

The most embarrassing Soviet breach of the eleventh commandment ("thou shalt not be found out") occurred on the Swedish coast near Karlskrona naval base in 1981: the "Whiskey on the rocks" incident in which a Soviet diesel boat of that ilk ran aground and had to be rescued amid a blaze of publicity. For about a year afterwards the Swedes suffered repeated attacks of "submarinitis", claiming intrusions by nuclear, diesel and miniature boats, dropping depth-charges to no known effect and producing photographs of mysterious depressions and track-marks on the seabed. It was not paranoia; it was persecution. In wartime it is called reconnaissance, in peacetime espionage; submarines are ideal for either.

Six Russian nuclear submarines are known to have sunk as the result of accident, fire or scuttling after an "incident". The most notorious case was in April 1989, when the one and only experimental "Mike" sub-marine, the *Komsomolets*, sank off Norway's Bear Island in the sub-Arctic, with the loss of forty-two of her crew of sixty-nine. The boat went down in 5,500 feet of water, but the crew had managed to shut down the reactor after a fire. A Russian freighter took her in tow but she sank on the way to Kola. The *Komsomolets* had been used as a test-bed for new systems and was carrying two torpedoes with nuclear warheads, containing a total of ten kilograms (twenty-two pounds) of plutonium covered by a layer of uranium. There was also uranium in the reactor to worry about as environmentalists and the Norwegian government considered a report at the end of 1992 that the boat's inevitable disintegration on the seabed would lead to an ecological catas-trophe, introducing radiation into the human food-chain via fish. The evidence of local radiation tests was comforting: nothing over officially tolerated levels was detectable three years after the disaster. A salvage operation using the latest miniature and remote-controlled recovery vehicles was possible – at a cost of at least $2 billion. But the 360-foot, titanium hull might break up in the process, compounding the problem instead of solving it. The "least worst" option seemed to be to leave well alone and hope for the best, relying on the depth of the water to stifle the problem. But international concern grew again in 1994.

This was merely one dramatic highlight of a much more menacing radioactive legacy of the defunct Soviet Union and its insatiable appetite for massive submarine forces, which had already made the Barents Sea a nuclear dump. The Norwegian Navy calculated at the end of 1992 that six submarine reactors had been ditched at the bottom of the eastern Barents Sea since the 1960s. A senior official of the former Soviet Union told a Norwegian newspaper that fifteen reactors had been dumped in the Kara Sea on the other side of the great island of Novaya Zemlya. Unwrapped, low-yield nuclear waste was dropped into the sea routinely: the Northern Fleet alone owned up to 12,000 cubic metres per year, a habit it expected to continue at least until 1998, when a waste-processing plant was due to open locally. And in a fjord near Murmansk, also on the Barents Sea, old nuclear boats lay rotting in rows. Waste from them and nuclear icebreakers was stored in hulks until a disposal plant was opened.

In this very area on 20 March 1993 the American *Grayling* (SSN 646, commissioned in 1969), 4,640 tons, collided with a 13,250-ton

Russian "Delta III". Clearly the hide-and-seek "games" were still flourishing after the Cold War. The second such incident in thirteen months might no longer have led to an international crisis, but it was not only the Norwegians who lost sleep over it.

On the other side of the Eurasian land-mass the Pacific Fleet indulged in similar profligate habits, albeit on a rather smaller scale: submarines and other warships lay crumbling as nuclear waste was dumped off Vladivostok and in the Bering Straits.

The Russian government banned such dumping in October 1992, but the Navy complained that its shore facilities for interim storage were already over-full after decommissioning thirty-three nuclear submarines. An intriguing piece of lateral thinking – the idea of using submarine reactors for power-plants – was discarded because of the technical difficulties (a Manila businessman suggested buying all six "Typhoons", mooring them in Manila Bay and plugging them into the Philippines' national grid, but local opinion was less than keen to import six potential Chernobyls). The three western nuclear-submarine powers had no magic solution to offer for disposing of nuclear waste, but were not caught dumping reactors or waste in the open sea (although Britain toyed with the idea before announcing its decision to refrain in 1994). Getting rid of nuclear waste needed a scientific breakthrough of the same magnitude as the harnessing of nuclear energy, the discovery of which threw up the problem in the first place. In 1994 the Italian particle physicist and Nobel prizewinner, Dr Carlo Rubbin, was hard on the heels of a possible solution, in which neutron bombardment of waste was to accelerate its radioactive decay from millennia to decades. Meanwhile old American, British and French nuclear boats lay in secluded berths waiting, like superannuated nuclear power stations, for a decontaminating miracle.

Nor should it be thought that the former Soviet Union had a monopoly of nuclear submarine accidents. The United States lost two nuclear boats in spectacular disasters. The first known fatal casualty ever among reactor-powered submarines was USS *Thresher* (Commander Wes Harvey), 220 miles east of Boston, in April 1963. She was 279 feet long, thirty-two feet in the beam and carried a reinforced crew of 129 (twenty-two above specification) at the time. After two years in commission, during which a long series of mechanical problems, often due to carelessness, had revealed themselves, this prototype of a new class was to undertake yet more diving trials following a thorough overhaul involving 100,000 man-hours. She set off from Portsmouth Navy Yard, New Hampshire, where she had been built to a Navy design, on 31 March, with the ill-named rescue ship *Skylark* (Lieutenant-Commander

Stanley M. Hecker), to which she was connected by open-line telephone.

At least twice on her last mission *Thresher* had to undergo running repairs of serious faults: an internal water leak and a seawater-valve failure, during the correction of which a fault was also found in the torpedo door-shutters. At 7.47 a.m. on 10 April she started a slow, deep dive. Five minutes later she told her companion that she had reached 400 feet and was "checking for leaks". The submarine was descending corkscrew fashion so as not to lose contact with her escort. At 9.13 a.m. *Thresher* signalled that she was "experiencing minor difficulty" and was "attempting to blow". Four minutes later came her last recorded transmission, the phrase "900N", an incomplete or coded message never explained. Aboard the *Skylark* via the unresponsive ship-to-ship telephone line the submarine could be heard breaking up, presumably the victim of another massive leak.

After a search of ten square miles of Atlantic Ocean, a brilliant technical feat by the manned bathyscaph *Trieste* found the wreck at a depth of 8,400 feet in June. Apparently it had imploded; fragments were scattered over a wide area. The search was officially abandoned early in September when dredged-up items that could only have come from *Thresher* were identified beyond dispute. Although advances in deep-water exploration techniques made it a racing certainty that the United States Navy re-examined the wreck at least once, the cause officially remains "unknown".

The loss of USS *Scorpion* (SSN 589) five years later officially remained just as mysterious for a quarter of a century. The submarine was commissioned on 29 July 1960, had a length of 252 feet and a beam of thirty-one, displaced 3,513 tons and carried a crew of eight officers and eighty-five enlisted men. She was designed and built by Electric Boat. After eight years of apparently trouble-free service the boat exploded underwater in mid-Atlantic 400 miles south-west of the Azores on 24 May 1968. The enquiry once again attributed the loss to unknown cause. But in 1993 naval veterans more than hinted to an American reporter that the submarine had been diverted to the aid of an American Polaris boat which was being badgered by at least one Soviet attack submarine. The missile boat had, unusually, been picked up by the Russians as she left the Polaris forward base in south-western Spain.

Since the whole point of Polaris and its successors was total concealment, the Soviet shadower had to be shaken off, and *Scorpion* was assigned this highly dangerous task, the veterans said (quoted by Ed Offley of the *Seattle Post-Intelligencer*). This might be done by lashing the "enemy" with loud active-sonar "pings" or by creating underwater disturbances to confuse his sonars. Two or three American hydrophones, ostensibly on the seabed (but one of them might well have been on the Polaris submarine involved), picked up the sound of the explosion, perhaps caused by one of the boat's torpedoes going off after being accidentally armed.

A piece of identifiable wreckage was photographed on the seabed by a towed sledge attached to the naval research ship *Mizar* on 27 June; the wreck proper was found nearby on 29 October. Photographs taken on the latter occasion suggested that the 100-foot-long central section containing the "power train" (reactor, turbines and drive) had disappeared – or been recovered. The bow section showed a large and jagged hole forward on the starboard side. If the scenario of Soviet interference and American counter-interference is correct, the incident would stand as one of the most serious in the Cold War. In May 1993 reporter Offley cited one naval source as saying that the communications unit where Warrant Officer John A. Walker of the spy-ring worked in 1968 had control of *Scorpion* at the time of the disaster.

According to deterrent theorists, nuclear weapons, latterly based on submarines more than anywhere else, preserved the peace between east and west for the four decades between the end of the Second World War and the rise to power of Gorbachev. Whatever one may think of nuclear deterrence there is a logical flaw in this argument, the fallacy known as *post hoc, ergo propter hoc*: if A preceded B, then A caused B. What the nuclear deterrent did not do was preserve world peace. The Americans and Russians confronted each other through surrogates in "Third World" countries in the Middle East, south-east Asia, Africa and Central America. Iraq knew the west had nuclear weapons yet seized the west's client, Kuwait; the Argentines knew Britain had them yet seized the Falkland Islands. But the designated roles of the 300 or so nuclear submarines, whether SSBNs, SSGNs or SSNs, of the five owner navies were clear enough, at least until the Cold War ended. The tasks assigned to some 400 diesel-electric boats owned by forty-six countries were rather more straightforward. It remains to summarise what submarines did operationally in the "limited wars" of the half-century of purported peace after 1945.

In September that year the Soviet Union and the United States partitioned Korea, just freed from brutal Japanese occupation, into North and South. As the Cold War deepened, each Korea claimed the other and each superpower backed its client. In June 1950 North Korea invaded the South and three years of intense fighting ensued between them, the North strongly supported by Moscow and very directly by Communist China and the South sustained by the United Nations (the United States backed by the Commonwealth and the western allies).

"Given the length of the seaborne supply line and the shortage of escort vessels, a serious submarine offensive would have faced the United States with a choice of accepting defeat or resorting to high-yield [nuclear] weapons. Quite possibly this situation was appreciated by the other side." This crisp assessment comes from the official *History of US Operations: Korea*, by James A. Field, Jr. In the first five months of conflict the Americans picked up eighty "possible" submarine contacts; in the second five months they noted sixteen. Many "chases" and "attacks" took place but nothing was found (or lost). The Communist powers did sow mines, the old Russian favourite, but otherwise did very little at sea, leaving it open to the UN and the Allied Navies, which did not organise a single convoy. The comparatively few escorts available were used to protect the carrier task forces of America and Britain and for blockading purposes.

The American Seventh Fleet and Naval Forces, Japan, deployed at least eight submarines in and around Korean waters. Their flotilla leader was USS *Segundo*, a 1944 boat (SS 198) 312 feet long, displacing 1,526/2,391 tons and armed with two dozen torpedoes for ten tubes. Patrol reports from some of these boats were declassified by the US Naval Historical Center in Washington at my request. They and other sources revealed that their main contributions were in the areas of coastal photographic reconnaissance of the Korean peninsula, surveillance of radar along the Chinese coast, and searching for hostile submarines (four Soviet "S" class boats were sighted by USS *Pickerel* in the Sea of Japan in October 1950). No American submarine fired a shot in anger during the Korean War, which ended with an armistice in July 1953.

American involvement in Vietnam went back to 1950, when President Truman began to send aid (eventually worth $2.6 billion) and advisers to help the French there, as part of the worldwide American confrontation of Communism. After the fall of Dien Bien Phu and the defeat of the French in May 1954, the Americans switched their aid to South Vietnam. The North Vietnamese started trying to destabilise South Vietnam and Laos from 1959, whereupon the US Seventh Fleet sent forces, including an ASW group of two submarines and a carrier, to support the American "presence" in Laos, Cambodia and Thailand. Under Kennedy more aid and advisers went to Vietnam in 1962. Three conventional submarines were sent to help the south Vietnamese Navy, among other things in ASW training, from 1960 to 1964.

At the beginning of 1962 the American Pacific fleet acquired the first sixty-man SEAL team (*sea-air-land*) for covert operations on hostile coasts, waterways and harbours. These teams consisted of naval personnel trained in guerrilla, counter-insurgency and sabotage operations; the older British equivalent was the Special Boat Section of the Royal Marines. SEALs could be delivered by plane, helicopter, surface vessel large or small – or by submarine. Two veteran boats of the Korean War, *Perch* and *Sealion*, were taken out of mothballs and turned into SEAL transports in 1964, when three more submarines were added to the Seventh Fleet. But the main naval activity in Vietnam from 1965, as American ground troops were committed in large numbers, was in the air from carriers (apart from coastal and river patrols with the South Vietnamese Navy). Once again, leaving aside clandestine missions behind the North Vietnamese lines, the main role of submarines in the south-east Asian conflicts between 1950 and 1975 was reconnaissance and coastal patrol. No US ship or submarine was lost, except for one destroyer sunk by an American mine.

SEALs meanwhile became a permanent fixture in the US Navy's armoury, and a large handful of former SSBNs were converted to deliver them (any US boat could be so adapted). They carried "dry deck shelters" for SDVs (SEAL delivery vehicles, miniature submarines not dissimilar to those used by the Russians for their "Spetsnaz" commandos) and bunks for up to fifty extra men as well as their equipment: SSBNs with their missiles and launching tubes removed offered plenty of space for such purposes. The British also carried out such clandestine operations, including in the Falkland and Gulf Wars.

Submarine warfare reached the Third World in December 1971 when India and Pakistan, not for the first time, went to war; each Navy had four submarines. The Indian Navy was considerably larger and included the carrier *Vikrant*. One Pakistani submarine went after her when she launched an air-strike against Chittagong in East Pakistan (now, as a result of this war, Bangladesh). She attacked with torpedoes, missed and was depth-charged by three escorting frigates, but got away unscathed. Another Pakistani boat, the *Ghazi* (ex-American *Diablo*, SS479, originally commissioned in 1944), was laying mines off the north-eastern Indian port of Vishakhapatnam when she succumbed to an internal explosion from one of her own mines. A third submarine, the *Hangor* (one of three members of the highly successful, small French "Daphne" class bought by Pakistan) was more fortunate: on 9 December 1971 in the Arabian Sea she fired no fewer than nine torpedoes at the Indian frigate *Kukri*. Three of them struck home and 191 sailors out of 288 aboard were lost when the victim went down in three minutes. The four

Indian boats patrolled but saw no action, as the Pakistani surface ships stayed at home for the duration.

Among the many military confrontations, rearguard actions and colonial disengagement struggles in British history since the Second World War, the Falklands War of 1982 stands out as a unique naval and military (as distinct from political and diplomatic) triumph. The Falkland Islands are at the opposite extremity of the Atlantic Ocean from the United Kingdom but under 400 miles from Argentina, which consistently laid claim to them for well over a century as "las Malvinas". The United Nations recognised them as British. The military junta in Buenos Aires, embroiled in overwhelming social and economic problems for which the only answer it could find was brutality, tried the favourite ploy of frustrated dictators down the ages – diverting attention from domestic incompetence to a foreign enemy. There had been smaller crises between Argentina and Britain over the bleak islands in 1948, 1966, 1968, 1973, and 1976, involving protests, demonstrations and even illegal landings.

At the end of March 1982 a group of "scrap dealers" landed on the even more remote island of South Georgia, part of the Falkland Islands Dependencies, upon possession of which Britain's claim to a share of Antarctica rested. The only British "presence" in the region was the ice-patrol ship HMS *Endurance*; the British government's known desire to withdraw this last flag-bearer to save money had encouraged General Leopoldo Galtieri, head of the junta, to believe that Britain would not fight for the Falklands. The first British reinforcements sent to the area were three nuclear attack submarines: HMS *Spartan* from that other British colonial leftover, Gibraltar, on 31 March, and *Splendid* and *Conqueror* from the main nuclear submarine base at Faslane in Scotland in the first days of April.

On 2 April, however, the equivalent of a division of the Argentine Army invaded the Falklands and occupied them. The British Prime Minister, then Mrs Margaret Thatcher, supported by Admiral Sir Henry Leach, First Sea Lord and Chief of Naval Operations, swung the government and the country behind sending a task force to take back the hitherto disregarded islands. A Navy now devoted almost exclusively to anti-submarine warfare was suddenly required to mount an invasion, under carrier air cover, 8,000 miles from its base. Admiral Sir John Fieldhouse, C-in-C Fleet, was in overall command (and direct command of the submarines); Rear-Admiral John "Sandy" Woodward led the task force at sea; Major-General Jeremy Moore led the invasion force of two brigades, made up of marine commandos, paratroops, Gurkhas and guardsmen. Half a million tons of merchant shipping, starting with three big liners (including the world's largest, the *Queen Elizabeth II*) were hired.

Woodward's task-force of thirteen ships, including two carriers with a total of twenty Harrier jump-jet fighters and twelve Sea King helicopters, arrived in the British-declared "Total Exclusion Zone" (TEZ) of 150 miles' radius round the Falklands on 1 May, a remarkable achievement in the time. *Spartan* was already inside it; *Splendid* was patrolling to the north-west and *Conqueror* to the south-west, both between the zone and Argentina, on the lookout for major Argentine naval units. These included the light aircraft-carrier *Veintecinco de Mayo* (25th of May) and escorts and the heavy cruiser *General Belgrano* (Captain Hector Bonzo), 13,645 tons, with two destroyers. Argentina also had two modern, German-built type 209 submarines, difficult to detect.

On the afternoon of 1 May Commander Chris Wreford-Brown, captain of HMS *Conqueror*, reported contact with the *Belgrano* (an American-built ship of Second World War vintage) and her escorts, armed with the formidable French Exocet missiles, sailing slowly and apparently aimlessly about forty miles south-west of the TEZ. The submarine had first found the group's oiler and waited until "clients" arrived to refuel. It was not until 1993 that Lady Thatcher disclosed that the carrier group had also been sighted (probably by *Splendid*) behaving similarly, outside and to the north-west of the TEZ at about the same time. As the group was just inside the twelve-mile limit of Argentine territorial waters it was left alone. Woodward said in his book that he saw the two main Argentine naval groups as a potential pincer against his task force and wanted "to take out one claw". On Sunday 2 May the British Chief of Defence Staff, Admiral of the Fleet Sir Terence Lewin, asked the "War Cabinet" for permission to sink the *Belgrano*. It was granted by lunchtime.

The deed was done at 3 p.m., about thirty-five miles outside the TEZ and with the *Belgrano* heading away from it at twelve knots. Hit at either end on the port side by a pair of old Mark 8 torpedoes (a modernised Second World War design rather than the Royal Navy's latest, high-technology but temperamental Tigerfish) fired at 2,000 yards, the old cruiser went dead in the water, burst into flames, listed heavily to port and sank within half an hour, with the loss of 368 lives from a crew of more than 1,000. Nothing like it had happened anywhere since USS *Indianapolis* was torpedoed in July 1945. After dropping some depth-charges ineffectually (the *Conqueror* by this time was observing from eleven miles away) the two Argentine destroyers left the scene at top speed – quite rightly, in view of the presence of a hostile submarine. *Conqueror* was the first nuclear boat to fire a shot in anger and remained

so for the foreseeable future. When she came home she flew the traditional skull and crossbones of a submarine that had sunk a ship on a
war patrol. Her captain was awarded the DSO.

Despite the daring exploits of Argentine pilots, operating at the limit
of their planes' range, in destroying several British ships with Exocets
during the successful counter-invasion, the sinking of the *Belgrano* and
the high loss of life was a diplomatic disaster for Britain. The inept
political handling of the Falklands crisis was compounded when the
government issued a series of shifting and shifty statements about the
attack, indicating underlying moral confusion.

There is no need to judge the rights and wrongs of the Falklands War
to suggest that a resolute statement, at the outset of a controversy
exacerbated by jingoistic headlines and the *Conqueror's* skull and crossbones, might reasonably have said: "The *Belgrano* was a major naval
unit of a country which had recently and without warning invaded
territory internationally recognised as British. It was at sea and capable
of posing a threat to the British task force legitimately preparing to
recapture the Falklands. It was therefore sunk. We regret the loss of life,
which would not have occurred but for the Argentine invasion of the
islands ..." No such hard-nosed but straightforward explanation was
ever offered, as a series of angry questions in and outside parliament
extracted a series of contradictory replies. Hindsight enables us to conclude that the British submarines should simply have stayed in touch
with the main Argentine units, firing only in self-defence or if a real
attempt was made to interfere with the task force. The submarines had
little else to do. On the other hand the terrible sinking of the obsolete
cruiser deterred the rest of the Argentine Navy from taking any further
part in the conflict: it went back to port and stayed there.

The nuclear submarines, joined by the diesel-electric *Onyx*, were
therefore diverted to other purposes. It is known that British special
forces were landed not only in the Falklands but also in Argentina, for
reconnaissance purposes if nothing else. The submarines acted as air and
radar pickets off the Argentine coast; they also landed the small Special
Air Service and/or Special Boat Section teams, a task for which the
rather smaller diesel boat was best suited.

Argentina deployed at least one submarine during the conflict, the
Santa Fé, (an ancient, ex-American "Guppy") which was caught and
crippled by British ASW helicopters at South Georgia on 25 April, the
day British forces detached from the task force recaptured the island.
On the same there was alarm on the British central Atlantic island of
Ascension over a "possible contact" with an unknown submarine; the
task force ships gathered there at the time therefore put to sea and sailed

in circles like the Grand Fleet in 1914. But nothing was found. On 14 June the Argentines surrendered to the much smaller British invasion force at Port Stanley, the Falklands capital. It would have been much cheaper to pay the 1,700 people on the islands £1 million each to go away.

From the end of the Second World War the Middle East, source of an increasing proportion of the oil which underpinned the western world's standard of living and simultaneously the setting for the Arab-Israeli conflict, was the principal source of international crises. Eventually the two superpowers, Britain, France, the entire Arab world and more became players in this perennial and dangerous drama.

Having tried and failed to expand to his east at the expense of Iran, Saddam Hussein resolved in August 1990 to move in the opposite direction, against Kuwait, regardless of the sheikdom's western nuclear friends. Kuwait had been part of Iraq under Turkish rule but was hived off after the First World War. Saddam Hussein wanted its territory, its oil and its access to the sea. American and Allied bombers attacked Iraq as the US assembled a "coalition" of western and Arabs powers to protect Saudi Arabia and recover Kuwait in Operation Desert Storm. The latter took 100 hours to drive the broken Iraqi Army out of Kuwait.

The US Navy deployed 100 vessels, eighty of them combatant, and 245 merchant ships in the Gulf War. The British and French sent an Army division each, their own naval and air forces plus troop- and supply-ships; other western navies sent ships.

The Americans deployed four SSNs in support of these operations: *Chicago*, *Louisville*, *Philadelphia* and *Pittsburgh*, all "Los Angeles" attack boats armed with, *inter alia*, the new Tomahawk Land-Attack missile (TLAM). As a ship- or submarine-launched weapon this was new to the American Navy (but not to the Russian, which had had something similar, if not so sophisticated, for years). The former pair were in the Red Sea, the latter stayed in the Mediterranean. The Persian Gulf itself is too shallow for large submarines; but cruise missiles could strike from 600 miles away. On 19 January, *Louisville* fired the first submarine-launched Tomahawk ever used in combat, followed by seven more; shortly afterwards *Pittsburgh* launched four. American surface ships however fired a total of 276, suggesting the submarine contribution was experimental rather than necessary. The Americans later claimed an eighty-five per cent accuracy rate for the Tomahawks; those who saw them coming in over Baghdad and elsewhere were amazed by their precision.

The shallowness of the Gulf made some American naval officers reflect on the wisdom of an exclusively nuclear submarine service; as noted above, one diesel boat was taken out of mothballs in 1993, ostensibly for ASW purposes but possibly for others also. The British said in 1967, when HMS *Onyx* was commissioned, that she would be the last diesel boat to join the Royal Navy, as well as the last of the successful, long-lived "Oberon" class. But in 1983 Britain ordered a new class of "Upholder" diesel-electrics, of which three had joined the fleet by 1993. An American source told me that a British conventional submarine did go into the Gulf during Desert Shield on a secret mission – so secret that the Americans were unaware of it. When they detected it they prepared to destroy it until they discovered whose it was. It did become public knowledge that the British had special forces behind Iraqi lines before the main landward assault, though not how it was done.

We have briefly seen how the once truly formidable superpower Navy of the USSR, built up by Gorshkov, was rapidly reduced to a sorry condition by the end of the Cold War and Russia's desperate economic problems. Still to come at time of writing was a redistribution of some of the fleet among the Commonwealth of Independent States, notably Ukraine, which broke away from Russia when the Soviet Union was wound up. Even so, the indigent Navy of the Russian Federation retained a horrendous arsenal of nuclear weapons representing a dual threat: silently to the environment if they were allowed to decay; and explosively to the world at large if political instability led to a new dictatorship in Moscow. Presidents Yeltsin and Clinton may have been all smiles whenever they met, but the latter's Navy obviously kept a wary eye on the former's; hence the collisions mentioned above. And if the American SSN *Halibut* could, as was revealed in 1994, lower monitors and cameras to inspect a "Golf II" ballistic diesel submarine sunk three miles down north-west of Hawaii as early as 1968, we can be sure that the two rivals would continue to spy on each other's wrecks as well (Russian prowess in this area was demonstrated by a commercial expedition to the wreck of the *Titanic* in 1987, using Soviet midget submarines).

They usually refrained from saying so, but doubt about Russian political stability was one of the main reasons why the three western powers with nuclear boats would keep them for the foreseeable future. Another argument for their highly expensive retention was the threat of nuclear proliferation, the acquisition of nuclear weapons by volatile nations.

Britain and France clearly hung on to their hugely costly ballistic nuclear submarines as proof of their entitlement to a place at the top table. This was symbolised by their permanent seats on the United

Nations Security Council, in the absence of such not inconsiderable powers as Japan, Germany and India. One of the very few things the five permanent members had in common was their ownership of such boats. No other nation had them or seemed likely to acquire them. But the British government proved in 1993 that it would rather sacrifice any item of public expenditure in its unprecedented debt crisis than this totem of status, by deciding to complete its Trident programme regardless.

The United States, in its new and ignominious position as the world's largest debtor when it had so recently been the world's wealthiest nation, also engaged in a fierce and much more public debate in the 1990s about the future of its nuclear submarines after the Cold War. The Navy set out to woo Congress and a would-be cost-cutting Clinton administration in the time-honoured American way: by lobbying, public relations and salesmanship. A distinguished naval historian was invited to prepare a glossy brochure extolling the value of American's nuclear submarines. When it appeared late in 1992, it revealed facts about them and their capabilities which the secret agents of the old Soviet Union would have killed for; the observer accustomed to British paranoid secrecy could not have imagined the Royal Navy going public like this, even in defence of its dearest (in every sense) equipment.

The brochure argued that SSNs would extend their range from hunter-killer/ASW work to "multi-mission capabilities" with anti-land and anti-ship Tomahawks added to their armoury. They would show the flag; they would go into forward areas ahead of other forces; they would deny sea areas to other navies and blockade ports; they would deliver SEALs in special operations, carry out surveillance, reconnaissance, sigint interceptions and radar patrols; they would support surface forces. A sharply reduced SSBN force would still be the main deterrent to nuclear adventurism or threats against the United States (terrorists were not mentioned).

In the highly uncertain world of the 1990s a sceptic might ask: is that all? Diesel boats with the latest electronics, electronic counter-measures, stealth technology and submarine weaponry cost half as much and could carry out the majority of these tasks without the added risks of reliance on nuclear power. Are these amazing but staggeringly costly nuclear weapons systems, among the most ingenious of human technical achievements, to be no more than underwater missile-silos against an unidentified enemy, reactor-powered picket boats, billion-dollar dinghies for commandos? Few in the west seemed prepared to address such embarrassing questions in the immediate aftermath of the Cold War, not even when the American, British and French governments were desperate for savings in a prolonged recession. Stealth at sea obviously retained its irresistible appeal to all forty-six submarine-owning nations, not just the five with nuclear boats.

Unofficial analysts suggested removing the nuclear power-plants from the "Ohios", replacing them with diesels and concealing them in the North American Great Lakes, from which they could hit any likely target with the latest missiles. They could be moved secretly from time to time but could be left virtually uncrewed except for maintenance purposes as their missiles could be fired by remote control. A Californian tycoon in the defence industry suggested that the United States should buy all six Russian "Typhoons", gut them of their missile sections and link them in pairs by a pontoon-style deck. They could then be used as 50,000-ton, underwater assault boats, complete with jump-jets, helicopters, landing-craft, Marines and their weapons. They would be capable of approaching an area of tension at high speed and unseen.

Such bouts of lateral thinking did not include practicable suggestions for the non-military application of superfluous nuclear submarines other than as generators of electricity. Despite the voyages of the *Deutschland* in the First World War, the idea of mercantile submarines did not catch on, not even when huge ones were available. It seemed so much simpler to send everything by ship. The advantages of minimum collision risk and maximum calm on passage were never attractive enough to warrant the extra cost. And there were far too many places around the world to which it would not have been wise, permissible or even possible to send a vast nuclear submarine. A few "leisure submarines" were in use in places as far apart as Scandinavia and Hawaii, but it was impossible to imagine a big nuclear boat being reduced to such a means of making a living.

At an exhibition entitled "Conversion '93" in Birmingham, England, in 1993, the Russian shipbuilding industry revealed how it was trying to diversify from building nuclear submarines and other naval vessels. Among the propositions on offer was a 250-metre (800 feet) submarine for carrying oil or containers (even longer than a "Typhoon"); its advantages would include immunity from bad weather and from pirates in the Far East. SSBN conversions with sailors to run them were also available. The ex-Soviet yards were prepared to build conventionally powered leisure submarines, including two-person midgets with pedals and optional battery-power for viewing marine life. There was, however, no discernible rush to take advantage of these high-technology mutants.

The commercial future seemed to lie with advanced industrial countries such as Germany, the Netherlands and Sweden, making diesel submarines for export as well as for their own small navies, and perhaps Japan, whose diesel-electric "Yuushio" class in the 1980s came closest to SSN performance standards. Although the Japanese had not entered the export market by 1994, they were reported to be trying to develop air-free but non-nuclear propulsion – half a century after the German Professor Walter came closest to this goal. If they achieve an objective abandoned by western submarine-builders in the 1950s they will doubt-less create yet another lucrative export market for themselves.

All the leading navies found themselves after the Cold War with surface fleets and aircraft very much geared to ASW but no immediate sub-marine threat to contend with, officially at least. Spending on ASW represented a naval investment second only to that on the nuclear systems themselves as submarine and anti-submarine technology ran an unending race. Active sonar, which did so much for victory in the Atlantic, remained in use but took second place in the electronic age to passive (the hydrophone immensely improved), because a submarine could detect the sonar ping and react before the transmitting vessel received its echo.

In addition to the hydrophones dropped by the superpowers on the seabed to detect passing submarines, the Americans deployed SURTASS (Surveillance Towed Array Sensor System) in special "civ-ilian" ships to trawl electronically for submarines. Surface warships and submarines listened for alien boats with smaller towed arrays of hydrophones. Aircraft and helicopters dropped sonobuoys for the same purpose and were equipped not only with highly sensitive, new magnetic anomaly detectors but "sniffers" for spotting exhaust emissions from the schnorkels of diesel submarines; modern radar routinely pinpointed objects even smaller than the tiny head of the modern schnorkel. Com-munication with submarines (and attempts to intercept them) also con-sumed huge amounts of taxpayers' money. Boats received Very Low Frequency signals (requiring vast landbased transmitters) by means of a towed antenna one-third of a mile long, or a buoy floated to the surface. Even more sophisticated Extra Low Frequency signals could be received as deep as 330 feet, a great if costly breakthrough. But advanced sub-marines still had to come very close to the surface to acquire satellite signals updating the Ship Inertial Navigation System (SINS), on which missiles and the boats themselves relied for their pinpoint accuracy.

Among the many weapons deployed by surface ships, and ASW submarines, were wire-guided torpedoes crammed with electronic coun-ter- and counter-counter-measures and released from their wires once locked onto a target. Other torpedoes, used by aircraft but also ships and submarines, were entirely automatic. There were rockets for short-range attacks and the Russians and Americans also deployed longer-range, high- or low-trajectory rockets, some with nuclear warheads. The US Navy, for example, from 1964 had the nuclear SUBROC (reproduced by the Russians from stolen plans as the SS-N-15), scrapped by the Americans and replaced by the more usable, non-nuclear Sea Lance only in the 1990s. By attaching rocket motors to "smart" torpedoes, their speed, range and effectiveness were enhanced even further. The Soviet and successor navies favoured multiple ASW rocket-launchers.

In the highly disorderly "new world order" which followed the Cold War, the five nuclear-submarine navies could be expected to keep the best of their existing boats, to complete outstanding contracts for new ones and then, strapped for cash, to allow their nuclear fleets gradually to run down, leaving superannuated boats unreplaced for as long as possible. America, Britain, France and Russia all cut nuclear submarine construction, bases and maintenance facilities in the post-Cold War recession, thus compounding its effects on employment.

Conceived as a weapon for the weak, the submarine became the ultimate weapon of the strongest powers in the nuclear age. But the ballistic version faced redundancy, thanks to improvements in the missiles it was invented to carry; and for that reason the attack version also stood to lose its main target and much of its credibility.

After the Cold War which had conjured it into existence, the true submarine, the nuclear boat which embodied real stealth at sea, had become more of a financial millstone than an indispensable asset to the five nations which deployed it. The submersible diesel-electric torpedoboat however still soldiered on, deadlier than ever.

APPENDIX

Operational submarines in service worldwide in 1993

(Sources: IISS; USN; author's files)

Key SSBN: nuclear ballistic-missile submarine
SSGN: nuclear guided-missile submarine (cruise etc)
SSN: nuclear submarine (hunter-killer)
SSG: guided-missile submarine (diesel-electric)
SS: submarine (diesel-electric)

ALBANIA 2 SS
ALGERIA 2 SS
ARGENTINA 4 SS
AUSTRALIA 5 SS
BRAZIL 5 SS
BULGARIA 2 SS
CANADA 3 SS
CHILE 4 SS
CHINA 46
   1 SSBN
   5 SSN
   1 SSG
   39 SS (including 1 with ballistic missiles)
COLOMBIA 4 SS
COSTA RICA 4 SS
CROATIA 1 SS
CUBA 3 SS
DENMARK 5 SS
ECUADOR 2 SS
EGYPT 4 SS
FRANCE 17
   4 SSBN (plus 1 refitting)
   5 SSN
   8 SS

GERMANY 22 SS
GREECE 10 SS
INDIA 15 SS
INDONESIA 2 SS
IRAN 1 SS
ISRAEL 3 SS
ITALY 8 SS
JAPAN 17 SS
KOREA (North) 26 SS
KOREA (South) 4 SS
KUWAIT 3 SS
LIBYA 6 SS
NETHERLANDS 5 SS
NORWAY 11 SS
PAKISTAN 6 SS
PERU 9 SS
POLAND 3 SS
PORTUGAL 3 SS
ROMANIA 1 SS
RUSSIA (Commonwealth of Independent States/250 former Soviet Union)
   55 with 832 strategic nuclear missiles (SSBN)
   36 with cruise missiles (SSGN)

59 mainly hunter-killer with torpedoes and some cruise/anti-ship
missiles (SSN)
2 experimental nuclear boats
(SSN)
8 diesel-electric with cruise missiles (SSG)
80 diesel hunter-killer with torpedoes (SS)
10 diesel, miscellaneous uses
(SS)

Of the foregoing, the
Northern Fleet has 126
(including 34 SSBN, 21 SSGN
and 38 SSN); the Pacific Fleet has
86 (21 SSBN, 15 SSGN and 21
SSN); the Baltic Fleet has 20 (all
diesel-electric); and the Black Sea
Fleet – to be distributed later
among Russia, Ukraine and
Georgia – has 18, all diesel.

SOUTH AFRICA   3 SS
SPAIN   8 SS
SWEDEN   12 SS
SYRIA   3 SS

TAIWAN   4 SS
TURKEY   12 SS
UNITED
KINGDOM   21
    2 SSBN (plus 1 refitting, 4
    building)
    13 SSN
    6 SS
UNITED
STATES   112
    All are nuclear-powered
    25 with 504 strategic nuclear
    missiles (SSBN) (10 older
    SSBN, withdrawn from patrol,
    excluded)
    18 armed mainly with cruise
    missiles (SSGN)
    69 mostly hunter-killer, armed
    with torpedoes and some cruise
    missiles; including four capable
    of special operations (SSN). Two
    more building.

VENEZUELA   2 SS
YUGOSLAVIA (Serbia &
    Montenegro) 10 SS

TOTAL worldwide 705, including 294 nuclear

Bibliography

Allaway, Jim: *Hero of the* Upholder (Airlife, Shrewsbury, 1991)

Anderson, Cdr William R., USN, with Blair, Clay, Jr: *Nautilus 90 North* (Hodder & Stoughton, London, 1959)

Bagnasco, Emilio: *Submarines of World War Two* (Arms & Armour Press, London, 1977)

Barnett, Corelli: *Engage the Enemy More Closely – the Royal Navy in the Second World War* (Hodder & Stoughton, London, 1991)

Beesly, Patrick: *Very Special Intelligence – the Story of the Admiralty's Operational Intelligence Centre 1939–1945* (Hamish Hamilton, London, 1977)

——*Room 40 – British Naval Intelligence 1914–1918* (Hamish Hamilton, London, 1982)

Berg, John: *The Soviet Submarine Fleet – a Photographic Survey* (Jane's, London, 1985)

Blair, Clay: *The Atomic Submarine and Admiral Rickover* (Henry Holt, New York, 1954)

——*Silent Victory – the US Submarine War Against Japan* (J.B. Lippincott, Philadelphia/New York, 1975)

Böddeker, Günter: *Die Boote im Netz* (Bastei-Lubbe, Bergisch-Gladbach, 1983)

Botting, Douglas: *The U-Boats* (Time-Life Books, Amsterdam, 1979)

Breemer, Jan: *Soviet Submarines – Design, Development and Tactics* (Jane's Information Group, Coulsdon, Surrey, 1989)

Brennecke, Jochen: *Jäger/Gejagte – Deutsche U-boote 1939–1945* (Heyne, Munich, 1991)

Buchheim, Lothar-Günther: *Das Boot* (Piper, Munich, 1973)

Calvocoressi, Peter, Wint, Guy, and Pritchard, John: *Total War – the Causes and Courses of the Second World War* (second edition, Viking, London, 1989)

Chack, Paul, and Antier, Jean-Jacques: *Histoire maritime de la première guerre mondiale* (three vols, Editions France-Empire, Paris, 1969–71)

Chief of Naval Operations, Office of: *The US Navy in "Desert Shield" and "Desert Storm"* (Washington, 1991)

Compton-Hall, Richard: *Submarine Boats – the Beginnings of Underwater Warfare* (Conway Maritime Press, London, 1983)

——*Submarines and the War at Sea 1914–1918* (Macmillan, London, 1991)

Coote, John: *Submariner* (Leo Cooper, London, 1991)

Corbett, Sir Julian: *History of the Great War – Naval Operations* (five vols, Longmans, London, 1920–31)

Crane, Jonathan: *Submarine* (BBC, London, 1984)

Cremer, Peter, and Brustat-Naval, Fritz: *U333 – the Story of a U-Boat Ace* (Bodley Head, London, 1984)

Dobson, Christopher, Miller, John, and Payne, Ronald: *The Cruellest Night – Germany's Dunkirk and the Sinking of the* Wilhelm Gustloff (Hodder & Stoughton, London, 1979)

Dönitz, Grand-Admiral Karl: *Die U-bootswaffe* (Mittler, Berlin, 1939)

——*10 Jahre und 20 Tage* (Athenäum, Bonn, 1958)

Ellis, John: *Brute Force – Allied Strategy and Tactics in the Second World War* (André Deutsch, London, 1990)

Field, James A.: *History of US Naval Operations – Korea* (US Naval Historical Center, Washington, 1962)

Frank, Wolfgang: *Die Wölfe und der Admiral* (Bastei-Lubbe, Bergisch-Gladbach, 1983)

Friedman, Norman: *Submarine Design and Development* (Conway Maritime Press, London, 1984)

Gorshkov, Admiral of the Fleet S.G.: *Sea Power of the State* (second edition, Voyenizdat, Moscow, 1979)

Gray, Edwyn: *Few Survived – a Comprehensive Survey of Submarine Accidents and Disasters* (Futura, London, 1987)

Hackmann, Willem: *Seek & Strike – Sonar, Anti-Submarine Warfare and the Royal Navy, 1914–54* (HMSO, London, 1984)

Halpern, Paul G.: *The Royal Navy in the Mediterranean 1915–1918* (Temple Smith for Navy Records Society, London, 1987)

Hastings, Max and Jenkins, Simon: *The Battle for the Falklands* (Michael Joseph, London, 1983)

Herlin, Hans: *Verdammter Atlantik* (Heyne, Munich, 1983)

Herrick, Robert Waring: *Soviet Naval Theory and Policy – Gorshkov's Inheritance* (US Naval Institute Press, Annapolis, 1988)

Hessler, Günter: *The U-Boat War in the Atlantic 1939–1945* (HMSO, London, 1989)

Hezlet, Vice-Admiral Sir Arthur: *The Submarine and Sea Power* (Peter Davies, London, 1967)

Hill-Norton, Admiral of the Fleet Lord, and Dekker, John: *Sea Power* (Faber and Faber, London, 1982)

Hinsley, F. H. *et al.*: *British Intelligence in the Second World War* (three/four volumes, HMSO, 1979–84)

Hough, Richard: *The Great War at Sea 1914–1918* (Oxford University Press, New York, 1983)

Howarth, Stephen: *To Shining Sea – a History of the United States Navy 1755–1991* (Weidenfeld & Nicolson, London, 1991)

—— (ed.): *Men of War – Great Naval Leaders of World War II* (Weidenfeld & Nicolson, London, 1992)

Humble, Richard: *Undersea Warfare* (Basinghall Books, Birmingham, 1981)

Jameson, Rear-Admiral William: *The Most Formidable Thing – the Story of the Submarine from its Earliest Days to the end of World War I* (Rupert Hart-Davis, London, 1965)

Jane's Fighting Ships of World War I (Studio Editions, London, 1990)

Jane's Fighting Ships of World War II (Bracken Books, London, 1989)

Jones, Geoffrey: *Autumn of the U-Boats* (William Kimber, London, 1984)

Kemp, Peter (ed.): *The Oxford Companion to Ships and the Sea* (Oxford University Press, 1976)

Kimball, Warren F.: *Churchill and Roosevelt – the Complete Correspondence* (three vols, Collins, London, 1984)

Kolesnik, Eugene M.: *Nato and Warsaw Pact Submarines since 1955* (Blandford Press, London, 1987)

Kuznetsov, Admiral of the Fleet N.G.: *Memoirs of Wartime Minister of the Navy* (tr. Vladimir Krivoshchekov, Progress Publishers, Moscow, 1990)

Lawliss, Chuck: *The Submarine Book – a Portrait of Nuclear Submarines and the Men who Sail Them* (Thames & Hudson, London, 1991)

Le Fleming, H.M.: *Warships of World War I – Submarines (British and German)* (Ian Allan, London, undated)

Lewin, Ronald: *Ultra Goes to War* (Hutchinson, London, 1978)

Liddell Hart, B.H.: *History of the First World War* (Cassell, London, 1970)

Literatur und Bildung, Gesellschaft für (ed.): *Die Wehrmachtberichte 1939–1945* (three vols, Cologne, 1989)

Lloyd George, David: *War Memoirs – Volume III* (Ivor Nicolson & Watson, London, 1933)

Longstaff, Reginald: *Submarine Command – a Pictorial History* (Robert Hale, London, 1984)

McGeoch, Ian: *An Affair of Chances – a Submariner's Odyssey, 1939–44* (Imperial War Museum, London, 1991)

Marder, Arthur J.: *From the Dreadnought to Scapa Flow – the Royal Navy in the Fisher Era, 1904–1919* (five vols, Oxford University Press, 1961–70)

Marolda, Edward J., and Price, G. Wesley: *A Short History of the United States Navy and the South-east Asian Conflict, 1950–1975* (Naval Historical Centre, Washington DC, 1984)

Mason, David: *U-Boat – the Secret Menace* (Ballantine Books, New York, 1968)

Middlebrook, Martin: *Convoy: the Battle for Convoys SC 122 and HX 229* (Penguin, London, 1978)

Miller, David: *Submarines of the World* (Salamander, London, 1991)

—— *Modern Sub-Hunters* (Salamander, London, 1992)

Milner, Marc: *North Atlantic Run* (University of Toronto, 1985)

Moore, Captain J.E. and Compton-Hall, Commander R.: *Submarine Warfare Today and Tomorrow* (Michael Joseph, London, 1986)

Morison, Rear-Admiral Samuel Eliot: *History of the US Naval Operations in World War II* (fifteen vols, Little Brown, Boston, 1947–62)

Padfield, Peter: *Dönitz – the Last Führer* (Gollancz, London, 1984)

Polmar, Norman: *Atomic Submarines* (D. van Nostrand, Princeton, NJ, 1963)

Poolman, Kenneth: *Periscope Depth – Submarines at War* (Sphere Books, London, 1984)

Prien, Günther: *Mein Weg nach Scapa Flow* (Deutscher Verlag, Berlin, 1941)

Quigley, Dave J.: *Under the Jolly Roger – British Submariners at War 1939–1945* (Portsmouth Publishing & Printing, 1988)

Rohwer, Jürgen: *The Critical Convoy Battles of March 1943* (Ian Allan, London, 1977)

—— *Axis Submarine Successes 1939–1945* (US Naval Institute Press, Annapolis, 1983)

—— (with Jäckel, Eberhard, eds.): *Die Funkaufklärung und ihre Rolle im 2. Weltkrieg* (Motorbuch, Stuttgart, 1979)

—— (with Hümmelchen, Gerhard): *Chronology of the War at Sea, 1939–1945* (second edition, Greenhill Books, London, 1992)

Roskill, Captain Stephen W.: *The War at Sea 1939–1945* (three/four vols, HMSO, 1954–61)

—— *The Secret Capture* (Collins, London, 1959)

—— *Naval Policy Between the Wars* (two vols, Collins, London, 1968–81)

Rössler, Eberhard: *The U-Boat – the Evolution and Technical History of German Submarines* (tr. Harold Erenberg, Arms & Armour Press, London, 1981)

Rowland, Peter: *Lloyd George* (Barrie & Jenkins, London, 1975)

Ruge, Friedrich: *The Soviets as Naval Opponents 1941–1945* (Patrick Stephens, Cambridge, 1979)

Rusbridger, James: *Who Sank Surcouf? – the Truth about the Disappearance of the Pride of the French Navy* (Century, London, 1991)

Schaeffer, Heinz: *U-Boat 977* (William Kimber, London, 1953)

Schofield, Vice-Admiral B.B.: *The Russian Convoys* (Pan Books, London, 1984)

Service Historique de la Marine (Ed.): *Les marines de guerre du Dreadnought au nucléaire: Actes du colloque international, Paris, 1988* (Vincennes, 1991)

Showell, Jak P. Mallmann: *U-boat Command and the Battle of the Atlantic* (Conway Maritime Press, London, 1989)

Spector, Ronald H.: *Eagle Against the Sun – the American War with Japan* (Free Press/Macmillan, New York, 1984)

Sueter, Commander Murray F., RN: *The Evolution of the Submarine Boat, Mine and Torpedo: from the Sixteenth Century to the Present Time* (second edition, J. Griffin, Portsmouth, 1908)

Terraine, John: *Business in Great Waters: the U-Boat Wars 1916–1945* (Leo Cooper, London, 1989)

Trevor-Roper, H.R. (ed): *Hitler's War Directives* (Sidgwick & Jackson, London, 1964)

United States Navy: *The US Navy in "Desert Shield" and "Desert Storm"* (Office of Chief of Naval Operations, Washington, 1991)

van der Vat, Dan: *The Grand Scuttle* (Hodder & Stoughton, London, 1982)

—— *The Ship that Changed the World* (Hodder & Stoughton, London, 1985)

—— *The Atlantic Campaign* (Hodder & Stoughton, London, 1988)

—— *The Pacific Campaign* (Hodder & Stoughton, London, 1992)

Waters, Captain John M., Jr.: *Bloody Winter* (revised edition, US Naval Institute Press, 1984)

Weddigen, Dr Otto: *Unser Seeheld Weddigen* (August Scherl, Berlin, 1915)

Weir, Gary E: *Building American Submarines 1914–1940* (Naval Historical Center, Washington DC, 1991)

Werner, Herbert A.: *Die Eisernen Särge* (Heyne, Munich, 1984)

Whitestone, Nicholas: *The Submarine – the Ultimate Weapon* (Davis Poynter, London, 1973)

Williams, Mark: *Captain Gilbert Roberts, RN, and the Anti-U-boat School* (Cassell, London, 1979)

Winton, John: *Convoy* (Michael Joseph, London, 1983)

Woodward, Admiral Sandy, with Robinson, Patrick: *One Hundred Days* (HarperCollins, London, 1992)

Index